T0348071

Culture and Politics in Economic Development

This significant new book examines the importance of culture and politics for economic development. Volker Bornschier utilizes new empirical evidence and an interdisciplinary approach in order to investigate the most pertinent issues that effect economic development and growth in the contemporary developed world.

Culture and Politics in Economic Development will provide the reader with a comprehensive understanding of this dynamic topic through its analysis of such generic issues as democracy, education and trust. Bornschier's exploration of the formation of the European single market and its impact on European growth and entrepreneurship is also a key feature.

This insightful book will prove invaluable to students and academics in sociology, economics and political science as well as general readers who are interested in understanding current development issues.

Volker Bornschier is Professor of Sociology at the University of Zurich. He is the author of twenty books, volumes and course textbooks, as well as numerous articles in leading social science journals, most recently his monograph on world society, *Weltgesellschaft* (2002).

Routledge frontiers of political economy

Culture and Politics in Economic Development

Volker Bornschier

Routledge
Taylor & Francis Group

LONDON AND NEW YORK

First published 2005
by Routledge
2 Park Square, Milton Park, Abingdon, Oxon OX14 4RN

Simultaneously published in the USA and Canada
by Routledge
270 Madison Ave, New York, NY 10016

Routledge is an imprint of the Taylor & Francis Group

Transferred to Digital Printing 2006

© 2005 Volker Bornschier

Typeset in Times by Wearset Ltd, Boldon, Tyne and Wear

British Library Cataloguing in Publication Data
A catalogue record for this book is available from the British Library

Library of Congress Cataloging in Publication Data
A catalog record for this book has been requested

ISBN 0-415-35454-4

Contents

PART III
**Beyond the nation-state: supranational and
transnational links**   153

PART IV
Persisting differences and the change in the societal model 203

Illustrations

Figures

Tables

Boxes

Preface, acknowledgements and overview

Although I have been a student of economic sociology for more than three decades, this book is on my research during the last six years. Most of these research projects were supported by generous funding from the Swiss National Science Foundation, and I would like to thank them here for that help.

During the time I was working on the various issues of economic sociology I benefited very much from the ideas and help of the excellent collaborators in my team at the Sociological Institute of the University of Zurich. In the various steps of research and teaching – not forgetting our research seminars and workshops – they helped enormously to clarify and critically evaluate ideas and to motivate students as well as to supervise their work. Together we learned a lot and also put together many conference papers and articles. I would like to thank them cordially. In alphabetical order my thanks go to: Mark Herkenrath, Claudia König, Michael Leicht, Michael Nollert, Sandra Rothböck, Bruno Trezzini, Hanno Scholtz, Thomas Volken and Patrick Ziltener. My other collaborators during that time with whom I did not work on issues of economic sociology will forgive me that they are not included in the focused list above. Also several of my advanced graduate and doctoral students deserve my thanks for their fresh inputs and additional findings, which I mention at the appropriate places.

I am also grateful for the many comments – including, of course, the critical ones – I received from colleagues and students at professional conferences and academic presentations. The comments of anonymous reviewers of our professional journals also helped in many instances to clarify issues.

Last but not least I would like to thank Marianne Schindler, Ute Ruggenthaler and Simon Milligan, whose effective help was indispensable in editing the several previous papers on which this book is built, very much indeed. My special thanks go to Simon Milligan who skilfully went through the whole manuscript and thereby improved it considerably. However, the responsibility for the present book which resulted from these drafts and for all remaining errors, inconsistencies and shortcomings in the text is solely mine.

For better orientation I will give an overview at the beginning. Chapter 1 on topics of economic sociology is in its first part a sort of general introduction for the reader, with a first clarification of concepts, distinctions and positions, while the second part examines different ways of modelling economic development. The sociological model of growth and structural change is then further elaborated and tested in the appropriate chapters of this book. This is a speciality of this book: to develop arguments and then to put them to the test.

Each of the four parts of the book are introduced with an overview which I reiterate here for the reader's benefit.

PART I Why and to what extent do cultural resources matter?

The focus of this part is on generalized trust as a cultural resource, which has attracted increasing attention from sociologists and economists. In the first chapter we address the significance of non-economic predictors of economic success, particularly generalized trust in its capacity for social capital formation. First, the concepts of 'effective social order' and 'social capital' are located in the sociological and economic tradition in order to deepen the debate over the economic significance of social capital. We reflect on the following mediated linkages: the cultural, structural and political characteristics of societies are shown to be related to the capacity for the formation of social capital among the population. The latter help specific forms of social capital in the economy to prosper, which is then seen as a factor for comparative economic success. We develop a new sociological growth equation and test it in samples of thirty-three and twenty-four countries. This allows us to consolidate the finding of the pioneering study by Knack and Keefer. Indeed, generalized trust turns out to be an important predictor of economic growth between 1980 and the end of 1998.

In an innovative new step, the next chapter considers generalized trust not only in its function of making existing actions and arrangements more productive but also in its second, newly discovered function, i.e., of making people more open towards change. We demonstrate this by examining the early proliferation of Internet usage using a sample of thirty-four developed and newly industrializing countries as well as a subsample of twenty-one rich societies.

Whether that new proposition is tenable is the question we address in the last chapter of this part. Does generalized trust really foster openness to change in general and in social spheres beyond the Internet? We approach this question by applying a different methodology. We rely on interviews with about 22,000 people from fifteen rich democracies. The support that we find for the proposition, by analysing three additional indicators to measure the inclination to change, raises new questions that are discussed in the last chapter of this section. What are the sources of generalized trust at the individual level? What are the implications of a culture of trust for theories of entrepreneurship?

PART II Democracy, political styles, trust and formal education

The leitmotif of this part is that politics matters. We argue in favour of this perhaps unoriginal position by distinguishing political forms, political outcomes and different political styles within the same political form.

We start with a chapter that asks whether the political form of democracy fuels economic growth and change. This is hardly a new research question in cross-national work but I argue that all previous cross-national studies erred when they directly related democratic measures to economic growth. I claim that the effects must be modelled as mediated by characteristics of societies which, and people who, are influenced by democracy as a specific set of institutions, and focus on education and generalized trust as mediating variables.

In the next chapter we address formal education in more detail as one political outcome. Worldwide, the educational system is to a very large extent under the aegis of the state, and this should result in variation according to political form. Although many cross-national studies exist that relate education to economic growth, it is theoretically unclear why education should spur economic growth. I then offer a combination of two favourable, albeit separate, effects education has on economic growth, i.e. (a) by legitimizing society in the eyes of citizens and therefore limiting social conflict, which is favourable for investment, and (b) by improving the qualifications of the workforce, providing better training and, thus, easier absorption of the knowledge relevant for improving production and distribution. This 'double dividend' of educational policy efforts is then put to its first cross-national test.

In the last chapter we consider developed countries at a very similar level of formal democracy and focus on different political styles. We consider degrees of negotiated capitalism (referred to in the literature as democratic corporatism) and liberal or Anglo-Saxon cultural heritage. As one would expect, different political styles produce different outcomes and – even more interesting – the same outcomes in a different way. I shall demonstrate the latter by showing how generalized trust is differently 'produced' in rich democracies. The findings in this chapter have very interesting consequences for the question of persistence and change which are addressed later in the book.

PART III Beyond the nation-state: supranational and transnational links

Up to this point, the arguments have considered characteristics of national societies and individuals. In this part we enter the discussion of the emergent state forms at the supranational level, most advanced in the case of the European Union (EU). How can the patterns of economic and political integration be explained and what are the consequences for economic growth and for convergence at the level of the member states?

Discussion of the co-evolution of state and capitalist development has belonged since Max Weber and Otto Hintze to the classics of sociology. Considering the five centuries of European modernity, one observes in comparing the different societies that the state forms were dissimilar for about three centuries before ending up in a convergence phase of about one and a half centuries. In the last third of the twentieth century, a new divergence occurred in state forms as manifested by the EU, which is, like the fully-fledged nation-state, a European social innovation. While this new state form certainly does not make the established nation-states obsolete, it adds a new supranational level.

In the first chapter we ask how such new state forms relevant to the political economy actually come into existence (what are the actors and circumstances) and consider what connections there are between the change in the societal model and an upgraded role for technology. The next chapter reflects on the consequences of this new supranational state form for economic development. The third is on the equalization of life conditions in the union as reflected in the high ideological value accorded to cohesion. Have poorer member states in the EU actually converged faster? If so, has this been due to economic factors (market creation and enlargement) or political ones in the form of transfers? Our findings also have some general implications for the relationship between state and market, which has been under debate for quite a while, and we come to this at the end.

PART IV Persisting differences and the change in the societal model

Societies at a roughly similar level of economic development differ in political style as well as in terms of culture, both at the level of individuals and as manifested in their institutional practices. Will such differences in the developed world – sometimes quite considerable in extent – vanish in the course of time as standard convergence arguments would say, or will they persist? If so, why? This is a very interesting question for our evolution theory. As a test, I consider the change in political styles as represented by different degrees of negotiated capitalism over the period 1960–95 . Such an analysis is pertinent to the claim of a general restructuring of the state in the era of economic globalization. We will conclude that differences between varieties of capitalism not only persist but that there tends to have emerged an even stronger polarization in the developed world during the last decades. Thus the two theses on the state–economy relationship under the aegis of economic globalization, i.e. the 'thesis of erosion' and the 'thesis of compensation', need to be reflected upon again. Both seem to receive some empirical support, depending, however, on different trajectories of political development.

I conclude the book with a chapter on the difficulties of the transition from the Keynesian societal model to the new societal model of the extended market sphere in the telematics era. Why is this transition so difficult and why does it take so much time? How has social change been brought about for different groups of developed countries and what role has the EU played in that change in Western Europe? Do the different patterns of economic growth in the 1990s make sense in the light of the theory of discontinuous change that is applied? This chapter fits together several arguments and findings which have accumulated throughout the book.

Let me add at the end of this overview that this book does not, of course, address all questions which might be of interest. Several other issues which I consider relevant are the topics of my recent monograph *Weltgesellschaft* (World Society). The quantitative approach which I use in the present book has not only merits but also shortcomings, since the great questions of economic history can hardly be directly addressed. Why, for instance, could the enormous global divergence in wealth appear over the last five centuries? In *Weltgesellschaft* I also addressed such issues, as several others have before – with competing arguments – for example, David Landes in *The Wealth and Poverty of Nations* or Ken Pomeranz in *The Great Divergence*.

Finally, the reader may wonder why questions of distribution and social inequality do not receive the treatment they deserve. This is not because I think that these issues are not of great importance; quite the contrary since I have often published on these issues before. The reason is that, with Hanno Scholtz and Thomas Volken, I recently started a comprehensive research project on inequality in comparative perspective. The innovative focus of this project is on the perception and evaluation of inequality as well as on the social and economic consequences of this more subjective side of the matter. The latter, which is shaped very much by culture, would have been a marvellous additional topic of the present book, in which I argue that culture and politics are significant factors in any economy. However, this research (again funded by the Swiss National Science Foundation) runs for another two years, and to communicate its results, when they have finally been consolidated, will thus need another book.

1 Topics of economic sociology in this book

Introduction

The first part of this chapter is a sort of general introduction for the reader, with a first clarification of concepts, distinctions and positions, while the second part examines different ways of modelling economic development. The sociological model of growth and structural change will then be further elaborated and tested in the appropriate chapters of this book. This is a speciality of this book: to develop arguments and then to put them to the test.

Let me make it clear right from the beginning what I understand by the term economic sociology. It is the sociological study of the economy or part of it. For instance, in this book the theme is economic development. The use of the label economic sociology to circumscribe the discipline is not at all intended to play sociology off against economics. By education, I am at the same time a sociologist and an economist, so the reader need not fear being seduced into a belief that sociologists have the right ideas and economists are wrong. That is not going to happen in this book. Neither will I give a summary of the broad field of economic sociology. There are excellent works available and I would like in particular to mention Richard Swedberg's 'Economic Sociology: Past and Present' for its lucidity and wealth of explanation, which the reader may wish to consult as a starting point.[1]

Of course, the topic of sociology is broader than that of economics, since sociological study includes all kinds of social phenomena and social actions and not only economic ones. Social actions that are not intentionally aimed at improving the efficiency of economic processes are also the topic of sociology, such as religion, the family, education and so on. This is not to say that such topics not directly connected with economic functions may not become indirectly relevant to the economy. A seminal recognition of such links was Max Weber's notion of economic behaviour, in which he introduced the analytical distinction between *economic* and *economically motivated* action, the latter aiming at economically valued resources without using economic means in the strict sense (Weber [1921]

1972: 31). Let me give examples to make this clear. The economy is only apparently a closed system, and thus is not distinct from other societal domains. Of course, the economy is the sphere of economic action, yet it is permeated by economically motivated behaviour (see Weber [1921] 1972). The latter happens, for example, if social power is used to gain economic advantages. Trade union power, for instance, can be used to acquire or expand participation in financial and organizational power, obtain wage increases, and achieve joint management in plants. Social power can also be used to influence legislation that concerns economic action, such as regulations about working hours and safety. Associations of firms, be they cartels or concerns, can be used in a similar fashion. Their activities are thus not confined merely to mutual agreements concerning markets, quality and prices. Furthermore, in many important respects, cultural power is also economically motivated. For example, in connection with the issue of education, one can observe that gradations in formal education form the basis for establishing exchange ratios between the culturally powerful and others in society. Finally, state power as a political form of social power is, after all, economically motivated. States tax economic activity and produce public goods, i.e. prerequisites for action. These themselves constitute factors of production; protection, i.e. social order and stability, enters the economic process at varying degrees of quality and cost, and will be discussed in several chapters of this book.

The social foundation of economic action

Economic action is social action in a certain sphere. Max Weber ([1921] 1972) saw the economic activity of an individual as social action, though he added the qualification that it should take account of the behaviour of someone else. This, I would argue, is most often the case since, for example, competition or information on prices presuppose at least the virtual or imagined presence of others.

But I would like to go a step further in emphasizing that both economic action and economically oriented action are basic to social life, and related in a fundamental way to freedom. The notion of efficiency that is used implies something other than the concept of efficiency used in physics. In physics the term effort, earlier also called effect, refers to the work performed as a result of a given force applied over a given time. Human action is more: the possibility and the claim to freedom, to autonomy of action. Ralf Dahrendorf (1979: 202) has argued that freedom signifies autonomous human action, and that different actions do not differ in dignity or meaning. Like Aristotle before him, Dahrendorf distinguishes between two components of human action, work and activity. In this duality, activity (*vita contemplativa*) refers to the individually chosen component and work (*vita activa*) to the externally determined component. For Aristotle, this ordering also implied a hierarchy of social classes. In his conception, the many were forced to lead a 'practical' life in order to make a 'contemplative' life possible for the few. Dahrendorf (1983: 89) states: 'This distinction has accompanied the passing centuries. No distinction has determined the formation of social classes more strongly than the one between "those who must work" and "those who do not have to work" '.[2] Yet 'the claim to freedom is always absolute. Limitations of freedom occur, but this does not make them tolerable' (Dahrendorf 1983: 91, my translation).

Freedom's various limitations cannot be detailed here. Instead, we shall now turn to some considerations concerning the important link between the striving after liberty and the striving after economic efficiency. Given a fixed time budget (twenty-four-hour day, limited life span) the claim to autonomy of action is limited by indispensable work which has to be done to secure survival. Autonomy of action can only increase if the time for necessary, i.e. existential, work is reduced. Time savings can either be used to reduce work time, thus rendering possible more free choice – true autonomy of action – or to improve the result of work so that consumption beyond basic needs becomes possible. No matter how time savings are used, they are always inspired by an attempt to enhance the results of efforts. This leads directly to economic efficiency. The economist Andreas Paulsen (1968: 9) once advanced a similar idea:

> Like all creatures man needs a minimal amount of nutrition, clothing and housing to survive. If by his economic action he can only meet these basic needs, he lacks the true freedom of economic decision-making between alternative possibilities. Only a surplus sets activities free and renders possible the unfolding of all the values of civilization. Thus, one may say that economic action is oriented towards the acquisition and utilization of a surplus that goes beyond the basic needs of man as a natural being.
>
> (my translation)

Although the surplus from work as a consequence of increasing economic efficiency may be distributed quite unequally, striving after liberty in the sense of self-realization and after economic efficiency are closely linked. Striving after efficiency includes individual realization and freedom as well as economic efficiency. Striving after greater freedom, namely autonomy of action, lies at the very core of striving after economic efficiency (economy of time). Yet, the latter does not necessarily have to lead to more freedom for everyone. Any extension of the room for action is subject to, and is embedded in, social power struggles. For this reason, not only the claim to equality, but also the claim to liberty, is very conflictive.

Under the modern capitalist division of labour, the claims to freedom and economic efficiency are integrated in a particular way. The use of energy for work, for activity, or any creative act must at least be compensated for by the exchange value of the outcome. Only this compensation justifies the use of energy under capitalist conditions. Here, the individual claim to freedom must find a compromise with economic efficiency. The success of human creation is determined by its profitability. For this reason one may say that acts of creation that do not feed their creator, either because they lack a market or because there is no effective demand for them, cannot be realized or, alternatively, must be subsidized (e.g. the arts). There is no possible resolution to this contradiction. Non-capitalist social systems, like traditional society, are organized around rigid normative structures. In such societies action is not subordinated to the demands of economic efficiency, yet at the same time they do not admit individual claims to freedom.

Therefore we come to the first conclusion: economic sociology is not an enterprise in competition with economics. When it comes to economic phenomena, sociology simply becomes economic sociology. Of course, there is always competition among different views of modelling and analysing phenomena with scientific rigour, but that is normal science. I myself side with the position that we have questions to solve and that there are different possible ways of doing so. Which one is more fruitful should be decided by empirical evidence.

Thus, my position is somewhat different from an argument often put forward when sociologists analyse economic facts and processes. They speak of the notion of 'embeddedness' which, although it might be a good slogan, is in a certain sense a misleading term, a fact to which Richard Swedberg (1987) has already drawn attention. The notion of the embeddedness of the economy in society was first spelled out by Karl Polanyi ([1944] 1978) who studied in his *Great Transformation* the disembedding of market society. It was Mark Granovetter (1985) who, in a very influential article, later applied the metaphor of embeddedness to the issue of what he called 'new' economic sociology. In a paper originally published in 1992 (see Granovetter 2000), he suggested a self-confident programme for the 'new' economic sociology, i.e. to conquer back lost territories from economists, who had increasingly narrowed their perspective. The problem with embeddedness is, however, that one can argue that the economy must always be framed by society; the study of the embedded part itself need not then be sociological. This could well result in a division of labour in which sociologists study the social frames of the economy while the study of the economy itself is delegated to economists, who study it according to their own paradigms, such as the presently hegemonic neoclassical approach.

My earlier statements should have made it clear that I am against such a possible interpretation of 'embeddedness'. The direction of economic sociology since the classical writings[3] has been quite straightforward: economic structures and processes are social systems and part of the larger social system. There is, then, no need for a 'new' economic sociology. All we need are good, theoretically based propositions for explaining what we define as the issues.

Before we come to the question of economic development and the enigma of economic growth, let me say something about two terms that occur in the title of this book.

Politics and culture may matter

In this book I argue, on the basis of evidence, that culture and politics are relevant to economic development – we shall come to a qualification of this at the end of this discussion.[4] For many readers, the assertion that culture and politics matter is hardly a novel idea. Yet mainstream economic growth models that have been prominent over recent decades mainly manage without reference to explicit notions of politics and culture (see pp. 15–17). This is not to accuse economists, since scholars from the other social sciences could have done that. But economists have not examined the issue, at least not to a satisfactory degree. To consider culture and politics in economic development is then a venture for all who are interested in development.

Better than arguing that the economy is embedded in society is to argue that the economy, culture and politics form a whole in a world politico-cultural economy. This is not common sense in the social sciences. The political scientist Robert Gilpin once pointed lucidly to preferences according to disciplines: 'Economists don't believe in power; political scientists, for their part, do not really believe in markets' Gilpin (1975: 7). To this I wish to add that, as economic sociologists, we would do better not to *believe* in anything, but to consider that culture, power on the part of states and corporations, and markets may all count. But how?

Culture, as a repertoire of learned and transmitted ideas, manifests itself at the collective as well as the individual level. It is a stock of positive knowledge and concerns values, norms, customs, technologies and modes of procedure. It has an ideational component relating to human consciousness as well as an objective expression in cultural artefacts and objects, e.g. books and machines. If it then refers to the totality of the life of a society – values, practices, symbols, institutions and human relationships – why should it be helpful in explaining social facts and development?

The answer lies in the degrees of freedom manifested in culture. Its potential variance ultimately begins with the manner of thinking and therefore with the imagination of alternative worlds, as well as its intersubjective mediation. Despite such alternatives, a group's culture is obliged to establish its manner of dealing with the world as the only correct, admirable and reasonable way. The self-evident behaviour of groups is based on this cultural principle. Groups normally live simultaneously under a kind of 'democracy' concerning participation in the common culture and a 'dictatorship' concerning positive knowledge. Within any given culture, there is then a certain tension between the knowledge of everyday practice, which produces identity and meaning, and the fact that it is possible to imagine alternatives. Therefore, culture is not unchangeable, yet a relatively constant factor in looking at groups and individuals.

What makes elements of culture interesting for comparative analysis is that you cannot predict them from purely material conditions. To make this less abstract I would like to point to our findings that the level of generalized trust in a society is only very poorly related to the level of average material wealth (see Chapter 2) and that the trust in other people that individual respondents report in interviews is only very poorly predicted by the hard facts of their ascribed and achieved social status (see Chapter 4). The very notion of culture simply stands for the possibility of looking at the world differently and of organizing society differently. Cultures may exist and have existed without a political order, but in the modern world the social order – as guaranteed by the state – is the embodiment of institutionalized culture at the collective level.

The arena of politics is, then, linked to culture. The imposition of rules governing social life and the conflict over it is in the very nature of politics. The outcomes of this conflictive process can be determined from below – 'by the people' – or set from above by autocratic powerholders. Such crudely differentiated forms of politics will later be discussed with more refinement in Chapter 5, when we address the varieties of democracy. The political culture as a subset of a society's overall culture is, however, not only determined by the political form. Moreover, in the same political form different political styles are not only possible but also empirically discernible, as we will show in more detail in Chapter 7.

What the term economy circumscribes has already been addressed above. Note that economic links have always, to a certain degree, transcended the borders of social orders organized by states, and not only since the catchword globalization became fashionable. The very fact that there exist many states means that the economic and the political spheres are necessarily linked in the world economy and that there is also economically motivated competition between the social orders guaranteed and protected by states. This notion of a competition between social orders has been developed in detail elsewhere (Bornschier [1988] 1996), but for our purpose here it is important to see that the social and material infrastructure provided by what has been termed social order, governed by state and culture, enters economic life. I emphasize that social order – also termed protection following Frederic Lane's protection rent theorem – is a territorially bounded public utility. Production, trade and financial transactions are conditional upon social prerequisites. They require support and protection. Property rights must be respected and people have to be motivated or obliged to engage in exchange relationships. These functions are by no means a secondary factor of production but at least as important as labour, knowledge, organizational resources, financial means and credit (Hintze [1929] 1964: 431). In my view, social order and protection has hitherto been an overly neglected element of national economic production functions. Governments, which can be viewed as political businesses, produce 'order' and sell this public utility to capitalist enterprises as well as to citizens under their rule. By means of supplying this utility, governments affect the quality of their territory in the framework of the world political economy.

This view is not only relevant for the production function when comparing societies but also for the theory of social evolution. The different supplies of social order – within which, for reasons of brevity, I here subsume culture and politics – compete in the world political economy. This competition acts as the social arena of selection. For long term economic development, the characteristics of a social order may be functional (i.e. they foster economic development in comparative perspective), dysfunctional (i.e. they impede economic development), or functionally irrelevant (i.e. they have no effect on comparative economic development at all). While functional irrelevance may be of little interest for the theory of economic development I would like to stress here that it is a good thing. It makes for the plenitude of cultural forms which for many of us represents the very essence of what makes social life rich and interesting, again both understood at the level of societies as well as individuals. Therefore, we need to qualify the relationship. Culture and politics are not necessarily relevant for economic development. To find out which elements are and which are not is then the task of economic sociology as it tries to explain development.

Economic development

Before we come to statements on what is thought of as important in economic development, let me first clarify the notion of economic development. Economic development contains two elements, growth and structural change. This is not only a substantial distinction to which social evolution theory draws our attention; it is also obvious. If one looks at human history, the forms of making a living have changed dramatically, from hunting and gathering to pastoral, fishing and horticultural societies, from these to simple and advanced agricultural societies, to industrial societies and, most recently, to knowledge-based society. In this advanced industrialized world today, only a comparatively small fraction of the active population physically touches a product, while the large majority is adding value through the creation, the management and the transfer of information.

Such great changes in the life of mankind, although very interesting in themselves, are not the topic of this book. Instead, we are concerned with the structural change from the Taylorist–Fordist way of using technologies and organizing production and consumption which became fashionable in the 1920s, diffused in the 1930s and led to the big boom after the Second

World War, to a new way of doing things which gradually emerged in its first manifestations in the 1970s, crystallized in the 1980s and started to diffuse on a large scale in the 1990s. I call this the new societal model of the extended market sphere in the telematics era, and see this as a new manifestation of a recurrent sequence of technological styles. I have had the opportunity elsewhere to explain this in more detail.[5] Whether readers are informed about the details of how I model this together with changing normative theories and a supportive politico-economic regime, and whether they like the idea, is not important here. The changes of the last two and a half decades are obvious and it is this change that is the topic of this book, regardless of whether one agrees that it is a recurrent phenomenon or not.

Economic growth

Economic growth is the second component of what is here summarized as economic development. Let me start with a few facts about economic growth. If one looks at the data for economic growth over very long periods, then it becomes obvious that growth has oscillated between phases of comparatively high and low growth. Angus Maddison (1995, 2001) has attempted the immense task of gathering figures for very long periods. In Figure 1.1 we take his periodization to demonstrate a regular sequence of high and low growth over time.[6] We distinguish between what Maddison calls Western Offshoots – USA, Canada, Australia, New

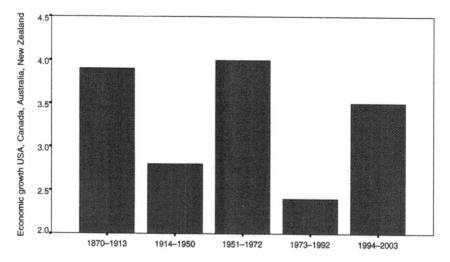

Figure 1.1a Estimates for economic growth in Western Offshoots: USA, Canada, Australia and New Zealand, weighted averages of real growth (net of inflation) (sources: growth periods from Maddison until 1992; since 1993 from IMF).

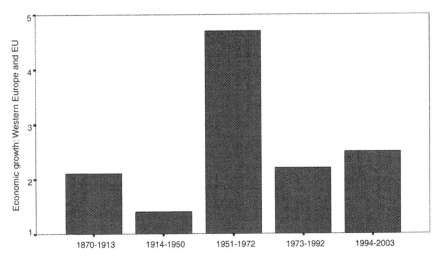

Figure 1.1b Estimates for economic growth in Western Europe and the EU, weighted average of real growth (net of inflation) (sources: Western Europe from Maddison until 1992; EU from IMF since 1993).

Zealand – and Western Europe. Note that the first group always had a much higher population growth, mainly through immigration from Europe. In Figure 1.2 we consider a single country to demonstrate the wave-like character of the booms and busts over time.[7] Switzerland is taken as an example case because its growth was less directly affected by the world wars.

These ups and downs in economic growth have attracted much attention in what has been called the long-wave literature (for an overview, see Bornschier 1996: Chapter 4). These regularities need to be taken into account in theories of economic development, and we will come later in the chapter to models of techno-economic change that try to model such discontinuities in economic growth over time.

Comparing a cross-section of countries over a smaller period of time reveals the second basic fact: growth rates vary considerably. Let me refer to figures presented by Jonathan Temple (1999: 117) in his review of the new growth evidence. In order to provide an impression of the huge range of economic growth Temple lists ten growth miracles and ten growth disasters over the period 1960–90. The figures relate to growth rates of output per worker. It only roughly represents labour productivity, since differences in working times are not controlled for.

In plotting economic growth against initial level (see for example Temple 1999: 117) one observes that economic growth differs at every level of material development. Furthermore, there is no general evidence for what is called convergence, i.e. the faster growth of less-developed

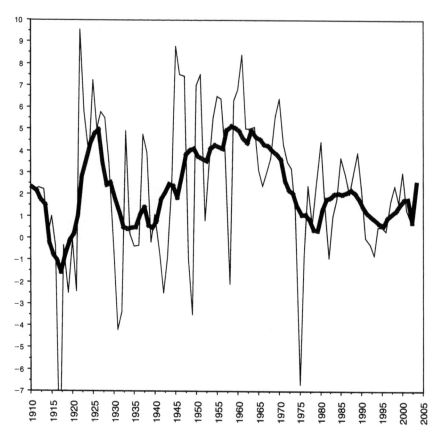

Figure 1.2 Estimates for economic growth in Switzerland (1910–2003). Yearly growth rates and moving average in bold; see note 7.

economies. This will be discussed more extensively in Chapter 2, where I call this the straggler effect. This seems to be the better term, since the term convergence suggests that the attempts of less-developed societies to catch up are finally successful. One may, empirically, find a straggler effect working, but convergence has not been the result, not since the big wave of decolonization after the Second World War and not since the 1980s. Temple (1999: 117) states in his overview:

> Overall, the figures and tables suggest that many of the most import-ant poor countries do not seem to be catching up to the USA's level of income. Instead, countries have roughly maintained their place within the world income distribution over the last thirty years or so, with little tendency for reduced income dispersion, and perhaps even some divergence.

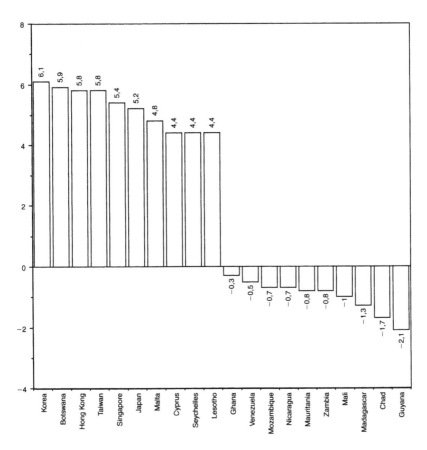

Figure 1.3 The range of economic growth demonstrated by listing ten growth miracles and ten growth disasters over the 1960–90 period. The growth
measure is: annual growth rates of output per worker (source: Temple
1999: 117).

Note
Approximately 160 countries in the world lie somewhere between these growth miracles and
disasters.

I recently published figures for the period between 1980 and 1997 on
the dispersion in average income per capita levels – expressed in purchasing power parities – for 103 countries which actually indicate an increasing
dispersion. Figure 1.4 presents the increasing dispersion of income levels
for 103 countries.[8]

The enigma of economic growth

As a sociologist, one is immediately inclined to ask about the functions of
economic growth for modern society. Of course, in the time before the

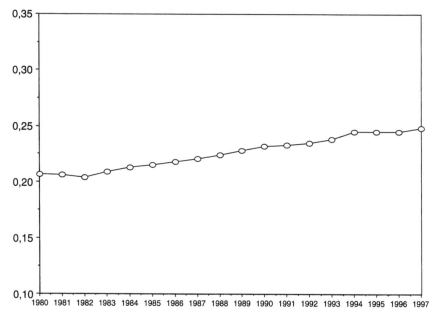

Figure 1.4 Dispersion of average income levels (at purchasing-power parities) from 1980–97. The dispersion measure is the mean logartithmic devia- tion (source: Bornschier 2002: 281 or Bornschier 2002b: 125).

breakthrough of the capitalist market economy there was growth; popula- tions grew and so did total economic output. What was peculiar is that effi- ciency increased only very slowly, and gains in total production were eaten up – literally – by an increasing population. Angus Maddison (1995) has performed the immense task of compiling data on growth for more recent periods of mankind, i.e. since 1500, see Table 1.1. Only after 1820 do the gains in economic productivity begin to exceed the increase in population (in some areas of the world), so that wealth per capita started to increase.

Why has growth become so important for sustaining modern society? I have already referred to the links between productivity and the possibility of freedom. Not only freedom but also equality is a core value of modern

Table 1.1 Historical growth records in the world aggregate

People and economic product	Annual compound growth rate (%)	
	1500–1820	*1820–1992*
World population	0.29	0.95
World economic product	0.33	2.17
Economic product per capita	*0.04*	*1.21*

Source: Figures from Angus Maddison 1995: 20.

society. At the same time, capitalist society is unequal. This is not to say that it is more unequal than earlier forms, but, crucially, this inequality co-exists with the claim to equality. In this context, economic growth is essential for social pacification. It nurtures a collective illusion of upward mobility and is capable of integrating even the less well-off part of the population: they can always rely on getting tomorrow what the upper strata, as social groups of reference, already have. This needs growth, and that is why growth is so important.

Economic growth means that there is always something that can be distributed, and the distribution is therefore not a zero-sum game. A while ago Albert O. Hirschman indicated the telling distinction between 'divisible' and 'non-divisible' conflicts:

> Typical conflicts in a society that is geared to a market economy revolve around the distribution of the national product to different classes, sectors or regions. Although these conflicts may differ, they are generally either 'more-or-less', i.e. divisible, conflicts or categorical 'either–or' i.e. non-divisible, conflicts. These conflicts are characteristic of societies that are split into rival ethnic, linguistic or religious groups.
> (Hirschman 1993: 26; my translation)

To emphasize the function of growth in modern society is, however, not to explain the differences in growth, why there is plenty together with scarcity, be it in comparisons over time or between societies.

Why, then, do there exist such considerable differences in economic growth between societies? If we are honest, then we must confess that we know little about it, although many economists have made it their focus of study. But let us first start with common sense. In the first place one has to consider that the economy has always grown or shrunk, for as long as mankind has been on the globe. This was even the case for hunters and gatherers, who collected more when climate and other factors were favourable and less when they were not. Their total production and consumption of food was dependent on the number of people who could engage in economic activity. As mentioned before, there was economic growth, since the total economic activity grew along with the number of people in the group. This is no different today; an economy grows if more people are engaged in it. Second, it grows in term of output if more tools and (later in human development) machines are used. Common sense then tells us that growth can be improved by technological progress.

Common sense arguments point to several variables which have also attracted attention in academic inquiry for a long time: the growth of physical capital and labour. But there are a substantial number of paradoxes. Robert Solow (1957), to whom we come again a bit later in the chapter, observed that only a small portion of the increase in labour productivity in the US between 1900 and 1950 could be accounted for by the increase in physical capital intensity. The vast majority of the increase remained unexplained. A bit less than half a century later, William Easterly and Ross Levine (2000: 1) had to confess:

> After accounting for physical and human capital accumulation, 'something else' accounts for the bulk of output growth in most countries and this 'something else' accounts for the majority of cross-country differences in both the level of gross domestic product (GDP) per capita and the growth rate of GDP per capita.[9]

We can call this 'something else' the enigma of economic growth, although I would like to mention here that, in the analyses later in the book, we will find that the growth of physical capital is a very strong (normally the strongest) predictor of economic growth in cross-national comparison. Yet this evidence is not quite free of important question marks. First, it is an ex-post analysis. During a certain period of time, investment in stocks grew because income grew. This is quite reasonable if investment is a certain portion of income that is not used for consumption. Second, the growth of total stock of physical capital may well include other factors, a qualitatively improved stock of capital and indirect effects of 'something else' that have spurred capital formation. Be that as it may, we have to solve the question of that 'something else'.

Of course, one may point to various reasons why some countries prosper while others fall back, whether such factors are conventional or novel. For example, one can make the case that it is geography and its consequences (productivity of soil, problems of diseases) that counts. This is not convincing in general. Why do the two Koreas differ in plenty? This is hardly because of geography, except that the dividing line was drawn on the basis of geography (47th latitude).[10]

To help to shed some light on this enigma, this book looks at elements of culture and politics so as to improve the explanation of economic development. How, in what forms, and to what extent do both matter – in addition, of course, to the undisputed classical growth factors? More precisely, among the cultural aspects I will focus on generalized trust, which has received considerable interest as a source of social capital among both sociologists and economists. The very broad sphere of politics will not only be represented by degrees of democracy as a political form but also by political styles and their different political outcomes. To more fully represent the political sphere, we also include new state forms at the supranational level, like the EU. In the concluding chapters we inquire into the persistence of societal traits in the transition to the new model of the extended market sphere of the telematics era, and how this shift came about despite the differences we find among developed countries. The main, albeit not exclusive, methodological approach used in this book is the cross-national comparison, which is sometimes called a quasi-experimental type of research design.[11] In some of the analyses we do not confine ourselves to country comparisons but also include data at the individual level (see especially Chapter 4). This quantitative approach is supplemented for some analyses by qualitative research based on interviews and documents (see especially Chapter 8).[12]

Before we come to these issues in their specific chapters, let me add my introductory remarks on modelling economic growth and techno-economic change. While distribution and inequality are topics which I have addressed regularly in my previous work, such questions are not included here; they need a separate book.[13]

Approaches to economic development – an overview

Sociology has a less extensive record of formal modelling than economics, so we shall begin with economic approaches; this will make clear what the sociological theory of economic growth and change is all about when the reader encounters it later.

For decades, economic growth theory has been based on the neoclassical, Solow–Swan model (Solow 1956, Swan 1956). Only in recent years, beginning in the 1980s, was it challenged or, as Gregory Mankiw (1995) put it, supplemented, by endogenous growth theory.

The starting point of the Solow–Swan model is a Cobb–Douglas production function (assuming constant returns to scale) of the following type:

$$Y(t) = K(t)^a L(t)^{1-a} \tag{1}$$

Where Y indicates total output or income, K physical capital and L labour.

The Cobb–Douglas function, which I admired as a student for its simplicity, attempts to reduce the enormous complexity of economic life by simply focusing on the two input factors at the aggregate level. Such generalization is what macrotheory normally does; what counts is the quality of insights available from the abstraction.

The question to be solved by the neoclassical model is: what is the growth rate like in the long run? Taking rates of growth of population and savings as exogenously determined, the Solow–Swan predicts that, in the long run, the economy approaches a steady state which should be independent of initial conditions (see Mankiw 1995: 277). Then the steady state growth is solely dependent on the rate of savings, the rate of population growth and on the rate of technological progress (Mankiw 1995: 277). Remember that all these mentioned factors which then make for differences in growth are exogenous, i.e. there is no immanent theoretical explanation for them.

This said, I have already pointed to some characteristics which make neoclassical growth theory a less than attractive starting point for my studies on growth differences in this book. Technological progress, population and savings growth are not explained. Furthermore, relying on steady state growth, the model, as Mankiw (1995: 283) has shown, 'does not predict the large differences in income observed in the real world'. This simply means that in the real world other variables must exist which explain growth differences or, to put it differently: 'If countries are in different steady states, then rich countries remain rich, and poor countries remain poor.' (Mankiw 1995: 284). We then have different steady states for each economy, as Mankiw says, but I disagree with him that this is only or mainly 'determined by the saving and population growth rates' (Mankiw 1995: 284).

To find out what the reasons are for such different growth rates, typically for countries over a longer period of time, is the purpose of comparative sociological growth theory, to which we come after a brief discussion of some extensions of the neoclassical model.

Endogenous growth theory

In the absence of technological progress, economic growth per capita of employed labour unit should, theoretically, eventually disappear due to diminishing returns on physical capital investment. This is not what has happened, nor what will happen. Therefore, why not include this technological progress into the model? Actually this is the basic idea behind endogenous growth theory. As Mankiw (1995: 296) put it: 'A simple change in the production function can dramatically alter the predictions about economic growth.' The extended Cobb–Douglas production function is as follows:

$$Y(t) = K(t)^a (A(t)L(t))^{1-a} \tag{2}$$

Where A indicates the level of technology or the human capital available which has become endogenous. There exist two schools with different emphases on how to interpret A in formula (2). Romer (1986, 1994, see also Whiteley) claims that is chiefly research and development which is the key to technology and which makes the economy grow above the steady state rate, while Lucas (1988) assumes that it is mainly the greater stock of human capital, formal education and learning by doing which drives and makes for different growth rates.

Be that as it may, formula (2) implies for endogenous growth theory that differences are not only dependent on savings and population growth rates but also on technological progress, as well as the capacity of the population to absorb and apply that growth of progress, very abstractly denoted by A(t). When it comes to the absorption and application of new technological tools like the Internet, which will be discussed in Chapter 3, it becomes clear that, for understanding international differences in the

absorption of technological knowledge, the direct payoffs from endogenous growth theory need to be improved. This is also what Mankiw (1995:
300) is saying: 'Models that emphasize unmeasurable variables such as
knowledge are hard to bring to the data.'[14] This should not, of course,
detract us from trying to refine the construction of theory so that they
become testable, and this is one of the salient efforts of the research this
book reports (for the issue mentioned in this paragraph, see especially
Chapters 3 and 6).

In principle one can incorporate other social, cultural and political
factors into a production function from which testable propositions can be
deduced. We need, however, to specify how they should interact with the
classical factors of production, physical capital and labour.

Comparative sociological theory of economic growth and change

While the details of the sociological arguments will be presented in the
various chapters of the book on specific issues, I would like to give some
sort of general summary here of the different directions that are possible.

We start with the question of economic growth and acknowledge that
the classical factors of production as spelled out in formula (1) are also
valuable for macrosociological approaches, since they are, theoretically
and empirically, well established predictors of growth, although they might
not explain all the differences in comparative perspective or might themselves need to be explained sociologically. For economic growth over a
certain period of time it follows from equation (1):

growth of income $[Y]$ = growth of physical capital $[K]^{b_1}$ growth
of Labour $[L]^{b_2}$ $\qquad\qquad$ (3)

In this multiplicative baseline model growth indicates: $Y(t+1)/Y(t)$,
$K(t+1)/K(t)$, and $L(t+1)/L(t)$. The exponents represent elasticities, i.e.
they inform us which percentage change in the right-hand side of the equation goes together with a percentage increase in the left-hand side variables. The reason why I do not divide the whole equation by the value for
labour is explained in Box 1.1.

To the baseline equation of the growth model in formula (3) we add
two kinds of vectors, representing social characteristics of theoretical
interest, in comparative perspective.

In comparative static perspective we add a vector called C; it denotes
characteristics of the social context within which the economic activity
takes place. In fact, C denotes a bundle of socially and economically relevant information which we will spell out in more detail in the following
chapters. Some examples will be given below.

When one wants to explain change in dynamic perspective, we need to
add a vector called D. D symbolizes the dynamics of two related but only

---

Box 1.1 Why I rely on total income (or product) as the dependent variable and control for labour

I have not divided the baseline growth equation in formula (3) by labour to achieve a growth of output per unit of labour input in the function of growth of physical capital per unit of labour input. This transformation is normally made, and for theoretical purposes it is in order. But for relating such formulas to real data, researchers use population weights as proxies for labour. Comparable labour figures are not available, since the number of labourers is no indication of labour input; some work longer days or have fewer holidays, some are only active part time. The product per work unit would be the desirable measure, indicating labour productivity. But such figures are not easily and reliably to hand for different countries. When researchers do use population as a weight to arrive at per capita figures, this is not only a very questionable proxy but it also changes the meaning. The product per population is not a measure of eco-nomic efficiency or, more precisely, of labour productivity, but a measure of average wealth, which is something quite different. The easiest way to understand that difference is to imagine that the same product per population can either be produced by a smaller propor-tion of highly productive workers or by a larger proportion of less productive workers. Given the huge demographic differences in comparing societies, one should therefore rely on growth of total income and control for the growth of labour input. The latter method is less biased since it is measured as a growth rate. If labour input is not comparable across societies, this will affect the growth rate less, as long as incomparabilities between countries remain the same over the growth period.

---

partly matched cycles that theoretically account for techno-economic change. We shall come to this soon. First let me formally present the two models.

In comparative perspective (comparing cases), with the new element in the equation in bold:

$$\text{growth of } Y = \text{growth of } K^b{}_1 \text{ growth of } L^b{}_2 \, \mathbf{C^b{}_3} \tag{4}$$

In dynamic perspective (comparing one case or a cross-section of cases over time), with the new element in the equation in bold:

$$\text{growth of } Y = \text{growth of } K^b{}_1 \text{ growth of } L^b{}_2 C^b{}_3 \, \mathbf{D^b{}_4} \tag{5}$$

In both of the models, represented by formulas (4) and (5), the impact of contextual or dynamic factors can work both indirectly or directly. The best way to communicate this distinction is by pointing to examples. An overview is found in Table 1.2. We first focus on contextual factors in comparative perspective, which are denoted by C in the above formulas.

Comparative static models compare economic growth across different societies. The growth period should be long enough to ensure that differences are meaningful and not affected by differences in links to the world business cycle. About fifteen to twenty years are sufficient in order to obtain such typical growth rates. The countries to be compared may differ in theoretically relevant social characteristics and processes. Although such traits of nations may change, they typically change very slowly and can be taken as fairly stable for comparative purposes. Take, for example, education: increasing levels of schooling will affect the overall proliferation of education in a society only gradually. One should furthermore only compare those countries with the relevant basic institutions. Throughout this book the focus is on capitalist economic growth, so the societies to be compared should be market economies.

In principle, we can thus choose between two approaches. The first of these assumes that the historic constellation of social forces – be it from structure or culture – is unique; this translates then into a so-called singularizing approach which offers an individual account for every case of the complex influences of society on the opportunities of economic growth. Such comparative case studies have their own value due to the wealth of information they can process for single societies, and I have done such

Table 1.2 An overview of different sociological approaches in modelling economic growth and techno-economic change

	Comparative static models	*Dynamic models*
Social characteristics affect indirectly	*Model I* $dY = dKdL$ $dK = f(C)$ $dL = f(C)$	*Model III* $dY = dKdL$ $dK = f(D,C)$ $dL = f(D,C)$ $C = f(D)$
Social characteristics as part of the economy	*Model II* $dY = dKdLC$	*Model IV* $dY = dKdLCD$

Notes
This is a simplified presentation: d for example in dY stands for $Y(t+1)/Y(t)$, and so on. The exponents in the equations (representing elasticities) have, for purposes of simplification, been omitted.

comparative case studies, too, for instance on Japan in comparison with the Atlantic West and Korea, Taiwan and Malaysia in comparison with Latin American cases (Brazil, Mexico, Argentina). In this book, however, we do not follow this approach.

The second methodological approach, which is applied in this book, is to work with theoretical generalizations that suggest social factors relevant for economic growth. Such factors are present in the societies to be compared to a different degree. Societies then can be scaled according to such factors, which one calls a variable. The art of this type of quantitative comparison of society, which is called the cross-national (sometimes also cross-sectional) approach, is then to generalize and to have far fewer variables you consider to be theoretically relevant than cases you compare. The reason is very simple (and called in technical jargon the degrees-of-freedom problem); the more your number of variables approaches the number of cases, the more likely you are to find one relevant factor for every case. Then you move in the direction of the singularizing approach just described. Later in the book we will often work with comparatively small samples of about two dozen societies. In such situations it is necessary that one confines the theoretical models to a small number of predictors which are really independent, so that every variable does not measure too much of what is covered by another variable. In other words, too many variables which contain too little independent information will make it almost impossible to effectively test theoretical propositions.

In model I of Table 1.2 the theoretical impact of social characteristics is thought of as being merely indirect. A classical statement in sociology can be taken to give a first example. Max Weber argued that the cultural–religious pattern of 'inner ascetism', especially present in certain protestant denominations, combined achievement motivation with economizing,[15] which was historically important for economic development and the spread of modern capitalism, since it led to more savings and demand for their use in productive investment. This is then an historical example where an element of the socio-cultural context embodied in C led to faster growth of capital formation and thereby to more economic progress. Although capital formation does not, at first glance, seem to be a sociological topic, there have been contributions to this from an economic sociology perspective which studied the capital accumulation of firms. This process later culminated in a view of the role of transnational corporations in economic development that might be summarized as 'capital is not capital, the source is what matters', a hotly debated issue since it first entered the top journals of our profession.[16]

Another example comes from social demography, which has a lot to say about development of the potential labour force due to fertility differences across countries and time. The same is true for labour regulation policies (including the stance of states and societies on child labour and minimum wages). Such examples point to links between social facts and the availability of labour and economic growth.

Political programmes designed to legitimize society by satisfying demands for upward mobility via the educational system may result in the increased proliferation of education in society and therefore affect the quality of labour available in the economy (at the same time they may somewhat reduce the quantity of labour, since people that are extensively educated enter the economy later).

Our examples make clear that the source of differences in context characteristics that indirectly work on economic growth can be both culturally and politically based. This type of modelling is termed stepwise, as known from path analysis in sociology.

Model II in Table 2 is different since it uses the idea that social factors are part of the economic process, in terms of formalization; they directly enter the production function. In this model, to take a metaphor, social facts are the lubricants of economic transactions. This is plausible since capital and labour are very abstract categories, and models of the mentioned Cobb–Douglas type tell us little about the specificities of the social processes in an economy. Cultural and political factors enrich this dearth by pointing to variables that are to different degrees favourable for co-operation, for meeting contracts and improving productivity at the work place and in distribution. It should be recalled, too, that they influence consumption, without which, of course, there would be neither economic activity nor economic growth.

Such factors as generalized trust, which we will discuss and test in this book, are cultural, yet are also embodied in institutions, not only political ones but also in commerce. There are many studies that demonstrate in businesses how the feeling of just and legitimate procedures within the firm foster productivity and innovation.[17] This is then an example that the mechanisms that are supposed to work in the economy at large are also verifiable at lower levels, not only in firms but also among individuals, as shown by experiments which we shall briefly discuss in Chapter 4.

A further example of cultural factors being directly part of the economy are value preferences. Value priorities, as measured by post-materialism in the seminal work of Ronald Inglehart (see his first elaborated statement in 1977), affect economic processes to the extent that they are proliferated, and they do this by shifting the utility functions, as argued by Volker Kunz (2000).

Lastly, cultural attitudes, such as the sense of duty (*pacta servanda*), which make for greater predictability of action, with considerable implications, also support the general proposition that cultural characteristics may make the economy run much more easily because they make the same amount of classical factors of production more productive.

Factors facilitating economic exchange (or impeding it, since not all social traits have a positive outcome) are, needless to say, not confined to the purely cultural sphere but can also be purely political. I shall here indicate just a few examples, since we have ample opportunity later in the book to dwell more on this (see especially Chapters 5–7). Democracy is a complex set of institutions with many consequences; by allowing freedom of coalition and thereby determining the basic framework of how labour can bargain with capital, for instance, it indirectly, yet in some cases profoundly, affects the economy. Different political styles within democracies develop distinct ways of regulating the economy, which in turn affect the way it operates. We come back to this by examining varieties of capitalism.

In sum, in model II of Table 1.2, social factors are directly part of the economy, and in formalized terms, part of the production function. Although the basic idea is similar to what endogenous growth theory suggests for technology and human capital, the scope of social factors I consider relevant in comparative sociological growth theory is much broader. Economists have increasingly become interested in including political institutions as well as culture in their models of growth (see, among many others, Knack and Keefer 1995, 1997 and Temple 1999, for an overview).

In Figure 1.5 I add an illustrative, though not an exhaustive, synopsis of the various ways in which social variables enter the world of the sociological modelling of comparative growth in models I and II which were listed in Table 1.2.

Dynamic sociological modelling: analysing economic change

Although there exists excellent and groundbreaking work by the economist and sociologist Joseph Schumpeter[18] on change which applies a

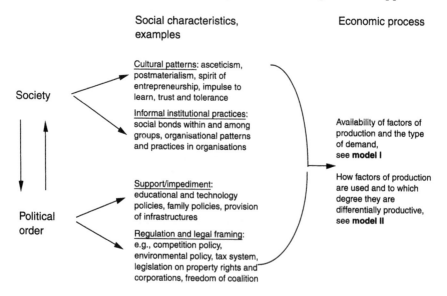

Figure 1.5 Examples of the way society and its characteristics enter the economic process; a non-exhaustive list to exemplify the Models I and II in Table 1.2.

dynamic, rather than merely comparative static, approach, not much progress has been made on theoretically modelling the process of discontinuous change in technological styles and the corresponding matching of the politico-institutional subsystem.

Endogenous growth theory in economics gives value to the role of technology (as neoclassical growth theory also did, albeit as an exogenous factor to its model) but has no understanding yet of discontinuous technological evolution, and even now has not developed tools to include that discontinuity in its modelling.

Central to the sociological understanding of technological evolution is that it is discontinuous (as Joseph Schumpeter stressed) and that it is the result of an interplay between two social subsystems, the techno-economic and the politico-institutional. This latter was the original and groundbreaking idea of Carlota Perez[19] in following and, at the same time in very important respects, overtaking the first doyen of innovation research in the twentieth century.

Although I had the opportunity to present my ideas based on Perez's stimulating work elsewhere (see note 19) and although we come to this later in the book (Chapter 3), some basic considerations should be mentioned here.

Assume that a new technological style (originally a term of Perez's) has in its cyclical development distinct phases in being built up and in being diffused throughout the economy in order to change again. Furthermore, consider, following Perez, that the technological style cannot flourish – be fully developed and diffused throughout the economy – without the matched provisions of infrastructures and regulations provided by the state sphere. Furthermore, take into account that the cycles of the style and the matching of the state are not completely chronologically matched due to the different rationales which govern social action in the two spheres. Then a complex process results, a dynamic of two related but only partly matched cycles, which are described in Box 1.2.

$D(t)$ is the term we use to represent the result of the complex interplay of the two related, but only partly matched, social processes that make in our view for discontinuous technological development, see details in Box 1.2. This may have an indirect and a direct effect on the economic growth rate, see also Table 1.2.

In model III of Table 1.2, the dynamics of technological style change, $D(t)$, affect the economy indirectly through their impact on capital and labour. According to the values of $D(t)$, investors may be more or less willing to invest according to expectation, being a function of $D(t)$. Furthermore, capital and labour may be affected by booms and busts, the latter affecting the 'creative destruction', which Schumpeter stressed, or restructuring and downsizing, which are relatively new to our vocabulary.

Finally, in model IV of Table 1.2, it is assumed that, irrespective of the size of labour and capital inputs, the state of the development of both

Box 1.2 The interrelated but only partly matched cycles of technological style and politico-economic regime development

For technological style as well as politico-economic regime I distinguish between four phases. For the *regime*, these phases are: (1) formation; (2) unfolding; (3) saturation and signs of dissolution; and (4) decay. The social impact of the politico-economic regime oscillates between growing and diminishing problem-solving capacity:

(1) Formation   (2) Unfolding

Minimum ⟶ Maximum
problem-solving ⟵ problem-
solving
capacity   (4) Decay   (3) Saturation capacity and
phenomena of dissolution

For *technological style* (which I use synonymously with what Carlota Perez calls 'techno-economic subsystem') the following phases can be distinguished:

1   elements of a new technological style become linked;
2   the style crystallizes and diffuses;
3   the diffusion process becomes saturated as elements of a new style emerge; and
4   the technological style becomes more heterogeneous.

The social process of the technological style oscillates between decreasing and increasing homogeneity. Once a new style has been fully diffused, homogeneity reaches its maximum:

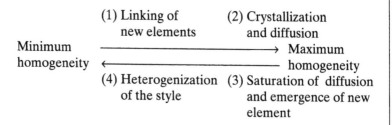

Thus, we have two social processes which are related to each other and oscillate between two states in four phases. Both social processes are decisive for economic management processes and for the conflict cycle during the course of the societal model.

The problem-solving capacity of a politico-economic regime refers to the institutional infrastructure of economic processes and is thus an important aspect of the macroeconomic production function. It creates the preconditions for economic growth. The phases of the technological style, on the other hand, are decisive for profits and industrial expansion. During the linking phase (1) quantum leaps in productivity lead to increased or renewed profit margins for certain groups of enterprises, but not for all. The reinvestment of profits for a harmonious dissemination of the style remains modest, however, because the expansion of consumption is limited. During these phases, there is a tendency to favour financial against industrial investments.

This changes during the crystallization phase (2). Cumulative upward processes result from the expansion of consumption and the reinvested earnings accruing from the quantum leaps in productivity. Still, it is important to note that the gains and industrial reinvestments as a whole result from the adoption of the new technological style because this includes the quantum leaps in productivity. Thus, the more the style has diffused, the weaker the aggregated growth surges.

For our purposes, we assume that the two unfolding processes oscillate regularly between lesser and greater problem-solving capacities of a regime, on the one hand, and between lesser and greater homogeneity of the economic units with respect to the technological style, on the other. 'Regular' means that we are positing a constant rate of the social process.

If the phases follow each other at a constant rate, harmonious swings like those of a sine function result. Thus, problem-solving capacity and homogeneity can be represented as functions of time. Yet this image of harmonious swings must not be misunderstood as an occurrence of one and the same thing. Rather, I interpret them in the following way: although each technological style and each politico-economic regime is historically unique, they follow similar processes of emergence and decay in the course of time.

We must keep in mind, however, that the processes arising from the technological style and the politico-economic regime do not occur simultaneously. In terms of harmonious swings there is a phase displacement. The foregoing theoretical argument explaining this refers to different logics of social management. Decisions affecting the components of the technological style are made in a decentralized way, guided by the market, on the basis of actors' individual utility calculations. However, decisions concerning the components of the politico-economic regime require the prior formation of consensus and collective action. These processes are not value-neutral but closely linked to values and interests.

From this follows the aforementioned lack of coincidence of the two processes, even if the intention exists to bring them together. The time lag of the politico-economic regime is the result of two factors:

1   The extent to which both processes are intentionally linked to each other;

2   The rate of the process of consensus-building, i.e. the rate at which collective decisions can be taken.

The first factor refers to the relationship between the economy and the state, which has varied historically as well as between societies. Despite the new role of the interventionist state after 1932 (see figure below to this Box) the United States preserved a more liberal view of the relationship between the economy and the state. Thus, notwithstanding notable successes during the formation phase of the new regime (1933–45) this hampered the unfolding of the regime after 1945. The second factor relates to the political order and its mechanisms of collective decision-making. I assume that the time lag grows longer under more democratic decision-making processes. Authoritarian systems can more quickly adopt the regime to the style, but they do not reach as durable a level of basic consensus as democracies do.

These considerations about different time lags will be taken up again later. First, however, one must make certain simplifying assumptions central to our model. I assume a displacement of one-quarter of a phase, whereby the formation phase (1) of the regime and the crystallization phase (2) of the style are linked to each other. The new technological style starts before its crystallization as new elements have begun to unfold significantly earlier. In the crystallization phase all elements are present and linked but not homogeneously distributed over all enterprises.

In the figure below both processes – problem-solving capacity (regime) and homogenization (style) – are depicted with a phase displacement of one-quarter. The development of these processes over time can be represented as two phase-displaced sine waves. The full unfolding of the regime only takes place after the technological style has reached its maximum homogenization.

Change or development, D(t), we call the result of the complex interplay of the two related, but only partly matched, social processes that make in our view for discontinuous technological development. This may have an indirect and a direct effect on the economic growth rate, see Table 1.2.

In model III of Table 1.2, the dynamics of technological style change, D(t), affect the economy indirectly through its impact on capital and labour. According to the values of D(t), investors may be more or less willing to invest according to expectation, being a function of D(t). Furthermore, capital and labour may be affected by booms and busts, the latter affecting the 'creative destruction', which Schumpeter stressed, or restructuring and downsizing, which are relatively new in our vocabulary.

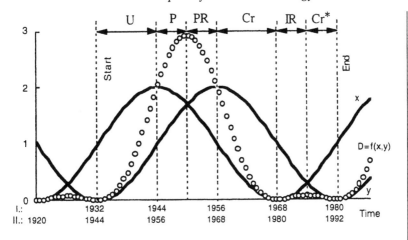

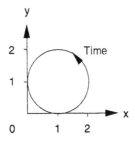

Phase-displaced cycles of the diffusion of the technological style and of the problem-solving capacity of the politico-economic regime and the ensuing probability of economic expansion in a dynamic model (D)

Notes
U (upswing), P (prosperity), PR (prosperity/recession), Cr (crisis), IR (interim recovery), Cr* (depression, renewed crisis).
Periodization for the last cycle from Bornschier [1988] 1996:
I   The periodization for the pioneers like Sweden, US, Switzerland, New Zealand.
II Adjusted periodization. Due to the Second World War the formation for large parts of the developed countries – excluding the United States and other societies not destroyed or restricted by the consequences of war – was delayed (new beginning after the war). The new beginning is dated to 1944/5 when the new world order of the post-war era was created (Bretton Woods, Yalta).
x(t); diffusion (homogenization) of the technological style.
y(t): problem-solving capacity of the politico-economic regime.
$D(t) = y(t) \times (t)$, indicating the ensuing probability of economic expansion.

Finally, in model IV of Table 1.2, it is assumed that, irrespective of the size of labour and capital inputs, the state of the development of both cycles, D(t), will make for different economic growth rates over time. This may be the consequence of varying legitimacy, trust, and optimism, which are affected over time by the joint cycle, D(t).

(Source: Bornschier 1996: 152–5)

cycles, $D(t)$, will make for different economic growth rates over time. This may be the consequence of varying legitimacy, trust, and optimism, which are affected over time by the joint cycle, $D(t)$.

Summary (see also Table 1.2)

(I) Political and social factors may determine the availability and amount of factors of production and thus indirectly influence the outcome in the economy.

(II) Political and social factors influence how, and how effectively, factors of production are used. Social characteristics such as socio-cultural orientations (generalized trust and tolerance) or socio-institutional practices of cooperative economic institutions differently affect, for example, transaction costs, and thus determine how effectively factors of production are used and thereby how economic growth is affected.

Political and social factors together with economic factors jointly determine socio-political and socio-economic change. We have pointed to the joint effects of the politico-institutional and the techno-economic subsystem on technological change. This can again be modelled indirectly (III), or directly (IV).

While (I) and (II) model reasons for differences in growth in comparative perspective, (III) and (IV) explain techno-economic change with a dynamic theory suggesting discontinuous technological change and booms and busts in economic growth. The latter is also the topic of long waves of growth in capitalist development. Indeed, I suggest an explanation for these Kondratiev cycles of about forty-five to sixty years length.[20]

In the various chapters of this book I develop the sociological models discussed in this overview further and put propositions derived from them to an empirical test. Rather than other characteristics, this link between theory and data is the speciality of this book.

PART I

Why and to what extent do cultural resources matter?

The focus of Part I is on generalized trust as a cultural resource, which has attracted increasing attention from sociologists and economists. In the first chapter we address the significance of non-economic predictors of economic success, particularly generalized trust in its capacity for social capital formation. First, the concepts of effective social order and social capital are located in the sociological and economic tradition in order to deepen the debate over the economic significance of social capital. We reflect on the following mediated linkages: the cultural, structural and political characteristics of societies are shown to be related to the capacity for formation of social capital among the population. The latter help specific forms of social capital in the economy to prosper, which is then seen as a factor for comparative economic success. We develop a new sociological growth equation and test it in samples of thirty-three and twenty-four countries. This allows us to consolidate the finding of the pioneering study by Knack and Keefer. Indeed, generalized trust turns out to be an important predictor of economic growth between 1980 and the end of 1998.

In an innovative new step, the next chapter considers generalized trust not only in its function of making existing actions and arrangements more productive but also in its second, newly discovered function, i.e. of making people more open towards change. This we demonstrate by examining the early proliferation of Internet usage using a sample of thirty-four developed and newly industrializing countries as well as a subsample of twenty-one rich societies.

Whether that new proposition is tenable is the question we address in the last chapter of this part. Does generalized trust really foster openness to change in general and in social spheres beyond the Internet? We approach this question by applying a different methodology. We rely on interviews with about 22,000 people from fifteen rich democracies. The support that we find for the proposition, by analysing three additional indicators to measure the inclination to change, raises new questions that are discussed in the last chapter of this section. What are the sources of generalized trust at the individual level? What are the implications of a culture of trust for theories of entrepreneurship?

2 Trust and growth

The issue of trust in the sociological and economic traditions[1]

The idea that trust fosters reciprocity and cooperation is hardly a new one, as evidenced by the classical writings of, for example, Alexis de Tocqueville, John Stuart Mill and Georg Simmel.[2] The more specific proposition, that the extent to which citizens are willing to cooperate with each other on the basis of interpersonal trust will affect the efficiency of political and economic institutions and thereby economic progress, is quite recent and, through the seminal work of Robert Putnam, Francis Fukuyama and James Coleman, has triggered a lively ongoing debate.[3] I understand this willingness to trust others, often strangers, without expecting that they will immediately reciprocate this trust, as a cultural resource, as an enabler if not a necessary precondition of modern social capital formation. But is social capital a sociologically meaningful concept, or does this fashionable social science term simply conceal a hegemonic claim on the part of our neighbouring discipline, economics? Intuitively, social capital has positive connotations and appears to be associated with 'good social order'. This offers us a point of entry into the discussion and an opportunity to put the various questions about social capital in sociology and economics in relation to each other.

Effective social order as a source of success in the competitive world milieu is a central thesis in my evolutionary explanation of Western society. This notion has been evaluated on the basis of both historical material and rigorous statistical tests using cross-national comparisons of core countries covering almost four decades in the postwar era.[4] What is an effective social order? We can say that, if the members of a society grant legitimacy to a social order, then this order becomes effective, although it must be acknowledged that the concept of legitimacy, like the concept of social capital, is elusive. We turn next to the relationship between effective social order and social capital.

The sociological tradition has, since its inception, discussed the question of societal order by focusing on the negative end of the continuum of social order. Social disorientation and disorganization – two facets of the understanding of anomie in the sociological tradition of Emile Durkheim and Robert Merton respectively – describe the variable absence of effective social order. We now expand this scale towards the positive end of the continuum, where we find variable degrees of qualitatively good social order.

Such considerations relate to the concern of a growing number of economists who seek to take into account non-economic factors of economic success. Because they want to grasp the sources of the efficiency of an economic system in accordance with the central theme of economics, they name these non-economic dimensions 'social capital'. In so doing, the definition of capital is broadened. A quotation from Simon Kuznets expresses what is meant here:

> Labor, in its most abstract meaning, which has been most closely approximated in Marxian discussion, i.e. as elementary socially useful labor time, unadorned by investment in training and education, is then the first productive factor. Everything else, whether it is investment in the training and education of active participants in production, or investment in material stock, or an element of enterprise, is capital – in the sense that it provides conditions for augmenting product per manhour.
>
> (Kuznets 1958/59: 5)

The meaning of this broader definition of capital becomes clear by contrasting it with the narrower definition of capital as physical capital: 'Physical capital includes all permanent facilities that serve production, living and administration, as well as the stock of reserves' (Kleinewefers and Pfister 1982: 301). In the broader definition, however, capital becomes a combination of things that is socially shaped in a diverse manner (cf. Bornschier 1988: 55, 1996: 45f.). In the framework of another definition of capital, we encounter the differentiation displayed in Table 2.1.

I claim, in unison with a growing community of researchers, that factors

Table 2.1 Types of capital

Type of capital	Producers of this type of capital
• Physical capital	Capital goods industry and construction industry
• Human capital	State, school, trade associations, training in companies
• Technological capital	Procedural knowledge, technical: science, R&D within companies
• Social capital as organizational models in firms and in the economy	Procedural knowledge – organizational: entrepreneurs and managers
• Social capital as conditions relevant for economic transactions	State, civil society, interest groups and family

like physical capital and investment of labour can only partially explain economic success; in addition, human capital, technological capital and the social capital of a country are also important for its affluence and its competitive strength. Francis Fukuyama's 1995 book, *Trust: The Social Virtues and the Creation of Prosperity*, certainly contributed to the wide attention paid to the importance of non-economic factors, and hence to social capital.

If one wants to evaluate the thesis that effective social order, based on legitimacy, is also economically advantageous, then legitimacy in turn can be seen as necessary for the formation of social capital. Consequently, in pursuit of the sources of economic efficiency, we see that there is no difference between the two. To be sure, the idea of effective social order is much broader than that of social capital. Effective social order can be a goal and value in itself, and it can also be relevant outside the sphere of economics in all remaining areas of society. This concludes our clarification of the partial identity of two theoretical concepts, which at first glance may appear quite distant from one another.

With this, we come to an initial description of effective social order, its meaning as social capital, which will later be elaborated even further: specific forms of social capital can be formed more easily if the members of society attribute legitimacy to social arrangements. These facilitative factors develop their economically extremely relevant productivity through their moderation of ever-present latent conflict, allowing trust, tolerance, confidence and, with these, cooperation to take the place of mistrust and confrontation. Through this facilitation of social cooperation, existing contexts of action in the economy become more productive and new contexts of action are more easily created.

In order to pursue the question of how social capital influences economic efficiency, one must first outline a model of aggregate economic performance and of growth. We do so in the next section of this chapter, in which we specify relevant contextual factors for the development of economic efficiency and bring a discussion of the straggler effect and social capital to the foreground. In the subsequent section we report on previous empirical work using indicators for social capital. Finally, in the concluding section, we report and discuss our new results.

The equation for estimating economic growth

The growth model

In order to model aggregate economic results (Y) beyond the undisputed influence of the classic production factors of capital (K) and labour (L), we introduce an additional group of variables, which are intended to represent characteristics of the social context and socially created resources (C):

Growth of Y = f (growth of K, growth of L, C)   (1)

C signifies an effect on total economic performance (Y) that is not explained by the change in physical capital (K) and labour (L). Socially created resources like the training of employees and entrepreneurs (an element of C) or the socially created context created by the organization of firms or through institutions of conflict resolution or through the values and motivations of the economically active population (further elements of C) have a potential influence on economic growth in comparative perspective.

Economic sociology is especially interested in the characteristics of social organization (C) that could be significant for economic growth. Therefore, we perform a comparison of societies in which the elements of C vary in order to be able to test whether economic growth is actually influenced by the group of variables we designate as C. We proceed from the view that the elements of C referred to here in individual societies vary only little over shorter time spans, such that their value for $t+1$ agrees largely with that for t. From the whole group of social context factors (C), we examine in this chapter only four whose contribution to economic growth is plausible and whose effect has already been discussed in the literature:

$$C = f (H, T, ¥, S) \tag{2}$$

In formula (2), H represents an index for the aggregate of the average existing human capital (quantity and quality) among the economically active population. T is an index for the technological capital. ¥ signifies the forces that are responsible for convergence, i.e. the forces which cause less-developed countries to grow faster than those which are economically more advanced. I call this the straggler effect, empirically represented by the difference in per capita wealth with regard to the leading nation in the comparison. S indicates an index for the existing social capital among the economically active population, for which various dimensions and operations are proposed in the literature, and which will be elaborated further below.

When we include the elements of social structure from equation 2 in equation 1, we obtain the growth model (3) that will be empirically evaluated later in the chapter:

$$\text{Growth of } Y = f \text{ (growth of K, growth of L, H, T, ¥, S)} \tag{3}$$

Equation (3) represents a multiplicative model of economic growth indicating that the effects of increases in physical capital and labour depend on the level of education, technology, distance in average wealth with respect to the highest value for average wealth in the comparison, and social capital. In other words, all elements interact with each other and are greater than the sum of their individual parts. In order to estimate this equation with linear statistical techniques one needs to transform the model, see technical note.[5]

The arguments in the literature for the influence of human capital (H) and technology capital (T) on economic growth – to which we come later in this book – are hardly controversial; therefore we devote ourselves in the following to a closer examination of the remaining contextual factors, the straggler effect (¥) and the conditions for social capital formation (S).

The straggler effect

Proponents of the straggler effect claim that the economy grows more quickly in societies with lower average value in average wealth or physical capital. Societies are thus expected to catch up over time. However, this is not necessarily valid; this becomes obvious if one differentiates between a traditional and modern sector in a society. The straggler effect does not come into effect (or not fully into effect) for a very long time in a society in which modernization has not progressed sufficiently.

The following arguments can be made for the negative connection between the level of development and the growth potential of an economy:

1   Neo-classical growth theory with the emphasis on physical capital. Growth is – if all other factors that influence growth are held constant – inversely proportional to the level of economic development (measured as product per capita); this is because a diminishing return on capital is to be expected (see, for example, Barro and Sala-i-Martin 1995). Between two countries with structurally comparable characteristics, the poorer country will grow more quickly. In other words, highly developed economies grow more slowly than less-developed economies.

2   a   Potential learning from models. Backwardness need not mean a disadvantage (Gerschenkron 1962), because stragglers can profit from the accumulated knowledge of those societies which are already advanced through imitation. Thus, the stragglers can close the gap. For this kind of catch-up development, stragglers need less time than the pioneers did. These advantages of backwardness result in a so-called straggler or catch-up effect. Although the outcome is very similar to the prognosis in (1) above, it is explained differently.

    b   Reference group behaviour, an argument to answer the question: what is the origin of the drive to learn from models? For societies located at lower levels of the international stratification system, their positional difference with respect to the most developed societies produces a drive to level these positional differences through catch-up development (for an early statement, see Heintz 1972).

The greater the positional difference to the reference group, the stronger this drive. Such a drive was, for example, strongly manifested in Japan's catch-up industrialization.

3   Saturation thesis. This argument emphasizes the declining motivation of members of society in the course of economic development. People in rich societies are less motivated to strive for greater affluence because of the level of general affluence already achieved. Greater affluence has a declining marginal utility for many people in rich countries. This thesis can be found in the postmaterialist theory of Inglehart (1977, 1997) and in the development theory of Heintz (1973).

The two remaining arguments discuss variables that restrict the impact of the straggler effect:

4   Modernization theory in its economic variant, emphasizing the capacity to save. In poor societies, the greatest part of what is produced needs to be used for subsistence. Because the surplus is low, hardly anything can be saved. Only with increasing affluence can the rate of savings be increased (for an influential statement, see Rostow [1960] 1990). The opportunities for growth are therefore dependent on the level of development or, more precisely, on the rate of savings, which is dependent on the level of income.

5   Modernization theory in its sociological variant, emphasizing the diffusion of institutional and individual modernity. The backward societies embrace individual and institutional modernity gradually at first (Kerr, *et al.* 1960). With the spread of modernity the traditional barriers to development are removed, allowing catch-up development to proceed more quickly. Here too, the prediction is made that the economic growth rate correlates positively with the level of development.

If we take all five arguments regarding the relationship between the level of development and the speed of economic development seriously, then growth potential must be a curvilinear function of the level of development. This has been repeatedly shown through empirical studies (examples include Bornschier 1980: 176, World Bank 1998: 198). It first increases among societies at lower levels of development, and then declines at higher levels of development. If one wants to specify the straggler effect in a linear fashion (distance from the highest level of average wealth in the comparison), we must restrict ourselves to those countries with sufficiently diffused modernity of institutions and individuals relative to those that are further behind. As mentioned in the introduction, we therefore restrict the comparison to developed and newly industrializing countries where the modern sector, in terms of institutional and economic practices, is already well developed.

How should social capital be conceptualized?

Ideological elements should be excluded from the concept of social capital. Social capital must not be seen as something that is good per se. I say this because social capital, just like physical capital, has different time-bound and societally constrained manifestations which take effect differently in different social areas, for instance through specific job structures in a particular technological style, or linkages and cooperation among firms. Thus, there is no such thing as the ideal type of social capital. In a given society, the aggregate social capital is as abstract and undifferentiated as the total physical capital, with the difference that the aggregate social capital of a society is harder to calculate than the aggregate physical capital. In the latter case, we at least have money as the form in which different manifestations of physical capital can be expressed.

Various elements of social capital forms, such as typical organizational patterns in a technological style or procedures of industrial dispute resolution, are not of themselves productive, even if they continue their unmodified existence as social practices, and even if they were once productive at an earlier time. This is theoretically just as evident as in the case of specific, historical manifestations of physical capital, which are no longer productive today because they were replaced with modified forms or rendered obsolete by competition.

The formula of James Coleman (1990: 302), which starts with the notion that social capital equals 'the ability to socialize easily', reverses the relationship. It is much more plausible that we assume the following: 'the ability to socialize easily' is the prerequisite for creating concrete, but historically variable, forms of social capital more easily. Thus, it is preferable that we look for variables that can express the capacity 'to socialize easily.' Which qualities are now especially important for modern, that is, strongly knowledge- and innovation-based economic growth? Here it is helpful to fall back on the differentiation between strong ties and weak ties introduced by Mark Granovetter (1973).[6] Strong ties might manage a large flow of information within social networks; at the same time, there are disadvantages to such ties, for example, impediments to learning, which represent the danger that those linked by such ties will conform to each other's thinking. There is a further consideration: because the extent of individuals' sociability is limited, networks of social relationships with strong ties perforce cut people off from contact outside their habitual circle. These networks are more exclusive than those with weak ties. As compared to strong ties, weak ties have the advantage of greater inclusiveness with respect to various other networks, and they facilitate the kind of learning that comes from crossing boundaries. The objection can surely be raised that networks of weak ties are sooner inclined to instability. This danger can, however, be avoided by the institutionalization of networks and relationships, a practice common in the context of firms.

What does the capacity to create social capital depend on in a society that is based on non-exclusive networks? The legitimacy of societal arrangements in accordance with the central values of modernity (autonomy/freedom, economic efficiency, equality, and security) is surely a considerable promoting factor.[7] What is also very important is the generalized trust in a population, which from our point of view is dependent on legitimacy. In addition, tolerance should also be cited as a condition for facilitating the formation of social capital of the non-exclusive type.[8]

Because the individual components, such as trust, which facilitate the formation of aggregate social capital in a society are more easily measured than the aggregated social capital itself, we will restrict our analysis in this chapter to those components which enable, rather than represent, social capital formation. This is also consistent with the literature that considers trust as a proxy for social capital. If in the course of this chapter we speak carelessly of the 'social capital indicator', we will not be quite precise, because we have in mind indicators, i.e. trust supplemented by tolerance, that are enablers of or latent forms of social capital and are not, in themselves, social capital.

How should determinants and mediations be specified?

In order to make visible the connections in which social capital can be seen, an illustration is offered in Table 2.2. This presents exactly what we will restrict ourselves to in the empirical part of this book.

Earlier studies of the influence of social capital

The role of legitimacy in creating economic success

Country comparison studies have previously been conducted that make the connection between the capacity of a society for social capital formation and economic growth. I (Bornschier 1989, 1996: 328ff.) tested the capacity for social capital formation in the following way. Effective social order based on legitimacy was measured using the absence of political mass protest (frequency of political mass protest events 1948–77) as a proxy. In order to guarantee the validity of the absence of mass protest as indicator for legitimacy, comparison of societies was restricted to stable democracies with constitutional states in which the articulation of dissent is only suppressed to a limited extent, since this behaviour is legally protected as a civil right. In the model predicting comparative economic success from 1955–80, this legitimacy – namely the ability of the institutional practices to moderate political conflict – was seen to be an indirect proof of the possible significance of social capital. For eighteen countries a strong positive correlation between comparative economic success and the straggler effect was found. In addition, legitimacy (the absence of political

Table 2.2 The mediation of social capital

Exogenous variables	→	Capacity of the population for social capital formation	→	Forms of social capital in the economy	→	Dependent variables: comparative economic success
Cultural and institutional heritage, political forms and outcomes (see Chapters 5 and 7)		Generalized trust and tolerance, indicating also the legitimacy of a society		Totality of specific arrangements and conflict management		Economic growth (see Chapter 2) Economic change (see Chapter 3) Openness towards change in general (see Chapter 4)

Notes
Specific forms of social capital remain unmeasured. The whole structure of the mediation presented in the above will not be the topic of this chapter, which focuses on trust and economic growth. The analysis of trust and economic change will be the topic of Chapter 3 while Chapter 4 addresses the question of trust and the openness to change and to entrepreneurship. The impact of exogenous variables will be addressed in Chapters 5 and 7.

mass protest) also had a substantial correlation with economic success. This correlation – although statistically highly significant – was smaller than the straggler effect correlation. Additional control variables had little or no influence on these results. The results of the study by Erich Weede (1996) – conceived as a critical re-examination of these research results – suggested certain instabilities when additional variables were introduced (e.g. age of the democracy as a measure of institutional sclerosis). It did not, however, disprove the earlier finding of the positive influence of more successful social conflict management on economic success.[9]

Trust and tolerance as predictors of economic growth

The work discussed in this chapter relies on earlier studies of Knack and Keefer (1997) as well as Leicht (2000). In both of these country comparison studies, trust is a dimension being tested, but tolerance is only introduced in Leicht's study. Using a sample of twenty-nine countries, Knack and Keefer demonstrate that generalized trust is significant for explaining economic growth, 1980–92. For the period 1990–98, Leicht (2000) finds that trust – measured as the common factor of trust in various institutions (for example social insurance, parliament, etc.) – is a statistically significant predictor of economic growth (controlling for level of development and education). In Leicht's analysis of the 1990s, Knack and Keefer's indicator for generalized trust does in fact appear to have a positive effect on economic growth, although it just fails to attain statistical significance. Since we consider generalized trust to be especially significant in the capacity for modern social capital formation, we want to examine the relationship between trust and economic growth over the entire time period from 1980–98 once again. In addition, we will examine the meaning of tolerance; up to now, only Leicht has used this construct and shown it to be a statistically robust predictor. Meanwhile, other work that relates generalized trust to economic growth has been published which corroborates the pioneering finding of Knack and Keefer (1997), i.e. Whiteley (2000), and Zak and Knack (2001), and their findings will be discussed later in the chapter.

The design and empirical results of the present study

Design

In the introductory chapter I presented the theoretical arguments as to why generalized trust should be considered as fostering economic growth, and this discussion will be extended in Chapter 3, when it is argued that trust is not only to be considered to make existing social relations in the economy more efficient by reducing transaction costs, but also encourages the propensity to early adoption of innovations. Here the focus is more closely on the design of our empirical evaluation.

In an earlier work I evaluated the role of generalized trust as a predictor for the ease of social capital formation in advanced countries, arguing that this specific cultural resource, generalized trust, is especially relevant for modern economic growth. In a first step we will therefore replicate this study, with some slight extensions, for the same sample of twenty-four developed countries. This sample includes the rich countries of North America, of East Asia, Oceania, Western Europe, and all member states of the EU as of 1995. In the listing below these are marked in *italic*. In a second step we extend the sample by including nine more cases from the group of the newly industrializing countries in order to estimate whether the effect of this cultural resource is of lesser importance in the larger sample which includes (richer) developing countries. The total sample includes thirty-three cases and is listed below.

Sample of the thirty-three countries, with the subsample of twenty-four richer cases in italics:

Argentina, *Australia, Austria, Belgium/Luxembourg,* Brazil, *Canada,* Chile, *Denmark, Finland, France, Germany, Greece,. Hong Kong, Iceland, Ireland (Republic), Italy, Japan,* Korea (South), Malaysia, Mexico, *Netherlands, New Zealand, Norway, Portugal, Singapore, Spain, Sweden, Switzerland,* Taiwan, Thailand, Turkey, *United Kingdom, USA.*

We consider long-term economic growth as our dependent variable, i.e. measured over the period between 1980 until the end of 1998. The choice of this long period covering about two decades has three reasons:

1 Stable differences in economic growth rates across countries can be expected only if long periods are considered, since shorter periods are characterized by conjunctional effects (see introductory chapter) which, if they are not perfectly matched in comparing countries, bias the true country differences in long-term growth.
2 The 1980s and 1990s span the transition to the new societal model of the expanded market sphere in the telematic era. It could be argued that generalized trust as an enabler of social capital may have been important in the previous societal model, but not, however (or not to the same degree), in the new societal model.
3 We wish to compare the results for our long growth period with those of Knack and Keefer found for the 1980s in their 1997 study and with those of Leicht (2000) for the 1990s.

When one wishes to use generalized trust as a predictor of economic growth one needs to ensure that the estimates are not blurred by two-way causation. The easiest way to take this into account is to measure generalized trust at the beginning of the growth period when its level, for logical reasons, cannot be affected by subsequent economic growth. The data basis for generalized trust is the 1980 wave of the *World Values Survey* (a product of the World Values Study Group coordinated by Ronald Inglehart).[10]

Generalized trust was measured in the *World Values Survey* by responses to the question: 'Generally speaking, would you say that most people can be trusted, or that you can't be too careful in dealing with people?' The percentage of the answers: 'Can be trusted' (ignoring the 'Don't know' answers) is the information we use.

A couple of our sample cases were, however, not included in the first *World Values Survey* wave of 1981. In previous research I overcame the lack of sufficient information by using a proxy variable. This was a non-discrimination or tolerance index that was developed by Leicht (2000).

The information for the tolerance index is based on different issues of the World Competitiveness Report (from the IMD/Lausanne and World Economic Forum/Geneva) and relate to the average for the years 1989 to 1991; earlier measurements are not possible. To construct the tolerance index, the following non-discrimination items were considered: (a) foreigners treated equally in all respects; (b) women granted similar career opportunities as men; (c) the extent to which the country facilitates integration of professional women in the workforce; (d) the degree of equal opportunity – the extent to which an individual can get ahead irrespective of background or sex.[11] The index reports informants' subjective evaluations of how they view social practices in a certain society.

Figure 2.1 indicates that trust and tolerance are highly correlated in the sample of twenty-four developed countries. This observation provides both a substantive information and a device to extend the measurement beyond the trust values reported for 1981.

The substantive information relates to our proposition that generalized trust is more common in legitimate societies. Non-discrimination or tolerance is without doubt an indication of legitimacy of a social structure vis-à-vis the principles of Western society. One can thus state that generalized trust indeed seems to be rooted in legitimacy of a social order.

The very high correlation between the non-discrimination or tolerance index for a given country and the average level of generalized trust therein enables us to use the tolerance index as a proxy for values for absent trust. In previous work I therefore averaged the scores for trust and tolerance to obtain our social capital index. In cases where information on the trust index was lacking, I substituted the value with the tolerance scores. This enabled me to include more cases in the analysis. On the Trust & Tolerance index all our twenty-four developed countries and the nine advanced developing countries, i.e. all our thirty-three test cases, have information.

Testing for the effect of Trust & Tolerance on economic growth does not tell us whether it is really trust that counts. In order to check for this

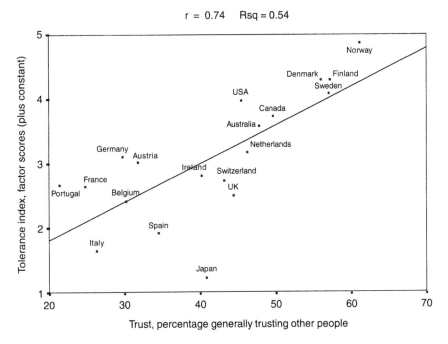

Figure 2.1 Trust & Tolerance.

we also consider here generalized trust alone. We need to rely on the 1990 wave of the *World Values Survey*, which contains more cases. These data are listed in Inglehart *et al.* (1998),[12] and I supplemented this information with figures for generalized trust in Taiwan and New Zealand from Pippa Norris (2000). But even so, trust values are lacking for three of the twenty-four developed countries (i.e. Greece, Hong Kong, Singapore) and for another two cases of the expanded sample (Malaysia and Thailand). In these cases I estimated the trust scores by using Trust & Tolerance as an instrument predicting the missing 1990 figures for trust.

We then have two measures that represent the ability for social capital formation: Trust & Tolerance, 1981/90 and Trust 1990. Both measures are highly correlated ($r = 0.84$, $N = 33$) and have, as we will see later, a similar growth impact. The second measure, Trust 1990, has the advantage that it exclusively measures trust but the disadvantage that it is measured in the middle instead of the beginning of the growth period 1980–98. But, given the limitations of data availability, using both indicators is the best we can do at the moment if we want to study long-term growth.

In sum, the analysis reported in this chapter replicates, and at the same time extends, the analyses performed by Knack and Keefer (1997) for the 1980s and Leicht (2000) for the 1990s. In addition I inquire whether the effect of generalized trust is stronger for modern economic growth, i.e. for more-developed countries. Knack and Keefer suggested the contrary in their study, evidence which we question on theoretical grounds. Furthermore, we estimate the theoretically based non-linear growth model mentioned earlier, which is an improvement over the earlier work. This non-linear specification of the estimation model had already been done in my earlier study but neither in the Knack and Keefer nor in the Leicht study.

The total test sample of countries, consisting of thirty-three cases (see p. 41) is somewhat larger than the original work of Knack and Keefer, who considered twenty-nine cases. It consists of rich countries and newly industrializing countries. Poor countries are excluded, not only due to lack of sufficient data on all variables (when one uses the *World Values Surveys* and the World Competitiveness Reports as data sources), but also on theoretical grounds – see our discussion on the convergence effect above. The thirty-three societies sampled are clearly less heterogeneous than a world sample of countries, in that modernization has proceeded to an extent that it makes sense to refer meaningfully to the aggregate society as well as the aggregate economy, not only in terms of statistical means but in terms of the actual status of those societies. As already mentioned in the introductory chapter, I do not consider transformation societies (the former USSR and the former state socialist countries of Eastern Europe). These transformation countries must be excluded from the sample, because the revolutionary events of 1989/91, including most notably the demise of the planned economy, make a comparative examination of growth between 1980 and 1998 impossible.

The test model, and why all variables are used in their logarithmic form

All variables will be analysed in their logarithmic form or, in the case of growth rates, as the first difference of logarithmic measures, because the multiplicative production model can only be tested through ordinary least squares regression after the logarithmic transformation of these variables.[13]

The estimation model is:

$$d \log Y_t = b_0 + b_1 \, d \log K_t + b_2 \, d \log L_t + b_3 \log ¥ + b_4 \log T + b_5 \log H + b_6 \log S + e_t$$

Here e_t is the residual of the regression; d is the operator of forward differences: (dX equals $X_{t+1} - X_t$),

for Y (total economic output): $d \log Y = \log Y \, 1998 - \log Y \, 1980$,
for K (total stock of physical capital): $d \log K = \log K \, 1993 - \log K \, 1985$, for L (total labour force): $d \log L = \log L \, 1997 - \log L \, 1980$.

Log ¥ 1990 symbolizes the inverted level of development (value subtracted from the largest figure in the sample) measured as the economic per capita product (purchasing power parities), and represents convergence, or the straggler effect,

Log T, average for 1985–95, symbolizes technological capital and is measured by scientists and engineers in research and development per million inhabitants. Log H, 1992, human capital, symbolizes the scope and quality of education,[14] log S symbolizes the measure for social capital and is the variable of main interest here. We have discussed the two alternative indicators in detail above: Trust & Tolerance 1981/90 and Trust 1990. The variables which are used as indicators for our theoretical constructs are given in an endnote.[15]

The results

The details of the empirically estimated parameters for the above model are given in an endnote while the findings in the main text are presented in reduced form.[16] The growth of the physical capital stock turns out to be the most important predictor of economic growth. The growth of the labour force, once physical capital growth is included, does not add to growth since its contribution to growth is already included in the former measure; on the average, the growth of physical capital and the growth of manpower correlate (with r = 0.55 in the sample of twenty-four developed countries). The convergence effect is very important and of almost the same size as physical capital growth. The social capital measures turn out to have a significant contribution to economic growth. This effect, as compared to growth of capital and convergence, is somewhat smaller but still very important and of about the same size for both of our measures, Trust & Tolerance and Trust.

The other predictors in our growth model – technological capital and human capital – have the expected positive sign, but fail to reach statistical significance. Only in the sample including developing countries does technological capital (remember, it was measured as the number of scientists and engineers in R&D) also turn out to be a significant predictor of growth.[17]

So far we have merely replicated our earlier findings, albeit with some minor extensions. In the next step we estimate whether the effect of the indicators for modern social capital formation changes when we include developing countries. It does, as evidenced by Table 2.3. More precisely, it becomes somewhat weaker although still clearly statistically significant.

We find the following strong (statistically significant) predictors for economic growth from 1980 to the end of 1998 when comparing the sample of twenty-four developed countries with the sample of thirty-three cases which also includes developing countries. The effect of growth of physical capital is of equal size in both samples. Convergence is of greater importance when we extend the development range, which is to be

Table 2.3 Explaining total economic growth from 1980 to end of 1998 (only significant predictors listed) for twenty-four developed countries and a larger
sample of thirty-three cases including developing countries. Estimations for
the alternative measures representing the ability for social capital formation: Trust & Tolerance 1981/90 and Trust 1990. Beta-weights are listed

	Twenty-four developed countries		Thirty-three developed countries and NICs	
	(1)	*(2)*	*(1)*	*(2)*
Growth of physical capital	0.69	0.67	0.73	0.72
Convergence	0.59	0.62	0.81	0.72
Technological capital	n.s.	n.s.	0.42	0.39
Trust & Tolerance 1981/90	0.44	not included	0.38	not included
Trust 1990	not included	0.45	not included	0.26

Notes
The displayed beta-weights allow a comparison of the relative importance of predictors of
economic growth. All listed effects are statistically clearly significant; 'n.s.' means not significant, and the variable was not included in the cleared up final estimate. The equation (1) uses
Trust & Tolerance and (2) Trust as predictors. We display here only effects which are
significant in at least one sample. Note that growth of labour force and extent and quality of
mass education have also been included in the multiple regression, but turned out to be
insignificant in both samples; see endnote 16.

expected. In addition, technological capital is still a significant predictor of
economic growth with developing countries in the sample. The size of this
effect is, once developing countries are included, of even greater importance than social capital, see summary in Table 2.3.

Conclusions drawn from our tests

For both of our two measures of social capital, Trust and Trust & Tolerance,
substantial growth contributions for the period 1980–98 can be found, of the
same size in developed countries. When one also includes developing countries in the analysis, then the two test variables differ in their impacts, Trust
& Tolerance having a higher impact than Trust. This is probably due to the
outliers Turkey and Brazil, with extremely low values on the trust variable.
Regardless of the differences in impact of the two measures for social capital
in the extended sample, their effect decreases from the sample of developed
countries to the one that also includes developing countries. This also holds
after recoding the trust values for Brazil and Turkey.

The implications for the effect of trust on growth are obvious. On the
one hand, the statistically substantiated impact of the cultural resource of
trust corroborates Knack and Keefer's finding (1997) in a larger sample.
On the other hand, the more substantial impact on growth in developed
countries is at odds with their claim (see also Zak and Knack 2001 for the
same claim using, however, a larger sample of forty-one cases). Contrary
to their finding for the 1980s we find that at higher levels of development

the cultural resource of generalized trust becomes more important for economic growth. In other words, generalized trust is especially important for modern economic development in advanced capitalism.

Further observations and clarifications

The predictors of economic growth are, in order of their importance: growth of the physical capital stock, straggler effect and social capital index (in the case of developed societies, whereas for the sample including newly industrializing countries technological capital explains a bit more than trust). Many cross-national studies are faced with the problem that the predictors are not sufficiently independent of each other. The desired goal of a multiple regression is to specify independent predictors, as is the case with the three predictors for growth in twenty-four developed countries. The social capital index Trust & Tolerance does not correlate with the growth of the capital stock ($r = 0.13$), and the growth of the physical capital stock is independent of the level of development ($r = 0.16$). A small correlation (albeit not significant in a two-tailed test) occurs between Trust & Tolerance and the level of economic development ($r = 0.36$), as displayed in Figure 2.2. Only if one adds developing countries does the

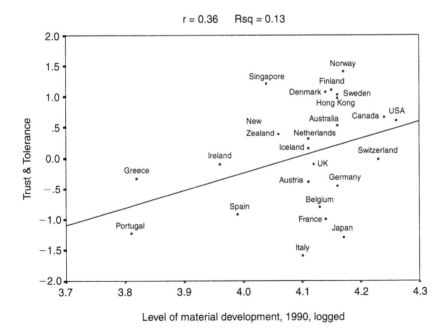

Figure 2.2 Level of material development (GDP per capita, purchasing-power parities, 1990) and Trust & Tolerance, the twenty-four richer countries of our sample.

correlation become more substantial and significant ($r = 0.60$, $N = 33$), as mentioned in the earlier work of Knack and Keefer (1997).

In other words, the three potent predictors of economic growth in more-developed countries over the 1980–98 period are virtually independent of each other. The level of material development in the richer sample cannot explain why the capacity for the formation of social capital in one case is abundant, while in the other case it is hardly present.

Our finding regarding the impact of cultural resources is rather solid; it holds for the Trust 1990 indicator as well as for the Trust & Tolerance 1981/90 indicator.[18] Furthermore, I have concerned myself with the problem of reciprocal causation raised, for example, by Mankiw (1995). It has been possible to confirm the effect of social capital on growth with help of instrument variables in a structural equation model, but no reverse effect was found. Finally, I have been able to show, through additional investigation, that the effect of social capital on economic growth remains even when the logarithmic transformation procedure is abandoned. Based on the aforementioned principal reasons, however, I hold the logarithmic form to be the most appropriate test of the theoretical model. Among the considerable number of recent studies investigating trust and growth, only Whiteley (2000) also uses the correct non-linear specification. In such a model, all variables are measured in logarithms and the coefficients that are estimated are elasticity coefficients. All other previous work uses linear models. Such Barro type cross-national regressions (see Temple 1999) have become very common but are, if at all, only loosely theoretically based and neglect the fact that elements of the production function interact.

Conclusions

We have come upon three strong and robust predictors of economic growth for the 1980–98 period for two dozen developed capitalist countries as well as for an expanded sample including advanced developing countries.

1   Growth of the stock of physical capital is the most important predictor of economic growth. Although this has been theoretically postulated for a long time, until now only a few sociological studies have measured and compared capital stock and its growth in large country comparisons.[19] Instead one has normally worked with investment rate as a proxy but, compared to capital stock, investment represents a fluid measure that is imprecise, and thus an unsatisfactory substitute measurement for the growth of capital stock.

2   The second most important predictor of economic growth is the straggler effect, which we have discussed extensively in this chapter. Here, earlier results are already available regarding the important role of

this convergence effect in more developed countries: Bornschier 1989 and Weede 1996, to name only the earlier sociological contributions. These results are confirmed once again and can therefore be considered very much established.

3   Social capital, as indicated by Trust & Tolerance or Trust alone, only occupies third position as an important predictor of economic growth in advanced capitalism. Yet the beta-weight is still considerable (see Table 2.3), at least in developed countries, while in the sample including the developing countries the impact of trust on growth falls behind that of technological capital (which is only significant in this extended sample but not in the sample of twenty-four developed countries).

The part of growth that cannot be explained by physical capital growth and the straggler effect when controlling for education is in fact not large, but this residual part correlates impressively with the residualized trust measure as our indicator of the ability of social capital formation (see Figure 2.3).

The basic finding reported in this chapter, that the cultural resource trust fosters growth, is, of course, not completely new. Indeed, the pioneering

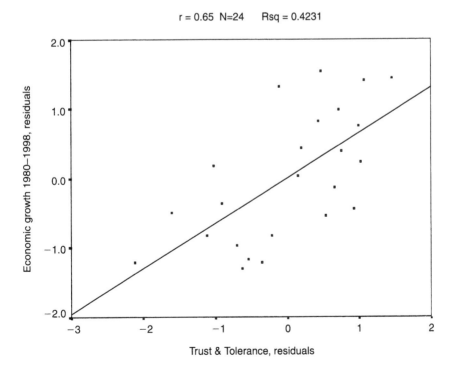

Figure 2.3 Trust & Tolerance and growth (partial plot).

work on the issue, that of Knack and Keefer, was published as early as 1997. A synoptic overview of the studies which have accumulated since then is presented and briefly commented on in the next section.

Comparing our results with other findings, and tasks ahead

The empirical debate with cross-national evidence for the relation between trust and growth starts with the pioneering work of Knack and Keefer published in 1997. In the five years since then five other studies have been published to test the claim again.[20] All but the study of Kunz (2000) – characterized by a specific measure of trust, small number of cases, short growth period – could establish a significant relation between trust and growth. The studies differ considerably in design, coverage of cases (between seventeen and forty-one), length of time periods covered between 1970 and 1998, and the number of control variables included. But such differences do not influence the finding of a solid effect of trust, as a cultural resource, on economic growth. The only point of disagreement relates to whether trust is more important for growth in developed or developing countries. In contrast to Knack and Keefer and Zak and Knack, I find a decline in impact when one adds less-developed countries and conclude that generalized trust is especially relevant for modern economic growth. Our measure of growth relates to overall economic output (controlling for the growth of the labour force), which is a measure of efficiency, while income per capita growth (used by the others, with the exceptions of Bornschier and Leicht) is a welfare indicator and less influenced by economic efficiency than by the number of people who have to share the product. I use a non-linear model specification (the only other study doing this is Whiteley's) and directly measure the growth of the total stock of physical capital (while all others use the investment ratio as a proxy). Therefore, I think that these results are more reliable and they suggest support for the view that trust counts more in modern economic growth.[21]

Years ago, the dean of neoclassical growth theory, Robert Solow, intervened in the debate about the role of social capital and demanded: 'but verify' (Solow 1995: 38). The pioneering work of Knack and Keefer and the studies that followed in the last years have done just that. By now there is considerable support for the view that generalized trust belongs to those cultural resources that create favourable preconditions for the formation of social capital, especially, I would stress, in the context of modern economic growth.

The basic question of trust and growth is thus empirically settled. New questions arise or become of great interest after that: (a) what are the sources of the considerable country differences with respect to generalized trust as a capacity for social capital formation? (b) Does this capacity also facilitate a faster transition into the network society of the telematic era?

The second question will be the topic of Chapter 3 and will be further elaborated by asking, in the subsequent chapter, what the functions of generalized trust are for innovation and for entrepreneurship in modern society. The sources of the remarkable differences in trust across countries will be addressed when we come to politics in Part II of this book.

3 Trust and technological change
The case of Internet diffusion

Framing the question[1]

Does the cultural resource of generalized trust merely foster economic growth – something which can now be considered a consolidated finding – or does it also make technological change, on which future economic growth will rest, easier?

In the introductory chapter I mentioned two until now little-connected approaches in studies of economic sociology. The comparative, static approach analyses social characteristics which help to explain comparative success in economic development in addition to the classic factors of production. This was done in Chapter 2 by pointing to social explanations for differences in long-term economic growth. The other approach is dynamic; it seeks to model socio-economic change by explaining how new ways of doing business with new technologies evolve from the logic of social systems. The discontinuous nature of technological development, or the sequence of distinct technological styles, is a case in point. Carlota Perez (1983, 1985) paved the way for a new understanding of this phenomenon. Decisively, she abandoned the Schumpeterian idea that the fundamental technological changes the capitalist system repeatedly experiences find an explanation in the logic of the economic system itself. Instead she modelled the evolution of discontinuous technological development through the interplay of two subsystems, which she termed the techno-economic and the socio-institutional, discussed in more detail below.

With the work reported in this chapter I attempt to bridge the gap between the static and dynamic approaches. This is expressed by the question with which we started. Cultural resources are not only understood as lubricants for economic growth but also as enablers of the early adoption of innovation. Beside bridging this gap, I would also like to enrich our understanding of discontinuous technological change by bringing in the social distinguishing marks that trigger what Carlota Perez has called the matching of distinct subsystems as a prerequisite of the effective evolution of technological change.

When we speak of cultural resources we again stress in this chapter the role of generalized trust. We therefore start in the first section with a discussion of trust, its role and functions. Then we address Perez's model of change in technological style. Bringing these two topics together results in propositions to explain the huge differences in Internet diffusion as a social practice. As usual in this book we then test our explanation with data and draw conclusions. While the thesis that trust fosters growth has been lengthily discussed and has found overwhelming empirical support in the short period since 1997, the issue of trust as a source of innovation is new.

Trust as a socio-cultural resource

Trust is a fundamental category for our understanding of social cohesion and modernization. In the earlier classic works of sociology this concept remained, however, rather subliminal. Only over time did it enter the sociological discourse more explicitly (see Misztal 1996). For early sociologists, however, trust vis-à-vis people who are not personally known has long been considered important, for example, by Max Weber ([1921] 1972) for propelling the rationalization of modern capitalism. In the view of Georg Simmel (1900) it made market exchange operate more smoothly. Ideas related to trust, though, have a considerable history within our discipline. Social cohesion of a modern type was stressed by Emile Durkheim ([1893] 1977) and the co-evolution of such new social bonds with long chains of social action in the expanding capitalist system was addressed by Norbert Elias (1969: Volume II). The term trust first entered the title of a treatise with that of Niklas Luhmann ([1968] 1974). In this treatise, as well as in following works, Luhmann (1979, 1984: 179ff.) also argued that trust enables the extension of the range of social actions through the reduction of complexity. For Anthony Giddens (1990), trust is crucial for the renewed modernization of modernity. In the last fifteen years, the notion of trust has become very popular in the social sciences (for example, Gambetta 1988; Coleman 1990: Chapter 5; Putnam 1993, Fukuyama 1995; Mizstal 1996) and has been conceptualized as a prerequisite of social capital, as we discussed in the previous chapter. In sum, the transition from personal trust in known people to generalized trust in unknown people is understood in sociology as a cultural resource that has made modern society possible and has thus unfolded capitalist economic development.

It is intuitively obvious that trust is basic to more or less all economic transactions, which could not, or could only at higher cost, become possible without its presence. This can be amply evidenced throughout all economic history and has already been recognized by the classics of sociology. But economic history is also rich in examples of closed networks as a foundation of social capital, within which people trusted each other because they belonged to the same ethnic group or to the same (extended) family clan. These forms of social capital, even if they were of high economic importance in traditional society and in early forms of capitalism, and come rather close to what Pierre Bourdieu (1983: 190ff.) understood as social capital, were effective on the basis of exclusivity and socially distinguishing, ascribed marks.

The ability to socialize easily is understood by James Coleman (1990: 300ff.) as social capital.[2] Such a social capital, based in ties with personally known partners must, however, be distinguished from one that is rooted in generalized trust vis-à-vis a generalized other. And it is this latter that has been crucial for modern economy and society. I therefore define generalized trust more precisely and relate it to the ability of modern social capital formation, the capacity for social linking across borders which facilitates learning and which becomes possible through generalized trust (see Chapter 2 and Bornschier 2000). As mentioned earlier in the book, this comes close to what Mark Granovetter (1973) expressed with his notion of distinguishing between strong and weak ties. Weak ties have the advantage of greater inclusiveness with respect to other networks and, therefore, are more favourable to the learning which stems from crossing boundaries. This is why Granovetter spoke of the 'strength of weak ties'. It is this openness and new cultural ability that I want to distinguish when I stress the term *generalized* trust as the basis of the successful unfolding of capitalism.

Functions of trust

The functions of generalized trust are twofold. The first, and for the most part exclusively stressed, advantage has its roots in amply available social capital, which makes social cooperation easier and functions as a lubricant in transactions. The lubricant metaphor goes back to Kenneth Arrow (1974) and has been often used since. The argument is that transaction costs, such as supervision, control, information-gathering and applying sanctions) are lower in a context where people trust. By bringing down coordination costs in the economy (as Kunz 2000 puts it) the lubricant of trust should add to economic efficiency and growth. This line of reasoning is rather widespread and has become practically standard in the cross-national empirical work on the trust–growth link.

What has hitherto been little addressed is the ability to make more and novel social actions possible. This is why I argue that generalized trust is important for social change and the diffusion of innovations. Granovetter (1973: 1366ff.) mentioned that weak ties in social networks make the diffusion of innovations easier, and Niklas Luhmann ([1968] 1974, 1979: 150) regarded generalized trust as a mechanism for reducing complexity. Tolerance vis-à-vis uncertainty is increased and so, thereby, is the capacity to act. While the first function suggests lower costs of control and should add to growth, the second emphasizes the greater inclination to take risks, which should favour change since new contexts of action are more easily created.[3]

This chapter is devoted to the task of empirically evaluating this second function of generalized trust. This is a novel step in the research on the economic consequences of trust, since the contributions up to now have exclusively inquired empirically whether trust actually makes existing contexts of action more productive, starting with Putnam's evidence (1993) from the comparison of regions in Italy,[4] qualitative evidence comparing a set of nations from Fukuyama (1995) and quantitative cross-national evidence from Knack and Keefer (1997). For a synopsis of the quantitative research since these pioneering works, see the previous chapter.

Measuring generalized trust and the new propositions

Starting with the cross-national research of Knack and Keefer (1997), one indicator for measuring generalized trust has been prominent, i.e. the question: 'Generally speaking, would you say that most people can be trusted, or that you can't be too careful in dealing with people?' As an indicator the responding category 'Most people can be trusted' is taken. This question has been included since 1981 in the various waves of the *World Values Survey* coordinated by Ronald Inglehart (see, among other publications: Inglehart *et al.* 1998). The phrasing of this question is not new. Almond and Verba (1963) used it in their five-country comparison at the end of the 1950s (Helliwell 1996). They then were astonished to observe the considerable differences in the average trust for societies which were not so different in their levels of material development. Almond and Verba were, however, not dealing with economic consequences but with differences in the structure of civil society and its impact on the functioning of democracy. Since then, this question regarding generalized trust has been used in many surveys, and it is quite astonishing that such a seemingly simple question has provided such rich information, not only across countries (starting with Knack und Keefer 1997) but also comparing individuals (first Alesina and La Ferrara 2000). Recently Thomas Volken (2002a, b) has suggested basing the complex construct of generalized personal trust on different indicators, which he takes from the *World Values Survey*. Yet responses to the classic question remain at the core of the common factor of generalized personal trust that he extracts from a group of items.

In the empirical part of this chapter I will use the same indicator for generalized trust – based on the question mentioned above about trusting others – Trust 1990, which is the same as that described and used in Chapter 2. Since the various measurements of our dependent variable – the diffusion of Internet usage – start in 1997, I use trust measures for the beginning of the 1990s. The trust figures of the *World Values Survey* of

1995 would have been an even better alternative, but too much information for our test sample cases is lacking.

Contrary to the hitherto accumulated cross-national studies on the economic consequences of generalized trust, in this chapter a new question related to the second function of generalized trust is addressed: does this kind of trust also speed up the early adoption of new social practices? This will be analysed with regard to the early adoption of Internet usage.

In short, why do we expect that widespread generalized trust favours the inclination to early adoption of an innovation? My hypothesis maintains that the scope of action reclaimed by trust (see also Luhmann 1974) nurtures – assuming a natural curiosity in humans – a willingness to investigate unconventional possibilities of action, which necessarily lie beyond socially structured, and thereby secure, routines. Trust is essential for handling the insecurity involved in innovation, not least since it makes humans more optimistic.[5] This is important, since trust cannot be explained by knowledge, as was discovered by Georg Simmel ([1908: 346] 1992: 346ff.).[6]This is logical since, if we know, we do not need to trust. To be sure, with more knowledge we can take better stock of possible gains and losses in evaluations involving trust (Coleman [1990] 2000: 97ff.). Yet generalized trust, beyond all considerations of trustworthiness in specific situations, remains an advance that tends to make people more optimistic and inclined to take a chance – and assists the adoption of innovations not least because their novelty precludes the exact evaluation of possible gains and losses.

This advance in trust is considered important for the early adoption of innovations in general, and especially also for the new medium of the Internet which, it should firstly be noted, implies frequent contacts with hitherto completely unknown others. Second, early users of the possibilities of the Internet – the 'early adopters' in the terminology of Rogers (1962, 1995, see also Mahler and Stoetzer 1995: 20), the dean of research on the diffusion of innovations – still act in considerable uncertainty whether the new medium meets their expectations or will in any case be economically useful at all. The exuberance relating to the evaluation of the 'new economy' during the second part of the 1990s and the extreme opposite at the beginning of the new century is a case in point for the uncertainty related to the possibilities of the Internet.

In such uncertain situations as the introduction of the Internet since the mid-1990s as a platform for social practices, generalized trust in the population is expected to be a relevant predictor in explaining the remarkable difference in Internet usage in the early diffusion phase. This is our first proposition. Our second proposition addresses the role of trust in later diffusion. To the extent that the originally new and little known becomes a standardized and routine social practice, the original source of early adoption becomes less and less important in explaining differences in usage across societies.

The Internet as a core element of the telematics era seen from the perspective of discontinuous technological evolution

People and the media are inclined either to neglect or exuberance, the latter most probably followed by a period of harsh disappointment. This is nothing new and is also true for the Internet. But contemporaries, even experts, often make the most unreliable prognoses. Let me cite but two short statements which make the point for computer development:[7] (a) 'There is no reason why anyone would want a computer in their home' (Ken Olson, Digital, statement in 1977); (b) '640K ought to be enough for anybody' (Bill Gates, statement in 1981). It is obvious to all by now how woefully wide of the mark such predictions were.

What is true is that the possible impact of the Internet on the change in social practices was dramatically underestimated or even neglected for quite a while. Since the second part of the 1990s, however, the impact has become more obvious. The Internet is likely to become the driving engine of a long economic upswing (termed a Kondratiev wave) and thus help to provide a renewed leading position for its country of origin, the USA, in the world political economy (see also Rennstich 2002a, b for arguments and evidence). In its country of origin, the Internet has occupied a prominent role in changed social practices for a couple of years; as early as the end of 1998 surveys, revealed that 37 per cent of the adult population in the USA were online daily and 32 per cent used the Internet at work.[8] Turnover of the US Internet industry (broadly understood) was 507 billion US dollars in 1999, compared to 350 billion for the automobile industry. The prognosis for the year 2003 was 2,800 billion for the Internet industry.[9] We know that this did not quite come out as predicted due to the end of the 'new economy' bubble, but the increase will go on and will be impressive.

But the most interesting fact, which we focus on later in the chapter, is that the spread of the Internet was very different in its country of origin, the USA, from the patterns and rates of adoption seen in other societies. This even holds if we look at countries with a similar level of material wealth. In order to account for this, I offer a new explanation based on differences in cultural resource. Before we come to this, though, I would like to put the Internet in the greater context of discontinuous technological evolution. The model developed up to now cannot account for the fact that the early diffusion of a new technological paradigm proceeds at a very different pace across different societies.

Change in technological style

Carlota Perez (1983, 1985, 2000) coined the term 'technological style' or paradigm to refer to a complex cluster of components, including basic materials, industrial procedures with their typical patterns of mechanization, the division of labour, organizational structure, corporate structure with its division of property rights, and the supply of goods with its specific patterns of distribution, consumption, lifestyle and leisure behaviour. Beyond the components of this cluster there are various complex and discontinuous processes that tend towards an unstable equilibrium during the upswing phase of a long wave of the Kondratiev type. Only with the combination of different elements during the later crystallization phase does a growth surge become possible. The new technological style then spreads to permeate all economic and social spheres. Finally, the spread leads to saturation, and the coherence of the now old technological style begins to dissolve; a new technological style then begins to emerge.[10]

Thus the Perezian model of technological style goes well beyond technology and the economy; it is a politico-economic model that addresses the question of changing economic and state spheres as well as their relationship with one another. In order to understand discontinuous technological change in the model of the sequence of technological styles, it is necessary to examine the links between two subsystems. Carlota Perez designates these two interrelated subsystems:

1   The technological style (or the techno-economic subsystem), which is characterized by faster adaptation due to the logic of more individualized choices; and
2   the socio-institutional subsystem (which I call the politico-economic regime), based on the collective logic of political choices, in which change is more conjunctive.

Both the technological style and the politico-economic regime (socio-institutional subsystem in Perez' terms) adjust to each other during a long-term economic upswing; Perez speaks of matching. The adjustment of the politico-economic regime (socio-institutional subsystem) is a necessary part of the effective evolution and diffusion of the new technological style. The institutional infrastructure that is able to support a new technological style is subject to a political logic; this needs to be defined, and new institutions need to be created in political changes, not only within nation-states but also in the world economy and the world polity.

A new technological style only starts to emerge when the old style reaches the limits of further diffusion and profits based on it decline. Even if the advantages of the new style become obvious, it cannot take off immediately. A struggle between the two styles, which can be compared with Schumpeter's (1939) notion of 'creative destruction', thus begins. The other important brake on emergence is the mismatch between the two subsystems:

> The transition to a new techno-economic regime cannot proceed smoothly, not only because it implies massive transformation and much destruction of existing plant, but mainly because the prevailing

patterns of social behavior in the existing institutional structure were shaped around the requirements and possibilities created by the previous paradigm. That is why, as the potential of the old paradigm is exhausted, previously successful regulating or stimulating policies do not work. In turn, the relative inertia of the socio-institutional framework becomes an insurmountable obstacle for the full deployment of the new paradigm. Worse still, the very diffusion of the new technologies, as far as conditions allow, is itself an aggravating factor because the new investment pattern disrupts the social fabric and creates unexpected cross-currents and counter-trends in all markets. Under these conditions, long wave recessions and depressions can be seen as the syndrome of a serious 'mismatch' between the socio-institutional framework and the new dynamics in the techno-economic sphere.

(Perez 1985: 445)

In order to overcome the mismatch, institutional adjustments are needed which require accompanying political action.

Besides modelling discontinuous technological change, the model originally proposed by Carlota Perez (and later elaborated by Bornschier [1988] 1996, Freeman 1992; Lipsey 1999) has three peculiarities which are worth mentioning.

1   The notion of a technological style goes far beyond innovations and their clustering in time. The distinction made by Christopher Freeman clarifies this point; incremental innovations occur continuously with regard to production methods as well as products. Radical or basic innovations are rather discontinuous events which cannot be explained by the improvement of known techniques and products. New technological systems evolve by networking innovations mainly stemming from basic innovations. Finally, changes in technological style or paradigm are those profound transitions which remodel the whole social system (Freeman 1992: 121). The whole set of conditions for production, providing services and distribution are affected, and cost structures are revolutionized. If such a fundamental change has established its dominant impact on engineers, designers and managers, then it can become the new technological system for decades (Freeman 1989: 48).

2   The matching of two distinct social subsystems, the techno-economic and the socio-institutional, are emphasized, while Joseph Schumpeter considered the great advances in innovation, brought about by daredevil entrepreneurs, as purely intra-economic phenomena. In contrast, the new model stresses that the socio-institutional subsystem needs to be remodelled through state action. The role of the state in the emergence of a new technological style is very obvious in the early development of the telematics era of the Internet (Lipsey 1999; Rennstich

2002a). Without the US government the Internet would not exist. This not only relates to the emergence of the Internet (see Box 3.1) but also to flanking initiatives to realize its potential impact (Müller 1996). Two core elements in governmental promotion in the 1990s were the Information Infrastructure and Technology Act of 1992 (Müller 1996: 17ff.) and the Clinton Initiative in September 1993, when the Clinton Administration formally launched its National Information Infrastructure (NII) initiative that, in rhetorical terms if not in dollars, ranks with the space race as a major technology centred policy initiative. The blueprint for the initiative, the *Agenda for Action*, defines the NII as the aggregate of networks, computers, software, information resources, developers and producers (Kahin 1996: 39)

The European Commission also speaks at the beginning of the 1990s of an accompanying and encompassing state strategy aimed at the 'preparation of the transition to a society in which information is seen as a basic material which is used in agreement between the social partners and on the basis of corresponding educational offers' (Commission of the EC, 1991: 10). In the course of the 1990s a competition

---

Box 3.1 The evolution of the Internet

This is an interesting story about the unintentional side-effects of social action. In 1969 the ARPA-Net (Advanced Research Project Agency) was founded in the USA. In order to avoid breakdown and decentralization in the event of an atomic attack, the American Ministry of Defence merged four mainframe computers into one national network.

In the 1970s and 1980s this net was opened to American universities and research centres. In 1982 a second generation of net software was started and became known as the Internet. The new communication standard, Transmission Control Protocol (TCP) and the Internet Protocol (IP, also called TCP/IP) made this possible. All kinds of computers and whole computer networks were able to be connected to the Internet. Because it was not easy to operate, and therefore not suited for mass use, scientists were more or less the only people using it. Then in 1991 in CERN (Geneva, Switzerland) Hyper Text Markup Language (HTML) was developed and the Internet transformed into the World Wide Web. The new communication standard expanded and simplified the technical possibilities of the Internet; information from different sources and places could be linked. At the beginning of the nineties the WWW was still mostly used by scientists and outside universities hardly anybody had access. This changed when Internet providers appeared who started to offer enterprises and households access to the WWW for a small fee. Through this, mass participation became possible and the diffusion process was started.

between governmental promotions to pave the way to a society shaped by the Internet emerged (see KIG 2000: II).

3 Single important elements of the future new technological style emerge in early manifestations (but not linked) long before, about twenty years, the new technological style becomes crystallized.[11] This can be briefly substantiated for telematics (a term that encompasses information processing and telecommunication). Digitalization rests on miniaturization of semiconductors, on the new basic material of the chip (see Figure 3.1).

Digitalization describes a process that certainly started with the development of computers but cannot simply be equated with the victorious career of the computer. Rather, the project of digitalization evolved in phases: digitalization of information processing and digitalization of information transmission. In crystallizing a core element of the new technological style, two types of standardization need to be distinguished. The first standardization relates to hitherto different media technologies

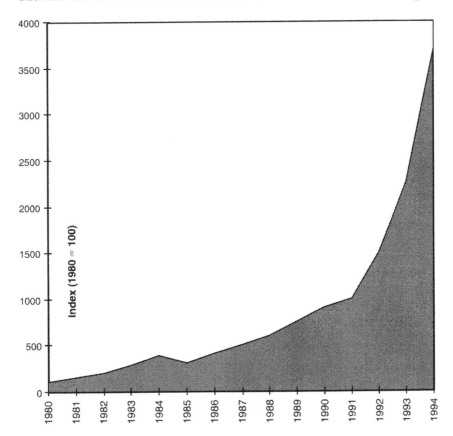

Figure 3.1 The importance of chips: share of the semiconductor industry in total US economic output (source: *World Development Report* 1998/9: 30).

such as text, pictures, sound and videos. The second relates to the standardization of communication and steering technologies, termed protocols. The latter made the networking of different technological systems, be it in offices, in plants or at home, possible. These technological systems are standardized not in terms of function or appearance, but in terms of their ability to communicate with one another. One prominent example of this is the link between mobile telephones and Internet services.

The origin of all networks which are trans-national, multimedia and interactive is the Internet (for the evolution of the latter see Box 3.1). The new technological system is not only identifiable from the emergence of new important lead sectors like the computer and telecommunication industries but is pervasive in its impact. It seizes the whole of society and the economy, not only creating new social practices but at the same time transforming existing ones, i.e. it becomes what has been termed a technological style.

This sketched model of discontinuous technological change offers a new understanding of the evolution of technological styles as the outcome of the interplay between the techno-economic and the socio-institutional subsystems. This is a clear improvement on the original modelling of the Schumpeterian line of reasoning (see second peculiarity in the numbered list above). But what shortcomings remain to be overcome? It is still socially underspecified, which I shall attempt to improve by considering cultural resources. First, though, let us look at Figure 3.2, a schematic synopsis of the model as it stands up to now:

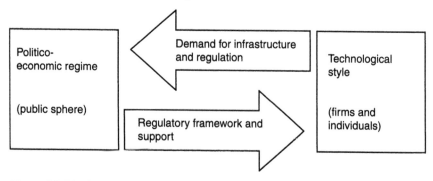

Figure 3.2 The interplay of techno-economic and socio-institutional subsystems.

From the emerging technological style, for example, stem requirements for policies to provide high-quality telecommunication infrastructure together with cheap access to telecommunication services, and to develop and improve the legal framework in areas such as electronic signatures, security of payment and international cooperation. For both state actors and interested economic actors (see Bill Gates 1995: especially Chapter 9) the risks of a 'digital divide' for the cohesion of society and the future of business are discerned and counteracting education and training programmes initiated.

This model is, however, socially underspecified in the following sense. The approval of the Internet in the early phase of proliferation, which is a necessary trigger for matching the techno-economic and socio-institutional subsystems, is completely neglected. It is the citizens who first demand Internet services who trigger the diffusion. Their early Internet practices not only foster the expansion of the Internet industry but also create the need for regulatory and supporting steps on the part of governments. Why does the frequency of early adopters differ across societies? I argue that this is due to cultural resources represented by the extent of generalized trust. If this is true, then such cultural resources are exogenous to the mutual matching process sketched above. By bringing in these social forces, we enrich our understanding of technological diffusion.

Compare, for example, Sweden and Finland with Japan and Korea during the 1990s. Both pairs of countries have a strong and research-oriented telecommunication industry and do not differ much in material wealth. However, the two Scandinavian cases range far ahead of the two in East Asia in terms of Internet usage. At the same time the two pairs also differ in terms of governmental support and regulation. To take the latter, however, as a cause of low levels of users completely neglects the fact that there must be sufficient users around to initiate such measures in the first place. This was so much earlier in the Scandinavian than in the East Asian cases. Such initial differences explain why the pioneering countries are able to maintain their lead for quite a while, despite the general increase in Internet usage around the world.

Internet diffusion in comparative perspective and the design of our empirical investigation

To find a valid indicator for international comparison of the Internet diffusion already achieved is not that easy. In the research reported in this chapter I use the figures for the proliferation of Internet hosts published in the *World Development Reports* of July 1997, January 1999, and January 2001. The definition is as follows:

> Internet hosts are computers connected directly to the world-wide network; many computer users can access the Internet through a single host. Hosts are assigned to countries on the basis of the host's country code, though this does not necessarily indicate that the host is physically located in that country. All hosts lacking a country code identification are assigned to the United States.
>
> (*World Development Report* 1999/2000: 285)

The huge differences in levels of diffusion of Internet hosts weighted by population size is presented in Figure 3.3 (the selection of the sample is explained later). But are these differences a valid representation of

Internet hosts per 10,000 inhabitants

Internet hosts January 1999

Internet hosts July 1997

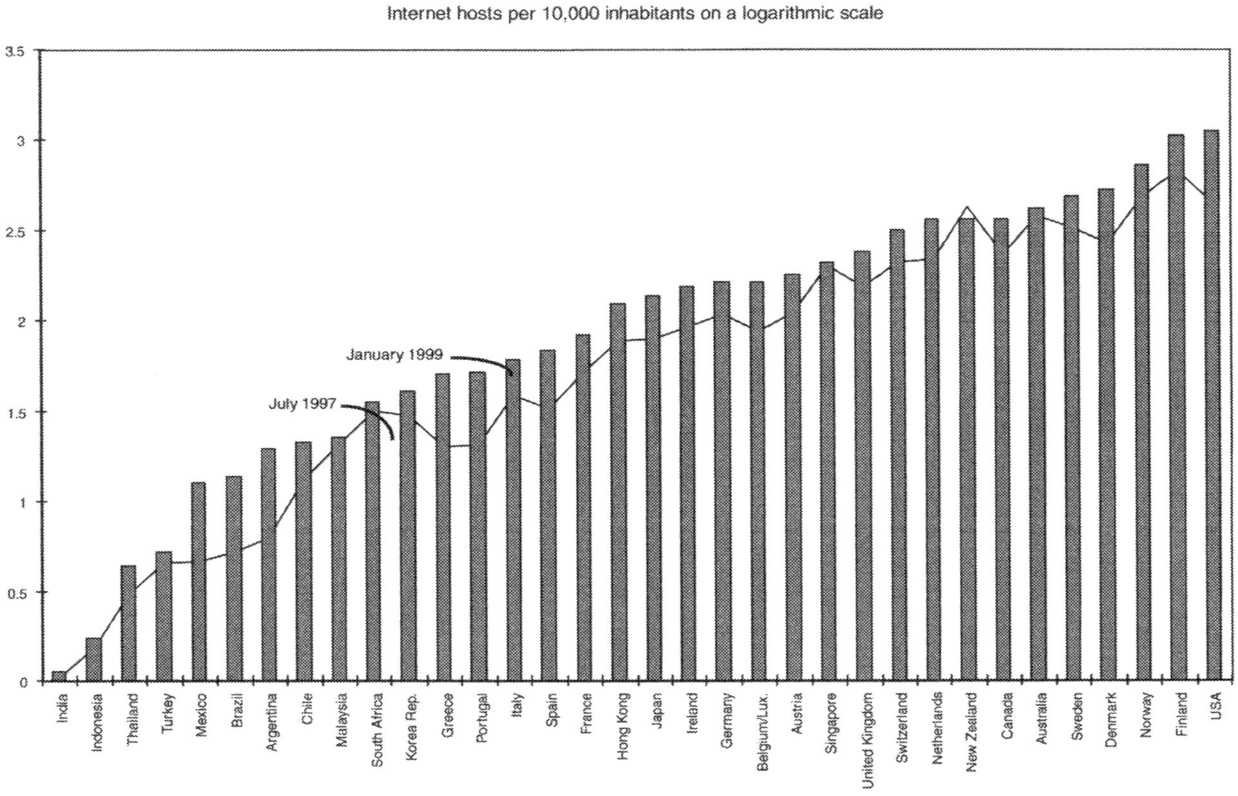

Internet hosts per 10,000 inhabitants on a logarithmic scale

Figure 3.3 The proliferation of Internet usage in cross-national perspective (July 1997 and January 1999).

Internet usage? The figures on Internet hosts are not without possible problems, to which the *World Development Reports* themselves point:

> Because Network Wizards (the source of these data at http://www.nw. com) changed the method used in its Internet domain survey beginning July 1998, the data shown here are not directly comparable with those published last year. The new survey is believed to be more reliable and to avoid the problem of undercounting that occurs when organizations restrict download access to their domain data. Nevertheless, some measurement problems remain, and so the number of Internet hosts shown for each country should be considered an approximation.
>
> *(World Development Report* 1999/2000: 285)

This might also be true because the different number of users who approach the Internet through a single host might call into question the international comparability of the figures. We therefore need to validate our measure. And we undertake additional analyses to assess whether the number of Internet hosts is a reliable representation of Internet usage in a population.

The first validation looks at the common element in different variables representing a cluster of components characteristic for the telematics era: Internet hosts, computers, telephone main lines and mobile phones (all weighted by population size and from the *World Development Report* source). Do these variables all represent a common factor? In a sample of thirty-four countries which include developing countries among twenty-one rich countries, one finds intercorrelations between +0.85 and +0.96, i.e. the single variables in the telematics cluster can statistically almost be substituted. Therefore, I rely in our factor analysis (principal component analysis) on the twenty-one richer cases, for which the intercorrelations are lower and therefore represent a more rigorous test of communalities.

The results of the factor analysis (principal components) are listed in Table 3.1 and imply the following. A common factor which represents 64 per cent of the variance in the four variables of the telematics cluster is extracted. This first factor is represented best by Internet hosts and computers. A second independent factor is also extracted and represented by mobile telephones. This is an interesting finding although we will not dwell on it here: at the beginning of the twenty-first century the rich countries proceed along a common path into the telematics era (factor 1 in Table 3.1). In addition, there exists also a somewhat different way for some countries via mobile telephones.

I undertake the second validation by matching our measures for Internet hosts with surveys on effective Internet usage in the population, see Figure 3.4.[12] The figures for the percentage of the population online are

Table 3.1 Factor analysis (principal components) of a cluster of variables representing the telematics era. The measurements relate to 1997, are
weighted by population and logarithmized. Sample of twenty-one rich
countries

	Factor 1	*Factor 2*
Internet hosts	*0.91*	−0.20
Personal computers	*0.87*	−0.39
Telephone main lines	*0.76*	0.07
Mobile telephones	0.61	*0.76*
Eigenvalue	2.56	0.77
Percent of variance explained	63.9%	19.3%

Note
Factor loadings above 0.70 are in italics.

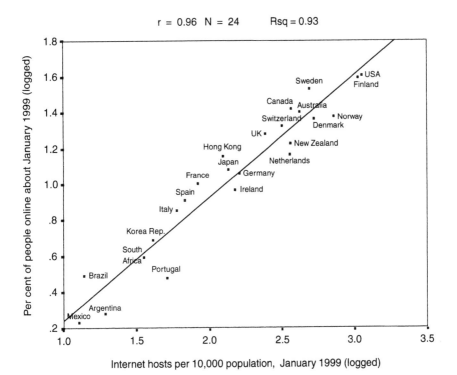

Figure 3.4 The second validation of the diffusion of Internet usage.

not always comparable, since the population group might differ and the
intensity of Internet usage is not always measured in the same way (in
most cases, at least once a month to classify as an Internet user). What are
clearly most important are the differences in the times of the interviews,
since Internet usage spreads considerably over time. From the results of

the available surveys I selected those which are most comparable and match as closely as possible to January 1999. These figures for twenty-four countries are displaced in Figure 3.4 and compared with those for Internet hosts. Our measure Internet hosts comes amazingly close to estimates for being online and the correlation is, in statistical terms, almost perfect. This is a convincing validation that adds to what was found with the results in Table 3.1. Nevertheless, I take Internet hosts (instead of per cent online) as a measure for Internet usage, since more, and more comparable, data are available, also for different points in time.

Our indicator for the diffusion of the new technological style is then the proliferation of Internet usage, as measured by Internet hosts at an early stage of Internet diffusion, to measure early adoption. It is not the change measured, for example, as a ratio between two points in time. This would be rather high for the late majority, or latecomers, after a certain time when early adopters have already paved the way.

Explaining early adoption of the Internet

The various predictors for early adoption are introduced in the form of propositions. The main hypotheses have been mentioned already; other facilitating factors have to be considered, too, in order to get an unbiased estimate of our main test variables.

1   As argued in detail, we expect that the cultural resource of generalized trust is favourable to the early adoption of Internet usage. Since generalized trust typically increases with education – comparing societies as well as individuals – we therefore need to control for the level of education in order not to assign trust part of the explanation that might actually be caused by education.[13]

2   Further, we expect that generalized trust as a predictor of differences in Internet diffusion will fade in the course of the development of the new technological style. Increasing familiarity with the new medium renders it standard. Further proliferation in pioneering societies, as well as the catching-up of latecomers, will then be less dependent on trust than on economic interests and advertising campaigns to increase markets, beside the matching achieved between the two subsystems.

3   The average material wealth of a society has an important influence on Internet diffusion. Most of the developing countries are too poor for a sufficient infrastructure and the number of users remains very small. Only from a certain level of economic development on can we expect that differences in material wealth might have an impact on the differences in diffusion that we find across countries. Since generalized trust tends to be somewhat more pronounced in richer societies, we need to control for the level of material development in order to estimate the true effect of trust.

4   Technological competence in the population: new technological systems are not easy to master and require quite a lot of technical competence from users. Therefore, the distribution of technical expertise in the population might co-vary with greater diffusion of Internet usage. To test whether this might affect the role our main test variable generalized trust plays, we need to control for this.

5   Tertiary education: in academia, computers and the Internet (for scientific exchange) have been used for quite a while by researchers and by students. We therefore expect that, despite the opening of the Internet to the general public since about 1993, countries with more widespread tertiary education will still have an edge. This favourable role of education does not pertain to mass education, even of high quality, but to university level education.

Our hypotheses refer to the phase of early adopters (Rogers 1962, 1995; Mahler and Stoetzer 1995) of an innovation like the Internet and may be of no or less importance once the new technological system has become established. One can think of other factors that might account for differences in early diffusion, like the degree of governmental support in general and educational policies (even in primary schools) in particular. But we have no suitably large sample of comparable data for this at hand. In our theoretical model such factors are, rather, dependent on early adoption. Given the lack of data, the study of those factors would rather require comparative case studies of the type we used by way of illustration. Finally, the deregulation of telecommunication markets and differences in Internet access costs might also account for early adoption, but recent findings suggest no or only a small effect.[14]

The country sample for evaluating the propositions

The test sample consists of thirty-four cases, developed and newly industrializing countries which have already been included in Figure 3.1. Due to the considerable and often revolutionary change from state socialism to market societies, transformation societies are not included. The People's Republic of China is still transforming from state socialism to a market economy and is, therefore, excluded from consideration.

The test sample of thirty-four cases is largely identical with the cases we considered in Chapter 2. From the sample of cases in Chapter 2, Taiwan and Iceland could not be considered due to lacking Internet data. In addition to the cases in Chapter 2 we considered South Africa, Indonesia and India, which results in a sample of thirty-four cases. From this test sample we have chosen a subsample of twenty-one rich societies, defined by a per capita product (purchasing power parity corrected) of more than 15,000 US dollars in 1997.[15] In addition, I have looked in more detail at a randomly chosen sample of thirty-four poor(er) countries. For these countries we have estimates for Internet hosts and for per capita product. The data base for predictor variables we want to use in this chapter is, however, lacking. More importantly, these additional cases do not differ notably in their very low levels of Internet diffusion. Since there is no variation, there is nothing that can be explained. I have analysed this additional, randomly chosen, sample of poor countries to demonstrate that, up to a certain level of material development, Internet diffusion is almost absent or negligible.[16]

Variables used in the empirical study and the test design

The predictor variables which measure the theoretical constructs are described in detail in endnotes (especially note 35). Here, therefore, we merely discuss some design questions. The variables to be explained, i.e. Internet diffusion in 1997, 1999 and 2001, is skewed, as evidenced in Figure 3.1. To apply linear estimation one needs therefore to transform them in order not to violate the requirement of regression analysis. This normalization is performed by a logarithmic transformation. Since the dependent variable is logged I have also logged the predictor variables. This means that the coefficients of the regression analyses represent elasticities (percentage changes of dependent variable are explained by percentage changes in predictors). The logarithmic transformation does not have an influence on the findings (as already demonstrated in full detail in Bornschier 2001a).

One can write the estimation equation for I_t (Internet diffusion, measured either in July 1997 or January 1999 or January 2001 as:[17]

$$\log I_t = b_0 + b_1 \log V_t + b_2 \log U_t + b_3 \log T_t + b_4 \log ¥_t + b_5 \log H_t + e_t$$

Here e_t is the residuum of the regression (error term).

V is an index of trust for 1990 as described earlier in the chapter.

U symbolizes the early proliferation of university education as measured by the tertiary student enrolment rates in 1970 (to represent early and not only recent widespread tertiary education).

T is an index of technological capital as measured by scientists and engineers in research and development 1985–95, weighted for population size, as used in Chapter 2.

¥ stands for the average material wealth or material level of development measured by gross domestic product per capita in 1997, corrected for purchasing-power parity.

H is an index for the extent and quality of mass education, based on subjective evaluation 1992 as used in Chapter 2.

The empirical results

In Figure 3.5 I have plotted the values for Internet diffusion in 1999 against average material wealth in 1997. Nigeria and China have been added to this graphical demonstration to show that, within the broad range of lower levels of development (from about 500 to 4,000 US dollars GDP), Internet diffusion does not increase with material development. Only after

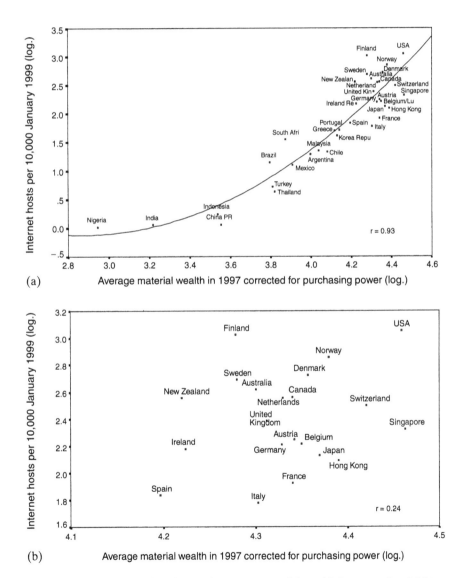

Figure 3.5 (a) Internet diffusion and average material wealth in a sample of thirty-six countries and (b) in a subsample of twenty-one rich cases.

that threshold does GDP per capita become a forceful predictor. This supports our expectation that material wealth determines the diffusion. This holds, but only after a threshold, and furthermore it considerably weakens when one considers only rich countries (between about 15,000 to 30,000 GDP per capita). The latter is demonstrated by a subplot (see Figure 3.5) that includes only the rich cases, where one finds no substantial correlation between wealth and Internet diffusion.

Let us now estimate which of the other earlier introduced predictors of Internet diffusion are able to account for country differences. All the statistical details are given in an endnote and the summarized results are presented here in the main text.[18]

We find that trust and early proliferation of university education are significant predictors of Internet diffusion, in addition to average wealth, in the sample of thirty-four countries. The control variables technological competence and mass education play no role at all. Only with regard to the latter was this expected. The relative importance of the variables in this full sample is: level of material development (average wealth), university education and trust.

In the subsample of twenty-one rich countries, average wealth no longer plays any role, and only trust and university education are the predictors (in this order of magnitude). This provides strong support for our first proposition that trust fosters the early adoption of innovations.

The two predictors of Internet diffusion, trust and early proliferation of university education in the population, are almost independent. In the full sample of thirty-four cases we find only a small and insignificant correlation ($r = 0.27$) whereas we observe no correlation at all for the subsample of twenty-one rich societies ($r = 0.05$). For rich societies the explanation of differences in Internet usage by differences in levels of trust is quite high and given in Figure 3.6.[19]

In an overview given in Figure 3.7, I now list the results for different time measurements of Internet diffusion (more details can be found in the endnote[20]). Remember that our second proposition suggests that the role of trust will become smaller in the course of further diffusion of an innovation such as the Internet.

We indeed find that trust as a predictor of Internet diffusion becomes somewhat less substantial in the course of time, but it remains significant. This suggests some support for our expectation that trust makes the early adoption of innovations easier. The role of trust, especially in rich countries, is, however, in the year 2001 still highly important in accounting for the very considerable differences in the spread of new social practices based on the Internet. We come back to the enduring effect of trust in the conclusion.

According to our results, the role of trust is somewhat fading in the course of the diffusion of the Internet while the role of early proliferation of university education becomes somewhat more important, for both the

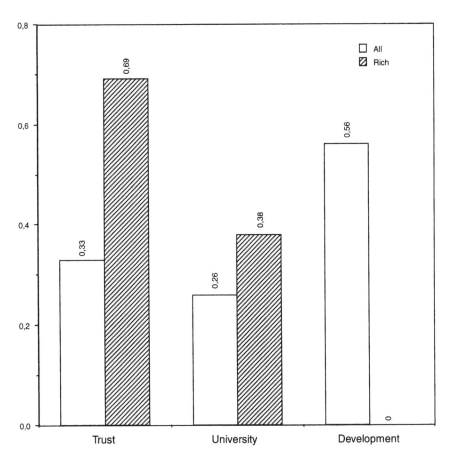

Figure 3.6 Internet diffusion in 1997: the graphical presentation of the relative importance of predictors (beta coefficients of the multiple regression are displayed, comparing all cases and the rich subset).

rich and the full sample. In the total sample average material wealth also becomes a bit more important over time.

As a result of our empirical inquiry we can conclude that, the higher the level of development, the less it is possible to explain the differences in Internet usage between societies in terms of the remaining differences in average material wealth. Instead, the cultural resource of generalized trust in the population becomes the pre-eminent predictor for the transition into the new technological style of the telematics era.[21] For the subsample of twenty-one richer countries this is again impressively demonstrated in Figure 3.6. Of all other evaluated predictors, only the early and broad proliferation of university education in the population has an additional predictive power, albeit smaller than that of trust (both variables are virtually

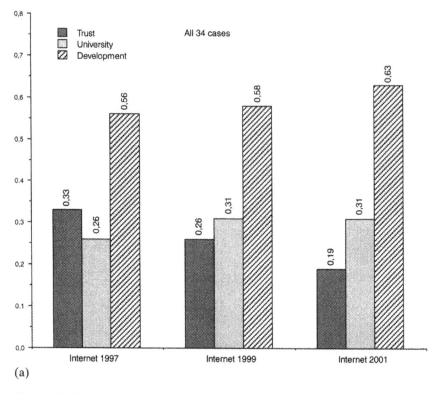

(a)

Figure 3.7 (a) Trust and Internet diffusion: the graphical presentation of the relative importance of predictors over time and (b) in a subsample of 21
rich cases.

statistically independent). Such an effect of university education in the
phase of early adopters is plausible, since well into the 1990s the Internet
remained largely in the domain of academia.

Discussion: are the empirical results trustworthy?

One could claim that the correlation between trust and early adoption of
Internet usage is spurious, because both are determined by a third unmeasured variable. This would be a classic case of a spurious relationship.
Economic growth could be such a neglected third variable causing a spurious relationship. That economic growth and trust are related was
demonstrated in Chapter 2, and, if growth were related to early Internet
diffusion, then trust would at best be an indirect cause of Internet diffusion. I therefore controlled for the average yearly economic growth
between 1990 and 1998. This was done by introducing growth as an additional predictor in the model for Internet diffusion. I could not find any

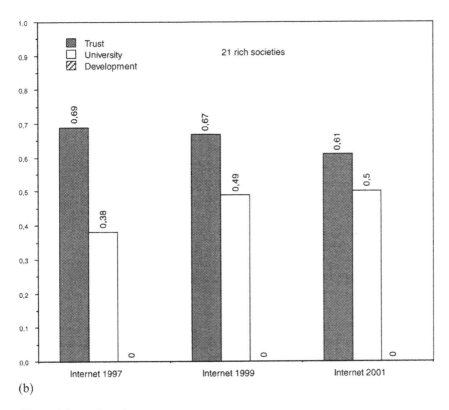

(b)

Figure 3.7 continued.

hint of a spurious relationship, since growth in the 1990s was not related to the level of Internet diffusion.[22]

In this chapter I have exclusively analysed established market economies, thereby excluding the numerous transformation societies of the 1990s. Furthermore, I only used the standard question for trust from the *World Values Survey* in 1990. Meanwhile, Thomas Volken (2002a, b) has extended the analysis in both respects to account for differences in Internet diffusion which he measures in the same way as introduced above.

Beside the sample of rich market societies which were also addressed in this chapter, Thomas Volken focuses especially on a sample of eighteen transformation societies. Furthermore, following arguments of Luhmann (1974) he suggests a distinction between system trust and generalized personal trust. He obtains measures for both trust dimensions by running a principle component analysis. The factor 'system trust' is represented by seven about equally high loading items, among them civil rights, political rights and freedom of the press. The factor 'generalized personal trust' is represented by again about equally high loading four items: generalized trust according to the standard question (see p. 55), liberal individualism (factor scores), amoral egoism (factor scores, with negative loading) and moral determination (all these items come from the *World Values Survey*, for details see the next chapter, and Volken 2002a, b).

In his empirical analyses Volken finds that both components of trust, i.e. system trust and generalized personal trust, are highly significant predictors of Internet hosts in 2000, both in rich market societies and in transformation societies. While both components of trust have a similar impact on rich societies (beta weight 0.61 for system trust and 0.57 for personal trust), in transformation societies the relative weight of system trust in predicting Internet diffusion is more important than personal trust (beta weight 0.94 vs 0.52). He explains that with the specific situation of the trust crisis in the transformation process. From Volken's analysis we can learn that outside the world of rich democracies it is useful to distinguish between both components of trust. In rich democracies, however, the items of the factor system trust correlate highly with generalized personal trust as measured with the question of the *World Values Survey*. The link between both was already foreseen by Niklas Luhmann (1974: 62) who expressed this both concisely and poetically: 'Die Hochbauten des Vertrauens müssen auf der Erde stehen' (The towers of trust have to be firmly planted on the ground). This tight connection between system und personal trust in long-established rich democracies is not guaranteed in underdeveloped and transformation societies and should be thus taken into account in future studies beyond the more developed social world.

Finally, Volken (2002a, b) used the same control variables that were discussed above, and again for rich countries as well as for transformation societies he found that only the early proliferation of tertiary education had an additional, albeit smaller, predictive power than the trust effects (beta weights for tertiary education: 0.38 for rich and 0.19 for transformation societies). Furthermore, he controlled for an index representing the costs of being online (Internet access costs relative to the total purchasing power) which had, however, no significant effect, neither in the rich nor the sample of transformation societies.

How does the trust–Internet diffusion link develop over time? I have argued that generalized trust which is able to predict differences in early Internet diffusion will fade in the course of diffusion. Increasing familiarity with the new medium renders it standard. The previously mentioned findings (of attenuating beta-coefficients and somewhat declining t-statistics over time) were interpreted as a first indication for that. Philipp Mathieu (2003) has replicated my earlier analysis by considering the yearly measures of Internet hosts per 10,000 population for the five years from 1997 to 2001 to find out with more rigorous methods whether the model is the same for all five years. He could not find, however, a significant decline of the impact of trust in pooling all the information from 1997 to 2001. In other words, although Internet diffusion markedly increased across the sample over the years from 1997 to 2001, differences in trust still explain the enduring differences in Internet host per 10,000 population. The likely explanation is that the Internet still has not become standard since ever new applications and products are always being developed, for which the initial advantage of trust keeps its facilitating role (Mathieu 2003).

Concluding remarks

Taking all empirical evidence from cross-nation research together, we have strong support for the proposition that the cultural resource of trust not only helps to speed up economic growth, but is also an asset for social change. To relate the early diffusion of innovations such as Internet usage with the cultural resource generalized trust is novel. The pioneering study of Bornschier (2001a) was reanalysed and extended in this chapter. Meanwhile the most recent study of Huang *et al.* (2003) also independently corroborated the trust–Internet diffusion link.

For sure, the impact of generalized trust in advancing early Internet diffusion also becomes plausible from micro-level studies (for example, WISO 2000). Such studies find that trust is the scarce resource in the Internet, a factor which retards commercial usage of the Internet. Such lack of trust is not always groundless. The German *Stiftung Warentest* tested 150 e-commerce services by means of simulated orders. In at least twenty-seven instances there was no delivery of the service, albeit 'particularly audacious ones who merrily credited the money to their own accounts' (Credit Suisse Bulletin 2000). Trust and security are thus broadly discussed issues. And trust also seems to play a very important role in the proliferation of e-banking.

Yet, new findings trigger new questions and to these we will come in the next chapter. Can the proposition relating trust to social change also be validated for other spheres of innovative behaviour? And does it also hold at the individual level, independent of the culture of trust in a society?

But before we come to this, let us briefly look back. Apart from demonstrating that there is more to trust than fuelling economic growth, this chapter also wanted to offer a more elaborate, less mechanical, understanding of technological change than was available from previous models. The cultural resource of generalized trust facilitates the transition to the new technological style of the telematics era, shaped by the Internet on which future economic growth opportunities will rest. Thus, trust not only influences economic growth but also the evolutionary advance of the economy and society. This adds to our understanding of technological change, which up to now has been socially under-specified, since it has not been able to account for the differential velocity of the transition.

The matching of the two subsystems, the techno-economic and the socio-institutional, is certainly important for a better understanding of the discontinuous dynamics of technological change. But the original impetus for this matching stems from the cultural sphere; it originates in pioneers venturing into new technologies. We found such an early adoption of the social practices associated with the Internet to be clearly associated with high levels of generalized trust. It hardly needs to be added that our explanation does *not* attempt to explain the Internet as such but its diffusion across countries.

4   Trust, innovation and entrepreneurship

The plan of this chapter[1]

Is the new proposition that trust promotes innovation – so far tested only against data for Internet diffusion – tenable? If so, one should also find support for it outside the specific field of technology. With Thomas Volken, I therefore extended the analysis and looked at another specific institutional sphere, the politico-economic: does generalized trust also predict the willingness to make fundamental economic changes? Then we looked at openness towards change in general. This was done by analysing: (a) the willingness to accept new ideas and (b) the propensity to act in order to bring change about.

Furthermore, we investigate whether the trust-change link also holds at an individual level. Remember, the hypothesis suggests that the scope of action that trust nurtures includes – assuming a natural curiosity on the part of humans – trying out unconventional courses of action which necessarily lie beyond socially structured, and therefore secure, routines. Trust is essential for handling the insecurity involved in innovation, not least because it makes people more optimistic. We will, therefore, change our methodology in this chapter and focus on individuals and national average. This is done by analysing a sample of almost 22,000 individuals from fifteen rich democracies. For these interviewees, documented in the *World Values Survey*, first, information is available about whether or not they trust in general and, second, their responses to various other questions, which one can take as indicators for a tendency to innovation. At the same time one can use average trust in the societal context within which these individuals live to find out whether it is rather the culture of trust – the average level of trust prevailing in a society – or the individually reported trust that determines the readiness of an individual to accept innovation.

As demonstrated in more detail below, Thomas Volken and I have found that people in rich democracies, who tend to trust, more often report a readiness to innovate (using the various indicator questions to be introduced later). But at the same time the level of trust in a society (the variable we have used up to now in our cross-national analyses) has a considerably greater positive effect on the individual answer to questions measuring readiness to innovate. This aggregate effect is an emergent property of the society in which people live and cannot be explained by individual characteristics. This discovery of both individual and societal factors in the link between generalized trust and innovation implies that individually expressed trust alone does by far not suffice to predict consequences, but that the proliferation of trust in a society needs to be taken into account. This finding has several implications, two of which we will discuss in this chapter: the first relates to the theory of entrepreneurship and the second to the sources of trust at the individual level.

Later in the book, when we have introduced the role of politics in economic development, we will address the question of where the remarkably large differences in the general level of trust come from, and we shall point to political and institutional factors to account for these differences between societies. But where does the individual propensity to trust come from? This is an important question, because the consequences of trust are determined by both individual and social characteristics. In this chapter we investigate the individual characteristics that make people trust others, again using the sample of almost 22,000 interviewees from fifteen rich democracies. This is a new step, since up to now the determinants of trust have only been studied systematically using US data (see Alesina and La Ferrara 2000). With my co-researcher I find that individual characteristics such as ascribed and achieved social status play some role, but that other cultural characteristics, as expressed in attitudes towards various indicator questions in the *World Values Survey*, are important correlates of trust. In other words, trust as a cultural characteristic is best explained by other cultural expressions, i.e. forms a cluster. This is not tautological; it illustrates that cultural variables are, to a considerable extent, not reducible to structure. This is why they should be taken into account in the study of economic development.

Entrepreneurship, as manifested in creativity and innovation, has long been seen as the engine of economic progress in capitalist society. Indeed, the doyen of innovation research in the twentieth century, Joseph Schumpeter, made the entrepreneur the core figure in his theory of economic change. Yet, while he insisted on the economic logic of the role of entrepreneurship, apart from the discontinuous availability of entrepreneurship over time he dealt little with the broader social roots of the ability to innovate, even though he also considered himself a sociologist. In other words, Schumpeter discussed motivations to innovation but did not consider where the specific abilities to be innovative come from. As I have said, we find that they are both individually and socially based. I will therefore discuss the implications of our results for the theory of innovation and entrepreneurship.

The chapter then concludes by summarizing the economic consequences of the cultural resource generalized trust which were found in the literature and in this book.

Trust and innovation – evidence from studying individuals and societal contexts

Design of the investigation

The following empirical tests all use individual level data from the *World Values Survey*. A sample of about 22,000 respondents in fifteen rich democracies is considered. These fifteen rich societies for a new step in the analyses are deliberately chosen. They represent most of the twenty-one rich societies which were the topic of research in the previous chapter and for the rich countries a remarkably strong trust-change link at the societal level was found when Internet usage was used as an indicator for change. The fifteen of the twenty-one rich societies comprise those cases which were surveyed in the 1990 wave of the *World Values Survey* from which we take three questions (that were included only in the 1990 wave) as the basis of additional measures for the openness to change. These fifteen societies are: Austria, Belgium, Canada, Finland, France, Germany, Ireland, Italy, Japan, Netherlands, Norway, Spain, Sweden, United Kingdom, United States.

The fifteen societies are rather homogeneous with regard to long established market society, level of wealth and institutional characteristics like the level and duration of formal democracy, i.e. except for Spain all cases have been democracies for at least half a century. Yet, they differ considerably with regard to the average level of trust among the citizens according to the earlier quoted question that is regularly used in the *World Values Survey*. The percentage of respondents who answer that other people can generally be trusted ranges in the sample of fifteen societies from 66.1 per cent in Sweden to 22.8 per cent in France.

This selection of representative material from fifteen societies allows us then to disentangle, less affected by other variables, the effects of: (a) the considerably varying average scores for trust which we consider as the extent of a 'culture of trust' as a societal characteristic and (b) the individual readiness to trust other people as expressed in the interview. To make it clear to the reader, we now change to an individual-level analysis, but consider at the same time average scores characterizing the whole society – the latter being the standard approach of cross-national analyses which we addressed in the previous chapters. We will consider three new indicators for attitudes towards change and predict the individual values of about 21,000 respondents by: (a) individual readiness to trust other people, and by (b) the 'culture of trust' as a contextual variable, measured by the average scores for trust in the respondent's society. We controlled for the average level of per capita material wealth and income inequality within the respondent's society. Since we are interested in both trust effects and use the controls only to obtain unbiased estimates, we do not report the results for the control variables. In most recent work (see endnote 1) we also included individual-level control variables (status characteristics: education, income, gender, age) which do not change the conclusions we draw from Tables 4.1–4.3 below.

The measure for generalized trust is the same as introduced in Chapters 2 and 3. While we have previously considered the percentage of people trusting as a macro-sociological characteristic of a society, in this chapter

Table 4.1 Summary of results for: 'This country's economic system needs fundamental changes', probability that a respondent agrees or strongly agrees

Predictor variables	Effect	Significance
Generalized trust of the respondent	positive	***
Level of generalized trust in respondent's society	positive	***

Sources: Based on *WVS* 1990, v335; 21,017 respondents from fifteen rich democracies.

Notes
The control variables were included in the above estimation.
*** indicates: very significant (probability of being the result of pure chance is less than 1 per cent).

Table 4.2 Summary of results for: 'New ideas are generally better than old ones', probability that a respondent agrees or strongly agrees

Predictor variables	Effect	Significance
Generalized trust of the respondent	positive	**
Level of generalized trust in respondent's society	positive	***

Sources: Based on *WVS* 1990, v324; 21,951 respondents from fifteen rich democracies.

Notes
The control variables were included in the above estimation.
** indicates: significant (probability of being the result of pure chance is less than 5 per cent).
*** indicates: very significant (probability of being the result of pure chance is less than 1 per cent).

Table 4.3 Summary of results for: making major changes. Scores on the scale ranging from caution to agreement with the statement: 'You will never achieve much unless you act boldly'

Predictor variables	Effect	Significance
Generalized trust of the respondent	positive	***
Level of generalized trust in respondent's society	positive	***

Sources: Based on *WVS* 1990, v323; 21,487 respondents from fifteen rich democracies; multiple regression.

Notes
The control variables were included in the above estimation.
*** indicates: very significant (probability of being the result of pure chance is less than 1 per cent).

we study individuals who responded to the trust question. This results in a dummy coded variable with values of 0 and 1, where 1 indicates that the individual agrees with the statement that most people can be trusted, and 0 indicates disagreement. The survey question is, to repeat, the following: 'Generally speaking, would you say that most people can be trusted or that you can't be too careful in dealing with people?' The effects of generalized trust on the test variables are then measured on the individual level. As mentioned above, we introduce at the same time the general level of trust in the society where a respondent lives as a predictor.[2]

The dependent variables represent indicators for the openess towards change and cover, when we also include the topic of the previous section, four dimensions: two institutional realms (technological and politico-economic), attitudes to change in general where we distinguish between openness to new ideas (affinity with new ideas) and the willingness to act (making major changes), see Box 4.1. In Tables 4.1–4.3 we present an overview of the findings.

In the first step we are interested in the influence of generalized trust on individuals' affinity with fundamental economic change. This institutional sphere is especially relevant, since the economic system stands at the very core of the reproductive system. As an indicator we take the question from the 1990 wave of the *World Values Survey (WVS)*, v335: 'This country's economic system needs fundamental changes.' The two responding categories: 'strongly agree' and 'agree' were coded as support, the others not. This results in a dependent variable that is a dummy, classifying the respondents according to their affinity with fundamental economic changes, with the value 1 for existing, and the value 0 for absent, affinity. Since we have a non-continuous dependent variable we cannot apply ordinary least squares statistical procedures but instead use what are termed logistic regressions. These are a bit more complicated than basic statistics. Therefore, we report the findings without technical details.[3] Basically, logistic regressions estimate the probability (and its significance) that, for example, a person who reports a general trust in other people is also classified as willing to make fundamental changes in the economy. The results are given in Table 4.1 (see endnote for more information).

Box 4.1 List of dependent variables for the openness towards change

With regard to institutional spheres:
for technological change (Internet diffusion), see Chapter 3;
for political change in the economy, see Table 4.1

Attitudes towards general change:
for information on the willingness to accept new ideas, see Table 4.2;
for the propensity to act in order to bring change about, see Table 4.3.

We find in Table 4.1 that both indicators for generalized trust, tendency at the individual level and proliferation in the respondent's society, have a significant positive effect on the individual's affinity with fundamental economic change. This holds after controlling for context characteristics (average material wealth and income distribution), and, in further research (see endnote 3), also for individual characteristics (income, education gender, age). We shall not go into details here since we use these additional variables only as controls in order to get an unbiased estimate for the two effects of trust.

The marginal effect of trust in a respondent's society is even more reliable than that of their personal trust in predicting the likelihood of their answer to the fundamental economic change question (not shown in detail). Therefore, we suggest that, besides the individual disposition to trust, the general societal level of trust has a strong influence on the individual's tendency to accept fundamental economic change. We interpret this important finding as follows. High levels of trust in a whole society may substantially increase that society's adaptive capacity. Changes in various spheres of life can be made more easily as people put more trust in others. This is of particular importance during periods of fundamental change, because agents who trust more are less inclined to interpret economic change as a zero-sum game. Cultural contexts which favour change will therefore more easily adapt to changes in the external environment, bringing about the matching process between different societal subsystems which has been recognized by Carlota Perez (see previous chapter) as the necessary precondition to boosting innovation and growth at the sensitive start of a new Kondratiev upswing.

We find, from the results of the tests (summarized in Table 4.1), that generalized trust not only favours early adoption of technological innovations, as discussed in the previous chapter, but is also associated with the propensity to agree with major changes in the politico-economic sphere. The latter holds both at the individual level and in the society at large. The predictive power of the culture of trust is, however, larger. We will discuss this after having presented the results for the other change indicators.

Trust and the affinity with new ideas

We now turn to the inclination to change in general, and first consider the aspect of ideas. The procedure is similar to the one just described. The dichotomous dependent variable is constructed from the answers to a statement of the *World Values Survey*: 'New ideas are generally better than old ones', which allows ten categories for rejecting or agreeing with the statement. The indicator variable is built by assigning those individuals who agree or strongly agree (values 7 to 10 of v324) to the group with a high affinity with new ideas. The results of the second test are reported in Table 4.2, which again simplifies the statistical output (see the previous endnote).

Analysing respondents from fifteen rich democracies at the beginning of the 1990s, we find in the summary of Table 4.2 a positive effect of generalized trust on the affinity with new ideas. Again, the level of generalized trust in the social context is more important than individual trust, which can also be seen this time from the significance listed in Table 4.2. This suggests that the individual's propensity to accept new ideas is less influenced by personal traits or characteristics than by societal factors which facilitate trust. Individuals who live in areas with high levels of generalized trust – we suggested speaking of a culture of trust – seem to have more resources for coping with uncertainty. Therefore their capacity to act as innovators in Roger's (1962, 1995) sense may be substantially greater when compared to agents in a low trust culture. As a consequence of this inclination to new ideas we should expect – all other resources held constant – a strong demand-side effect in the process of the diffusion of innovation, which of course will attract even more entrepreneurs and promotes further innovation.

Trust and the tendency to make major changes

The last indicator is less relevant to ideas than to action. The indicator question is variable 323 (v323) from the *WVS* 1990, which measures the general attitude towards change. The responding categories, ten in number, range from caution to boldness: 'You will never achieve much unless you act boldly' covers the codes from 7–10. This time a multiple regression was performed (for more information, see previous endnote).

Comparing respondents from fifteen rich democracies at the beginning of the 1990s, in Table 4.3 we summarize the very significant associations between individual trust, the average level of trust in the respondent's society and the average score on the indicator for the general tendency to act for change. Again we observed that trust on the level of the individual is significant, but the level of trust in the social context provides a better indication of the willingness to act in order to bring change about.

We can conclude, then, that trust is indeed a cultural resource for innovation. There is evidence for this proposition not only in the technological sphere (see Chapter 3) but also in the politico-economic sphere. Furthermore, the proposition holds not only for change in specific institutional spheres such as technology and the political economy, but also for change in general; we find both more openness to new ideas and a greater willingness to act in order to change associated with the cultural resource of generalized trust.

In looking simultaneously at the trust a person has and at the level of trust in the society where the person lives, one finds that both account for the individually expressed inclination to change. Therefore, we wish to look at the correlates of trust at the individual level. What makes people trust? This will be the next question addressed in this chapter.

Since we have also found evidence for the general level of trust in society being a more important predictor of change than individual trust,[4] we need to ask what that might imply for the theory of entrepreneurship, which, it should be recalled, used to focus on the individual. This will begin a theoretical clarification that also needs further papers or books. And this clarification cannot yet address the question of why the general level of trust in one society is so much higher than in another. This discussion will be postponed until we have examined political and institutional differences between societies in Part III of this book.

What makes people trust?

Where do the consistent differences in generalized trust come from? This question has, as yet, only been insufficiently addressed in empirical research. First, there is one study that looks at individual data, but only for the United States (Alesina and La Ferrara 2000). Furthermore, there are studies that are restricted to mere experimental settings (Yamagishi *et al.* 1998; Kollock 1994; Molm *et al.* 2000) and, finally, there are a few cross-national analyses (Knack and Keefer 1997; Bornschier 2001b; Zak and Knack 2001) investigating predictors of the level of trust in the society as a whole. While we come to the prediction of this overall level of trust later in the book, in this chapter we want to look at the individual determinants of trust.

Predicting trust of individuals in fifteen rich countries

With my co-researcher I considered a sample of 14,321 interviewees from fifteen rich countries for which all necessary information is available. The details of the multiple logistic regression are omitted here,[5] while an overview is given in Table 4.4. The average level of trust in the fifteen rich countries, which differs considerably, is controlled for in order to estimate the effects of individual characteristics. Three groups of predictors will be distinguished: (a) ascribed characteristics, (b) achieved social status – both of which have been studied already by others – and (c) other cultural attitudes of respondents, which is a new contribution (following the studies of Bornschier and Volken 2002; Volken 2002a, b; Halpern 2001).

Comments on the findings summarized in Table 4.4

Ascribed characteristics

Similar to the results of Putnam (1995, 1996), Alesina and La Ferrara (2000) and Glaeser *et al.* (2000), we find a substantial effect of the respondent's age on his inclination to trust. People tend to trust more with increasing age. Whether this finding reflects an age rather than a cohort

Table 4.4 Probabilities of individual characteristics predicting trust in other people

Predictor groups	Effect	Significance
Ascribed characteristics		
Age	positive	***
Gender	none	–
Married	none	–
Children	none	–
Divorced	negative effect	***
Religion	none	–
Achieved social status		
Education	positive	***
Income	positive	***
Cultural attitudes		
Liberal individualism	positive	***
Amoral egoism	negative	***
Moral determination	positive	**

Sources: Based on *WVS* of 1990–3; sample of 14,321 interviewees from fifteen rich countries.

Notes
** indicates: significant (probability of being the result of pure chance is less than 5 per cent).
*** indicates: very significant (probability of being the result of pure chance is less than 1 per cent).

effect cannot be decided on the basis of our cross-section data.[6] The other personal characteristics are not significant predictors except for the personal experience of divorce. This result corresponds with that of Alesina and La Ferrara (2000); the possibly traumatic experience of divorce substantially upsets trust in general. In line with the authors mentioned using data for the US, our extended sample of respondents from fifteen countries reveals no substantial effects of religious affiliation on trust, once the average level of trust in the context has been controlled for. However, when looking only at individual level data (without controlling for the large differences in average trust in the fifteen societies) we find significant effects of religious affiliation (not listed). This could imply some support for Weber's thesis on Protestantism – protestant denominations tend to trust more and Catholics less than the base category. The finding that the religious effect vanishes once average trust in the society is controlled for may indicate that actual religious affiliation in modern Western society is less important than the impact these religions have had over the past and which is still residually present in generalized ethical norms – also incidentally noted by Weber.

Achieved social status

Education and income go together with higher individual trust, a relationship supported by several studies (Putnam 1995; Alesina and La Ferrara 2000; Glaeser *et al.* 2000). Again the interpretation is ambiguous. It is not clear whether education works as a cognitive resource which enables the reduction of complexity, and thereby catalyses more security and trust, or whether education works rather as a ticket to social circles which, for whatever reason, already trust more. Similarly the interpretation of the income effect is ambiguous. In this case, too, a causal link via social networking is not implausible. Alternatively, one can make the case that an asymmetry of status implied by high income is a resource that, potentially, enables sanctions for untrustworthy behaviour to be threatened and is therefore taken into account by the weaker party when thinking about defecting from any agreement. With some confidence, the more powerful actor can therefore assume the weaker party to be trustworthy (Molm *et al.* 2000). Income as a power and status resource thus indirectly fosters trust. Analogously, Glaeser *et al.* (2000: 830) find that high-status individuals can capitalize on their power resources by generally receiving more trust and trustworthiness than they themselves are ready to give in social exchange. In this sense they create negative externalities, which in turn is the reason why the general level of trust is higher in symmetric exchange relations, which are governed by norms of reciprocity (Molm *et al.* 2000).

Cultural attitudes: liberal individualism, amoral egoism and moral determination

While personal characteristics and achieved status have already been considered by Alesina and La Ferrara (2000), considering other cultural attitudes as determinants or concomitants of generalized trust is new (see Bornschier and Volken 2002). The logic which leads us to expect such links may be expressed as follows. The ethical and moral conceptions of actors not only structure their own value-led actions; at the same time they also signify expectations towards the behaviour of others. In a fuzzy situation between 'knowledge and ignorance' (Simmel 1908) it is therefore prudent to make sure of the motivation of another by imagining how one would act in that other's place (Luhmann 1974). Thus, in following this practical imperative, the morally judging actor always reflects not only himself but also others, i.e. the prevailing moral.

Three different attitudes to moral judgement have been considered in our research and turned out to be relevant in determining whether a person trusts a generalized other or not (further details in Bornschier and Volken 2002). We term them liberal individualism, amoral egoism and moral determination. The first two dimensions result from a principal component analysis. The extracted factors, together with high-loading items, are displayed in Table 4.5. The items subjected to a principal component analysis (for a similar approach, see Halpern 2001) come from the *World Values Survey* of the 1990 wave. The interviewees each placed themselves on a scale ranging from 1 (never justified) to 10 (always allowed), thus stating to what extent they believe that such morally sensitive forms of behaviour are justified. Liberal individualism: factor score of the first factor extracted by a principal component analysis. The factor represents morally contested attitudes and values towards the body and personal intimacy, e.g. homosexuality, prostitution, abortion, divorce, euthanasia and suicide. High-factor scores indicate a high tolerance towards these morally contested forms of behaviour. Amoral egoism: factor score of the second factor, see Table 4.5. The factor refers to approving forms of behaviour which in a wider sense belong to the subject of collective goods: claiming government benefits which one is not entitled to, avoiding transport fare (the classic free rider), cheating on tax, buying stolen goods and accepting bribes. High-factor scores indicate that one is highly permissive towards actions that deplete the public good.

The third dimension, which in Table 4.4 is used as a predictor of personal trust, is moral determination, a dummy coded variable with values 0 and 1, the latter indicating that one agrees with the following *World Values Survey* statement: 'There are absolutely clear guidelines about what is good and evil. These always apply to everyone, whatever the circumstances.'

The first factor, liberal individualism, represents various attitudes towards the body and personal intimacy. People who prefer an affirmative attitude

Table 4.5 Dimensions of individual moral orientations and attitudes in fifteen rich democracies, 1990

	Factor 1	*Factor 2*
Claiming benefits not entitled to	–	0.674
Avoiding transport fare	–	0.714
Cheating on tax	–	0.741
Buying stolen goods	–	0.697
Accepting a bribe in duty	–	0.664
Homosexuality	0.748	–
Prostitution	0.743	–
Abortion	0.755	–
Divorce	0.769	–
Euthanasia	0.680	–
Suicide	0.622	–

Source: Basic data from the *WVS*.

Notes
Method applied: principal component analysis with varimax rotation.
Variance explained mounts to 52 per cent. Only factor loadings > 0.6 displayed.

towards morally contested behaviour not only express more tolerance but also a preference for individual freedom and self-responsibility. To the extent that behaviour such as abortion, suicide, or euthanasia is evaluated as always justified, one may argue that a primacy of the individual vis-à-vis society prevails, since at least potentially adverse side effects remain unconsidered. Simultaneously stressing individual responsibility, the ability to make judgements and the right of both privacy and intimacy points to a cultural cluster in which the individual is considered to be capable and therefore also trustworthy. Indeed we find substantial effects of the syndrome termed liberal individualism on individually expressed trust vis-à-vis others: see Table 4.4 for this new empirical evidence.

The second extracted factor, amoral egoism, is predominantly constituted by items reflecting a lack of civic virtues, signifying an anti-civic moral or a free-rider mentality. People who score high on this dimension reflect a moral orientation of reckless opportunism. This is why – following Edward Banfield – we term this dimension 'amoral egoism'. Assuming an anthropologically rooted norm of reciprocity and a prudent inspection of the motives of generalized others under conditions of ignorance, it is hardly surprising that we can predict a low probability to trust for people who score high on amoral egoism. See Table 4.4 for this new finding.

Finally, we evaluate the impact of the determination with which a person believes him- or herself to be able to morally evaluate issues. Under the heading 'moral determination' are gathered all those people who opted for a universalistic moral stance on the relevant items in the interview. Individuals are classified as being characterized by moral determination if they agree with the following statement: 'There are absolutely clear guidelines about what is good and evil. These always apply to everyone, whatever the circumstances' (from *World Values Survey*, 1990).

We find a positive effect of this moral determination on trust, see again Table 4.4 for evidence of this new hypothesis. Obviously, people with a universalistic moral orientation are better able to generalize trust. This may relate to the high probability that, according to the universalistic account, others are supposed to have the same orientation, by which, *eo ipso*, trust can be built up (similar to Max Weber's travelling salesman). This ability to generate trust through projection has been substantiated by Macy and Skvoretz (1998) in computer simulations. It is important, however, to note that this projection cannot completely rest on self-deception, since trust without experience is unrealistic, as has already been stressed by Niklas Luhmann.

The relative impact of groups of variables in predicting individual trust

Up to this point our discussion of the influences on individual trust has been confined to the significance of the impact resulting from different variables. What remains to be answered is the following question: What are, in terms of relative importance, the different contributions of the various groups of variables as predictors of trust?

We compare ascribed characteristics (age, religious affiliation, primary group relations such as being divorced), status characteristics (education, income), and cultural attitudes (liberal individualism, amoral egoism, moral determination). The procedure of comparing the relative impact is described in Bornschier and Volken (2002); here we only mention the results.

Ascribed characteristics together increase the probability (0.15) of making the right prediction whether a person trusts or not. The two status characteristics education and income are, with an increase of 0.23, clearly of greater importance. The most important variables in relative terms, however, are those representing value orientations and attitudes. With a predicted probability of 0.40 they have almost double the size of the impact of status variables, and a bit less than three times the size of the ascribed characteristics. To generally trust other people seems fundamentally to be a question of moral attitudes and orientations. This can be expressed by the somewhat tautological observation that culture is best explained by culture.

That generalized trust is indeed part of a broader cultural cluster which includes the variables mentioned so far has been revealed by Thomas Volken (2002a, b) in cross-country research. In a sample of forty-seven societies, he extracted various factors (factor loadings in brackets). One factor he found is characterized by common loadings of:

general trust	(+0.78)
liberal individualism	(+0.79)
amoral egoism	(−0.71)

This cross-national evidence corresponds very closely to what we have reported in this chapter at the individual level for respondents from fifteen rich democracies, see Table 4.4.

Yet, as mentioned earlier, individual trust is only one predictor for innovation. What also counts – indeed, our findings suggest, what counts more – is the general level of trust in a society. This culture of trust is not reducible to individual preferences. What implications might this have for theories of entrepreneurship? We come to this in the last substantive treatment before we summarize.

Implications for theories of entrepreneurship

The entrepreneurial triangle

Innovation, we find, is less explained by individual trust than by average trust in society. This causes us to look for a clarification of the social root of the enabler of innovation, i.e. that component that cannot be explained by characteristics of the individual. What are the implications for theories of entrepreneurship and innovation? Before this question can be adequately addressed, we need to develop an understanding of what exactly is meant by the terms entrepreneur and entrepreneurship and how theories of entrepreneurship and diffusion of innovation explain the success or failure of innovation.

Joseph Schumpeter informs us that entrepreneurship essentially consists of doing things that are not generally done in the ordinary course of business routine; it is a wider aspect of leadership (Schumpeter [1947] 1989b). In his view, the defining characteristic of the entrepreneur is therefore simply the doing of new things or the doing of things that are already being done in a new way. The entrepreneur gets things done (Schumpeter [1947] 1989a). However, the entrepreneur, as Schumpeter argues, does not necessarily have to be embodied in a particular physical person: 'Every social environment has its own ways of filling the entrepreneurial function' (Schumpeter [1947] 1989b: 260).

Although Schumpeter conceptualized the entrepreneur as a specific societal function in his later work, he paid little theoretical attention beyond the idea of a supply-led process of creative destruction. Thus, the broader social roots of the ability to innovate and diffuse innovations were left systematically under-reflected. Subsequent research on the subject of the innovation and diffusion of new technologies has substantially filled this gap by taking into account several context factors that enable the entrepreneurial function to perform efficiently and effectively.

In a macro perspective, the institutional framework and policy initiatives – often seen as national systems of innovation (Freeman 1988; Dosi and Orsenigo 1988; Boyer 1988; Perez 1983, 1985; OECD 1999) have been widely discussed, and communication processes have been recognized as being of core importance in the demand-led diffusion process (Rogers 1962, 1995). Furthermore it has been pointed out that the capacity to innovate is inherently coupled with the context's stock of human capital (Romer 1990), the accessibility of credit (see Miller and Garnsey 2000) or the presence of other resources, in particular a common infrastructure which allows markets to supply innovation in the first place (e.g. automobiles are fundamentally dependent on service stations and an extended infrastructure of motorways).

In a micro perspective, it has been argued that the firm must be understood as a self-organizing system propagating innovation. This 'corporate entrepreneur' (Fecker 2001) uses specific capabilities – human, technical, financial, real and social capital – to realize new ideas, but at the same time innovative projects are taking place within a given cultural context. Culture, however, is the emergent product of specific and generic capabilities and the surrounding social structure. Others have focused on how the entrepreneur makes use of specific resource capital (firm-specific capabilities) and institutional capital (the industry's infrastructure and legitimacy, norms and values) in order to promote the 'entrepreneurial culture' or 'entrepreneurial story', which functions to identify and legitimize new ventures (Lounsbury and Glynn 2001: 546). In this view, what is particularly important are links to gatekeepers – e.g. the investment bankers who play a central role when it comes to deciding whether and when an IPO will be able to go forward, or how much attention the IPO is given by institutional investors. To put it more generally, networks of weak ties (Granovetter 1973) are a central resource which not only enable entrepreneurs to communicate more efficiently but may also be a source of information and innovation as well. Larson (1992), in her study of high-growth entrepreneurial firms, concludes that these corporate agents sustain innovation and high growth by sharing a common pool of strategic as well as administrative knowledge. At the same time these successful networks are governed by norms of fairness, reciprocity and trust (Larson (1992); see also Lorenz 1999). The role of trust in processes of innovation has been further explored by Yli-Renko *et al.* (2001). They find substantial effects of social capital on knowledge acquisition and, mediated through knowledge, on the firms' capability to produce a greater number of new products, develop greater technological distinctiveness and reduce overall sales cost. In short, plentiful social capital puts firms in a very competitive position.

Recently, Miller and Garnsey (2000) have pointed out that theories of diffusion and theories of entrepreneurship should be linked in order to overcome the shortcomings of each of the particular theories. While on the one hand theories of diffusion underestimate the important role of the 'agent of change', theories of entrepreneurship very often lack an adequate understanding of the social context. These authors have, therefore, proposed a theoretical framework which integrates the opportunity structure, the capabilities of the entrepreneur and the resources at hand.[7]

Indeed, the three elements (opportunities, capabilities and resources) may be seen as a general common characteristic of most of the micro theories presented, however distinct their contents. At the same time many of these micro theories of entrepreneurship have recognized the productive power of trust and social capital. However, they generally conceptualize it, similarly to Pierre Bourdieu (1980, 1993), as a specific, private asset which results from personal ties. Although there is nothing wrong with understanding trust as a resource that may be individually used, this picture only tells half the story. Trust is, as Coleman (2000: 300) notes, an element of the social structure. As such, it goes far beyond the limited scope of just an individual firm or entrepreneur. It is produced and reproduced on the societal level and therefore must also be understood, just as the availability of a common infrastructure or other public goods, as an asset of the national context. Of course, this does not exclude private forms of trust or social capital.

The entrepreneurial function, we may now say, certainly contains more than just one parameter, the entrepreneur. It must also be thought of as reflecting aspects of the wider societal context, which provides opportunities and resources and allows for the development of capabilities. In other words, the micro perspective needs to be complemented by the macro perspective, and vice versa.

A first step in this direction has been taken by the recent work of Stern, Porter and Furman (2000). In their proposed model of 'national innovative capacity', the authors draw on three theoretical areas: the macro-oriented ideas-driven endogenous growth theory put forward by Romer (1990), Porter's (1990) cluster-based micro theory of national industrial competitive advantage, and the broad literature on national innovation systems.

While this approach is certainly very promising, it completely neglects the role of trust and social capital, as do macro theories of innovation in general.

Six issues which need further consideration

We argue that, while the importance of a fruitful link between micro and macro approaches to entrepreneurship and innovation have been recognized, the role of trust and social capital as a context-specific general resource has not been sufficiently reflected and needs further clarification. While micro theories treat trust and social capital as private goods, macro theories tend to neglect them completely. Why, then, should trust in the national context be important for the entrepreneurial function?

Trust facilitates learning alliances

First of all, networks of legally independent corporations are becoming much more important (Maskell 2000; OECD 1999) and alliances are shifting from traditional risk or resource sharing alliances to learning alliances (Lane and Lubatkin 1998). However these learning alliances – as will become clear when discussing the next point – require a much higher level of trust in order to facilitate and assure cooperation between otherwise competing agents.

Trust facilitates information-sharing

As information becomes the most important tradable good – as implied by the concept of the information society – firms in their struggle for competitive advantages (time to market, costs, etc.) are fundamentally dependent on knowledge and information sharing (Yli-Renko *et al.* 2001; Lane and Lubatkin 1998; Larson 1992). However, the process of information sharing is fragile and may result in market failure (Arrow 1970). Since information is only of value to the 'buyer' if it is not already in his possession, he wants to evaluate it. For the 'seller', the dilemma is that once he has uncovered the information, the 'buyer' may not be willing to pay for it, even though the information is of value to him. Trust is the resource that may overcome this specific form of market failure and facilitate cooperation under conditions of uncertainty (Kollock 1994; Yamagishi *et al.* 1998; Maskell 2000). Thus, the higher the level of trust in a context, the greater the probability that entrepreneurs will be able to share information and knowledge, learn from each other's experience and so introduce innovations more quickly, more effectively and more efficiently.

Trust facilitates cross-border cooperation

Because competition is becoming more intense as borders wither away and barriers to entry for foreign competitors become lower, trust and, more generally, social capital may become a competitive resource that is valuable and very hard to imitate. The general ability to extend trust to members of neighbouring nationalities may for instance considerably reduce coordination costs in cross-country business interaction, and therefore enhance overall competitiveness by pushing the limits of cooperation much further.

Trust enhances the demand for new products

The success of the entrepreneur is greatly dependent on the demand of the markets as well. Therefore, the greater the affinity with new ideas in a context, all other resources held constant, the greater the probability that an innovation will be in demand. Since innovations always carry a certain amount of risk with them, trust is needed to bridge the lack of knowledge and uncertainty, so contexts that facilitate trust are more inclined to accept new ideas and create a climate that makes successful entrepreneurship more likely. Evidence for this may be derived from the findings concerning the diffusion of Internet hosts (Bornschier 2001a; Volken 2002a, b). In addition, one may argue here that high levels of generalized trust allow for better and more extensive flows of information (Granovetter 1973), which in turn help to reduce the level of uncertainty which prevents agents other than innovators from adopting the new idea (Rogers 1962, 1995).

Trust facilitates institutional reforms

The higher the level of trust in a context, the greater the social, political and economic adaptability of that context, as indicated by the openness towards fundamental economic change. This is of particular importance in times of creative destruction, when different societal subsystems need to be re-matched in order to boost a new Kondratiev upswing (Perez 1983, 1985). Social contexts which are able to exploit their trust potential in an early phase of the creative destruction will produce an institutional framework that is highly conducive to entrepreneurship and therefore magnifies the innovative potential of the context itself.

Trust facilitates human capital accumulation

Knowledge is increasingly becoming the crucial key factor for the success of the entrepreneur. This makes his project highly dependent on the availability of knowledge workers on the one hand and consumers with an adequate cognitive capacity to adopt his innovation on the other hand. Societies with very low trust resources on all levels may substantially suffer from a lack of these knowledgeable agents, since under conditions of low trust there may be no or too few incentives to invest in human capital. This is especially true when the culture of low trust stems from rampant nepotism or a climate of outrageous corruption.

Generalized trust in a context should, for the above reasons, be considered by theories of entrepreneurship and innovation as a cultural resource that unfolds its powers both by influencing the opportunity structure and the capabilities and resources of the entrepreneur.

As a cultural resource, trust is bound to the very structure from which it originates. It is hard, if not impossible, to move or export it, so it can be regarded as a competitive advantage of the social context as a whole. While recently there has been much talk and anxiety about the mobility of footloose global financial capital, that sort of capital is far from the only resource that is part of the production or entrepreneurial function. Trust as a form of social capital is another resource, and, I dare to say, it is especially valuable in attracting the agents of the financial markets. A culture of trust, as recent research shows, is well suited to facilitating investment (Knack and Keefer 1997; Zak and Knack 2001) and provides the entrepreneur with necessary venture capital. Thus it seems that, although the entrepreneurial story (Lounsbury and Glynn 2001) certainly is of some importance, it is of no use if told in a low trust culture, since its inherent uncertainty in such a context will prevent agents from believing it.

Given the importance of trust for the entrepreneurial function, we will have to clarify further its determinants. One additional step will be made after having introduced politics and institutions, see Chapter 7.

A short summary of the economic consequences of the cultural resource generalized trust

This chapter dealt with social and cultural sources of creativity and innovation. It adds to our knowledge of cultural resources in economic development, which includes growth and structural change. More specifically, we investigated the effect of generalized trust on the willingness to change and on entrepreneurship.

In putting together the evidence of the last three chapters it becomes clear that, yes, cultural resources matter in both the aspects of economic development, growth and change. The cultural resource of generalized

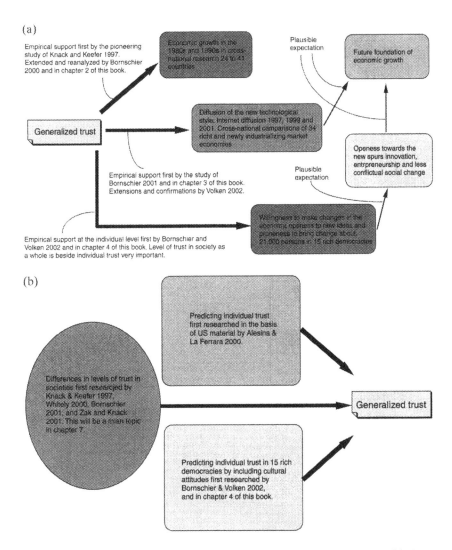

Figure 4.1 Consequences and determinants of trust: overview of results. (a) Generalized trust: economic consequences of this cultural resource. (b) Determinants of the cultural resource generalized trust.

Note
The recent study of Huang *et al.* (3003) independently corroborated the empirical trust–Internet diffusion link.

trust is a single element in a sea of cultural traits, but it clusters with other cultural elements which are favourable for modern life: liberal individualism, absence of amoral egoism and moral determination.

The best way to summarize the findings of the three chapters is by using a graph which summarizes the findings we now have: see Figure 4.1.

PART II

Democracy, political styles, trust and formal education

The leitmotif of this part is that politics matters. We argue in favour of this perhaps unoriginal position by distinguishing political forms, political outcomes and different political styles within the same political form.

We start with a chapter that asks whether the political form of democracy fuels economic growth and change. This is hardly a new research question in cross-national work, but I argue that all previous cross-national studies erred when they directly related democratic measures to economic growth. I claim that the effects must be modelled as mediated by characteristics of societies which, and people who, are influenced by democracy as a specific set of institutions, and focus on education and generalized trust as mediating variables.

In the next chapter we address formal education in more detail as one political outcome. Worldwide, the educational system is to a very large extent under the aegis of the state, and this should result in variation according to political form. Although many cross-national studies exist that relate education to economic growth, it is theoretically unclear why education should spur economic growth. I then offer a combination of two favourable, albeit separate, effects education has on economic growth: (a) by legitimizing society in the eyes of citizens and therefore limiting social conflict, which is favourable for investment, and (b) by improving the qualifications of the workforce, providing better training and, thus, easier absorption of the knowledge relevant for improving production and distribution. This 'double dividend' of educational policy efforts is then put to its first cross-national test.

In the last chapter we consider developed countries at a very similar level of formal democracy and focus on different political styles. We consider degrees of negotiated capitalism (referred to in the literature as democratic corporatism) and liberal or Anglo-Saxon cultural heritage. As one would expect, different political styles produce different outcomes and – even more interesting – the same outcomes in a different way. I shall demonstrate the latter by showing how generalized trust is differently produced in rich democracies. The findings in this chapter have very interesting consequences for the question of persistence and change which are addressed later in the book.

5 Democracy's indirect role for growth and technological change

Framing the question[1]

Is democracy good for growth? The debate on this issue is hardly new, neither among scholars nor among interested parties.[2] If one looks at single cases like Singapore since the 1960s and the People's Republic of China since its economic reforms began in the 1980s, one might doubt that democracy is an indispensable prerequisite. Yet, in order to reach general conclusions, empirical evidence should not rest on single cases. Consequently, over the last decades numerous cross-national studies addressing the issue have been undertaken. However, the results of over thirty studies are ambiguous. As we enter this seemingly overstudied field, I seek to give fresh impetus to the inquiry. I argue that the inconclusiveness of the results obtained so far are due to a flawed research design. These studies went astray by relating democracy directly to economic growth in a Barro-type series of ad hoc regressions (see Barro 1996); such an approach entirely ignores the complexity of the relationships involved. Necessarily, the channels through which democracy, as a set of political practices, affects economic growth must be indirect, whether via institutional outcomes or via empowering people. Such outcomes then affect investors and workers and, only through these, economic development.

Therefore, I explicitly specify indirect theoretical paths through which democracy as a set of institutional practices may affect economic development, and focus in this chapter on two forms of capital formation: at the individual level and at the social level. These two forms of capital, which will be examined through education (as human capital) and generalized trust in the population (as an enabler of social capital formation), are thought of as being especially sensitive to different political systems. This is not to say that physical capital formation is not affected by political structures and outcomes – indeed our previous research on the links between democracy, socio-political stability and investment in physical capital – suggest that it is.[3] But the foci of the present study are education as human capital and generalized trust in the population as mediators of social capital. This brings the study of political forms close to what we have discussed and will further elaborate in this book.

Differing from previous work, Hanno Scholtz and I not only explicitly specified indirect effects of democracy but also considered two different measures for the final outcome, i.e. economic development. The first indicator is the sheer economic growth rate of the per capita product – which has so far been the standard measure – and the second is a new measure, that of techno-economic change, which we have discussed in Chapter 3.

Figure 5.1 summarizes our indirect design linking democracy to both economic growth and techno-economic change. It also depicts six relationships we are going to analyse in the empirical part of this chapter. These paths refer to that from democracy as political form to human and social capital formation, and from these intermediates towards economic growth and techno-economic change. Data availability determines the estimating and control procedures for the different paths.

The chapter is organized as follows. I will briefly define what is meant by democracy as a political form, discuss previous opinions and results on the issue of democracy and development, and then argue why we can expect this political form to be associated with more education and generalized trust. Then I report our tests whether the indirect links of democracy to economic growth and techno-economic change can be empirically established in cross-national research. While the effects on education and generalized trust on economic growth and techno-economic change are less in dispute (see Chapters 2–4 as well as the next), we need to establish not only arguments but also empirical links between democracy on the

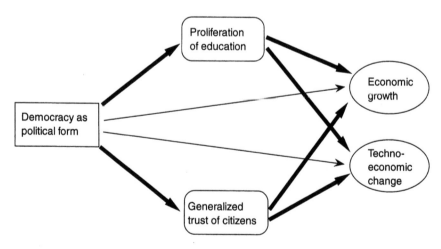

Figure 5.1 Modelling indirect effects of democracy

Note
The bold lines indicate indirect effects, the thin ones direct ones which might be empirically observable as long as not all relevant direct links have been specified.

one hand and education and generalized trust on the other. These are, then, the main theoretical and empirical contributions of this chapter, arguing that democracy as a political form is likely to increase education and generalized trust and therefore is good for economic development. The two subsequent chapters will deal in more detail with the role of education in economic growth and on how developed democracies enhance generalized trust.

The novel findings presented in this chapter contribute to a better understanding of political forms in economic development, since such indirect effects have been missed by previous cross-national research on the consequences of democracy as a political practice.

The notion of democracy as a political form and the issue of its role in development

I here refer to liberal political democracy, which is organized around the ideal of equal participation in political matters but does not extend to democracy in economic matters. Indeed, it exists to different degrees within capitalist societies, which are characterized by a highly uneven degree of control over capital and economic decisions.

In successive social movements this political form, including political participation, rule of law and human rights, separation of political powers and countervailing powers such as trade unions and critical movements, has become increasingly established in the form that we call democracy in today's developed countries, and also diffused in waves to the developing parts of world society, albeit to different extents and seldom in fully-fledged forms, so that we can speak of this political form as being a variable in cross-national research.

There have been excellent contributions to our scholarly understanding of democracy; among the many writings on democracy we would especially like to point to Robert Dahl's (1971) classical statement. I can thus be brief here in saying that we can speak of a democratic form of government if:

1 There is a free competition among citizens concerning ideas, opinions and interests (the dimension of pluralism).
2 Office holders are elected in unrestricted and fair ballots where all adults can participate with an equal vote (the dimension of participation).
3 Political office holders are responsible to the elected representatives (the dimension of responsibility).
4 All citizens are protected against arbitrary political encroachments by human rights, freedom of opinion and expression and of information, by the freedom to associate and other individual rights (the dimension of civil rights).

This description of four dimensions makes clear that the political form of democracy is multidimensional, something also taken into account by the various models put forward to measure democracy empirically.[4] The definition, however, does not take into account various other aspects of political organization and political styles in democracies, to which we shall come later in the book. We consider these aspects as differentiations within the form of political democracy.

In the contemporary developed world, democracy is hardly contested by significant groups. But in parts of the underdeveloped world it still is, especially by power holders. This is not hard to understand, since autocrats are hardly interested in power-sharing and controls, which democracy basically implies. More interestingly, even among social scientists who would not normally argue against democracy in their own developed countries, doubts have been raised about whether democracy is the best form in which to bring about late development. These opinions stand against those expressed by scholars who see democracy as an indispensable step to initiating development. We can be brief here in summarizing the positions (see Bornschier 2002: 405ff.): The authoritarian position (or the conflict model between democracy and late development) claims that democracy is hardly the best form to pursue late development since, among other reasons put forward, hard choices need to be made in order to fuel capital formation in late development, and these are difficult to implement if people have a say in politics. The contrary view of compatibility, or the democratic position comes to exactly the opposite conclusion, and argues that democracy is good for late development because of its inherent pluralism, legitimacy and political stability. There also exists, however, a skeptical position, which argues that the special circumstances which historically lead to the democratization of today's developed countries, including civic culture, civic virtues and the acknowledgement of the supreme right of individuals and their freely elected representatives vis-à-vis political powers, might be historically specific and so not necessarily available to late developers. Finally, a position has been advanced that can be called the tandem position, which argues that market society and political democracy are necessarily linked due to intrinsic mechanisms of mutual legitimization (see Bornschier 1997). Merely partial modernization will make society less legitimate, and this is seen as a long-term handicap. We will come to this again later in the chapter.

The empirical issue of democracy and development

Empirically, one finds that certain core elements of democracy, such as the right to vote for all adult citizens (universal suffrage), have become a universal norm; countries which do not at least claim to practise it have become a tiny minority among the currently existing 200 sovereign states (Markoff 1996: 144). Certainly, the discrepancy between norm and reality is in many societies considerable. But, from the sociological point of view, both the norm and behaviour which deviates from it are important.

In cross-sections of countries, one basic fact is obvious: the higher the level of material development, the higher democracy scores, as measured by a variety of scales. This holds even when we only compare societies outside the developed world. Yet, correlation of this type does not necessarily imply causality; it could well be that the increase of democracy follows material development and the new composition of classes it implies, as explained in the famous Lipset argument. In contradiction to this, causal evidence would imply that the extent of democracy attained furthers subsequent economic development. On this issue, however, the findings are inconclusive. Since 1974 more than thirty cross-sectional studies of the effect of democracy on growth have become available.[5] Most of these studies (about 60 per cent) find no statistically significant effect of democracy on subsequent growth. In the minority of studies which find a statistically significant relation, those reporting a positive one prevail in a ratio of about seven to three. Despite this, the conclusion would appear quite obvious: no trustworthy empirically proven relationship can be demonstrated, and this would not warrant the addition of a new study to this seemingly overstudied field.

However, such a conclusion would be premature, since these studies related measures of democracy directly to economic growth and simultaneously controlled for many variables that are both affected by democracy and affect growth. One example is the work of Robert Barro, who initiated an influential school of comparative economic growth studies by putting as many variables as could conceivably be influential into the equation for estimating growth, the so-called Barro-type regressions (see also Temple 1999). In 1996 he published a piece entitled 'Democracy and Growth' where he reported no effect of democracy on growth after simultaneously putting factors like investment, the rule of law, market freedom, government consumption and human capital as predictors in the growth equation (for a recent discussion, see Plümper and Martin 2003).

The logic of indirect effects implies, however, that once mediating variables are put into the growth equation together with the indirectly working variable, the latter will lose (part of) its effect. Therefore to conclude that democracy does not affect growth, as Barro (1996) did, is simply wrong unless one fully explores the possible indirect effects with an adequate design. We look at this question again, using an adequate design as depicted in Figure 5.1.

Why the political form of democracy and the proliferation of trust and education are linked

In order to underpin our indirect approach theoretically, the focus is on the links between democracy and education on the one hand and trust on the other. The subsequent effects of education and trust on economic development are less in dispute and have been established in cross-sectional research; for trust see the chapters in Part I and for education the next chapter.

Democracy and trust

Let us start with trust. Democracy as a political form which mitigates the difference between interests, and thereby limits violent forms of conflict resolution, is a reflection of the legitimacy of a social order. This legitimacy is seen as a pillar of generalized trust in the population (see also Chapter 2). Our argument runs as follows. Modern societies are forced to find solutions to solve the conflict between their core values of freedom and equality, since this legitimacy is based on a compromise between both that is acceptable for the citizens (see Bornschier [1988] 1996). We also argue that economic freedom in the market society and political freedom with universal suffrage operate in tandem first (Bornschier 1997).[6] The fact that economic freedom and political freedom began to evolve in proto-forms at the same time was not a historical accident. This necessarily parallel design did not survive and does not justify itself simply as a superior, affluence-creating power, but much more as a peacemaking form for the management of freedom and equal opportunity. The rationale for this will be briefly outlined. The very fact of political regulations, on which market society necessarily depends, simultaneously facilitate and impair the taking of economic chances by active individuals, even if the rules are minimal. Even if these rules were to be strictly the same for everyone, and arranged in the form of a law-based state – something we assume here – they restrict the freedom of individuals differently. This restriction is in no way just when viewed in the context of freedom. In order to make freedom of action and political regulation compatible, the political rule-setting process must be established according to the principle of equal opportunity and individual freedom of choice. In this way, all individuals have, in principle, the same chance with their votes to introduce their personal preferences into the formation of the political will. Thus, the market and political democracy are inseparable as institutional solutions if full legitimacy is to be warranted.

This argument then suggests that democracy, which includes political participation and universal suffrage beside human rights and the rule of law, represents system trust. This system trust not only bolsters the generalized trust of citizens but is its prerequisite. Trust of individuals must of course be related to supportive evidence, not only in daily life but also in the trustworthy functioning of institutions like the set embodied in what we call democracy. Niklas Luhmann ([1968] 1974: 62) expressed this both concisely and poetically: 'The towers of trust have to be firmly planted on the ground.'[7]

While system trust and personal trust are seen to be related, the intrinsic nexus of the latter with democracy is, in addition, more dialectical. Indeed, it goes beyond political participation and universal suffrage, since it also includes other important elements of democracy: checks and balances, controls in the form of parliamentary inquiries, and opposition taken as a matter of course.

Luhmann (1974: 78f.) once pointed our attention to the relationship between trust and mistrust, the latter not supposed to mean simply the opposite, but the functional counterpart, of trust. If we consider the problem of trust as one of risk-taking, then there always exists the problem of at least latent mistrust. We never have enough information to be sure that trust is justified but, by our will, we have to negate such inherent doubts. This possible mistrust can, however, be externalized to institutions, which then function as a way of effectively making people trustful. Furthermore, such institutions cannot be regarded simply as the foundations on which the generalized trust of citizens rests, for example through the enforcement of laws. Instead, institutions may function as a complement to personal trust by institutionalizing mistrust.[8] This is where the very form of democracy enters, since the above-mentioned core characteristics also represent institutionalized mistrust.

Democracy and education

The market and formal education are two institutional realms crucial for legitimizing modern society with its central values of equality and efficiency. Freedom and equality are contradictory, a problem that needs to be solved in order to legitimize capitalist market society. The way this comes about can be also termed the social magic of the market and has been developed elsewhere (Bornschier [1988] 1996: 32f.). The argument runs as follows. Given the existence of a claim to liberty, equality in an absolute sense is a contradiction, because in this form it would admit no claim to freedom. We have to recall that freedom of will finally leads to inequality. Neither in the biological (genetic) nor in the social sense (and not even as a result of the freedom of will) is it possible to consider people as equals. This paradox between the claim to equality and the multifaceted diversity of people constitutes at the same time a productive force and a contradiction which historically has made more equality possible in Western society. It is precisely the impossibility of realizing finally and fully the claim to equality which keeps this issue alive. The paradox can be resolved only by raising the problem of the claim to justice. If persons are equal in principle, dissimilarity per se is not an argument for inequitable treatment or value statements that transform dissimilarity into inequality. Instead, justice demands that inequitable treatment or the assertion of inequality be justified. From an anthropological and natural rights point of view, this justification is not discretionary. Rather, it remains linked to rational judgement and thus to equality in principle, despite dissimilarity.

Which institutions can help to resolve the problem of justice in valuation? In modern times the problem has been delegated to a large extent to an anonymous and so called value-neutral institution: the market. The formula is: people deserve what they earn (the play on words in German is telling: *Jemand verdient, was er verdient*). In the course of the development of market society, economic concentration grew and the increasing numbers of employees instead of self-employed posed a problem; the delegation of the question of justice to the market alone did not suffice any longer. Formal education moved alongside market success in justifying differences in earnings. Beside state-regulated markets, this is then the second state-governed sphere relevant for justifying distributional inequality; remember that, worldwide, the vast majority of the educational system is under the aegis of the state.

Let us briefly reflect on the relevant function of formal education in modern society. The second form of social magic, i.e. the myth of equal opportunity through schools, is relevant here.

The system of formal education is a pillar of equality, albeit a problematic one. The modern school system is an attempt to institutionalize the principle of equal opportunity, just as democracy attempts to do the same in the political sphere. Right from the start, when all primary school pupils start in the same grade, individual performance alone is supposed to decide one's progress and final position in the educational hierarchy. Because formal education is functionally linked to society's positional structure, the educational system contributes to the acceptance of an uneven positional structure created by formal organizations in capitalist market society.

Although individual capacities and performance are supposed to be the exclusive factors governing educational progress, reality of course always limps behind this idealistic claim. In addition, the legitimizing role of the educational system remains linked to uneven positional structures during a given historical phase, being conditional upon the current technological style. The number of pupils reaching the various grades cannot depend merely upon individual will and performance, for educational capital is also bequeathed. The children of parents with higher schooling have 'natural' advantages that can only partially be democratized, hence the tendency of educational stratification to be reproduced over generations. The overall outcome is a contradictory dynamic. If one attempts to preserve the legitimizing function of education, access to it in the form of upward mobility must be opened up and democratized to counteract those forces tending towards unequal opportunities. The result of this is necessarily educational expansion (for evidence, see Bornschier [1988] 1996: Chapter 9). This is seen as the result of status competition for educational certificates. But this is not a purely mechanical process either, since politics necessarily enters.

Let me recall what the dialectics of status competition imply: the higher the educational levels reached by the parents, the higher their aspirations to preserve status. Thus, the higher levels of the educational system can only be kept open through equal opportunities that link educational success solely to cognitive capabilities if the number of students at the highest levels increases; this has been the case since the establishment of compulsory schooling (see Bornschier [1988] 1996: Chapter 9). Collective, i.e. public, decisions are certainly required for increasing the volumes of students at higher educational levels. Thus the state, which attempts to institutionalize the value of equal opportunities through education policy, must meet the mobility aspirations of the lower classes. At the same time, the aspirations of the educated to preserve status for their offspring operate in a universalistic way, through educational success. Thus, schools and universities can only be kept open if they expand.

The conclusion for the democracy–education link is thus quite straight-forward. Democracies have to obey the demand of legitimacy, since people have a voice, and it is public decisions which are ultimately responsible for educational expansion. Therefore, democracies pursue, other things being equal, a more expansive educational policy. The reader will have noticed that I do not here discuss the intrinsic value of education for individual productivity at the workplace but the logic of legitimizing society by offering legitimate channels for the distribution of positions and income in society.

Empirical evidence

Before we come to the empirical links between democracy and our two mediators, generalized trust and formal education, in order to establish the necessary conditions for the indirect effects of democracy on economic development we need to say something about the data and the design.

Democracy data

There are three main indices which try cross-nationally to translate polit-ical reality into numbers: those of Tatu Vanhanen (2000, see also 1997), of the Polity project of Ted Robert Gurr and his team (Gurr 1974, Jaggers and Gurr 1995, Marshall and Jaggers 2000), and of Freedom House, start-ing with the work of Raymond Gastil (Gastil 1982). A fourth, the newer approach of a team in the World Bank Development Research Group (Kaufmann *et al.* 2001) merges normalized data from different sources, therefore providing a non-transparent measure containing a huge amount of expert information. But this index is available only for 1997/8 and 2000/1, and for us it can only serve as a benchmark.

Of the first three indices mentioned, each has its own merits: Vanhanen provides a measurement which very transparently describes political reality instead of institutional forms; Freedom House explicitly states the two different notions of democracy, and the Polity index (Jaggers and Gurr) codes a large number of institutional characteristics, going back in history as far as possible. And as they try to measure the same thing, the correlations, at least between three of the four, are high.[9] These are given in Table 5.1. For most analyses we rely in this chapter on the data from the Polity project (Jaggers and Gurr).[10]

Before we come to the results concerning the indirect effects of democracy on economic development, I would like to comment on the samples of countries and the data used for the intermediate variables (trust and education) and the ultimately dependent variables (economic growth and techno-economic change).

Samples

In order to test the links depicted in Figure 5.1, one has to rely on different samples of countries. This is due to lacking data, especially for trust. The number of cases on which the results rely thus vary and this will be mentioned when we come to the figures that express the size of the effects. It is, then, needless to say to specialists that the analysis is thus not a path analysis in the strict sense, although Figures 5.1 and 5.2 could suggest that.

All the country comparisons in this chapter contain many more developing countries than have been included up to now in the empirical tests reported in this book. The reason for this is very simple. Within the OECD world, the differences in democracy measures are comparatively small (see Bornschier 2002: 121; Jaggers and Gurr 1996). In other words, we have too few differences to be related to our intermediate variables. This is also the reason that we need to include former state socialist countries, on their way to market societies, in order to have enough cases to estimate the link between democracy and trust.

Trust

The broadest database for trust and by now frequently used in international comparison is provided by the *World Values Survey* (Inglehart 1990; Inglehart *et al.* 1998). In these surveys the question was: 'Generally

Table 5.1 Cross-tabulation of Freedom House dimensions

	Freedom House	*Jaggers & Gurr*
Jaggers & Gurr	0.89**	–
World Bank	0.82**	0.79**

Source: Berg-Schlosser 2002 for correlations with World Bank; own calculations.

Note
All correlations significant below the 1 per cent level.

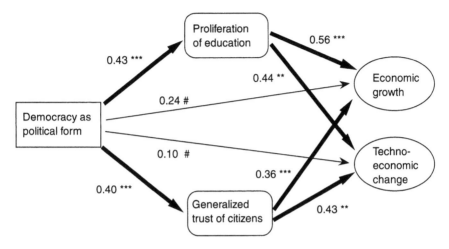

Figure 5.2 The empirically observed indirect effects of democracy on economic
development: a synopsis of our preliminary work.

Notes
The listed figures represent standardized effects, also called beta effects. They inform us
about the relative importance of effects. The number of observations on which the coefficients are based, as well as the controlled variables to obtain the result, are referred to in the
text.
\#   statistically not significant (p > 10%);
**   statistically significant (p < 5%);
*** statistically very significant (p < 1%).

speaking, would you say that most people can be trusted or that you can't
be too careful in dealing with people?' The percentage of people who trust
is our indicator, as in previous chapters. The trust question has been asked
not only in the *World Values Survey* (*WVS*), but in other surveys, too.
Norris (2000) uses trust data from shadow surveys to include New Zealand
in her sample, a country that has not yet been included in the *WVS* survey
waves. Such additional information is added to our data set, which relates
to the third wave of the *WVS*, 1995–8, and allows a comparison of up to
fifty-four countries.

Education

To find an indicator for educational expansion that is equally informative
for less-developed countries and highly developed ones is not easy. In the
next chapter we will address this question in more detail. Education at the
basic level (compulsory education) is already universal in rich countries to
the extent that that there are no meaningful differences, while the proliferation of basic education still differs among poorer countries. The case with
tertiary education is that proliferation among the whole population has, as

compared to rich societies, only started in poorer countries. The proliferation of secondary education is then the most suitable indicator for educational expansion if one wants to compare countries at very different levels of development. Here, we use the data on the proliferation of education attained at the secondary level provided by Barro and Lee (2000).

Economic growth

The economic growth rates are calculated on a per capita basis. These long-term averages are based on the Penn World Tables by Summers and Heston (1988, 1996), who use purchasing-power parities. This allows for an analysis more pertinent to the situation and life chances of the people in the respective societies (while figures at exchange rates are more relevant for transnationally traded goods). The sample for economic growth is based on the data set from Levine and Renelt's study (1992), provided by the World Bank.[11] It covers data averaging from 1960 to 1989 for 119 countries.

Techno-economic change

As discussed more fully in Chapter 3, the world economy is undergoing a structural change in its technological style, towards an even higher level of economic integration via electronic communication (telematics). This change started slowly during the 1970s, accelerated during the 1980s and experienced a take-off during the 1990s. That change is, however, very uneven with regard to diffusion levels of indicators of the telematics era, even if one compares different developed societies and even more so when the bulk of developing countries is included. As in Chapter 3, I consider a variety of variables representing the physical infrastructure of the telematics era: Internet hosts, mobile phones, personal computers, telephone mainlines and in addition here, fax machines, newspapers and radios. These data are provided by the *World Development Reports* of the World Bank, all standardized by population size.

A factor analysis (principle component analysis) was performed, similar to the one for twenty-one rich societies in Chapter 3, for a world sample of 104 countries with the extended variables mentioned above.[12] Almost all the variance of the seven included measures of the telematics era is represented by just one factor, representing 77.6 per cent of the variance common to the seven indicators. This common factor reflects to a very large extent the level of development as measured by the material per capita product (purchasing-power parities corrected figures). In order to obtain a useful indicator of techno-economic change that measures something that is not already included in the level of material development, one therefore has to control per capita product as the measure of material development. The justification and procedure is as follows. A sensible measure for economic change is not one that informs us about how much telematics infrastructure is built up (and used) because of a country's level of material development, but about how much new infrastructure is built up relative to a country's level of material development level. Thus, one needs to residualize the telematics variables. This simply means that one only considers such differences between countries which are not implied by differences in average material wealth. This is then our measure for techno-economic change.

Empirically substantiated indirect links

In Figure 5.2 we come back to our theoretical model of indirect links between democracy and economic development and add the weight of empirically substantiated relationships to it. This is an illustration of the relationships found in subsequent steps of the analysis, and cannot be interpreted according to standard path analysis, since the analysis had to rely on different samples. In the following paragraphs I wish to comment on the various empirically substantiated paths displayed in Figure 5.2.

Democracy → generalized trust.

We are empirically able to establish a very significant relationship, as suggested by our theoretical proposition. This is for a sample of fifty-one countries (controlling for the level of material development). Remember that the trust measure is our standard one (percentage of people trusting) and the democracy measure includes both Freedom House components.

Generalized trust → economic growth

The relationship between trust and economic growth, as we found in Chapter 2, has also been established for a sample of fifty-four countries – so far the largest in which the relationship was ever tested (the sample also includes former state socialist countries). Trust is measured 1995–8 and economic growth in the second half of the 1990s.

Generalized trust → techno-economic change

The association we found in Chapter 3 for Internet diffusion is confirmed for forty-six countries with a broader indicator for technological change. The significant coefficient (the number of cases is between thirty-five and forty-six, depending on the number of control variables) still holds after controlling for education, level of development and democracy (measure from the Polity project). Democracy has only an indirect effect on techno-economic change, as evidenced by its insignificant direct effect once trust and education are included.

Democracy → education

As suggested by our proposition, democracy and educational expansion (measured by the proliferation of secondary education in the population) are very significantly associated for a sample of 106 countries which cover all levels of development. Education is measured in 1960 and democracy with the data from the Polity project. This still holds after controlling for per capita income as an indicator of the level of material development, which also has a positive effect on education. The conclusion is that educational expansion cannot be explained by material development alone; in addition, democracy has an independent favourable effect, of about the same size and significance (effect of development on education not shown in Figure 5.2).

Education → economic growth

As reported in many previous studies, we find a significant association between the diffusion of education (1960) and economic growth (1960–89) for a world sample of 101 countries. We will come back to this in the next chapter. The positive effect of educational expansion on subsequent economic growth still holds after controlling for per capita income (one observes a significant straggler effect, not displayed) and for democracy. Once education and trust are included in the growth model, it turns out that democracy has no significant positive direct effect on growth any more. This is what we expected from the logic of indirect effects.

Education → techno-economic change

Education not only adds to economic growth but helps to foster techno-economic change. We find a significant effect of education on techno-economic change for a sample of ninety-seven countries (level of development is not included as a control since the change measure is net of level of development). When trust is included as a predictor, the sample drops to thirty-five cases. Even then, education still has a significant effect on techno-economic change, of about the same size as trust. This is very similar to the results reported already in Chapter 3 for Internet diffusion in thirty-four countries, where education (there we considered tertiary education) and trust were significant predictors which independently explained techno-economic change. As mentioned above, democracy loses its direct effect on techno-economic change once the variables trust and education, through which favourable effects are mediated, are included.

Conclusion and review

The results appear to substantiate our claim that democracy has favourable effects on economic development, which was demonstrated by those mediated through educational expansion and higher levels of generalized trust. For these mediators I proposed theoretical reasons which here receive their first empirical support.[13]

The bulk of previous studies on democracy and economic development erred by dismissing consideration of the beneficial indirect effects of democracy. Only one of the previous studies explicitly followed the same step-wise design and found the following causal chain:[14] the impact of democracy on socio-political stability is positive in that study; this stability then has favourable consequences for investment, which is one of the most important predictors of economic growth (see the results in Bornschier 2002: esp. 412). This previous study, which could also establish positive indirect effects of democracy for a sample of seventy-eight countries over the 1965–85 period, indicates that more than the intervening variables which were considered in this chapter need to be studied to get a full understanding of the role of democracy. The aim of this chapter was, however, not to provide such a complete analysis, but to demonstrate that the whole field needs to be re-analysed, and can hardly be considered to be an overstudied area.

As demonstrated with the links between democracy and education and generalized trust, I not only suggest a fresh impetus for the seemingly overstudied field of democracy's impact on economic development (both growth and change) but also link the political form of democracy to education, which will be discussed in the next chapter. Furthermore, democracy is related to trust as a cultural resource, as discussed earlier in the book. How political styles within the form of democracy are related to the capacity to generate trust among citizens will be the topic of the chapter that concludes the second part of the book.

Studying the clustering of the culture of trust with political styles in democracy will add to our understanding of the considerable differences in trust between societies. As we have seen, these exist alongside the clusters of cultural attitudes at the individual level, of which trust is a significant part (see Chapter 4). Having done that, we will look at the clustering of culture in different spheres, including politically relevant features of culture and those characterizing the everyday life of citizens which, when at the workplace or shop is, of course, also economically relevant.

6 The double dividend of expanding education for development

Why do we study the role of education?

In the previous chapter, I advanced the argument that democracy is expected to lead to educational expansion in order to make plausible the indirect links between democracy, educational expansion and accelerated economic development. Empirical evidence for both links was found. More education in the population was related both to more democracy and to faster economic development. While the first link has not often been studied, the latter has; there is plenty of evidence from cross-national studies that education is a good predictor of economic growth, alongside investment in physical capital, the straggler effect and other control variables. Indeed, we presented evidence so far in the book that education not only adds to economic growth but eases structural change, too (see last chapter as well as Chapter 3 on Internet diffusion).

At the same time I stressed at the end of my theoretical reasoning in the previous chapter that my point was not to discuss the intrinsic value of education for individual productivity but its ability to legitimize society by offering channels for the distribution of positions and income in society. If educational expansion does not necessarily result in higher average individual productivity at the workplace, though, why is it good for growth? Do we not then have a problem accounting for the empirically substantiated positive effects on development?

I would argue that we do not have such a problem if we take account of arguments other than those proposed by human capital theory. This is what we do in this chapter, by arguing that there is not one, but at least two, ways in which education might theoretically be beneficial for development.

The common sense argument, which is also the assumption of human capital theory, says that schooling provides qualifications which would otherwise not become available, at least not to the same extent, if schooling were shorter and less widespread in the population. Here, schools (used as a generic term for all levels) both socialize and implant knowledge and skills; in short, schools are thought of as the 'great socializers'.

Pupils leaving school have more knowledge, and this represents human capital, which is, of course, supplemented by, for instance, practical experience and continuing education after formal schooling. This stock of education is thought, in human capital theory, to make workers more productive; therefore, they gain more as workers or entrepreneurs. This not only holds at the individual level but also in the aggregate of society, where the individual stocks of human capital add to the aggregate stock. That sounds plausible and reflects common sense. But we have a problem when we want to explain the growth of income, either of the individual or of society at large, since more education is associated with a higher level of income. Growth of income in the aggregate would only result if schooling (human capital) were expanding. Interestingly, the latter cannot be substantiated by empirical evidence. We come to a discussion of this problem later and will evaluate arguments why the level of education should have a continuous, not just a temporary effect.

We find the idea of the function of education as legitimizing society less often applied in cross-section work. This argument goes beyond what was once called the allocation function of education in critical treatments (schools thought of as the 'great sorters'), but it uses the link between level of education and access to positions in society as a necessary precondition. Only because level of schooling gives access to social positions can education legitimize society, and it does this if, and only if, access to education is more open than other routes to status in society. Guaranteeing this relatively greater openness is what makes educational expansion necessary, as was argued in the last chapter. In such a perspective, the proliferation of education in a society – as long as it represents at least partial social mobility – is indirectly favourable for economic development. It helps to limit the ever-present distributional conflicts in society and makes people more motivated to engage in what they regard as a legitimate society. In short, via links to socio-political stability (which spurs investment, as theoretical reasoning and empirical evidence suggest) and motivation which makes people, other things being equal, more productive at the workplace, education can be thought of as beneficial for economic development.

These links, of course, the one via better qualifications and the other through the legitimization of society in the eyes of citizens, need not be mutually exclusive. And while the theoretical reasoning is quite different in each case, they both should fuel economic development. This is why I propose that more emphasis on education in a society may result in a 'double dividend', a metaphor intended to combine the arguments for human capital theory and those from the theory of increasing legitimacy due to educational access.

Although its main topic is education, this chapter is also intended to add to our understanding of the broader question of the role of politics in development. This is simply because education is, worldwide, mostly organized under the aegis of the state (including its lower-level organs, which very often structure and finance educational policy). In any case, the expansion of education needs public decisions and spending.

This chapter is organized as follows. First I will illustrate the astonishing expansion of education in the world today, which in many societies has surpassed comparable modernization of the socio-economic structure. This exposition is followed by an overview of findings on the link between education and economic development. Then some theoretical question marks are added to the human capital argument and I indicate some fallacies in previous empirical work. Then I compare the arguments of the human capital theory and the theory of expanding education as a legitimizing device, pointing to some limitations of the applicability of the latter. Finally, we will come to our recent empirical findings, which suggest that both perspectives add to our understanding of the role of education in development. This is followed by a brief summary of the double dividend argument.

Educational expansion in world society

When compulsory basic education was introduced in what are now the developed countries during the second half of the nineteenth century, a spiral of educational expansion was triggered which has lasted until today. This spiral has two distinct components. On the one hand, the length of compulsory education has considerably expanded over time. On the other hand, the frequencies of pupils at intermediate and higher levels of education has increased, which has led – with a certain time lag – to a corresponding shift in the educational distribution in society at large (see Bornschier [1988] 1996: Chapter 9). The second part of the process is demonstrated by the educational attainment of different cohorts in Western society born between 1875 and 1945 in Figure 6.1.

Soon after the Second World War, this expansion, which had been taking place for a hundred years in the core societies of the West, started to occur in the mostly colonized developing countries. Since 1960 this process has accelerated and is depicted in Table 6.1, which offers average figures for the world and for the developed and developing parts of it separately. Note that these are average figures and that one has to take into account that educational expansion in the developing world also varies considerably with level of development and with degree of democracy, as demonstrated in the previous chapter.

Of course, there are still considerable differences not only between the developed and the underdeveloped part of the world but also within these groups. To explain such differences and their consequences is, of course, what comparative approaches are about. As early as 1977 John W. Meyer and his collaborators aptly called the general trend a 'world educational revolution' (Meyer *et al.* 1977; Meyer and Hannan 1979: Chapters 3–5; see

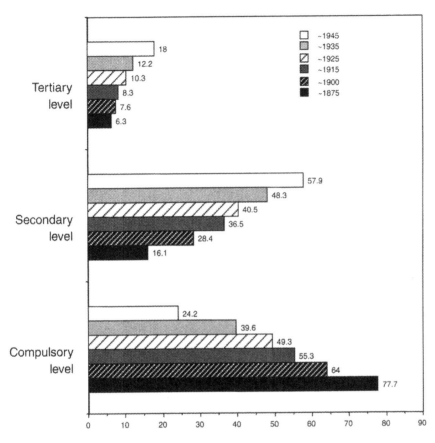

Figure 6.1 Educational attainment of birth cohorts, born between 1875–1945 in a pooled sample of eight Western core societies (source: figures for graphical presentation in Bornschier 1996: 224).

also Sanderson 1995: 304–17). Certainly the socio-structural and material circumstances in most societies could not hope to match this revolution. And this is one of the first issues that raises doubts about the general applicability of human capital theory. Given the increase in education, the material conditions should have increased correspondingly, which was, however, not the case (see Bornschier 2002: esp. Chapter 2). The obvious mismatch between educational and economic expansion is less of an enigma if the contending perspective is applied. Education is, according to this, a legitimate device to distribute positions; at the same time education is a positional good. If everybody attained more education, total product would be distributed by requiring more education for every item of income. Actually, the truth seems to lie between the positions. Increasing

Table 6.1 Educational attainment at various levels in world society, 1960–99. Percentage figures for 82–90 countries

	n	World	Richer countries	Poorer countries
Only primary school completed				
1960	82	17.1	27.3	9.2
1965	82	17.5	28.2	9.0
1970	84	16.5	26.8	8.8
1975	87	15.5	23.7	9.2
1980	88	14.8	21.8	9.9
1985	88	14.3	19.4	10.8
1990	90	13.8	18.2	10.9
1995	88	13.6	16.6	11.5
1999	88	13.4	15.7	11.8
Secondary school completed				
1960	86	5.1	9.7	1.9
1965	86	5.2	9.8	1.9
1970	86	6.3	11.8	2.4
1975	87	7.2	12.8	2.9
1980	88	9.0	16.6	3.8
1985	88	9.5	16.7	4.5
1990	90	10.6	18.7	5.2
1995	88	11.9	20.4	6.1
1999	88	12.1	20.1	6.5
Tertiary school levels completed				
1960	88	1.5	2.6	0.7
1965	88	1.6	2.8	0.8
1970	86	2.1	3.6	1.1
1975	87	2.7	4.5	1.4
1980	88	3.6	5.9	1.9
1985	88	4.3	6.7	2.6
1990	90	5.3	8.1	3.4
1995	88	6.3	9.5	4.2
1999	88	7.4	11.1	4.8

Sources: Calculated by Claudia König (figures from Barro and Lee 2000, update from 1994) for Volker Bornschier's research seminar. For world data and country groups the unweighted country averages are used. The division into poorer and richer countries is given according to the *World Development Report* (1997: 258f.); the borderline is approximately between Venezuela and S. Africa.

education might have added to the overall product, but not to the degree it expanded.

In developed countries, the educational system integrates almost all citizens, although to a different degree, since citizens differ according to levels attained. At least the citizens with no education at all, i.e. the illiterate, are a tiny minority (if one does not apply concepts of functional illiteracy). However, in world society the illiterates are quite a large proportion of the population, and in poor countries even today they are still the majority, once one considers only women. Table 6.2 gives figures for the development of literacy from 1980 to 1995. In Table 6.2 only developing countries are considered, since in these countries the official figures for literacy amount to almost 100 per cent.

With the increase in education over time (see Figure 6.1 and Table 6.1), the average level of educational attainment has increased and growing numbers have become integrated into society via the modern device of the educational system. But there are still considerable numbers of illiterates, especially in poorer countries, who are left out (see Table 6.2). These groups are not only marginal to the system of promises of education by, for instance, having only low-level certificates; they are completely excluded and thus entirely untouched by the myth of equal opportunities through schooling, in which every person starts at the same level. In my view the proportion of non-integrated is a very important fact that limits the legitimizing function of education. Obviously, some, if not many, illiterates may aspire to a better lot for their offspring, but illiterates nevertheless represent a group outside the immediate legitimizing logic of education in modernizing society. And this is why we need to consider this group later in the chapter, too, in order to investigate more completely the consequences of the educational situation in societies.

Table 6.2 Literacy in total population (percentages for 1980–95)

	n	*1980*	*1985*	*1990*	*1995*
Men and women					
Societies with low income	*49*	41.0	45.7	50.2	54.9
Societies with middle income, lower category	*34*	69.7	73.9	77.4	80.6
Societies with middle income, higher category	*14*	75.9	79.4	82.6	85.1
Men					
Societies with low income	*49*	52.1	56.6	60.8	64.9
Societies with middle income, lower category	*34*	77.1	80.4	83.2	85.7
Societies with middle income, higher category	*14*	81.6	84.2	86.7	88.6
Women					
Societies with lower income	*49*	30.2	35.0	40.0	45.0
Societies with middle income, lower category	*34*	84.9	68.0	71.7	75.5
Societies with middle income, higher category	*14*	69.4	74.0	77.9	81.2

Source: Calculated by Claudia König (UNESCO, http://www.uis.unesco.org/en/stats/stats0.htlm) in Volker Bornschier's research seminar.

Note
For the country groups the unweighted average was used. The division of the group of developing countries was made according to the *World Development Report* (1997: 258f.).

Some further comment on explaining educational expansion

We have already touched in the last chapter on the basic reasons why education expands in the modern world.[1] The core concept is legitimacy. The legitimizing content of education is based on its ability to integrate modern society by its functioning as an institution. We thus have to concentrate on the potential integrational function of education, which, to become effective, must meet two conditions.

1   The model of interpreting the world in which the educational system is anchored must accord with the dominant culture in other domains of society, which are ordered around rationality and progress.
2   The distribution of status in the educational system must be legitimized by conforming to the two central principles of striving after efficiency and equality. Formal education fulfils these two conditions like no other institution, which is why it belongs to those very important key systems absolutely essential for the integration of modern society. The myth of progress runs through both science and economics and essentially reflects the desire to control nature and to limit insecurity. Thus, euphoria and periodic skepticism and animosity towards science and growth go hand in hand.

The system of rules of institutionalized education attracts broad assent because the principles of efficiency and equality appear to be very thoroughly embedded in it. The 'social magic' of the school derives from symbolic equality, as each person starts their educational career at the same level. Later, performance measured in grades, i.e. personal achievement, is central to advancement within the system. No doubt it is a myth that only talent and performance count, a myth that neglects the inheritance of educational status resulting from differing cultural capital endowments and class-specific differences in aspirations.

Further, the legitimizing power of the school is based on the fact that graduates at the highest educational levels have also gone through the same lower levels. By such linkage of different levels, school is legitimized by principles only really relevant at the very top, i.e. in the universities: autonomy, critical ability and the reign of reason. Mass education, on the other hand, remains confined to the teaching of obvious cultural elements and standard knowledge. The comprehensive school thus obscures the fact that the school system determines the number of pupils at different levels by selectivity. Reforms that favour a stronger anchoring of equal opportunity aim at loosening the ties between educational opportunities and social origin, and at a greater permeability between the different levels. Both measures would result in a democratization of education.

Various studies have critically pointed to the absence of equal opportunities in the acquisition of education (see Bourdieu and Passeron

1970). This was discussed in the previous chapter, and you will recall the conclusion, that schools can only be kept open if they expand.

The competition for educational status cannot be separated from the need of employers for certified and legitimate differences in qualification, which usually constitute a first selection criterion for job applicants. Societal expectations are the outcome of the normative strengthening of the correspondence of rules between educational status, job position and income. These expectations are necessary prerequisites for educational status competition – i.e. the pressure for upward movement as well as, for some, for the preservation of status. Yet it is only possible to legitimize the social differentiation of occupations if educational access routes remain open and are not too obviously conditional upon social origin.

The conventional form of educational expansion surely cannot continue forever; this has already become obvious in the developed world, where continuing education and training have become the new wave of educational expansion. I cannot examine this here in detail, for which see Bornschier and Aebi (1992) and Bornschier (1996: 241f.).

Education promoting material development

The importance of education and training for the wealth of nations was stressed by Adam Smith as long ago as 1776. Yet, it took a considerable time until such variables were actually included in cross-national studies to explain economic development. Before the new endogenous growth theory in economics inspired cross-national work that included education as a predictor, several sociological works had already addressed the issue (see Scheidegger 1981, who reviewed earlier work and added new analyses).

The very close correlation between measures of the proliferation of education in a society and the level of material wealth, as indicated by per capita product, has been mentioned earlier. In world samples a large part of education (measured at the secondary level) can be explained by per capita product (for 106 cases the common variance is 61 per cent using the data set by Levine and Renelt 1992). But is education really capable of speeding up economic development? If so, how can we explain that?

A brief overview of studies

In cross-national empirical work two kinds of designs can be found.

1   Growth of education is correlated with the growth of the economy (controlling for other variables relevant for economic growth). Studies with such a design do not find effects of education (see, for example, Jess Benhabib and Mark Spiegel 1994).

2   The level of the proliferation of education is correlated with sub-sequent economic growth. Such studies overwhelmingly find positive and statistically trustworthy associations, see Jess Benhabib and Mark Spiegel (1994), Michael Graff (1996), as well as overviews of additional studies: Norman Gemmel (1998), Johnathan Temple (1999), Axel Weber (1998); for a recent overview that covers twenty-two cross-national studies on education in the population and subsequent growth, see OECD (2001: 95–8).

Why do designs of the first type (growth rates of education correlated with growth rates of income) fail to find the effects of education? This is due to lack of common sense in specification. Benhabib and Spiegel (1994) wonder that in their pure growth rate model, the growth of human capital (education) between 1965 and 1985 has no effect on economic growth in the same time (their Table 1). The reason is not difficult to find. If education capital grew substantially between 1965 and 1985, this necessarily implies that many people were schooled during this time. First, that involved costs (resources which were not available for physical capital formation). Second, many people must have been in school during this time span and so, of course, could not be productive in the economy. The authors do not perceive this and wonder: 'The most surprising result concerns the coefficient on the log difference in human capital. The log difference in human capital always enters insignificantly, and almost always with a negative coefficient' (Benhabib and Spiegel 1994: 149.)

They then find no effect until they use the second type of specification; education (alternatively termed human capital) at the beginning of the growth period is used as a predictor and the original level of per capita wealth (to cover the straggler or convergence effect) and capital formation during the growth period. Then and only then, does the proliferation of education have a positive effect on subsequent economic growth (see Table 4 of Benhabib and Spiegel 1994: 159). In other words, more wide-spread education than predicted by the level of material development is positive for economic growth at every level of development. This is the result that further studies (see references above for overviews) which follow the second design find.

Within the second type of specification, a 'puzzling finding' or 'strange finding' has been entering the discussion for a while. It relates to the different effects of education of men and women: 'The results of education show the puzzling pattern described in Barro and Lee (1994) in which the estimated coefficient of male attainment is significantly positive ... whereas that of female attainment is significantly negative ...' (Barro 1996: 6). In the same tenor are Barro and Sala-i-Martin (1995: 431), Perotti (1996) and Gemmel (1998: 131). In fact, this discussion is entirely unwarranted, since the anomalous findings rest on grotesque methodological fallacies in combination with lack of common sense.[2] Both the education of women and of

men are positive for economic development, but since the economic participation rate of women is lower than that of men (and varies across countries), the positive effects are more indirect in the case of women, affecting
health and child care as well as pre-school education and fertility.

Apart from this abstruse and definitely aberrant 'finding' relating to
gender differences, one can conclude that the findings from the second
specification then suggest support for human capital theory, to which we
will come soon. Yet, one could also interpret the finding of a positive
effect of education on subsequent economic growth in terms of modernization theory. Attending school enhances individual modernity and is
associated with more rationality, which would then be a cultural resource
that would be associated with economic development rather than an effect
of educational content per se (see the synopsis of arguments later).

Before we come to a brief further discussion of why these positive
effects exist, I would like to mention a novel finding presented by Michael
Graff (1996), which draws our attention away to the question of educational distribution. Instead of merely measuring education in terms of
average years of schooling in the population, Graff introduces the following significant improvements. He considers educational inequality of the
kind that favours higher education at the expense of basic education. He
supposes that such educational inequalities have negative impacts on economic growth. In the case of pronounced educational inequalities, higher
education tends to be a means by which elites try to secure supremacy
rather than a useful resource in terms of human capital. Graff sees the
resulting negative consequences as a consequence of conflict potentials
that go together with educational inequality. Indeed, he finds empirical
support for the adverse effect of educational inequalities. Therefore, in
countries with educational inequalities, there is indeed a lower growth
contribution to higher education than in countries that follow a more
balanced education policy (Graff 1996: 292).

This finding may build a bridge between human capital theory arguments and the contending view of legitimacy, since Michael Graff's study
(1996), although pursued in a human capital framework, in certain aspects
comes close to what is addressed by the understanding of education as a
legitimizing device. A pronounced educational inequality limits the effect
of legitimization, since certain groups are excluded or discriminated
against. Thus, we need to control for that when we test legitimacy theory.
This is done later in the chapter when our own empirical work on the issue
will be reported.

Human capital theory and the theory of education as a legitimizing device: competing or complementary views?

Before I come to summarize the two theoretical views (see the schematic
overview later) and to a test of the different effects on economic growth

they claim, let me discuss the human capital suggestions to explain the link between the level of education and economic growth, and address some problems involved. I have mentioned the first problem already; education may not act solely through knowledge but as an enabler of cultural attitudes such as individual modernity and higher rationality. This would be then an example of the indirect effects of schooling.

From a human capital theory background, one could advance arguments for positive direct effects. This means that a higher level of human capital in a society may add to the productivity of the classic factors of production. In adding education to the growth model developed in Chapters 1 and 2, one would expect an effect comparable to that of the cultural resource of generalized trust. Societies with different levels of education will not converge in their growth rates, since more education will make the same amount of standard factors of production more productive. The reason for this can be explained by an easier absorption of the knowledge relevant for productivity wherever education is higher.

The education of individual workers, which sum up to the stock of educational capital in the aggregate, may also have positive external effects that are dismissed if one only adds individual knowledge. This would mean that the higher productivity of one educated person may also enhance the productivity of others. A problem with this is that such possible effects do not accrue to education alone but to networking, which is normally considered an element of social capital. The second problem is that external effects may not necessarily be positive. The inequality of education and its possible consequences, as discussed above, is a case in point.

Last but not least, one can assume the presence of collective effects of education. The average stock of human capital is in some sense a collective good which helps to produce and to absorb new knowledge. This will then foster technological progress applied in running the economy. One problem with this plausible consideration is that it dismisses the fact that education also regularly embodies status-securing elements ('ständische Elemente' as Max Weber put it) aimed at maintaining privileges, which may inhibit the diffusion of knowledge necessary for beneficial collective effects. Furthermore, the diffusion of expert knowledge from research laboratories to application is a very complex process that is organized quite differently in various societies; to look at average schooling as the only condition which fosters that diffusion may well be, to say the least, simplistic.

Despite these problems, there are plausible reasons from the viewpoint of human capital theory why a country with a higher level of education should have a permanently higher economic growth rate. The arguments for the theory that education is a legitimizing device have been already put forward, together with qualifications in the case of pronounced educational inequality and of the exclusion of groups to the social magic of participating in a 'zero hour' when all pupils seem to start at an equal level.

The latter exclusion is especially pertinent where widespread illiteracy exists.

Figure 6.2 schematically summarizes the two ways in which education should be good for growth. the first one stresses the content of education as such or its impact for cultural attitudes, which actually goes beyond the standard human capital arguments. The other schematically depicts the legitimacy arguments.

Of course, neither schematically presented view excludes the other, and they could well be combined. Actually this is what will be suggested in the empirical demonstrations, which then go beyond anything that has been done in empirical research so far.

The human capital approach, both in sociology and in economics, assumes direct effects. The better equipment of workers with knowledge, as indicated by average level of schooling, has a direct positive effect on the overall productivity of factors.

The argument that the educational institution legitimizes social inequality (which is only formulated within sociology), suggests a model that also allows for indirect effects. Opening the access to social positions through education may temper the ever-present social conflict quite considerably, which would then result in more socio-political stability, and would enhance the motivation of the economically active, be they employees or employers. Both these assumed beneficial intermediate consequences will

---

Education contents: abilities and knowledge
Education changes personal characteristics and the store of knowledge

(a) Individual modernity and higher rationality
→ lower transaction costs → higher economic growth from the same inputs
(b) Higher learning ability of the working population, which allows for greater absorption of knowledge, also helpful for R&D
→ more technical progress → higher economic growth

Societal function of education: legitimation
Wide access to education increases the legitimacy of society
→ Instills more hope of just distribution
→ reduces socio-political conflict
→ favourably influences investments in conventional capital
→ increases work motivation and through this achieves
→ higher economic growth

Figure 6.2 Schematic presentation of different views of education.

positively influence another intermediate variable, the propensity to invest in physical capital due to the greater stability of expectations and higher growth assumptions brought about by the presence of a more motivated workforce.

Empirical tests

In order to assess whether the propositions from both lines of argument receive some empirical support, I present first the results of preliminary work from one of my research seminars, estimated by Thomas Gehrig (1999).[3] Figure 6.3 shows the results.[4]

The comment on the results in Figure 6.3 is as follows. The efforts of educational policies (measured by total government spending on education as a share of all government spending) improves the legitimacy of society in the eyes of its citizens, as expressed by socio-political stability. This link is statistically significant for the world sample of seventy-four to seventy-six societies. Socio-political stability is itself good for economic growth, expressed by a significant effect (this is mediated to a considerable extent by positively affecting physical capital formation as our further analyses show, not shown in Figure 6.3).

At the same time, the emphasis of government spending on education positively affects economic growth, which I see mediated by the proliferation of education in the population (not measured in the preliminary analysis, but see Figure 6.4). This link suggests indirect support for human capital arguments. The size of that part of the population excluded from education, measured by the illiteracy rate, reduces socio-political stability, and thereby negatively affects economic growth. If the overall integration of society through the educational system is still small (high illiteracy) or remains small even with increasing economic development due to a policy of educational inequality, then the institution of education which is so important for legitimizing inequality in society is less able to fulfil its task.

The effects of the emphasis on education in development on the one hand seem to be mediated in the way human capital theory would expect. On the other hand they are mediated in the way the theory of education as legitimizing device predicts.

In a second empirical test, performed with my collaborators Mark Herkenrath and Claudia König, we went a step further by including a measure of the proliferation of education in the adult population.[5] Furthermore, for an extended sample of eighty-three cases we used the non-linear model, introduced in Chapter 2, to estimate economic growth. In our path-analytical procedure we control for several variables which also affect or might affect economic growth (mentioned in Figure 6.4). Due to lacking data, we could not include the measure for trust in such a large sample. Three variables are of interest here: educational spending, educational attainment and conflict, and we address their direct and indirect

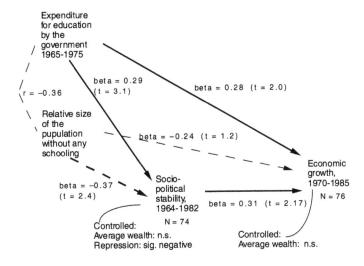

Figure 6.3 The double benefit of educational efforts: the first empirical test. A
step-wise prediction for a world sample of 74 to 76 cases. The listed
coefficients represent the relative weights in the model (in brackets are
the t-statistics which tell the statistical significance; levels of at least 2
can be considered substantial) (source: my research seminar with
model estimations by Thomas Gehrig (1999). Explanations on the variables are provided in the note below. The chronological delay in
measuring the variables was deliberately applied in this pilot study in
order to avoid false causal inferences due to mutual influences the
variables have on each other (in statistical jargon: in order to avoid
simultaneity).

Note
The measures employed in Figure 6.3 are the following. Economic growth per capita
1970–85: logged quotient for the figures at the beginning and the end of the growth period
(databased on Summers and Heston, taken here from Barro und Lee 1994). Socio-political
instability over the 1964–82 period, index covering various dimensions of political instability,
taken from Gupta (1990), the original scale was inverted to represent stability. Government
spendings on education as a share of all government expenditures, averaged for the years
1965, 1970 and 1975, as well as the share of population without schooling, again averaged for
1965, 1970 and 1975, come from the data compilation of Barro and Lee (1994).

effects on economic growth.[6] This new analysis covers the whole 1975–95
period. Educational spending is the weighted average value of public
spending on schooling over the period 1975–95.

The actual educational attainment rate in the population over twenty-
four years is our measure to capture the economically valuable human
capital in the labour force, measured five years after the beginning of the
twenty years' growth period. The figures are based on the percentage of

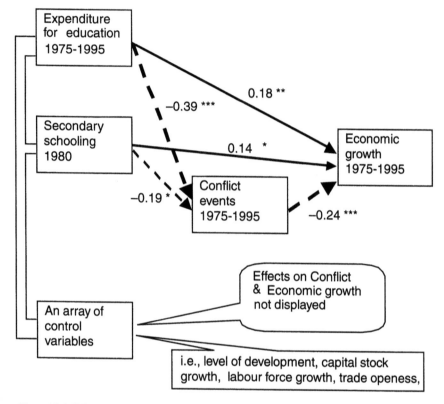

Figure 6.4 Educational spending and secondary schooling completed in the adult
population: direct effects on economic growth and effects mediated by
conflict (source: Bornschier, Herkenrath and König (2003)).

Notes
*   significant at a 1% level of confidence;
**   at 5 per cent level;
*   at 10 per cent level.

those who completed secondary education and left school afterwards to
work, to get additional vocational training or to go on to tertiary education.
For a world sample of societies this is the most appropriate way to capture
the proliferation of education in the population. These figures, which have
only recently become available, are taken from Barro and Lee (2000).

The educational spending of governments increases, of course, educational attainment in the population. This is certainly a gradual process,
since the educational attainment of the older cohorts is not affected by
current government spending. In our sample of eighty-three cases we
nevertheless find a considerable correlation between government spending
on education (average over 1975–95) and the educational attainment in
the adult population in 1980 (r = 0.64).

The intervening variable of special interest in our path model is the intensity of social conflict, which we measured by the weighted sum of anti-government demonstrations, general strikes, riots, political assassinations, guerilla activities and attempted revolutions (all in per capita figures, and furthermore, weighted by severity of the conflict dimensions). The basic data come from Arthur Banks's Cross-national Time-series Data Archive (Banks 2002).

The results of our path analysis are displayed in Figure 6.4. Conflict is substantially reducing the economic growth performance, the same as others have revealed in cross-sections and as we found already in Figure 6.3 (where we studied with sociopolitical stability the inverted scale of conflict). The positive effect of educational attainment in the population which we find in Figure 6.4 is in accordance with other findings as well as ours in the previous chapter. And this effect is what the human capital argument suggests. Expenditures in education, controlling for educational attainment in the population, also adds directly to growth and most probably functions as a proxy for the quality of education which is also – albeit not exclusively – a question of government efforts in the field. Therefore, the direct path from educational expenditures to growth can also be considered in line with the human capital argument.

The indirect effect of educational efforts as well as their long-term outcome (proliferation of education in the population) are pertinent to the legitimation argument and again suggest support for it, see Figure 6.4. The educational efforts of governments significantly reduce conflict and thereby add indirectly to economic growth. The same, albeit to a somewhat lesser extent, is also true for the proliferation of education among the citizens. This corresponds with the finding (in Figure 6.3) of the role of the part of the citizens integrated in society through schooling.

A test for both direct and indirect effects of education and educational efforts on economic growth is what we presented in the empirical part of this chapter. Our previous preliminary results could be checked and consolidated by the new analyses which we presented in Figure 6.4. And as a result of the empirical support of both lines of arguments which we introduced in the theoretical section I wish to suggest the conclusion below.

Drawing conclusions

The proposition of a 'double dividend' of educational efforts in development receives support in our studies. Never before have the two functions of the educational system been tested in the same design. The thesis suggests:

1   In the short and medium term educational effort of government can contribute to legitimizing society, which is reflected as tempering conflict in society.

2   In the longer run such a policy improves individual human capital and adds, with a certain delay, to a higher total stock of human capital in the economically active population of society. This adds to future growth, which again will bolster legitimacy. This proposition, supported by our evidence, suggests that there is more to education than the conventional human capital arguments specify. Education as a device to legitimize modern society is what counts, too.

7 Political styles and the production of trust in rich democracies

Introduction

Democracy as a political form is a topic I introduced in the first chapter of this section; I argued that it should be theoretically related to the level of trust, and indeed empirical evidence was found for this proposition. Here I would like to continue the analysis between politics and the cultural resource of trust,[1] yet the approach here is to control for the level of formal democracy by analysing only developed and rich democracies. By doing so, I investigate the relationship between political styles within rich democracies and trust.[2] This is to find out more about the reasons why levels of trust differ, even among rich countries which are all characterized by a high development of formal democracy, and to which characteristics trust, defined as a cultural resource, is related. Since political styles represent manifestations of (political) culture, we then look at the interrelationship of various aspects of culture. This will be done indirectly in a sort of path analysis: what are the meaningful social characteristics that go together with political styles, and what consequences do these have for the level of trust? Do rich democracies produce trust in the same ways or in different ones? For this analysis I take the trust measure from the 1981 wave of the *World Values Survey*, since our measure of political styles refers to the period 1960–89. Later in the chapter, a somewhat larger sample is used to look at the direct relationships between political style and trust in 1990.

Political styles will be conceptualized by using two dimensions. The first is represented by the degree of mediated, or negotiated, capitalism, which is discussed in the broad literature on democratic corporatism. This relates to consensus-based forms of cooperation in running the political economy. The second is represented by the socio-cultural heritage of liberalism, which is more pronounced in Anglo-Saxon societies. As we will see, both dimensions are interrelated but not identical. At low levels of negotiated capitalism we may find both a pronounced and an almost absent liberal heritage.

Political forms which make for varieties of capitalism may change over time. Many arguments, based on changes in the political economy due to new forms of organizing work (flexible specialization) and an increase in economic globalization since the 1970s, suggest such changes and, infrequently, a convergence towards the American way of running capitalism. To what extent this is the case will not be dealt with in this chapter but in Chapter 11, where we will not find significant changes in the political styles that are common to all rich democracies. This persistence of varieties of capitalism needs to be explained by a theory of social evolution, to which we also come in Chapter 12. The relative stability of political forms over time allows us to draw conclusions on their relationship with trust, even if the data are not recent.

Since we have already discussed the dependent variable of this chapter, i.e. generalized trust, in the three chapters of Part I, we shall go directly to the new variables which are considered as predictors of trust. Thus, the first task in this chapter will be to explain in detail what different styles in rich democracies mean, and how they have been measured in the literature. Then we discuss the findings of a two-step analysis investigating the effects of political styles on five distinct social characteristics and the effects of the latter on the level of trust. We will find that both our measures of political style are related to the level of trust, although this comes about in different ways. We shall then briefly discuss our findings, comparing them with what has been found up to now on the sources of trust, both at the societal and individual level.

Political styles mediating interests in the political economy

Often we speak of Western society or rich democracies to emphasize what they have in common. But such a collective term should not be taken to suggest that they are very similar in all respects. Indeed they are not, as our statements on political styles will show. Let us first focus on cooperative institutions in advanced capitalism. Such cooperative institutions at the macro-level have been termed neo-corporatism or democratic corporatism. I prefer the term negotiated capitalism, and will use it interchangeably for what others have called democratic or neo- or quasi-corporatism. I used to term this mediated ('vermittelter') capitalism in my lecture scripts. But, having looked at Harold Wilensky's latest book (2002) where he uses the term 'bargained capitalism', I think that the term 'negotiated' is more apt. Incidentally, Harold Wilensky has been at the forefront of the debate on corporatism in democracies. Yet Hicks and Kenworthy (1998) have recently reminded us of the fact that such cooperative institutions also exist to different degrees at the level of the firm.

A summary of key areas of cooperative institutions in advanced capitalism is given by Hicks and Kenworthy (1998: 1, 635), and I list it in Table 7.1 for its informative character.

Negotiated capitalism seems to be a better term than 'economic

Table 7.1 A listing of key types of cooperative economic institutions

Type	Summary
1 Business confederations	Centralized business confederations reduce rent seeking by individual firms and industries
2 Coordinated wage bargaining	Coordinated wage bargaining encourages wage restraint – facilitated by a centralized and/or concentrated union movement
3 Government and interest groups	Cooperation between government and interest groups generates productive, coherent state policies – fostered by coordination within interest groups and among government agencies
4 Tripartite neocorporation	Tripartite neocorporatism is conducive to rational macrolevel collective action. It may be centred in the economic system (as in Lijphart and Crepaz's (1991) neocorporatism) or in the political system (as in Hicks and Swank's (1992) social democratic corporatism)
5 Investors and firms	Long-term, voice-based relationships between firms and their investors permit long-time horizons for management
6 Purchasers and suppliers	Long-term, voice-based relationships between purchaser and supplier firms foster heightened communication and greater supplier willingness to invest and raise productivity
7 Competing firms	Alliances among competing firms lead to greater investment in R&D and employee training, permit quicker agreement on standards and provide assistance with matters such as financing, technology diffusion, design, accounting and marketing
8 Labour and management	An employment guarantee by firms generates greater cooperation between labour and management. Workers are more willing to share valuable knowledge, accept productivity-enhancing technology, and upgrade skills
9 Workers	Participatory teamwork arrangements result in greater work effort by employees
10 Functional departments	Multidivisional project teams that link various departments within firms yield a quicker, more effective transition from R&D through to production

Source: Alexander Hicks and Lane Kenworthy (1998: 1635).

integration' which Alan Siaroff (1999) recently proposed as an innovation. This is because, despite cooperation, the different interests of the various actors persist and are acknowledged by the other actors. Thus, negotiated capitalism represents a type of conflict resolution, and this should not be confused with integration. Despite participating in bargains which affect the political economy struck in such constellations, the divergent interests of the participants persist. This was what Emile Durkheim stressed in his foreword to the second edition of *The Division of Labour*.[3]

The cooperative institutions in the political economy reflect varieties of conflict resolution, and rich democracies differ remarkably in these. Let us start with a general description of negotiated capitalism.[4]

In societies with pronounced forms of negotiated capitalism (liberal or democratic corporatism), politico-economic bargains are regularly struck which affect the major issues of the political economy, not only in a narrow sense but also, increasingly, with regard to new issues like medical care and technology (for the latter at the level of the EU, see the next chapter). This pattern of conflict resolution presupposes some sort of basic national consensus and is made through trade-offs, for example, extensions of social policy in exchange for wage restraints. The actors involved are organized, centralized, co-opted interest groups of a limited number, and they strike such bargains under the auspices of governments. Such political styles may be informal arrangements or may even be provided for by the constitution, as, for example, in Switzerland. They transcend a clear separation of the public and the private (interest groups such as national business and employers' associations are private actors) since governments by law or custom consider the advice of admitted interest groups. The blurring of the public and the private takes place before action is taken on the part of parliaments or executives and after that in the course of implementation. That this involvement of private actors in politics is typical for democratic corporatism is stressed by Gerhard Lehmbruch (1977), whereas Philipp Schmitter (1977) rather emphasizes the structural aspects: a limited number of highly organized and centralized interest groups bargain under the auspices of government.

As just mentioned, there are differences in the exact conceptualization of democratic corporatism, which I here term negotiated capitalism. This refers to the role of the state and the extent to which it is involved, the same applies to the degree that labour is included at the national level. Despite reflecting different theoretical approaches, this implies that negotiated capitalism is a variable, and it is as such that I will use it.

I started with pronounced forms of organized capitalism. The other end of the variable is represented by a condition in which all the mentioned characteristics are more or less absent. Politically relevant interest groups are many in number and not matched. This absence of organized capitalism is then the opposite extreme of the scale, and not pluralism, which is often counterposed to corporatism (my negotiated capitalism). This reflects a confusion, since interests in negotiated capitalism remain plural, and democracies are, by definition, pluralist (see Chapter 5). Therefore negotiated capitalism in democracies cannot be the opposite of pluralism, neither does it represent a 'subclass' of democracies; rather, the manner in which capitalism is negotiated indicates a diversity of political styles in democracies. I was glad to read recently that Harold Wilensky (2002: 84) also argues against looking at pluralism as the opposite of democratic corporatism. On the issue of 'subclass', however, I disagree with him. Maybe I do not understand precisely what he means by subclass. Since the characteristic of democratic corporatism is a variable, though, the term class is misleading.

When one defines social capital as the ability of groups and people to cooperate in order to achieve common goals (as suggested by James Coleman, see Part I of this book), then it is obvious that the outcomes of negotiated capitalism represent a form of social capital. This political style deliberately aims at improving economic outcomes (and is, therefore, capital, see Chapter 2) and, furthermore, the consensus and conflict resolution it implies represent a special form of institutionalized trust, as introduced in the chapter on democracy. Therefore, I expect that negotiated capitalism as an institutionalized form of trust will go together with the personal trust expressed by citizens.

Political styles can also be distinguished in the structure of the political system. Indeed, the associated term 'consociational democracy' originally introduced by Arend Lijphart (1968: 6) has many overlapping meanings.[5] Lijphart (1984, 1999) followed this conceptual line in his work and contrasts the Westminster model of democracy (majoritarianism) with the consensus model (consociational democracy). The conceptual range from majoritarianism to consensus forms of democracy, once operationalized, overlaps, however, to a very large extent with measures of styles in running the political economy.

Measuring negotiated capitalism

The extensive literature on democratic corporatism is quite diverse concerning the details of theoretical focus. But the empirical scales that were suggested from this research on OECD countries are remarkably similar. Let us take, for instance, the scaling of eighteen OECD countries suggested by Nollert (1992), or that developed by Hicks and Kenworthy (1998).[6]

Hicks und Kenworthy (1998) proceed as follows. Over the period 1960–89 they scale eighteen OECD countries according to the ten cooperative institutions in advanced capitalism that were listed earlier in this chapter. In their empirical analysis, two dimensions emerged (extracted by factor analysis): one that represents democratic corporatism at the macro-level and one that can be called meso-level corporatism, at the level of firms. These factors are not completely independent, since they are significantly correlated ($r = 0.64$).

As our measure of negotiated capitalism we start with the factor scores for corporatism at the macro-level, for the period 1960–89, as determined by Hicks and Kenworthy. Before proceeding, a comment on the validity of these figures is necessary. The recent research of Alan Siaroff (1999) has demonstrated that the many scales of countries suggested in empirical work on democratic corporatism – he considers twenty-three scales from the literature and calculates an average score for the countries – all correlate very highly (and are in a statistical sense almost identical).[7] In Figure 7.1 Siaroff's average scores from the literature are plotted against those Hicks and Kenworthy found with their procedure. The very high correlation ($r = 0.91$) is a good indication of the validity of the scores from Hicks and Kenworthy's study that I use in this chapter together with the ones from Siaroff (1999); the latter are available for twenty-four cases.

To sum up, despite the several differences in the understanding of coagreement about locating certain countries on such a scale (I do not go into these details here), there is an amazing empirical correspondence regarding the almost two dozen scales developed and used in the literature.[8]

In the next step I plot my measure of negotiated capitalism against the

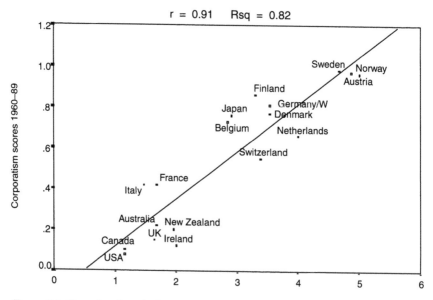

Figure 7.1 Negotiated capitalism, measures for democratic corporatism from Hicks and Kenworthy (1998) for the period 1960–89, and average scores from twenty-three studies, computed by Siaroff (1999).

material level of development, as indicated by the per capita product 1990, corrected for purchasing-power parities (ppp); see Figure 7.2a.

We find in Figure 7.2a that little negotiated capitalism is present at all levels of material development, while moderately and highly negotiated capitalism tends to be highly concentrated medium values on the income per capita scale. The dispersion of little-negotiated capitalism over all levels of average wealth becomes even stronger if one adds Spain, Portugal and Greece (not democracies over the whole period), which are not considered by Hicks and Kenworthy for the 1960–89 period. However, Siaroff has computed values for Spain, Portugal and Greece on corporatism after the shifts to democracy, too, and these all cluster at low levels of negotiated capitalism; see Figure 7.2b.

Liberalism as a socio-political and socio-economic heritage

There is no question that a consensus exists in the literature that some countries are least corporatist, again mentioned recently by Wilensky (2002: 91): the USA, UK, Canada, New Zealand, Australia and Ireland. All six are Anglo-Saxon countries, and we indeed find them in Figures 7.2a and 7.2b where the other literature locates them, at low levels of negotiated capitalism. But France and Italy, as well as Spain, Portugal and Greece, are all also characterized by comparatively low levels of negotiated capitalism (Siaroff 1999; see Fig. 2b).

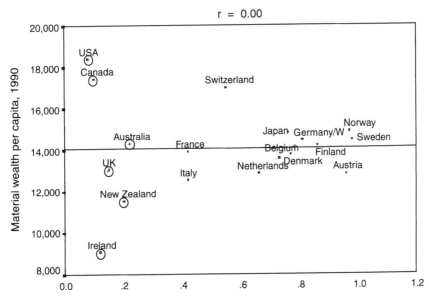

Figure 7.2a Average material wealth and negotiated capitalism for eighteen cases (measure for democratic corporatism 1960–89 from Hicks and Kenworthy (1998). The Anglo-Saxon cases are marked by a circle.

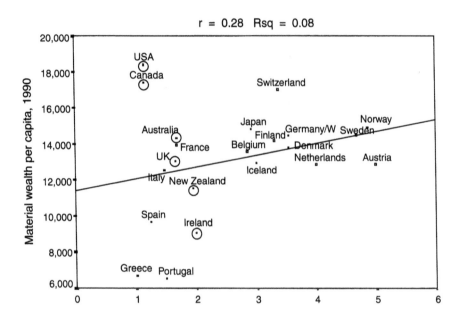

Figure 7.2b Average material wealth and negotiated capitalism for twenty-two cases (measure for democratic corporatism, average from studies compiled by Siaroff (1999). The Anglo-Saxon cases are marked by a circle.

Now, I wish to introduce a second aspect of political style. One can identify this as the liberal Anglo-Saxon cultural heritage, and thus begin to differentiate political styles in addition to a low level of negotiated capitalism. The Anglo-Saxon societies are characterized by specific historical trajectories that make them distinct from those of other rich democracies, even controlling for negotiated capitalism on which all Anglo-Saxon cases, along with several other cases, rank very low.

The historical origin of this Anglo-Saxon group is, of course, Great Britain, where the parliament in its modern form and as a distinct element of modern democracy first emerged. The group covers, furthermore, the former British settler colonies as well as Britain's first colony, Ireland. As mentioned, this group is represented in Figures 7.2a and 7.2b by six cases: the USA, UK, Ireland, Australia, Canada and New Zealand.

What makes the historical development of this group peculiar is that absolutist claims to political power were successfully countered at a relatively early date, on the one side by the rise of parliamentary power and on the other through the absolute claim of superiority of the individual manifested in the philosophy of John Locke. He perceived the state as something quite pragmatic, an explicit or implicit contract which must bend to the will of the majority. Even though the law-making (legislative) power is supreme, it does not exercise absolute power because it depends on a basic rational consensus. John Locke introduced these ideas during the English Enlightenment. Towards the end of the turmoil of the English Revolution, Locke moved to Holland to avoid political persecution (1683–88). Later on, he followed the Dutch William III of Orange, who ended the revolution in England. Locke's ideas were taken up in the subsequent constitution.[9]

Furthermore, in the British settler colonies the authority of the Crown was rather weak, not least because of the spatial distance from the centre of power. These societies were, in a sense, built from below by the settlers, and the coordinating level of the state emerged only gradually, rather in correspondence with the needs of civil society.[10] Historically, this Anglo-Saxon cultural cluster was associated with more pronounced liberalism and individualism as compared with societies on the European continent, and for centuries this liberalism shaped the arrangement of Anglo-Saxon states more than continental ones.[11] There, the all-power-usurping state was only democratized after long struggles for increased civil rights (Marshall [1950] 1965) and eventually became, in historical comparison, subdued to the will of the citizens.

These historical developments are now long passed, and one could simply say, so what? However, I would like to demonstrate that citizens in Anglo-Saxon countries differ in significant respects from their counterparts in other rich democracies even today. To do this, I shall contrast instances from the Anglo-Saxon group with examples from the group of Mediterranean European countries which, you will remember, also scores low on negotiated capitalism. Let me take two indicators from the 1990 wave of the *World Values Survey* which show something about the relative importance of freedom versus equality and about the importance of individual effort in legitimizing inequality.

Table 7.2 shows that, given the low level of negotiated capitalism in both Mediterranean and Anglo-Saxon countries, contemporary citizens in Anglo-Saxon countries on the average prefer more freedom if they choose between freedom and equality, and agree more often with incentives for individual effort. Differences with regard to citizens of countries with negotiated capitalism are on the average still there, but they are less pronounced. We may interpret this as indicating that the institutionalized priority of the value of equality in negotiated capitalism, together with effective devices to safeguard that in practice, may lead citizens to be rather more open to freedom and to individual efforts. However, if this institutional security is lacking, citizens opt much more for equality, except where an Anglo-Saxon cultural heritage is present.

In order to differentiate societies at a low level of negotiated capitalism I therefore introduce an additional variable to represent political style, liberal or Anglo-Saxon cultural heritage.

Table 7.2 An Anglo-Saxon cultural pattern beside low values for negotiated capitalism? An illustration with examples; questions from 1990 *WVS*

	Agreeing answers in representative surveys (%)	
	1 In doubt rather freedom	*2 Greater incentives for individual efforts*
Contrast group 1: Low values for negotiated capitalism (democratic corporatism) but Ango-Saxon cultural heritage		
USA	71	62
UK	65	58
Canada	61	63
Average for the group	*65.7*	*61*
Contrast group 2: Low values for negotiated capitalism but Mediterranean cultural heritage		
Italy	46	47
France	53	40
Spain	43	32
Average for the group	*47.3*	*39.7*
Control group: Higher and high values for negotiated capitalism, examples from three different cultural backgrounds (not Atlantic, Protestant, Catholic)		
Japan	46	34
Sweden	67	58
Austria	64	48
Average for the group	*59*	*46.7*

Source: Based on *World Values Survey (WVS)*, Inglehart *et al.* 1998, variables 247 and 250.

Notes

The two questions are:

1 A: 'I find both freedom and equality are important. But if I were to choose one or the other, I would consider personal freedom more important, that is, everyone can live in freedom and develop without hindrance.' H: 'Certainly both freedom and equality are important. But if we were to choose one or the other, I would consider equality more important, that is, that nobody is underprivileged and that social class differences are not so strong.' The percentages in Table 7.2 refer to the population that 'agrees with statement A'.

2 'Now I'd like you to tell me your views on various issues. How would you place your views on this scale? 1 means you agree completely with the statement on the left, 10 means you agree completely with the statement on the right, or you can choose any number in between.'

1   2   3   4   5   6   7   8   9   10
Incomes should be   There should be greater
made more equal   incentives for individual effort

The percentage in the population that agrees (codes 7–10) are depicted in Table 7.2.

The indirect and direct links between political style and trust

The first part of our empirical study of the links between political styles and trust takes place in two steps.[12] First we look whether and how five societal characteristics are related to political styles. Then we investigate whether these five societal characteristics may help to predict levels of generalized trust in the population. The five measures of societal characteristics come from my earlier interests in the sources of legitimacy in developed countries. The samples are relatively small due to lacking information on these interesting variables. Since the indicators should predict trust (the figures for 1981 are used)[13] they need to be measured not later than the dependent variable. Otherwise, causal logic would be violated; a later measure cannot be the cause of an earlier measured variable. The indirect study is informative because it tells us about possible mediating variables. Since this evidence rests on few cases, I would like to consolidate the finding of an effect of political style on trust in a larger sample where trust is measured in the period 1990–3 (the same as the 'Trust 1990' measure explained in Chapter 2) but no mediating variables are used.

Indirect effects of political style on trust

Let me start by introducing Figure 7.3, which lists the five mediating variables and at the same time shows how the measured concepts are related to each other (in a multivariate design which controls for other

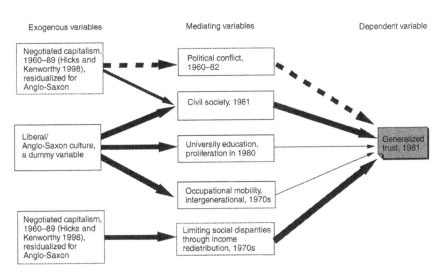

Figure 7.3 Summary of indirect effects of political style, mediated by five societal characteristics.

variables).[14] The figure summarizes two independent steps of analysis which rest on different sample sizes.

Five societal characteristics which I considered important in reflecting the legitimacy of society are used as possible mediating variables: political conflict, richness of civil society, opportunities for mobility through education, intergenerational openness of society and class equilibration through redistribution of income. We briefly comment on these mediating variables.

Political conflict

The period 1968–82, which is measured by events of political mass protest and political violence is the first variable to be considered.[15] This characteristic, if it is low or almost absent, has been used in earlier work as a proxy for the legitimacy of a social order (Bornschier 1989, 1996: 328–39; Weede 1996). Earlier in the chapter I proposed that negotiated capitalism, since it represents a form of conflict resolution, will have a lower level of political conflict. This is also established empirically. Increases in negotiated capitalism bring down the amount of political conflict and this supports generalized trust (conflict and trust correlate negatively).

Richness of civil society

The year 1981 is now considered.[16] The free association of citizens who organize themselves outside family and work integrates society at the meso-level, since the frequency of overlapping membership is measured. By this cross-border networking, the richness of civil society helps to establish and nurture trust among citizens. Actually, civil society is used in one branch of the literature influenced by Putnam (1993) as a measure of social capital. Empirically, we find the richness of civil society associated with trust.[17] But where do the considerable differences in the richness of civil society come from? As long ago as the first part of the nineteenth century, Alexis de Tocqueville observed large differences in the role of civil society in his transatlantic comparison.[18] One would expect that Anglo-Saxon societies, due to the peculiarities of their historical development, would rank higher on the indicator for the richness of civil society. This is indeed what we find in Figure 7.3. A less conventional finding seems to be that pronounced negotiated capitalism also goes together with a rich civil society (once Anglo-Saxon cultural heritage is controlled for). The effect is smaller but clearly significant. This is a new and interesting finding and we come back to it in our discussion at the end of this chapter.

Note that this figure summarizes two independent steps of analysis which rest on different sample sizes. The importance of effects and their significance are schematically presented. Bold lines indicate strong effects (dotted if negative), semi-bold medium-strong and significant effects, and fine lines indicate weak effects which are – given the small sample size – not statistically significant.

Mobility opportunities through opening tertiary education

The year 1980, which measures years of tertiary education in the population is now considered.[19] Primary and secondary education in developed countries are rather saturated but differences on the tertiary-education level are still considerable and therefore indicate educational openness. In the previous chapter we discussed the role of educational expansion in the legitimization of society. Empirically, we find Anglo-Saxon cultural heritage significantly related to a more open society as indicated by the proliferation of tertiary education in the population. In comparison to other societies, they tend to focus more on equality of opportunities rather than equalizing the outcome of status attainment. The empirical association would support that.[20]

Now we come to the link between higher education and trust. Without doubt, all available data for trust according to level of education show an increase, especially for higher education (according to the data of Inglehart *et al.* 1998). But knowledge and trust are different things, as was recognized by Georg Simmel and acknowledged earlier in this book. At the individual level we found a further association between education and trust and suggested explanations for that (see Chapter 4). In the analysis of this chapter, we find higher education and trust clearly related when taken alone, but controlling for the other variables this effect becomes small (and statistically insignificant). Therefore, it seems that education is not a very important independent predictor of trust in cross-national comparison.

Opportunities for occupational mobility (intergenerationally)

The relevant period for consideration of this is the 1970s.[21] The interpretation of equality as equality of opportunities allows, to the extent that it is effectively reflected in social structure, the establishment of a sense of social justice in the citizenry. To find a valid indicator for this in comparative perspective is not so easy. Therefore we need to rely on intergenerational occupational data. The data for non-discrimination, i.e. the index of tolerance which was discussed in Chapter 2, would be an even better alternative, and one indeed finds non-discrimination significantly related to trust ($r = 0.73$; see Chapter 2). But to preserve the coherence of the causal design (data for that non-discrimination index are available only after 1989) we cannot use them here.

In the case of equal opportunity measured with intergenerational occupational openness, one would expect that Anglo-Saxon societies have a certain edge over the others. Indeed, we can establish that empirically (see Figure 7.3). This openness as an indicator for justice is positively asso-ciated with trust but fails to be significant (even when one outlier is excluded). This problem might be created by an insufficiently large sample and a thus-far unsatisfactory indicator for openness. Although not estab-lished empirically with the indicator we here had to rely on, I suggest that the hypothesis of a link between equal opportunities and trust be main-tained, not least because, as mentioned, we find a strong association between non-discrimination and trust (see Chapter 2). Due to the incon-sistencies of times of measurement (trust measured in 1981, and non-discrimination around 1990) this cannot be interpreted causally for the moment.

Limiting income disparities with redistributive measures

We encounter more equality in outcomes in the 1970s. As several readers may not know, developed countries do not differ that much (at least they differ considerably less than developing countries) regarding income dis-tribution according to market processes (wages, salaries and profits). After taking into account taxation and redistribution of income through social policies, the differences increase (Swank and Hicks 1985: 134). And we see the extent of these differences related to political styles. More precisely, in negotiated capitalism social policy is to a considerable degree absorbed in general economic policy, as mentioned earlier in the chapter. Actually, in Figure 7.3 we find a strong association between the political style of nego-tiated capitalism and income redistribution through taxation and social policy outlays.[22] In Anglo-Saxon societies, political preferences and effect-ive policies should rather put a brake on redistributive claims; instead such societies tend to offer more mobility opportunities as a compensation. Yet, after accounting for the level of negotiated capitalism, we do not find any indication in our data for such a negative link with redistribution.

I should add here that the links of negotiated capitalism with inequality not only apply to redistribution after the economic processes but also to less unequal distributions of wages due to the strong impact that rather centralized unions have in the power cartel that runs the economy. We come to this again later when we discuss varieties of capitalism and point to the findings whether they make a difference in terms of inequality and economic growth (Chapter 11).

This was a brief discussion of the last of our five mediating variables: the social justice intended by redistributive measures materializes in the form of higher levels of trust in the population (see Figure 7.3), and this redistribution is theoretically and empirically linked to the degree of nego-tiated capitalism.

Summary of the indirect links between political styles and trust

All the five measures of societal characteristics show strong associations with levels of trust, but only three of them can maintain that effect after controlling for the other predictors.[23] These three are: political conflict management, richness of civil society, and justice through redistribution. Openness of higher education and of intergenerational occupational mobility have small but insignificant additional effects. This is perhaps due to the fact that these indicators inadequately measure equal opportunities in society, which I think is a valid proposition for predicting trust and which deserves to be further tested with better indicators (or causally adequate settings in the case of the indicator for non-discrimination, which also includes equality of opportunities between genders, see Chapter 2).

Political styles affect the intermediate social characteristics quite differently. Pronounced negotiated capitalism brings political conflict down and positively affects redistribution of incomes through taxation and social security spending. Anglo-Saxon cultural heritage is associated with a richer civil society and is favourable to the openness of opportunities.

Both political styles then operate differently in affecting the cultural resource of generalized trust. In the end, however, both political styles deliver; they both support generalized trust in the population. In an earlier, more detailed, version of this research I performed a test and found that Anglo-Saxon societies, as compared to the others in the sample, do not differ significantly in their levels of general trust (see Bornschier 2001b: 467). This certainly relates to the average level of negotiated capitalism as contrasted to Anglo-Saxon cultural heritage. Societies scoring high on negotiated capitalism, for example Norway or Finland, have trust values remarkably higher than any Anglo–Saxon case, whereas stragglers on the political style measure, such as Italy or France, have trust values lower than any Anglo-Saxon case. Thus, Anglo-Saxon cases cluster rather homogeneously around medium levels of trust, and the others are dispersed according to level of negotiated capitalism. This pattern has several implications which we discuss briefly at the end of this chapter and which will be followed up in Chapters 11 and 12.

Direct effects of political styles on trust

As a validation of the links we observed between political styles and trust let us briefly come to the direct associations between both in a larger sample of twenty-three cases with more recent data. Trust is now measured for 1990–3; it is the same 'Trust 1990' measure introduced in Chapter 2. By that time more countries had become democracies and are included in Siaroff's compilation (1999) for average scores on democratic corporatism from the literature. With some hesitation I added South Korea and Taiwan, although they could not yet be considered full democracies at the beginning of the 1990s and their political style scores had to be estimated, see note to Table 7.3.

The prediction of generalized trust for twenty-three cases in Table 7.3 is moderate (40 per cent of the variance explained). Both our two political style variables, negotiated capitalism and Anglo-Saxon cultural heritage, contribute about equally to that overall explanation. What makes a big difference is whether one includes Austria or not. In the latter case, we can explain 64 per cent of the differences in measured trust. Why Austria deviates (see also Figure 7.4) is an enigma; this may have substantial reasons or may simply reflect data errors (pertaining to trust, since the literature is in agreement that Austria ranks very high on negotiated capitalism, which is as mentioned measured with corporatism). The Anglo-Saxon (dummy) variable shows a somewhat smaller effect than negotiated capitalism, but notice that this variable has only a limited variation (for the six Anglo-Saxon cases it takes the value 1, for the other 17 the value 0).

Furthermore, we find in Table 7.3 that the level of material development is not significantly related to trust. The simple correlation is moderate ($r = 0.46$) but vanishes as soon as variables indicating political culture

Table 7.3 Generalized trust 1990 in rich democracies explained by political styles

Predictors	Relative explanatory power (beta-values)	Repetition, excluding one deviant case
Negotiated capitalism (average scores from Siaroff 1999, see also note below)	0.64***	0.84***
Anglo-Saxon cultural heritage (dummy variable)	0.50**	0.62***
Average income 1990, corrected for purchasing power parities	0.27	0.22
Total explanation R-square (corrected)	0.40	0.64
Number of cases	23	22 without Austria

Notes
** significant (below 5 per cent).
*** very significant (below 1 per cent).
Figures without asterisk: not significant (>10 per cent)
I have dared to include South Korea and Taiwan in the sample although they could not be considered full democracies by the early 1990s. Furthermore, I had to estimate their values for negotiated capitalism (see notes to Chapter 11). This might look questionable to some readers and I therefore report the beta-effects without Korea and Taiwan in a sample consequently numbering twenty-one cases: negotiated capitalism 0.65, Anglo-Saxon dummy 0.51, level of development 0.27 (all the statistical significances unchanged). There is, then, almost no change in the estimation of effects whether or not Korea and Taiwan are in the sample. What makes quite a difference (less in relative weight of coefficients than in total explanation), however, is whether one excludes the outlier Austria or not; see also Figure 7.4. There seems no easy explanation as to why Austria is such a deviant case (much too little trust as reported in the survey compared to its pronounced social partnership, at least at that time).

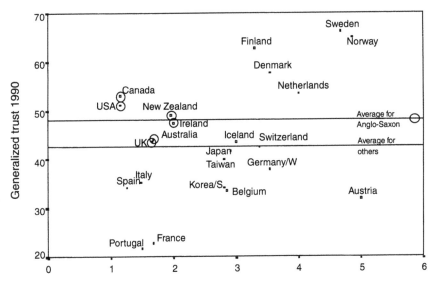

Figure 7.4 Trust 1990, contrasting the averages for Anglo-Saxon societies and the other cases in a sample of twenty-three societies; see also Table 7.3 and Chapter 2 of this text (source: Siaroff (1999); Korea and Taiwan own estimates).

are introduced. Also, in the sample of the nineteen cases earlier used in this chapter, there is a moderate correlation with level of development and trust in 1981, which also vanishes once other variables are simultaneously used as a predictor of trust. We will come back to this finding of an absent relationship between trust and level of development in the comparison with other findings.

In Figure 7.4 the values for 'Trust 1990' are plotted against the continuous variable negotiated capitalism and the Anglo-Saxon cases are marked. The differences between the average trust of these six cases and the other seventeen cases is not significant in statistical terms (by the way, one has to take into account the heterogeneous variance between the two groups, which is very obvious in the figure). With the additional research using more recent data it could be confirmed that both political styles deliver in terms of trust. But societies with low degrees of negotiated capitalism are handicapped if they are not of Anglo-Saxon origin. Since this seems quite historically ascribed, societies low on negotiated capitalism have either to climb up the ladder or they fall back, since all our findings so far suggest that generalized trust is a competitive resource in the political economy.

Comparison with other findings

This chapter has not only tried to demonstrate that political styles matter but also provided findings to address how they do so. In the cross-national literature only Knack and Keefer (1997) and Zak and Knack (2001) have started to look at determinants of trust. They look, however, at samples of twenty-nine and forty-one cases respectively, including many developing and non-democratic countries. Compared to these samples, one significant difference of rich democracies is that there exists no association between average material wealth and trust. A positive relationship between average wealth and trust was found, however, both by Knack and Keefer (1997) and by Zak and Knack (2001) for their more heterogeneous samples.

In rich democracies, trust is not a question of material wealth but of political culture, which makes for distinct social characteristics. And these cultural differences cannot be traced back to those in material wealth. To look at such effects of political styles in rich democracies is an innovative step in the analysis of the determinants of trust, and no other findings exist for the purposes of comparison. Concerning the variables which are considered as mediating, however, some comparisons can be made. Knack and Keefer find that, similar to the negative effect of conflict on trust in rich democracies, conflict (using however a rather crude proxy variable for it) is negatively related to trust.[24] We found that the degree of negotiated capitalism is a good predictor for low levels of conflict and this is consistent with Arend Lijphart's (1999: 263f., 266) conclusion from his study of thirty-six democracies that consensus democracies have a better record than majoritarian democracies with regard to controlling violence.[25]

The significant role of civil society in nurturing trust that we find for rich democracy cannot be established by Knack and Keefer when poorer and non-democratic countries are also included. This difference as well as the question of cause and effect demands further inquiry.[26] Also the recent finding of Markus Freitag (2003: 218), based, however, on individual data for Switzerland, questions that link since he finds 'no empirical support for the thesis that active membership in various kinds of associations fosters ... trust'. A similar conclusion is drawn by Delhey and Newton (2002: 19, 21) from their study of seven societies with individual-level data, since a link between voluntary organizations and trust can be found only in three of their seven cases and this is, furthermore, of low to only medium strength.[27] Yet, as our findings in Chapter 4 suggest, individual-level and aggregate effects may be quite different in strength. In the country sample studied in this chapter the richness of civil society varies markedly. Thus the culture of civil society may well be a sensible predictor in comparing rich democracies. Remember furthermore, that especially the Anglo-Saxon cultural heritage was found associated with the culture of civil society. Though the richness of civil society also increases with the intensity of negotiated capitalism, this contribution is less strong.

Regarding the role of education, Knack and Keefer, as well as Zak and Knack, report positive effects which are, however, not always clearly significant. The positive effects we find for our sample of rich democracies are not significant at all. Therefore, in comparing societies it seems questionable that the level of education turns out to be a substantial predictor of the proliferation of trust. This would be notable, since individual-level analyses have so far pointed to education as a good predictor of trust (see Alesina and L Ferrara 2000 and our findings in Chapter 4).[28]

Income inequality is used as a predictor of trust in the study of Knack and Keefer and that of Zak and Knack, and both find that income inequality acts negatively on the level of trust. I have not used income inequality, since the differences in rich democracies are not very large before taxing and social security transfers. Differences become greater after these transfers, and we find different efforts of income equalization by state action positively related to trust. Our finding that negotiated capitalism favours the extent of redistributive measures is consonant with theoretical arguments as well as the empirical findings. We will come to this again when we address accomplishments of varieties of capitalism.

Knack and Keefer report negative effects on trust for ethnic–linguistic heterogeneity. I have tested that, too (see Bornschier 2001b: 469) but never found a significant relationship with trust in rich democracies, whatever measure of heterogeneity I used. This suggests that ethnic–linguistic heterogeneity need not necessarily result in discrimination; a good historical example of this is Switzerland, multicultural but, since 1848, politically balanced. More recently, Zak and Knack (2001) have also found no linear relationship between trust and homogeneity. Further studies are needed to clarify this issue. Zak and Knack also tested an index for economic discrimination which has strong negative effects on trust. This corresponds to the high correlation between our non-discrimination index and trust, which was observed in Chapter 2 but could not be used in this chapter due to discrepancies in the times of measurement. That trust is significantly reduced by discrimination is also reported by Alesina and La Ferrara (2000), who use individual level data.

Democratic control of government and the independence of courts are found by Knack and Keefer to raise the level of trust. This is very similar to what we found in Chapter 5, where democracy was successfully introduced as a predictor of trust. In addition, Zak and Knack introduced several institutional characteristics which indicate system trust (such as absence of corruption, contract enforceability, investor rights). All these institutions significantly improve the level of trust. There seems to emerge a certain consensus, then, that culture, as expressed in such institutions and regularly improved on the average by democratization, counts in explaining different trust levels. We have added new findings to this emerging research by comparing different political cultures at roughly the same level of formal democracy.

Conclusion, implications and preview

A general comment on our findings in this chapter might state that several characteristics that stand for a 'good' social order are empirically related to the extent that citizens trust in other people. These include: the taming of political conflict; the provision of social cohesion by a rich, interlocked civil society; an open society with many mobility opportunities; the absence of discrimination, and the limitation of social disparities through the redistribution of income.

This cultural resource of trust, which we found to be helpful for economic development (Chapters 2 and 3), is, however, achieved and nurtured in different manners in rich democracies. We have considered two different political cultures or styles, the variable degree of negotiated capitalism and liberal Anglo-Saxon cultural heritage. These factors have made for rather distinct varieties of capitalism in the past. Will such differences persist?

Culture, including also political culture which, whatever its specific set of origins, may also include structural characteristics, tends to become embedded in a multitude of institutional practices, and this gives them a certain stability. This stability is, however, dependent on political outcomes. We were able to confirm that both political styles deliver in terms of trust. But societies not of Anglo-Saxon origin with low degrees of negotiated capitalism are hampered. Since this seems quite historically ascribed, societies low on negotiated capitalism have either to climb further or fall back, since all our findings so far suggest that generalized trust is a competitive resource for long-term success in the world political economy.[29]

For pronounced forms of negotiated capitalism and for the Anglo-Saxon approach to running the political economy, the prediction is that they will continue to be rather stable methods of managing rich democracies. Given all the talk about the change of the political sphere due to technology change and increased economic globalization, this seems to be a risky prognosis. We need to look at the possible change in political styles over the last thirty-five years, as we do in Chapter 11. There we ask whether one observes changes and, if so, how we can explain them. And in Chapter 12 we will look at how different political styles managed the techno-economic change that has led to a new societal model.

But before this can be done, however, we need to look more closely at one factor that has, without doubt, changed statehood in many rich democracies by adding a new supranational level to the political sphere in the fifteen member states of today's EU.

PART III

Beyond the nation-state

Supranational and transnational links

Up to this point, the arguments have considered characteristics of national societies and individuals. In this part we enter the discussion of the emergent state forms at the supranational level, most advanced in the case of the EU. How can the patterns of economic and political integration be explained and what are the consequences for economic growth and for convergence at the level of the member states?

Discussion of the co-evolution of state and capitalist development has belonged since Max Weber and Otto Hintze to the classics of sociology. Considering the five centuries of European modernity, one observes in comparing the different societies that the state forms were dissimilar for about three centuries before a convergence phase of about one and a half centuries. In the last third of the twentieth century, a new divergence occurred in state forms as manifested by the EU, which is, like the fully-fledged nation-state, a European social innovation. While this new state form certainly does not make the established nation-states obsolete, it adds a new supranational level.

In the first chapter we ask how such new state forms relevant to the political economy actually come into existence (what are the actors and circumstances) and consider what connections there are between the change of the societal model and an upgraded role for technology. The next chapter reflects on the consequences of this new supranational state form for economic development. The third is on the equalization of life conditions in the union as reflected in the high ideological value accorded to cohesion. Have poorer member states in the union actually converged faster? If so, has this been due to economic factors (market creation and enlargement) or political ones in the form of transfers? Our findings also have some general implications for the relationship between state and market, which has been under debate for quite a while, and we come to this at the end.

8 Transnationals and supranationals

The elite bargain towards EU

Approaching the transformation of statehood in Western Europe[1]

Among the great political events of the world political economy in the 1980s and 1990s belong, beside the collapse of state socialism, the significant changes in Western Europe. At a regional level, the EU initiated an effective cooperation among nation-states which surmounted a set of linked international regimes. How can we come to theoretical terms with this momentous development?

The simultaneous emergence of globalization and a tighter closing of the ranks by European states are only contradictory at first glance. The first implies a shift in power between the state and the economy in favour of the transnational economy, to which regional integration is an answer; it amounts to a new deployment of an old weapon by the state. Let me briefly mention some important processes in this context. In the world political economy, both economic enterprises and states compete with each other. On the other hand, economic enterprises and states are dependent on each other.

The supply of state-based order as a geographic, locational condition and the demand on the part of economic enterprises for the same must be united in practice. Here, negotiations are the typical form of exchange. The qualitative change in West European integration in the first half of the 1980s was a result of one such round of negotiations, an elite bargain between the European transnational firms and the European supranational political entrepreneurs represented by the Commission (Born-schier 1996: Chapter 14; 2000a).

How well can we, as contemporaries, be aware of the impact of events at the time, without the benefit of hindsight? If we are honest, not always so well. In the course of the 1990s it became obvious that, politically, Europe was on the move. But what entered public awareness then actually started ten years earlier, during the early 1980s. Let me cite one key protagonist in the decisive events, in fact one of the architects of the Single Market project, who commented as follows: 'There are turning points in history. Frequently only dimly perceived at the time but later clearly identified. The renaissance of the Community which was launched by the Internal Market Programme and, in its wake, the Single European Act is likely to prove such a turning point' (Lord Cockfield 1994: 157).

The impact that was underestimated by most contemporaries was only reported in the newspapers later. At the tenth anniversary of the Single European Act (SEA) one could read in the *Neue Zürcher Zeitung*: 'Modest treaty amendments with big effects … Ten years ago, on 1 July 1987, the Single European Act reforming the treaties of Rome were ratified. Contrary to the expectations of many experts the rather modest changes of the treaties had a great impact' (My translation).[2]

These quotes introduce a term that is not immediately clear especially with regard to its consequences. Therefore I would like to point to certain facts concerning the SEA; the somewhat curious terminology will also be explained.

The proposals of the Commission for a SEA were adopted in December 1985 by the European Council and formally approved by the Council of Ministers (ministers of foreign affairs) on 28 February 1986. The act, implying no less than the path to the EU, became effective after ratification in mid-1987 (with a half-year delay since Ireland had to amend its constitution, which was subject to an obligatory referendum).

The SEA is called single precisely because it regulates European policy cooperation by treaty and changed the existing treaties of the Community at the same time. Since its adoption the new superior body of the Community, the European Council (heads of state and government of the member states), coordinates political and economic policies with the President of the Commission, who is a member of the European Council with equal rights.

The intentions of the new formulation of the treaty are clearly evident. The SEA is explicitly understood as a step towards European union (see its preamble). The second part of the SEA (Part II) includes changes to the original European Economic Community (EEC) treaty affected by the new one, and the third part (Part III) regulates political cooperation in Europe. In the first instance, the provisions regarding the establishment of the internal market by the end of 1992 are worth mentioning. These conceptions of 'Europe 92' were most prominent in the headlines at the time.

The Community had already operated as a common market. However, despite the elimination of tariffs on intra-EC trade, the domestic markets of Community members had remained fairly fragmented due to non-tariff barriers that had proliferated and even intensified during the economic downturn of the 1970s. Only the completion of the internal market programme, which erased the variety of non-tariff barriers that sheltered domestic firms from competition, created, via deregulation or harmonization, a single market for merchandise, services, labour and capital. This provides both greater opportunities for economies of scale and economies of common governance. In terms of protection and regulation, this means a significant restructuring; the locus at which the public good is provided is the Community and no longer the single member state.

The renewed treaty also involved substantial changes in the institutional frameworks. The procedure for enacting law changed; the majority vote in the Council was extended. Now, for all decisions concerning the internal market, qualified majority votes are stipulated. In connection with the alignment of legal regulations, either a qualified majority vote or the mutual recognition of the equivalence of regulations in the member states is called for. Further, the participation of the European Parliament in formulating legislation and its budgetary authority have both been expanded. Finally, the treaty broadens the role of the European Court of Justice through coordination with the Court of First Instance.

In addition, the agreement concerning extensions of earlier authority of the EC, as well as new authority, is worth mentioning. The section regarding the progress of economic and social cohesion (Part V) represents a new jurisdiction. This area is supposed to shape the policies of cohesion and represents a collective good: solidarity.

What is more, the Community obtains the authority to support research and technological development to advance international competitiveness (Part VI). This section is designed to shape technological capital for international competition, which again is a collective good. Last but not least, environmental policy now partly falls under the jurisdiction of the Community (Part VII). Earlier authority has also been significantly extended, for example, in connection with social policy (improvement of working conditions, minimum standards, dialogue between social partners) and economic policy (the anchoring of the European monetary system and its corresponding institutional changes).

These elements of the renewed treaty, thus briefly described, allow us to speak of the Community's statehood with respect to the sphere of the market economy insofar as it provides public goods on its own rather than simply coordinating member state activities. For the first time, a supranational provision of such goods common to the Community is detached from the nation-states of the members. It should be made very clear that this did not abolish the nation-states: quite the contrary. The member states, although they lost competencies to the Community, remain powerful since they have the sole legislative power in terms of revision and extension of Community law.

Understanding the European relaunch

In the following I would like to draw attention to the circumstances and actors involved in the political package which was wrapped up in 1987. This is only superficially a purely historical inquiry; more pertinently, it allows the evaluation of theoretical ideas which stem from very different conceptions of the origin of institutions in the world political economy.

Here I shall approach the question of how important regulations in the world political economy come into being. More frequently it is the impact of new regulations in different spheres of the economy and society which are the focus of attention, while their genesis is not considered in detail.

In my subsequent considerations I shall focus on the interaction between transnational corporations with headquarters in Europe and supranational political entrepreneurs represented by the Commission. With this context established, I will go more deeply into the issue of the new technology policy and its anchoring in the model of the Community.

What happened?

This significant change within the Community during the mid-1980s became evident in two events which find their expression in two documents published by the Community: the Commission's White Paper (1985) for the European Council (heads of state and governments) regarding the completion of the internal market, and the SEA, adopted in December 1985 by the European Council and formally approved by the Council of Ministers (ministers of foreign affairs) on 28 February, 1986.

The White Paper was a political initiative of the Commission, and as such it was not exceptional. Within the European Community, the Commission is a supranational body whose independence from the member states was set out in the treaties of 1958. The Commission is, simultaneously, a partner of, and an opposition to, the Council (Fusion Treaty, article 15). Due to the multitude of its functions, the Commission plays a key role within the Community; it is its motor, has a right to make proposals in the legal process (which then are agreed upon by the Council) and has the exclusive right to propose initiatives. The plans, programmes and memoranda of the Commission are intended to advance the development of the Community; all this was agreed upon in the treaties of 1958, although the Commission's position vis-à-vis the Council was in fact weakened during the years of the Luxembourg compromise.

From a dynamic perspective, the historical dates of significant events are often the outcome of social processes that have already taken place, and this was indeed the case here.

The White Paper had already been prepared when Jacques Delors assumed the presidency in early 1985. The first initiatives of the Commission to establish the internal market can be traced back at least to 1981. The completion of the internal market project was worked out between the Commission and the European Roundtable of Industrialists (ERT). The ERT is an informal panel founded at the initiative of Commissioners Etienne Davignon and François-Xavier Ortoli in April 1983; it was initially composed of seventeen top European industrialists, and was later expanded to include forty members. Wisse Dekker, head of Philips, already an influential figure in the ERT and later its president, who formulated the 'Agenda for Action: Europe 1990', and Lord Cockfield, then vice-president of the Commission, under whose auspices the White Paper 'Europe 1992' was drafted, were bound together by far more than merely common intentions; from April 1983, the informal panel of the ERT (informal because it is not a body within the institutional framework of the Community) linked the representative of the transnational European economy with that of the Commission.

Naturally, formally and as foreseen by the constitution, the member states of the Community had to act to renegotiate the original treaty for the SEA. According to our hypothesis, the initiative did not originate in the Council (representing the member states). The Council only transformed the new project into applicable law. The renewed treaty brought about a marked extension and supersession of the original EC treaties. The SEA, with the single market as its core element, marks the transition to a new supranational level of statehood.

What were the consequences? The links between the political with the economic sphere, already close, transcend the nation-state for the first time in modern European history. Thus, the move towards European integration, towards a new and additional level of political activity, is also of great interest for political sociology.

Theoretical background

Let me draw attention briefly to my understanding of processes in the world political economy. The political and economic spheres are necessarily linked in the world; this is why political and economic entrepreneurs have to bargain to come to terms. States in the market economy cannot prosper without enterprises, which for their part need state services and protection (see Bornschier 1988: Chapter 14, 1996: Chapter 3).

That there is a world market for protection is an argument inspired by the work of Max Weber, Otto Hintze and Frederic C. Lane which emphasizes that social order, also termed protection, is a territorially bounded public utility. Production, trade and financial transactions are conditional upon social prerequisites; they require protection. Property rights must be respected and people have to be motivated or forced to engage in exchange relationships. Protection is by no means a secondary factor of production, but is at least as important as labour, knowledge, organizational resources, financial means and credit. In our perspective, protection is a neglected element of national economic production functions; it represents the social capital provided and maintained by states. Governments, which can be understood as economic as well as political contractors, produce order and sell this public utility to capitalist enterprises as well as to citizens under their rule. By means of supplying this utility, governments affect the locational quality of their territory in the framework of the world economy, thus creating a competitive global market for social order. In an attempt to keep their political and military equilibrium they are forced to produce the political preconditions for economic success. If they fail, or only perform unsatisfactorily, they can neither attain nor preserve core status in the world economy.

This view stresses that it is not the capitalist state per se that is most favourable to economic success, but any state that reconciles capitalist profit logic with claims to legitimacy among the citizens, based on demands for security, equality and efficiency. Although legitimacy is attached to a social order, it is suggested that its enduring effect rests not on ideology but on features of the social structure which reflect the meeting of such demands.

Comparing explanations for the move towards integration

The accelerated integration of Europe has spurred an intense scholarly debate (Sandholtz and Zysman 1989; Moravcsik 1991; Cameron 1992; George 1993; Bornschier 1994; Green Cowles 1995; Robinson 1995; Fielder 1997; Ziltener 1999) and Moravcsik's (1998, 1999); most recently, respectable contributions have not been aimed at closing but renewing the debate over the fundamental causes of European integration. Here, we very briefly discuss the controversy between neofunctionalists and neorealists in the debates of political science so as to clarify the particularities of our own approach.

Neofunctionalism and Neorealism

The analysis of Western European integration has revived the old controversy between neofunctionalists and neorealists (George 1991: 20–4), while some contributions represent a combination of perspectives (George 1992, 1993; Cameron 1992).

The central idea behind neofunctionalism is that of a 'spillover', and here a distinction is made between 'political spillover' and 'functional spillover'. Functional spillover pertains to the dynamics that occur when states decide to integrate certain economic sectors, forcing them to integrate further sectors in order for the integration of the first to succeed. These dynamics are seen as a result of the interdependence of economic sectors. Political spillover is the result of a new political reality in connection with the shift of political decisions from the national to the supranational level. As decisions are now made at the supranational level, relevant interest groups and other political actors shift their lobbying to the supranational level to influence the decision-making process. Those interest groups which benefit from integration then start pressuring their national governments into shifting ever more political functions to the supranational level. According to neofunctionalist theory, both spillover processes should be spontaneous and incremental, because they result from the internal logic of integration. They not only occur in the lower realms of politics, but move from these specific areas to higher political fields of state sovereignty such as defence, security and currency.

Neorealists, on the other hand, believe that, because governments have been elected by the people, and therefore have legitimized power, they remain the truly significant actors in the integration process and defend national interests. Neorealists do not believe that a spillover from low to high politics will occur. Defence, security and currency, which represent the essence of state sovereignty, will remain excluded from the integration process. Yet the neorealists see the power structure in the overarching and global context as an important element, reactively influencing states' decisions.

Neorealist explanations of this kind have various weaknesses, which stem from the fact that these perspectives regard nation-states as the only relevant actors and take too narrow a view of government motives. Neofunctionalism, on the other hand, has too limited an understanding of transnational actors, and neglects the possibly far-reaching initiatives they may engender.

Transnational corporations in search of a political entrepreneur

The theoretical perspective advanced earlier may overcome some of the theoretical limitations resulting from an approach centred on policy. As already mentioned, two kinds of enterprises are relevant for the processes of the world economy: states and firms. Thus, a framework is suggested that integrates the supply of, and demand for, order. Together with the rise and decay of societal models, this approach seems promising, especially when one focuses on questions of timing and of the protagonists behind the relaunch of European integration in the 1980s. According to our argument, states compete with each other not only in a politico-military sense – the classic form in which their competition has been understood – but also in the framework of the world economy, essentially mediated by the production factor of social order guaranteed by the state. Thus, states also compete in a genuinely economic way, and in addition, they are forced to recreate, improve, or qualitatively reorganize interstate regulatory mechanisms in case they should break down or prove insufficient.

The idea of competition for social order, or protection, on the world market enriches the theoretical apparatus in one important respect. The economic motives of political undertakings, and even more, the view thus implied that states are producers of economically valuable goods, become important. Such motives are added to the classic ones of security and power politics. In this our perspective differs from the neorealist approach. It also differs from neofunctionalism, because the economic motives of state actors become predominant when the world economy is central to status distribution and when transnational corporations increasingly force states to compete with each other as sites of economic activity.

If we start from the perspective of competition between political entities supplying order and economic enterprises demanding order, it is easy to assume similar strategies for states and economic enterprises. While competing they may cooperate, build strategic alliances, or even merge. Contrary to the neofunctionalist argument, such processes are not the automatic results of internal spillovers; rather, they are primarily generated by the competitive conditions of the world political economy. Such strategic alliances or even mergers are much more likely to happen – or may only be possible – if supra-national institutional preconditions are met and available for political entrepreneurship. This was the case with the European Commission, whose independent role was stipulated at its inception in 1958.

Our theoretical perspective thus differs in important respects from the functionalist and realist theories of international relations. The argument for the theory of protection rent is as follows. European transnational corporations asked the political entrepreneurs in Europe to provide them with the locational advantages their rivals were enjoying in the United States and Japan. This demand stimulated the negotiation of a new state project along the lines of a wide homogeneous market combined with strategic planning, particularly with regard to the ever more important production factor of technology.

This project was forged in the informal European Roundtable of Industrialists (ERT). With his paper 'Agenda for Action: Europe 1990', Wisse Dekker, a central figure in the ERT, created an important conceptual basis for the White Paper authored by the Commission's Lord Cockfield. The EC Commission acted as a political entrepreneur, launched and popularized the project, overcame the resistance of governments, and submitted it to the Council for decision.

In previous publications I have had the opportunity to spell out the theoretical explanation as well as to display detailed empirical evidence (Bornschier 1996: Chapter 14; 2000a). Rather than repeating more than is necessary for the general argument, I wish here to deepen consideration of the aspect of the emergence of a new technological style. How did the supranational state sphere react to that? Well, it acted, one might say, in the role of midwife to a newborn child.

The state meets technology

The notion of technological style was originally proposed by Carlota Perez (1983, 1985), and later developed by Bornschier ([1988] 1996). The advantage of Perez's approach in comparison with earlier conceptualizations of technological change (e.g. Schumpeter) is that she models the socio-institutional sphere, governed by states, as an indispensable element of technological style. Today we are witnessing a shift towards a new technological style. 'Telematics', or 'digitalization', is the new key project that has replaced 'automobilization'.

In order to understand discontinuous technological change in a model of the sequence of technological styles that shape markets, the structure of firms and lifestyles, it is necessary to refer to the work of Carlota Perez which, you will recall, is discussed in Box 1.2 and in Chapter 3.

In the case of the emergence of the telematics paradigm, the contradictions between the new technology and the old institutions explain the kind of limited economic recovery that occurred in the 1980s, while institutions like Keynesianism, welfare states and labour unions came under pressure or even deteriorated. Remember, the coherence of the technological style begins to dissolve as soon as the long wave's economic peak is reached. To reach an equilibrium of production and consumption, two kinds of inventions are necessary. Innovations aimed at saving labour in the productive apparatus alone (i.e. innovations that increase output with the same work–time input) lead to disequilibria if they are not linked to inventions that fascinate people so that they want to spend their leisure consuming these goods and services. In the Keynesian societal model, flow technology and Taylorism were examples of process innovations, whereas television sets and cars represented the second type of invention, leading to the supply of hitherto unknown goods and services.

European proposals for technology corporatism and protection

The supranational political entrepreneurs in Europe were well aware of these transitions by the end of the 1970s and the beginning of the 1980s. Etienne Davignon, at that time vice president of the Commission, is a case in point. In an essay 'Europe at the End or Before a New Upswing?' which he published in a volume edited by Ralf Dahrendorf (1981) – himself a former commissioner – outlined the policy recommendations which later became part of the new Community legislation. Davignon looks at the competition as one between industrial nations, spurred by the emergence of new competitors, involving structural adjustments of old industrial sectors and innovation with regard to new ones, among which he especially mentioned microelectronics, space and biotechnology. He suggested that in the competitive restructuring the resulting future world division of labour should neither be left to accident nor to fate but should instead be the result of concerted policies to foster innovations embedded in 'reasonable' decisions for investment and research. He especially pointed to the route Japan had already chosen in this field (Davignon 1981: 169). What he proposed was nothing less than an 'independent European answer'. Davignon's postulates were the following:

First of all, a market for the introduction of new products must be established, where the demand regarding the creation of European norms and standards, as well as the expansion of public demand, can be stimulated. Second, there must be real support to enable sufficient positioning in the world markets ... Finally, Europe should make it possible to improve the coordination of the respective national research and development activities.

(Davignon 1981: 183; my translation)

The point of reference is very obvious. Under the heading 'The Telematics Revolution: the Barriers Must Fall in Europe' Davignon points to the new technological revolution already going on in the core area of telematics:

The question is whether the Europeans – and this really concerns the whole continent and not simply a country or several countries – want to gain one of the first places in the current competition or whether they will content themselves to passively observe the strategies which their American and Japanese competitors are following. The answer is simple. Europe can no longer allow itself to stand aside when modern technology is on the agenda, otherwise it must accustom itself now to the fact that it will soon be ranked among the also-rans. Our autonomy is at stake.

(Davignon 1981: 184; my translation)

This project of technology corporatism and of social order, or protection, was clearly linked to the other core areas of the renewal:

We want to create a truly European market, a common market, which offers businesses the same chances as their American and Japanese competitors have.

(Davignon 1981: 185; my translation)

In order to legitimize his approach he continues:

Quite a few people ask themselves why the EC Commission does not concern itself with telematics. Furthermore, they say that on the telematics market everything appears to be going well and that business 'copes very well without the technocrats from Brussels'. But that only serves to confirm our diagnosis; that is, that in Europe one just muddles through ... Europe manufactures only 10 per cent of world production of highly developed electronic components, whereas the EC represents 25 per cent of the world market in this sector. That means that the distance to our competitors will increase. European industry must set itself the goal of producing one-third of the world

market in the area of telematics by the end of the 1980s. This is a difficult goal but it is attainable – and it is the unanimous opinion of all,
that is, of the governments, business and the EC Commission.

(Davignon 1981: 186; my translation)

From this early statement (published in 1981!) it becomes obvious that
protagonists in the Commission coded the transition towards a new European societal model in terms of competition with Japan and the USA, and
that early on they proposed a European answer in the form of a proposal
of the EC Commission (Davignon 1981: 187). This approach not only
made its impression on the later SEA (see pp. 156–7) but became part of
the official normative theory of the Commission. Karl-Heinz Narjes (1988:
396), then vice president of the Commission stated:

> It was not until 1980 that the Community was able to take a strategic
> view of science and technology. It was then that the Commission first
> stated its belief that it was not possible to devise a new model for
> society, to secure Europe's political and economic autonomy, or to
> guarantee commercial competitiveness without a complete mastery of
> the most sophisticated technologies.

By the early 1990s, the approach of technology corporatism and protection had become a standard core element of EC policy, justifying its
common procedure with regard to competitive pressure and insufficient
R&D funds in information technologies (Commission of the EC, 1991: 8).

> The Community therefore developed a global strategy in the first half
> of the 1980s in close collaboration with industry and with research
> institutions.
>
> (Commission of the EC, 1991: 10)

This is followed by a list of different elements, the support of business
as well as measures against side-effects and a vision of a

> preparation of the transition to a society, in which information is seen
> as a raw material, which is used in agreement with the social partners
> and on the basis of the corresponding offers for education and train-
> ing.
>
> (Commission of the EC 1991: 10)

It was not only protection inside the EC that was envisioned in these
tasks. In the words of the Commission:

> Considering the growing challenges in the area of Information and
> Communication Technologies the Community must prove its joint

action towards third party states. This applies to the bilateral relationship of the EC to the US and to Japan, as well as in international institutions like the General Agreement on Tariffs and Trade, International Standards Organization or International Telecommunications Union.

(Commission of the EC 1991: 71)

Concluding remarks

Our understanding of Western European integration that started in the first half of the 1980s is that an elite bargain was struck between European transnational firms and supranational political entrepreneurs in the Commission. It should be made clear that it was not European businesses as such which pushed the relaunch of European integration in the 1980s, since most of them took advantage of national protection within the early phase of the European Community, when non-tariff barriers to trade and many restrictions on investment and national monopolies still prevailed. Thus, neither was it the European business associations, which already existed at the Community level and represented numerous enterprises, but rather the transnational European business elite, with its considerable business stakes outside their headquarter countries, who was pushing to have the same opportunities as their global competitors by broadening their home base, thus allowing for greater economies of scale, and by obtaining support from strategic technology policy. This is not to suggest a conspiracy theory of European integration, since the position of European big business as represented in the European Roundtable was overt and publicly stated. This becomes evident from the first Policy Memorandum of the European Roundtable of Industrialists, which was officially transmitted to the Commission in 1983:

> Despite the efforts of the European Community to liberalize trade, Europe remains divided into national markets with different industrial structures. This prevents many enterprises from reaching the size necessary to withstand the pressure of competition from non-European concerns. But the European market must serve as a single 'home base' so that European firms can develop into powerful competitors on world markets.

This is not to say that all other business was against the project, but the others were fragmented in terms of interest and, on average, rather neutral; some would gain, some would lose. This divided position contrasts with that of the European transnational corporations, all of whom were on the winning side and possessed resources for taking advantage of the new possibilities.

Furthermore, our explanation does not completely neglect the political

Box 8.1 Selected evidence from documents and interviews with protagonists and contemporary witnesses

The findings have been documented in different reports and Bornschier (2000b) also offers an overall picture.

Our analysis of numerous documents gave us background information for the expert interviews; this supplemented our findings so that we could testify to the informal cooperation between transnational economy and the Commission. From a total of twelve interviews we conducted eight of these with temporary witnesses and four with informants, who either knew the Commission from inside or from their intensive research. Two vice-presidents of the Commission and two members of the European Roundtable of Industrialists were interviewed.

The findings of our interviews confirm the central role of the Commission of the EC in the genesis of the SEA. Furthermore, they also pointed out the close cooperation between the Roundtable of the European Industrialists and the Commission, which could not be shown through the analysis of the documents alone. Davignon and Cockfield were named throughout as the central and influental figures in the Commission, whereas, for the Roundtable it was mainly Dekker from Philips who was mentioned. It was Dekker whose paper 'Europe 1990' prompted the White Paper.

Selected references from our interviews:

How were the opportunities for contact between the European Roundtable of Industrialists (ERT) and the Commission created?

A member of the ERT answers:

> We value the fact that the European Roundtable of Industrialists not only engages in lobbying, narrowly defined, but also makes general proposals and elaborates general projects. We have access on a higher level than all the associations, unions, etc.; we are not lost among the many partners in dialogue, we speak directly with Commission presidents, with the heads of government or at least directly with the economic ministers.
>
> (Interview, 11th July 1995 with Helmut Maucher,
> President of the Administrative Council of Nestlé,
> and Member of the European Roundtable of Industrialists)

How great was the influence of the initiatives of the European Roundtable of Industrialists on the Commission? One of the protagonists answers this in the interview:

> I think *(the influence of the European Roundtable of Industrialists on the Commission and the White Paper) was* very strong, but not to the extent that the industry could more or less dictate what they have to do, that of course was impossible, but there has been a very, very fruitful cooperation between the Roundtable and the Commission ...
>
> (From an interview with Wisse Dekker)
>
> *Can it be said that there was a cooperation between the European Roundtable of Industrialists and the Commission?*
>
> ... it was mainly Wisse Dekker, then head of Philips, who launched an initiative via the European Roundtable. This initiative was in parallel with what Lord Cockfied set up in the Commission. And that is why Commission and Economy stood together and demanded the creation of a truly boundary-free home market.
>
> (From an interview with a contemporary witness,
> Hanns R. Glatz)

entrepreneurs of the existing nation-states in the Community. On the average, however, they needed to be pushed hard – a process which actually took many years, since their national constituencies were diverse in terms of the winners and losers created by deregulation. Thus, with respect to political entrepreneurs in Europe, our hypothesis is very clear: in the end it was the transnational level that was decisive.

By pointing to an elite bargain struck between the two European elites, both transnational and supranational, I do not imply that these two were decisive for other aspects of European integration. The formal role of the Commission, as spelled out in the treaties, may vary in its effectiveness. Before the 1980s the Commission was not always a strong actor in European politics, and in the 1990s this was, likewise, the situation. Once the project was successful, the European transnational elite turned instead to normal interest-group politics, albeit within a new institutional setting. The Roundtable is still active and has even expanded its membership over time, but it does not seem to be influencing further European state-building, although it has a big stake in moulding concrete policies within the framework achieved.

9 Regional integration and economic growth

The case of the EU

Introduction

In the preceding chapter I summarized our research on the remarkable relaunch of European integration since the 1980s and the actors involved therein. This and the following chapter reflect on the economic consequences of this change in the European political economy. Research into the policy fields which, at a supranational level, shaped those parameters which affect national growth included three core areas: market creation (deepening and expansion), technology policy, and regional, structural, and cohesion policies (see Bornschier 2000b).

The two main research questions relating to economic consequences which we wish to consider are the following:[1]

1 Did the EU provide collective goods for their members which foster economic growth in addition to the national provision of relevant development factors? We consider as relevant supranational collective goods those three supranationally regulated policy fields in the EU mentioned above. Is the access to these collective goods – the internal market, technology policy and provisions for cohesion – as provided by membership a factor that simply adds to national endowments, or does it make these national provisions more productive? This leads to the significant question of whether membership in the EU is actually beneficial for national economic growth.

2 Did EU membership actually accelerate economic convergence among EU countries, i.e. the catching-up of less developed members, or would such a convergence have happened anyway, dependent on a lower initial level of development? This poses the question of whether the strong emphasis on cohesion and convergence in both the rhetoric as well as institutional designs of the EU effectively translate into faster convergence in comparative perspective. The second core question is distinct from the first one, since EU membership could be beneficial for economic growth without fostering convergence.

The focus in this chapter is on economic growth; in the next one we will deal with the question of convergence in more detail. In order to answer the two research questions, the classic method of cross-national comparisons is applied, including thirty-three countries where non-EU members function as a benchmark. The design of this comparison will be detailed later in the chapter.

The question of whether European integration was economically important with regard to the three policy areas – internal market, technology policy and cohesion policy – can be divided into two. First, it is of interest whether the policies were indeed relevant, in the sense that they aimed at affecting those economic factors which are demonstrably favourable for economic growth, as evidenced in classic cross-national studies. Even if this turns out to be the case, it should be asked whether the specific EU regulations in these policy fields were actually economically effective. It is not so easy to determine this, even if one applies contrast cases as a benchmark. This is because the competing countries in the world economy were not idle in reshaping their own political economies. To include this information is, however, beyond the scope of this chapter. Yet three reasons suggest that one can, nevertheless, arrive at certain conclusions.

1   Regarding market creation – the removal of barriers to trade and expansion of the common market – European integration from the onset, i.e. since the European Economic Communities of 1958, obviously went further than other integration projects in the world political economy, for example the NAFTA.

2   With regard to research and technology policies, the situation is different. For a long time, both in political practice as well as in social science analysis, technology policy has received high attention as a competitive resource for economic growth. To find out whether the EU's efforts were effective on logical grounds is only possible if it can be demonstrated that the EU undertook more and/or better technology policies. Due to lack of data one therefore needs to confine oneself to the question whether the EU's technology policy was effective to the extent that it prevented the EU's members from falling behind its competitors in what has been labelled the triad (USA, Western European countries, and Japan). After all, national efforts (private as well as public) are predominant in building up the stock of technology capital; but EU policy has both added to them and coordinated their efforts.

3   With regard to the cohesion policy of the EU, to which we will come in detail in the next chapter, the situation is quite comfortable. While the creation of the internal market and the technology policy within the EU have been imitated in the course of time by other integration projects and state initiatives within the political world economy con-

cerning regional, structural and cohesion policy, the efforts of the EU are actually quite unique, since they are measures which attempt to balance wealth between countries which remain formally sovereign states. More efforts have been made towards equalization within nation-states (e.g. between the US states or regions in Japan), but this is irrelevant to our comparison of sovereign nation-states. However, a different problem arises in analysing the convergence efforts of the EU. The economic convergence effect among different societies has been solidly and empirically established, at least for more-developed countries, and proves to be quite strong in this context. Therefore, the question arises as to whether the effort the EU has made is justified by an even stronger convergence process than could have been expected otherwise.

Why should member countries gain an economic advantage?

The removal of barriers to trade and the extension of the market should result in a general increase of welfare, and the arguments for this are as follows. A larger market leads, via greater opportunities for the expansion of firms, to efficiency gains due to economies of scale. The efficiency gains are transmitted; because efficiency gains are conducive to the institutionalization of research and development, they speed up gains and are able to favourably affect capital formation, and via higher wages and salaries they expand consumption. These economically beneficial consequences again add to the growth of existing firms and to new firms, and they also accelerate the absorption of new knowledge in the economy. Therefore, the resulting rate of economic growth should be permanently higher than it would be otherwise, with no or less removal of barriers to trade and market extension.

As compared to trade across national boundaries, the common market, in addition to the mentioned favourable consequences, results in increased economies of common governance due to the harmonization of political regulation. Firms and consumers can sell and buy beyond their state boundaries but within the common market without the hindrance of diverse regulations. This advantage accrues more to members of the EU than to other countries trading in the world economy even if the relative importance of foreign trade is the same, since two-thirds of the 'foreign' trade of EU members takes place within the EU (figures for 1996).

The process of successive creation, deepening and expansion of the market can best be presented in a table as a short history of Western European integration, see Box 9.1.

The Internal market project that was developed with the aim of completely abolishing the barriers to free economic action between member states was not a new goal; the common market had been on the agenda since the foundation of the EEC. The various steps towards the realization

Box 9.1 Market creation and market expansion in Western Europe, 1945–2000

Date of agreement	Enactment	Measure	Countries involved
1944	1948	Market creation: Benelux Customs Union	B, NL, LUX
1951	23.7.1952	Market creation: Common Market for European Coal and Steel (ECSC Treaty) Implemented on 1 May 1953	EC 6 (D, F, Benelux, I)
1957	1.1.1958	Market creation: Common Market for industrial goods; common agricultural policy (Treaty of Rome) 1 January 1959 first reduction of tariffs by 10 per cent 1962–6 Agreement on agricultural, financial and competition system 1 July 1968; Customs Union completed 1 July 1977; Reduction of internal tariffs completed (EC 9)	EC 6 (D, F, Benelux, I)
1959	3.5.1960	Market creation: European Free Trade Area (EFTA)	EFTA 7 (GB, DK, P, SW, NW, A, CH)
1972	1.1.1973	Market expansion: EC entry of Great Britain, Ireland, Denmark	EC 9 (D, F, Benelux, I, GB, IRL, DK)
1972/3	1973	Market creation and expansion: free trade agreement EC – EFTA countries	EC 9 and EFTA (P, SW, NW, IS, A, CH, later plus NW, FIN)
1979	1.1.1981	Market expansion: EC entry of Greece	EC 10 (D, F, Benelux, I, GB, IRL, DK, GR)
1985/6	1.7.1987	Market creation and deepening: programme to create a single market by 31 December 1992; in mid-1995, 90% of measures are implemented by member countries	EC 12 (D, F, Benelux, I, GB, IRL, DK, GR, SP, P)
1985	1.1.1986	Market expansion: EC entry of Spain, Portugal	EC 12 (D, F, Benelux, I, GB, IRL, DK, GR, SP, P)

Date of agreement	Enactment	Measure	Countries involved
	3.10.1990	Market expansion: inclusion of the German Democratic Republic into the Federal Republic of Germany and therefore into the EC	EC 12
1992	1.1.1994	Market expansion: European Economic Area (EEA) Agreement Integration in Single Market, R&D policy, cohesion policy; not integrated: agricultural policy, foreign trade, economic and monetary policy	EU 12 plus FIN, SW, NW IS, A, FL
1994	1.1.1995	Market expansion: EU entry of FIN, SW, A	EU 15 (D, F, I, Blux, GB, IRL, DK, GR, SP, P, FIN, SW, A)
Since 1991/8		Eastern Europe enlargement: 'European Agreements' and negotiations for accession	

Note
Transition and implementation periods of different lengths have to be considered in the accession agreements; for instance, three and a half years (six years for financial regulations) for the enlargement of 1973; five years (seven years for freedom of movement of labour and trade with specific agricultural products) in the case of Greece; seven years (ten years for certain agricultural products and fishery) in the cases of Spain and Portugal; special regulations for the new provinces in Eastern Germany in the agricultural and transport sectors and for the single market implementation by 31 December 1995.

of that goal are mentioned in Box 9.1. Actually, market creation and expansion in Western Europe has not occurred through one or two 'big bangs' but has been a more or less continuous process of negotiation and implementation of trade liberalization since various interim regulations have often lasted almost up to the next step towards integration.

When we evaluate possible economic effects, it becomes clear that the welfare effects of market integration have increased over time. Given the hypothesis of the transmission of beneficial effects we need to control for the length of membership; members that entered earlier should have gained more.

Research and technology policy

On the threshold of the 1980s the architects of European technology policy designed measures to make Europe fit for the future and able to compete with the challenging competitors, the USA and Japan, in the main spheres of the new technological style. This has been treated in the preceding chapter, and a historical overview of this policy field can be found in Box 9.2.

If indicators of technology capital turn out to have had an empirical influence on the economic growth rate, then such policy initiatives were right and timely. But, as already mentioned, the competitors of the EU member states did not remain idle. We will therefore evaluate whether in the course of this competition the position of members of the EU changed.

Cohesion policy

Right from the beginning, i.e. even before the integration relaunch of the 1980s, European integration implicitly and explicitly politicized the question of cohesion within the community. This is relevant to whether that speeded the convergence of less-developed member states, i.e. whether they grew faster than non-members of a similar level of development. I have reserved a whole chapter (the next one) for this question, which has obvious implications for the question of late development. Here I wish to mention that cohesion and convergence undoubtedly belong to the ideological keywords of the European Community. Was this only rhetorical? During the 1980s and 1990s, several qualitative shifts also took place, such as the anchoring of regional policy in the Treaty with the SEA and several important political reforms. This transformed the original *juste retour* transfer system between the nation-states into a European system of cohesion policy, which to a large extent is implemented according to supranationally defined criteria and goals.

Method of evaluating economic consequences of EU membership

We here compare countries in a sample of thirty-three OECD and newly industrializing countries, the same selection as in Chapter 2 of this book. The period considered is from 1980 to the end of 1998 and is deliberately chosen. It covers, on the one hand, the remarkable extension of European integration, the enlargement of membership up to fifteen member states and the deepening of integration (as indicated by supranational EU regulation with regard to market creation, technology policy and cohesion measures). Among the thirty-three countries of our comparison there are only fourteen EU members, since Luxembourg is included in the data for Belgium. On the other hand the long growth period is chosen because a comparison of economic growth does not make much sense over shorter periods. If we want to make meaningful growth differences the dependent variable, we have to choose longer periods. First, as mentioned in the introductory chapter, the short term growth rates are to a large extent

Box 9.2 Research and technology policy

New forms of cooperation were the basis for developing joint R&D policies between the Commission and the European transnational enterprises. The roots of the R&D policy of the EU reach back into the late 1970s (Sandholtz 1992). Parker (2000) and Nollert (2000) both confirm the important role that the Commission played and the successful realization of their initiative function for the information and biotechnology fields. Especially in the field of technology policy cooperation between the Commission and the so-called Roundtable, the European Information Technology Industry Roundtable (EITIRT) was institutionalized for the first time. This new form of cooperation proved to be very successful and became the strategic role model for many more Commission projects. In 1983 the Council adopted the first research programme (1984–7), which initiated the breakthrough of European functions in this field of politics. In the wake of this, the EC strategically reoriented its activities and expanded it even further than the sectoral activities. In 1984 the European Strategic Programme for Research and Information Technologies (ESPRIT) was adopted. It was not only the (first) result of the very close cooperation between the Commission and Roundtable EITIRT, but it also influenced as a flagship the whole of the research and development policy and its targets and methods (compare Grande and Häusler 1994).

With the EEA (Art. 130 f–q EC Treaty) R&D policies were firmly anchored. Every outline programme had to be approved unanimously by the Council, whereas for single research projects a qualified majority vote sufficed. The second research outline programme for the years 1987–91, with a total of 5.4 billion ECU, showed where the new priorities of the European research and technology policy lay. Whereas in the first R&D almost half of the budget had been put aside for energy research, in the second programme this was drastically reduced and research for information and communication technology was focused on. The Maastricht Treaty generalized the Commission's task and stretched research and technology policy (Art. 130 f–p), thereby empowering the EC to go beyond the industrial area and 'support all measures of research that – based on some of the chapters of the Treaty – are considered necessary'. The third programme for research (1990–4) was increased from 5.7 to 6.6 billion ECU in December 1992. The fourth programme already had a total of 12.3 billion ECU (plus 1 billion in reserve) at its disposal. So, based on these new priority patterns in the *White Paper of Growth, Competitiveness, Employment* (Commission 1993), the areas of telecommunication, information, and innovation were then focused on.

determined by period effects of the world economy. Second, we want to focus on sustainable growth. Latin American countries, for example had their 'lost decade' in the 1980s, then recovered remarkably in the course of the 1990s to fall back again towards the end of that decade. Some newly industrializing Asian countries had very high growth rates for most of the time during the period considered but were brought down to earth with the Asian crisis in 1997. A long period is the best solution to neutralize these different growth patterns. Again, I want to stress that only cases which were market economies over the whole period are included, since the cases which shifted from state socialism to market economy after the revolutions of 1989/91 cannot be meaningfully compared.

The growth model and the equation for empirical estimation

The same growth model is applied that was already explained in Chapter 2 except that new predictors are added:

$$\text{Growth of } Y = f \text{ (growth of } K, \text{ growth of } L, C) \tag{1}$$

$$C = f \text{ (¥, T, H, S, M)} \tag{2}$$

Socially created resources (C) signify an effect on total economic performance (Y) that is not explained by the change in real capital (K) and labour (L) the undisputed factors of production. In the set of social context factors five variables are included, four of which we introduced in Chapter 2 (see also endnote 15); the new one is membership in the EU, M. The latter takes the value zero for non-members and values for members weighted according to length of membership.[2]

With the new variable, years of membership in the EU (and the former EEC), one can test whether EU members differ in their growth by taking non-members as a benchmark. It has been ensured that the control group does not differ too much in terms of significant variables, like level of development, from EU members. The contrast group of non-members in the total sample of thirty-three cases, the vast majority of them OECD members (see country listing in Chapter 2), has about the average level of material development.[3] However, despite the similar average, the contrast group which is used as a benchmark is more dispersed in terms of level of development than the EU members. The poorest non-EU country is Argentina, with 60 per cent of the average wealth of the poorest EU members, Portugal and Greece, and a couple of non-EU members are richer than the richest EU members, for example, the USA and Switzerland.

The test procedure: an overview

The new models that use logged differences in cross-national comparisons (as in Chapter 2 of this book and, for example, Firebaugh und Beck 1994; Benhabib und Spiegel 1994; Graff 1996; Bornschier 2000) have certainly produced interesting results. They suggest growth of total product by the growth of real capital. This, however, is a typical ex-post analysis. The economy grew because real capital input did so, too. But why did the stock of real capital grow? It is equally interesting and important to know which characteristics of an economy – which one knows ex-ante – were responsible for subsequent growth of the capital stock. Such characteristics would allow a true prognosis of the growth of real capital, which is one of the main sources of economic growth.

Therefore I choose, in this chapter, the following sequence of analyses. First, it will be briefly demonstrated that it is indeed the growth of the stock of real capital that considerably influences economic growth. Then the growth of capital is predicted in an ex-ante analysis, i.e. by using only predictors which one knows beforehand. Finally, the ex-ante and ex-post considerations will be combined to evaluate which variables influenced economic growth between 1980 and the end of 1998. Our main test variable, EU membership, enters both steps, as a predictor of capital stock growth and as a predictor of economic growth alongside capital growth and other variables relevant for growth. If EU membership is a significant predictor of growth beside capital growth, we want to know whether this effect is a singular, temporary phenomenon or permanent. This is investigated by contrasting our test variable, EU membership years, with two other possible ways of modelling (see p. 180). An overview of the various tests is given in Figure 9.1.

Empirical analyses

1 Economic growth (1980–98) and growth of physical capital (1986–93)

Figure 9.2 demonstrates the high correspondence between capital growth and economic growth. This is expressed in more technical terms by the high common variance of 69 per cent. This is, however, a typical ex-post analysis. At the end of the period we know that it was capital growth that counted, but capital growth is also dependent on economic growth. This is then a classical example of the problem termed simultaneity in cross-country regressions, i.e. that the right-hand-side variables (here capital growth) are not independent of the economic growth rate but are also jointly determined. We therefore come to an ex-ante analysis of capital growth.

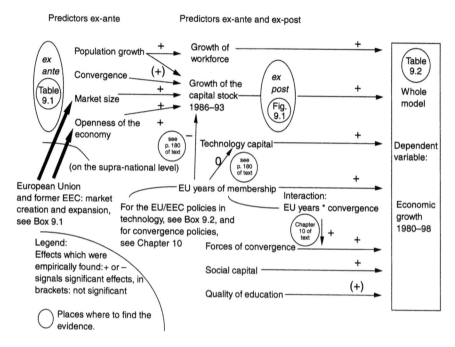

Figure. 9.1 Overview of the various investigations.

Note
The effect of EU membership on convergence is included in the overview but will be treated in the next chapter.

2 Determinants of capital growth, an ex-ante analysis

Which exogenous variables, known as ex-ante, influence capital growth? We suspect that due to economies of scale these will be the openness of an economy (trade as a share of total product) and the absolute size of the market (total product). Furthermore, we think that developmental late-comers or stragglers provide special opportunities for capital formation. Theoretically, the approximately known future growth of population is an ex-ante predictor, too. In accordance with this expectation, we find in our analysis a positive effect which, however, fails to be significant. One possible reason for this is that population growth and convergence forces are correlated (r = 0.59).

Table 9.1 presents the results of the ex-ante predictors of capital growth.[4] What is most important is the openness of the national economy, followed by the absolute size of the national economy and, with about equal weight, the convergence forces (indicating a comparative low level of economic development). Together one can, ex-ante, explain 40 per cent of the differences in capital formation.[5]

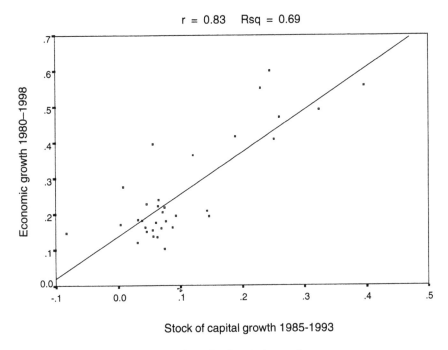

Figure 9.2 Economic growth and stock of capital growth.

Table 9.1 Capital stock growth between 1985 and the end of 1993 for the thirty-three countries under study. Listed are the figures indicating the relative importance of predictors (beta-weights of a multiple regression) which are highly significant

	Predictors
Openness of the national economy	0.81
Absolute size of the national economy	0.46
Convergence	0.50

Thus, we reach our first substantive empirically based conclusion: the EU policy of market creation and deepening, i.e. the Common Market or internal market programme which is detailed in Box 9.1, was in the following sense right and effective; it aimed at improving those conditions at a supranational level which turn out in our cross-national analysis (see Table 9.1) to be significant predictors of capital growth. And, as indicated at the beginning of our empirical section, capital growth is one of the most important single factors influencing economic growth.

3 Determinants of economic growth

Now we turn to economic growth as the variable of interest. Did years of membership of the EU add to economic growth over the 1980–98 period? It certainly appears to; Table 9.2 lists all the economic growth predictors and EU membership is among the significant ones.[6] The relative importance of predictors of economic growth are very much the same as in Chapter 2, except that we have an additional one: years of EU membership. As compared with the other predictors, EU membership has the smallest effect but is clearly significant.[7] Note that this is the direct effect; we shall come later to the indirect effects.

Now we examine further our variable, years of EU membership, since one might expect, as argued earlier, enduring and cumulative positive effects due to membership. Alternatively I have considered a variable of EU membership where the countries most recently admitted have the highest scores. If membership of the EU only adds to growth in a transitory way, i.e. by a surge in growth that fades over time, then this alternative specification 'EU recently joined' should have a higher impact on economic growth than 'EU years'. In addition, I consider a plain dummy variable which is unweighted, assigning the value 0 to non-members and 1 to members. The analysis reported in Table 9.2 is repeated, changing only the specification of EU membership. The results are given in Table 9.3 (only the effects of EU membership are reported).

We find that EU membership weighted for years has a significant effect on economic growth, while the membership variable calibrated to assign

Table 9.2 Predictors of economic growth 1980 until the end of 1998, thirty-three countries. Listed are the figures indicating the relative importance of predictors (beta-weights of a multiple regression) which are, unless otherwise stated, highly significant

	Predictors
Convergence effect	0.81
Growth of capital	0.70
Technology capital	0.51
Social capital (Trust & Tolerance)	0.38
EU years	0.30

Table 9.3 The effect of length of EU membership on growth

	Beta-weights in the multiple regression	*Statistical significance*
EU years	0.30	highly significant (p = 1%)
EU dummy	0.26	significant (p = 4%)
EU recently joined	0.17	insignificant (p = 19%)

the highest scores to the most recently admitted countries is insignificant. Our interpretation is straightforward; the beneficial effects of EU membership due to economies of scale and economies of common governance appear to be propagated and result in permanently higher economic growth. This follows from the above result, which is more substantial the longer a nation-state has been a member of the European integration.

Thus, we reach a further empirically substantiated conclusion: the advantages of integration for economic growth tend to be transmitted and result in permanently higher growth levels. Even if these are fresh, and perhaps preliminary, results, it is important to mention that they contradict the classic Solow–Swan economic growth model and the work that builds on it (earlier Cecchini 1988, more recently: Vanhout 1999), which suggests only a temporary surge in growth due to integration. According to this model, growth returns to its previous equilibrium rate. However, enduring higher growth rates due to integration, as we find, are also reported by Henrekson *et al.* (1997). In Chapter 10 we will qualify this general conclusion when we point to the fact that this is dependent on level of development.

4 How did the EU policy of supranational market creation influence subsequent national growth of capital in member states?

The Single Market policy of Western European integration since the 1980s and the opening of the nationally segmented markets was, one can say today, a success. Before, under the reign of the European Communities, national markets were still in many respects (e.g. services and investment) closed and protected. With the removal of these restrictions, the EU created the preconditions for faster capital growth. In the shorter run, however, the effects might not have been as favourable as theoretically assumed. This is due to the cross-boundary concentration of firms, which EU policy not only implicitly but also quite explicitly encourages, so as to obtain larger-scale businesses fit for world competition.

Thus, the Internal market programme resulted in two processes: (a) capital destruction following mergers and acqusitions through downsizing in order to limit excess capacities; and (b) new opportunities for capital formation due to larger markets and economies of common governance. Our earlier work revealed that until 1993 the overall effect was unfavourable (see Bornschier 2001). In predicting capital growth, EU membership had a negative effect. These results were preliminary, since only stocks of capital until 1993 were available to measure capital growth.[8] More recent replications have been able to use capital growth until 1996 but have still found an overall negative effect (see Bornschier, Herkenrath and Ziltener 2001, 2003; and the next chapter).

Our next conclusion is, therefore, that the positive growth contribution

EU membership had on economic growth (see Table 9.2) was counteracted (in part) by the negative effect the internal market programme had on capital growth in member states due to overall capital destruction due to cross-border mergers and acquisitions. Whether this structural adjustment becomes less important in recent times in compensating the beneficial effects of the larger market for capital formation is an open research question.

5 Technology gap with the competitors in the triad

In the earlier and more detailed version of the research that is reported in this chapter, I researched whether during the period between the mid-1980s and the mid-1990s a technology gap between EU member states on the one hand and the USA and Japan on the other hand opened (see Bornschier 2001). Three indicators of technology capital were evaluated: scientists and engineers in research and development, the number of personal computers, and the number of Internet hosts, all weighted according to population. All such indicators exhibit high correlations with economic efficiency, for which per capita income was taken as a proxy. Values above or under what would be expected according to the level of economic efficiency are measures of under- or over-performance in the technology race.[9] In Table 9.4, I present only the summary of our findings and conclusions.

In the USA and in EU member states (unweighted average), the three indicators for technology correspond to what can be expected on the basis of economic productivity. In other words, there is no technology gap due to EU membership. If EU members are less technology-based than the USA it is not due to the EU but explicable by differences in economic efficiency, and with increases in this, the gap can be expected to be closed. Japan is an overperformer on one of the three technology indicators but an underperformer in the other two. This seems to contrast with the

Table 9.4 The technology gap: summary of findings from three indicators of technology

	Japan	USA	EU members
1 Scientists and engineers in research and development	>	=	=
2 Personal computers	<	=	=
3 Internet hosts	<	=	=

Notes
> larger;
= about the same;
< smaller than expected on the basis of economic productivity.
EU members: unweighted average.
Further analyses and additional considerations are to be found in Bornschier (2001).

figures that are frequently released by the press, according to which Japan has not only surmounted the EU but also the USA in terms of research and development outlays as a share of total product. But such figures might be quite misleading, since they merely relate to the costs of technology investments, which should not be confused with results.

The conclusion to be drawn from the analyses cited here is that the research and technology policy of the EU was effective in that it politicized those resources which empirically affect economic growth early, at the turn of the 1970s to 1980s (see previous chapter). The supranational initiatives were also effective in that, in the terms of technology application I mentioned here, no gap opened vis-à-vis the USA, which the architects of European technology policy originally feared but seem to have effectively avoided. According to our technology indicators, Japan is not an overperformer; the higher investment it made in research and development during the 1990s has not resulted in correspondingly higher economic growth rates (see also Chapter 12).

Summarizing and concluding remarks

We started this chapter on the economic consequences of European integration with two questions. The evidence so far available about the first – what is the effect on economic growth? – has been examined in this chapter. The second – has EU membership accelerated economic convergence of formerly poor members? – has also been preliminarily approached in the research that is reported in this chapter, but since more data are available we will reserve a whole chapter, the next, for that discussion.

With the internal market programme launched in the 1980s, the EU, at a supranational level and according to this analysis of thirty-three nationstates, appears to have improved those parameters that stimulate capital formation. These parameters are the openness of the economy and the size of market. During the late 1980s and the early 1990s, however, capital formation within the member states did not take advantage of this, since the improved internal market led to structural adjustments through transborder mergers and acquisitions, which led to capital destruction. Specifically, the stock of real capital grew more slowly, per saldo, in EU member states than in our contrast cases. A sensible interpretation is that this is a transitory effect which, however, seems still to have been in effect in the mid-1990s.

The research and technology policy of the EU, which has been a significant part of restructuring integration since the 1980s, was effective in that the widespread fears at the threshold of the 1980s that Europe would be shaken off in the high-tech race did not come true, at least not according to the technology indicators that were considered. The effect of the third policy area, i.e. that of cohesion, will be the topic of the next chapter.

Did EU membership add to national resources and so to economic growth? Yes it did, according to our findings. After controlling for several other relevant factors which are favourable to economic growth, we find that membership had an additional positive effect. This direct positive effect, however, needs to be set against the unfavourable effect on capital growth just mentioned. Through the latter, this positive effect was (partly) lost through the consequences of the explicitly desired capital restructuring.

Our results suggest that the beneficial effect of integration is permanent, which contradicts classical growth theory as expressed in Paolo Cecchini's famous study, *The Costs of Non Europe*. One could argue that the move towards integration during the 1980s provided a growth bonus for all members and that it is even now unclear whether or not this was temporary. Against this, one can hold our finding that those countries with the longest membership benefited more from integration than the ones which only joined during the 1980s. This can only be explained by assuming that the beneficial effects of earlier steps towards integration were dynamically transmitted to the 1980–98 growth period, thus permanently adding to growth. The positive growth contribution of membership that we find seems to be rooted in higher total productivity, which was the more substantial the longer the membership.

Let us briefly compare our results with those from other studies. Our finding contradicts that of Vanhout (1999); against his study one can, however, raise some objections. He considers the aggregate economic growth of the countries integrated in each period. From the fact that this growth until 1974 was slightly over the long-term trend and afterwards below, he concludes that integration only produced a temporary growth spurt, as implied by neoclassical growth theory. His conclusion is, however, erroneous, for two reasons. First, economic growth until 1973 was almost double that of the rate since then (see Maddison 1995). Second, he does not control the different growth trajectories of each new member. Because of these objections, we argue that Vanhout's finding (1999) does not represent counter-evidence to our own.

The direct economic contribution to growth of integration has, until now, rarely been studied within a comparable research design. De Melo *et al.* (1992) study the role of membership in integration projects in a sample of 101 countries over the periods 1960–72 and 1973–85 and find no effects on economic growth. But they measure membership only as a dummy variable (whereas I consider also length of membership), and use inadequate control variables in a sample with huge differences in level of development. Landau (1995) also finds no effects of membership (again measured solely as a dummy variable); he considers, however, only a very small sample of seventeen OECD countries over the growth period from 1950–90. Baldwin and Seghezza (1996: 19) likewise report insignificant results with membership measured as a dummy variable. Thus, studies not controlling for the length of membership have not, up to now, been able to find effects on growth,[10] with the exception of the work of Henrekson *et al.* (1997). In a panel regression design of OECD countries from 1975 to 1985, Henrekson *et al.* find significant permanent effects of membership on growth although they only use a dummy (i.e. the dichotomy between membership or non-membership); in addition, they consider, beside EU membership, membership of the European Free Trade Association (EFTA). Since they consider various control variables, their finding seems to be quite robust. Their findings point in the same direction as ours and in my view we therefore can maintain the hypothesis of a positive economic effect on growth of integration. Membership should, however, also consider length, since we have demonstrated that this clearly produces more significant results.

In concluusion, we can say that the countries of the EU have effectively managed the turbulences of the 1980s and 1990s, stemming from the transition to a new technological style and the search for an adequate politico-economic regime, with an economic growth record that – given the level of development already reached by most EU member states – was competitive. The world can count on the continued existence of Europe, which is after all not so bad, since progress results from the competition of systems.

10 The political and economic logic of integration
The convergence policies of the EU

Framing the research question[1]

The notion of convergence and the empirical straggler effect, discussed in Chapter 2, means that less-developed economies with a certain level of modernization grow faster than developed economies. This effect is regularly found in cross-national samples and is, at least above a certain threshold of modernity, quite strong. In reflecting further on the economic consequences of the EU, I wish to focus in this chapter on the question: has EU membership accelerated economic convergence, i.e. have the less-developed members been able to catch up due to growth rates even higher than non-members with a comparable level of development? Two different arguments for an accelerated convergence effect due to membership are presented in this chapter. To decide empirically upon the question, again the classic comparative method is applied using the same sample of thirty-three countries as in the previous chapter and in Chapter 2, the non-EU member states in the sample acting as a benchmark.

With regard to the EEC and later EU, we more closely analyse one of those policy fields which influence the parameters for national economies at the supranational level, namely the regional, structural and cohesion policy. The transformation of these, and other, policy fields since the 1980s have been mentioned in the two preceding chapters and the details have been published elsewhere (see Bornschier 2000b).

As discussed in Chapter 9, the creation of the internal market and the technology policy within the EU have been imitated in the course of time by other integration projects and state initiatives within the political world economy. Yet, concerning regional, structural and cohesion policy, the efforts of the EU are actually quite unique, since – as we mentioned already briefly before – they are measures for balancing wealth between countries which formally remain sovereign states. More efforts have been made towards equalization within nation-states (e.g. between the US states or regions in Japan), but this is irrelevant to our comparison of sovereign nation-states. However, a different problem arises in analysing the convergence efforts of the EU. The economic convergence effect among different societies has been solidly established empirically, at least for more-developed countries, and proves to be quite strong in this context. Therefore, whether the effort the EU has made is justified by an even stronger convergence process than could have been expected otherwise is both a pertinent research issue and one which is unique to the EU.

The first section of this chapter presents two competing arguments, and the second section depicts an overview of the history of EU cohesion policy. In the third section, the new data my co-researchers and I collected is introduced. The fourth section starts with a replication of the earlier finding of a stronger convergence effect for EU member states and then expands the analysis to clarify the question of whether EU membership accelerates convergence through market access or through redistribution measures, or both. Finally, in the fifth section, we discuss the results and draw conclusions from the evidence we have so far. There I also wish to draw attention to the implications of our findings for late development beyond Western European integration.

Theoretical considerations

Why should member states benefit from integration and experience faster convergence? The economic logic of European integration is broadly debated. However, while the political logic – even though economically motivated – is just as relevant, it has hardly been discussed so far. The question is approached by referring to the 'EEC' as the new formation in Europe called itself for a long time.

The Community as an exchange system – an asymmetric surrender of individual power

Community is an important element in economic life, even in modern times. Like all other forms of exchange (anonymous market, bargaining market, organization), the association as a community is based on the surrender of valuable goods, possibilities or resources by members in order to achieve a benefit (Bornschier 1994). The giving of individual resources in reciprocal exchange (be it an association of individuals, firms, or societies) is the price of increasing the possibilities of the community as a whole. The main objective of such an exchange system lies in achieving or enhancing solidarity as a collective good. The aim is to be more effective in confronting competing actors in the external exchange system, or to have greater weight in determining the rules of the system, or both. Associations therefore build social power, which improves the competitiveness of the community. This power belongs to the collective and is rooted in solidarity. To achieve this goal of solidarity, the individually more powerful members of the association cannot fully deploy their power vis-à-vis the less powerful without threatening the cohesion of the community.

Therefore, the more powerful actors of the association have to donate potential individual power to other members of the association to participate in the increased solidarity. Although all association members benefit from this collective good, not all members pay the same amount for it. The benefits are the greatest for those members of the association who have the least individual power. The donation of possibilities and their redistribution within the association is the price of the collective good of solidarity and the cohesion of the community. Community as an exchange system is thus inherently a system with internal balancing transfers.

If this exchange system logic is applied to the European Community, then the redistributive character of political power at the supranational level is immediately apparent. Within the Community, and later in the Union, the smaller countries have always had a larger political weight, relative to their size, in all institutions of the Community. With the extension of the integration project, countries with lower levels of economic development joined, and consequently an economic balance had to be arrived at by transfers of resources. Advancing cohesion by means of an internal balance of finances within the community follows, thus, a political logic inherent to this exchange system. Of course, these politics within the association are also motivated economically, as mentioned above, but do not constitute economic action in a narrow or immediate sense.

These considerations suggest the stronger economic convergence of poorer community members as a consequence of the political logic expressed by an internal redistribution of economically useful means. Such a proposition can be confronted with the argument of the economic logic of faster convergence through market creation and expansion.

Market creation and market expansion in Europe

According to the economic theory of integration, the abolition of trade barriers and the expansion of markets result in a general increase in wealth. The arguments are as follows: market creation and expansion eliminates constraints that prevent enterprises from being as efficient as they could be and from employing their resources to the full. It establishes a more competitive environment which encourages them to exploit more opportunities. This leads to: a reduction in costs, due to a better exploitation of economies of scale associated with the size of production units and enterprises; to improved efficiency; to a rationalization of industrial structures, and to adjustments between industries on the basis of the play of comparative advantages. This in turn leads to an increase of the level of investment and consumption (economic gains of integration; Emerson *et al.* 1988; Molle 1991; Pelkmans 1997; Ziltener 2001). Therefore, the resulting economic growth rate will be above the growth rate which would be expected without, or with less, abolition of trade barriers and without market expansion.[2]

Here, I would like to draw attention again to the core argument of the previous chapter: unlike foreign trade (across national borders), a common market leads to increased profitability (in addition to the effects mentioned above) due to economies of common governance. Companies and consumers can sell and buy goods, invest or offer labour outside their own state, but within the common market, without the obstacle of different regulations or political structures. Members of European integration benefit from this advantage much more than non-members – even though the significance of foreign trade across national borders is the same – since about two-thirds of the foreign trade of EU states is within the EU.

The reason for accelerated convergence due to economic integration can be explained as follows. According to neo-classical theory, the law of decreasing marginal return on capital generally makes poorer countries, including closed national economies, grow faster than richer ones (Barro and Sala-i-Martin 1995). Furthermore, under certain conditions, international trade leads to convergence even without factor mobility (this follows from the Heckscher–Ohlin theorem in economic theory). Convergence, however, according to economic theory, is mainly propelled through the international mobility of capital and human resources, which are potentially larger due to integration and should thus strongly enhance convergence. This prediction is of special significance here. Integration theory describes these processes according to the following pattern:

> If wages are higher in the developed regions, labour will migrate to them from the less developed ones. Consequently, labour will become scarce in the latter and abundant in the former type of region, respectively, triggering an upward or downward movement of wages. On the other hand, if wages and the marginal product of capital are inversely correlated, capital will move to labour-intensive sectors in low-wage regions, diminishing the trend for labour to migrate outwards. Thus, economic growth would be faster in peripheral than in central regions, which would make for convergence.
>
> (Molle 1990: 177)

In sum, regional integration can theoretically lead to, or foster, convergence in two ways, through market integration and political regulation. The latter was described above as stemming from the community as an exchange system. It aims at balancing wealth so as to increase the solidarity of the association. This chapter seeks to examine whether more empirical evidence can be found for either of the two explanations.

In the following section we shall analyse the various measures of balancing wealth within the community and then view them within the broader framework of the history of Western European integration.

Cohesion policy during market integration

The process of the successive creation, deepening and expansion of the market has been overviewed in the previous chapter (see Box 9.1). Regarding an evaluation of possible economic effects, it becomes clear that market creation and expansion in Western Europe has not been the result of one or two 'big bangs' but a more or less continuous process of negotiation and implementation of trade liberalization. Market integration was consciously flanked by a series of measures to secure cohesion, to which we now come in detail; see Box 10.1 below.

Right from the beginning, i.e. even before the integration relaunch of the 1980s, European integration implicitly and explicitly politicized the question of cohesion within the community (Ziltener 2000b; cf. Anderson 1995; Borrás and Johansen 2001).

Structural Fund expenditure increased from 4.8 per cent of the EU budget in 1975 and 9.1 per cent in 1987 to 28 per cent in 1992. During the 1980/90s, several qualitative changes also took place, such as the anchoring of regional policy in the Treaty with the SEA and several important political reforms. This transformed the original *juste retour* transfer system between the nation-states into a European system of cohesion policy, which to a large extent is implemented according to supranationally defined criteria and goals. But the actual system still maintains a hybrid character. Following the Maastricht decisions, as much as 35 per cent of the Union's expenditure was reserved for regional policy in 1999. According to the *1st Report on Economic and Social Cohesion* (1983–93; European Commission 1996), the total sum of payments in the analysed period amounted to about 100 billion ECU.

'Cohesion' and 'convergence' undoubtedly belong to the ideological keywords of the European Community. This was not only rhetorical, as the total sum of payments mentioned earlier shows. The question is whether these measures also had an effect. The cross-national analysis later in the chapter will examine whether the convergence effect really was larger in the countries of the EU than would have been expected otherwise, and whether this convergence effect results from transfers or mainly from market liberalization. The efforts made to balance wealth, i.e. the accumulated cohesion payments to certain member states, as well as data on net transfers, are described next.

Transfers in the EU

Empirically evaluating transfers in the EU, there are two dimensions that have to be looked at: first, the net transfer flows between the member states and the EU institutions and, second, the payments from the EU to the member states as part of its regional, structural, and cohesion policies.[3] Therefore, my co-researchers and I gathered data for the twelve EU

Box 10.1 Regional, structural and cohesion policy

The ECSC Treaty of 1951 included financial resources for regions with problems resulting from economic structural change (transition aid). In the EEC Treaty of 1957, regional policy appears in different contexts. Cohesion as a political goal was included in the preamble (the member states were 'anxious to strengthen the unity of their economies and to ensure their harmonious development by reducing the differences existing between the various regions and the backwardness of less favoured regions'). However, no EC policies have been developed to achieve this goal; there was a large trust in the market mechanism itself.

The funds which were established with the Treaty of Rome had a regional policy dimension right from the beginning: the European Agricultural Guidance and Guarantee Fund (EAGGF), established in 1962, provided resources for the modernization of rural areas. The European Investment Bank (EIG) issued loans and guarantees to finance investment projects which contributed to the goal of 'harmonious development'. In fact these were mainly infrastructural projects. As a bank, the EIB applies the usual economic lending guidelines. The European Social Fund (ESF) was founded in 1960 to finance resettlement and retraining measures for workers and was increasingly turned into an instrument of European employment policy. The establishment of a European Regional Development Fund (ERDF) was part of a package deal which included the first EC enlargement round (Denmark, Great Britain and Ireland) as well as the project of a monetary union. The monetary union project, which was decided upon in 1969, was only possible with compensatory payments. In particular Italy, which repeatedly applied the instrument of realigning parties to strengthen the competitiveness of its export industries, asked for such payments. A pressure group with the accession countries Great Britain and Ireland as well as Italy was formed in alliance with the supranational actors which had significantly different motives behind the demand for compensatory payments. At the Paris summit in 1972 the ERDF, whose goal was the elimination of structural and regional imbalances within the Community, was established. Shortly afterwards, the EC was severely shaken by the oil crisis and the recession that followed. The monetary union project vanished without trace in the wakes of this anti-crisis strategies of the individual states. The planned regional fund did not fall victim to the crisis; it was introduced on 1 January 1975. With the fixed distribution ratio, the principle of the *juste retour* (fair return) was adhered to, that is, the claim of the member states to a balanced relationship between payments and receipts, and not a regional policy based on superordinate criteria. A coordination of the national regional policies was not intended, nor was there any anchoring of Community regional policy in the treaties.

With the EC's southern enlargement in the 1980s, a further extension of the Community's regional policy was to be expected. Using the term 'cohesion', the Commission suggested an ambitious package of social regional policy measures at the intergovernmental conference in 1985, with varying success in different sectors (cf. Ziltener 2000a). This resulted in Art. 23 of the SEA (Art. 130 a–e of the EC Treaty). This explicitly anchored regional policy in the Treaty, making it an integral part of Community policy. Art. 130a includes a general aim according to which the EC develops its policy to strengthen economic and social cohesion and continues to promote a harmonious development of the Community as a whole. This is effected by the specified aim of decreasing the gap between the regions and lag of the least-developed regions. The first Delors Package in 1988 fulfilled the SEA's 'promises' of regional policy within a complex package solution of financial policies (doubling the regional policy payments until 1993).

The Community's structural policy had five main goals according to a reform effected on 1 January 1989:

1   Aid of regions with a development backlog (action goals of ERDF, ESF, EAGGF). Such a backlog is determined if the region's GDP per capita amounts to no more than 75% of the Community average. The aim of the intervention is the development of the region's potential through investment aid, creation or modernization of infrastructure, etc. Four-fifths of the ERDF means is assigned to these regions. Of the means which were to be applied according to this goal until 1993, 16% were granted to regions in Greece, 33% in Spain, 25% in Italy, 18% in Portugal, and 6% in Ireland.
2   Transition of regions which were severely affected by regressive industrial development (ERDF, ESF goal). This is determined if industrial employment is significantly declining and unemployment is above EC average.
3   Reduction of long-term unemployment, especially the unemployment of youth.
4   Assistance for the adaptation of workers to industrial change (both goals of ESF).
5   Accelerated adjustment of agricultural structures and development of rural areas (EAGGF goals). The necessary conditions are a high proportion of agricultural employees within total regional employment, a low income level in agricultural and also a total regional production below average.

At the Maastricht summit in 1991, the peripheral countries linked their demand of increasing adjustment and compensation payments to their acceptance of the Monetary Union. A new fund was established, the Cohesion Fund (since 1993) for member states whose GDP per capita amounted to less than 90% of the EU average, This not only contributes to half (maximum of 75% in Goal 1 regions) of the finances for investments, as in the case of the Regional Fund, but can provide up to 90% (sectors: environment, infrastructure). The budget decisions necessary to realize the Maastricht decisions were enacted in December 1992 as the Delors II Package. As a result of the negotiations with the EFTA states, a sixth goal was added, namely to develop regions with a very low population density (<8 inhabitants per square km). Such regions in Scandinavia are treated as Goal 1 regions.

The step-by-step expansion of regional policy had its effect in the Community budget: Structural Fund expenditure increased from 4.8% of the budget in 1975 and 9.1% in 1987 to 28% in 1992. Following the Maastricht decisions, as much as 35% of Community expenditure was reserved for regional policy in 1999. According to the *1st Report on Economic and Social Cohesion* (1983–93), the total sum of payments in the analysed period amounts to about 100 billion ECU. For the four ex-EFTA countries, 5.9 billion ECU were projected in 1995–9.

member states from 1986–93 (published in detail in Bornschier, Herkenrath and Ziltener 2001, 2003), which include:

- total EU payments to its member states;
- total member state payments to the EU (agricultural levies, custom duties, VAT equities, financial contributions of member states);
- net position of member states (total EU payments to member states minus member state payments to the EU);
- EU regional, structural and cohesion policies: EU payments to member states (payments of the EAGGF guidance section, regional and social funds, without the payments of the EAGGF guarantee section, without the reimbursement of levying costs of equities and other payments), in absolute figures (million Deutsche Mark, DM) per year and accumulated over the period under consideration (1986–93); for instance, Belgium received structural payments amounting to 260 000 000 DM in 1986, which means 26.37 DM per capita.

Two new variables were created based on this data:

- EU structural policy payments to member states, i.e. EU payments to member states (payments of the EAGGF guidance section, regional

and social funds, without the payments of the EAGGF guarantee section, without the reimbursement of levying costs of equities and other payments, accumulated 1986–93, per capita).
- EU net position i.e. total EU payments to member states minus member state payments to the EU, accumulated 1986–93, per capita.

Figure 10.1 shows that the recipient countries of payments from the structural fund are also those countries with a positive net balance for all transfers. The correlation of 0.91 (84 per cent of variance in common, see Figure 10.1) implies that the two variables, EU net transfers 1986–93 and EU structural policy transfers 1986–93, cannot be simultaneously included in a multiple regression model. Since structural policy transfers conceptually describe redistribution according to the level of development more accurately, we need to rely primarily on this variable.

As Figure 10.2 shows, structural policy transfers are actually transferred to the poorer EU member states. However, Ireland receives more structural fund payments in relation to its wealth than the lesser developed members Greece and Portugal.

Testing the hypotheses

The empirical work on the economic benefits of EU membership in this chapter is a replication and an extension of previous results, the bulk of

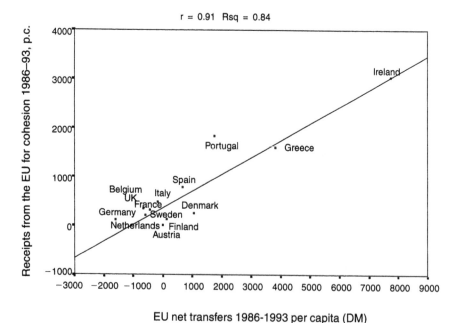

Figure 10.1 EU net transfers and cohesion payments.

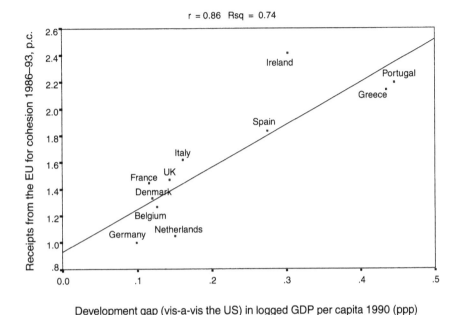

Figure 10.2 EU development gap and cohesion payments.

which were reported in the previous chapter. Therefore we can go directly to the results which are summarized in Table 10.1 and which will be explained in the text.

In the first two columns of Table 10.1, my earlier findings, presented in the previous chapter, are reproduced. All predictor variables and the sample of thirty-three cases are as introduced in the previous chapter, except that now the two additional variables are considered which are explained above, EU transfers and EU net position.[4]

Column 1 in Table 10.1 replicates the results of the former study (Born-schier 2001), which were mentioned in the previous chapter. They can be summarized as follows. The convergence effect, which has already been analysed intensively and proven to be quite stable (e.g. Bornschier 1989, 1996, 2000; Barro and Sala-i-Martin 1995; Weede 1996; World Bank 1998: 198), turns out to be the most important factor for the explanation of economic growth in our model. Its contribution to economic growth is even slightly larger than the effect of capital growth. Growth of manpower shows a significant coefficient, controlling for the other growth factors. Technology capital also seems to have a substantial effect on the dependent variable. Furthermore, the growth enhancing contribution of social capital, measured with our index Trust & Tolerance 1981/90 (see Chapter 2), proves to be significant once more. The effect of the variable 'quality of

Table 10.1 Predicting economic growth 1980–98: the basic model from Chapter 9 and its (non-additive) extensions with new variables

Predictors	(1)	(2)	(3)	(4)	(5)	(6)
Growth of physical capital stock	0.70** (8.48)	0.69** (8.92)	0.67** (8.91)	0.68** (9.09)	0.67** (9.31)	0.72** (9.00)
Growth of manpower	0.34* (2.30)	0.37* (2.67)	0.34* (2.44)	0.33* (2.49)	0.32* (2.89)	0.11 (1.14)
Convergence (low level of development)	0.81** (5.42)	0.69** (4.54)	0.70** (4.72)	0.71** (5.10)	0.71** (5.32)	0.63** (4.16)
Technology capital	0.51** (3.37)	0.43** (2.97)	0.41** (2.88)	0.41** (2.97)	0.41** (3.22)	0.35** (2.49)
Quality of mass education	0.08 (0.88)	0.14 (1.53)	0.15† (1.75)	0.15† (1.77)	0.15† (1.90)	0.06 (0.73)
Social capital (Trust & Tolerance)	0.38** (4.30)	0.35** (4.07)	0.36** (4.31)	0.37** (4.58)	0.37** (4.72)	0.30** (3.43)
EU years	0.30** (2.68)	0.11 (0.80)	0.01 (0.10)	0.01 (0.10)	–	–
Convergence* EU years	–	0.25* (2.12)	0.04 (0.24)	–	–	–
EU transfers	–	–	0.28 (1.42)	0.32* (2.63)	0.33** (4.05)	–
EU net position	–	–	–	–	–	0.21** (3.09)
R-square, corrected	0.86**	0.88**	0.88**	0.89**	0.89**	0.87**

Notes
Dependent variable: economic growth 1980 to the end of 1998;
N = 33;
OLS-estimates, columns 1–6 refer to six different models that were estimated.
Relative importance of predictors (beta-weights) shown as well as statistical confidence levels t-values in brackets.
** p < 0.01;
* p < 0.05;
† p < 0,1).

education' is slightly positive, but statistically insignificant. This might be due to the fact that five of the thirty-three values had to be estimated. Yet the variable that is of particular relevance to our research is EU years, i.e. the indicator of membership in supranational European integration we dealt with in the previous chapter.[5]

Compared to the effects shown by the other predictors in the model, the direct effect of EU membership on economic growth from 1980 until 1998 is relatively small (beta 0.30 at the most, see column 1 in Table 10.1). It is, nevertheless, highly significant and discussed in detail in the previous chapter. In addition, the effect remains constant even if the operational definition of EU membership is modified (i.e. if the new members of the expansion round in 1995 – Finland, Austria and Sweden – are coded as having the same values as non-members on this variable). As mentioned in the previous chapter, the positive direct growth effect of membership in the EU must be offset against possible indirect effects, however. I shall refer to this problem again below.

Accelerated convergence due to EU membership?

The main concern of this chapter is to study the process of convergence in more detail. European integration involved the question of cohesion within the Community/Union as a central political problem right from the beginning, i.e. even before its new departure in the 1980s. Initially, measures based upon the common agricultural policy constituted the main means of limiting the gap between incomes in the agricultural sector and developing industrial society (Rieger 1996). Later, particularly in the 1980s, new policies were added, and the respective financial measures were introduced; the EC funds have been described in Box 10.1 and the corresponding transfers were collected for the years 1986–93. Yet, the question as to whether these measures were successful remains unanswered. Was the process of convergence among the members of the European Union faster than could have been expected in countries not belonging to the community?

In order to give an answer to this question, my former study (Bornschier 2001) introduced a statistical interaction into the growth equation used here. This test is reproduced here, adding the interaction term 'EU years*convergence' to the growth model presented in Table 10.1. As indicated in column 2, the statistically significant interaction found earlier can be replicated. The existence of a significant interaction effect leads to the following conclusion: the process of convergence was faster and more notable among EU members than among other nations of the sample of thirty-three cases. Less developed EU members caught up faster than other poor countries. This finding of a significant effect pertains to the whole time period under study here, 1980–98.

As it has already mentioned, there are two competing explanations that could account for the accelerated convergence among EU members found in the original study and in our replication. On the one hand, faster convergence could be a result of the internal market from which the less-developed EU member countries benefited. On the other hand, it could also result from the transfers flowing to these countries. Both hypotheses seem plausible.

However, the two explanations are not necessarily mutually exclusive; indeed, they may be complementary. The faster convergence of the poorer EU countries, which are also characterized by relatively high agricultural production, could be the result of both politically motivated transfers (Common Agricultural Policy, cohesion, structural and regional funds) and the effects of extended market access. If this were the case, then the interaction shown in column 2 of Table 10.1 would become less significant if one considered the structural policy transfers as an additional predictor. If the interaction disappeared altogether, this would mean that the accelerated growth of poorer EU members (relative to non-members as a benchmark) was exclusively caused by redistribution measures.

In column 3 of Table 10.1, where the structural policy transfers have been included in the model, the interaction term is no longer statistically significant. As shown in column 4, the variable termed EU transfers exhibits a highly significant effect, and turns out to be an even better predictor than the former variable EU years, when the insignificant predictors are excluded from the equation (see column 5).

The interpretation of these results is straightforward: the ability of the less developed EU members to grow faster than non-members can be attributed exclusively to transfer payments. This finding supports our argument regarding the political logic of Western European integration. The fact that the payments indicated by our variable EU transfers actually flow towards the poorer EU countries becomes evident in our graphical analysis; see Figures 10.1 and 10.2.

The existence of a direct positive contribution of EU membership to economic growth, indicated in column 1 of Table 10.1, can be reinterpreted in the light of these new results. It is not EU membership per se that leads to the increased growth of EU countries. Rather, the poorer member states benefit from growth impulses that are created by convergence policy measures. Hence, the benefits of EU membership are distributed asymmetrically: the poorer member states are profiting, and the richer states, insofar as they are net payers within the EU, are financing that additional growth. In column 6 of Table 10.1, the net position is introduced as a predictor of growth, and the result clearly shows that net recipients enjoyed a growth benefit.

Discussion

According to the statistical findings presented in this and the previous chapter, EU membership actually does influence economic performance. The effect, however, seems to stem exclusively from the politically motivated transfer payments that are related to membership. Thus, only the group of relatively backward members can extract an economic profit from membership. While the countries of this group exhibit higher growth rates than other developing countries outside the EU, European integration has been unable to improve the economic performance of wealthier member states. Apart from the influence of transfer payments, there is no purely economic effect of integration on growth. The popular contention that European integration should lead to enhanced growth perspectives in all the participating countries has to be questioned.

Yet, having proposed this rather strong statement, some important issues remain to be addressed. For instance, the research design that underlies our results could be accused of not sufficiently considering the economic logic of integration. Economists usually conceive of market creation and amplification as creating important indirect effects on growth, with capital formation acting as the intermediate variable. Accordingly, one of the most powerful reasons for creating the Single Market was that some important investment, particularly investment in research-intensive areas such as the chemical industry, is not profitable except for big markets. Hence, the models presented in Table 10.1, which treat capital formation as a control variable that is held constant, somewhat underrepresent the economic theory of integration.

Thus, we need to turn again to the question of whether EU membership affects capital formation: do member countries actually accumulate more capital than others do, as is predicted by economic integration theory?[6] Although there is not much empirical literature on this issue, some preliminary answers can be found. Earlier research (Bornschier 2001: Table 4), mentioned in the previous chapter, concludes that EU membership has had a negative effect on capital growth. That study, however, is restricted to the years 1985–93, i.e. a relatively short period after the initiation of the Single Market project in 1986. The less than average capital formation observed by my earlier analysis could thus be interpreted as a short-term reaction to the creation of a common market. Since mergers and acquisitions were usually followed by the elimination of overlapping activities, the unification of formerly autonomous markets most probably resulted in the destruction of capital. Unfortunately, due to a lack of appropriate measures of capital stocks for the years after 1993, my preliminary tests do not allow any insights into the long-term effects of the Single Market project. However, in the meantime Gehrig and Gmünder (2000) have computed new capital stock estimates for the years 1994, 1995 and 1996 (and, in some cases, even for 1997–2000). Although these estimates still do not permit an assessment of long-term processes, at least they enable us to analyse short-term and medium-term effects separately. These additional results have been documented elsewhere (Bornschier, Herkenrath, and Ziltener 2001, 2003: 151ff.) and we here restrict ourselves to the presentation of an overview and conclusions.

The negative effect of EU membership on capital formation found so far also appears when the period under study is expanded to a maximum of years (1982–96). Comparing the results for 1982–9 with the ones for 1990–6 reveals that, in both sub-periods, the regression coefficients indicate a significant negative effect of EU membership on the accumulation of capital stocks. Even from 1990–6, growth of capital is slower in EU member countries than in comparable cases. If the Common Market has initiated what might be termed a cleansing process, then this process must have lasted much longer than expected. However, the negative coefficient turns out to be smaller in the period 1990–6 than in 1982–9, lending some support to the idea that the unwanted slowdown of capital accumulation will be reversed in the long run.

Finally, then, the economic arguments presented by many advocates of regional integration find virtually no support in the results of our tests. Capital stock growth that could act as an intermediate variable in the supposedly positive effect of integration on economic performance is actually found to be influenced negatively. Thus, the above-mentioned lack of any significant effect of EU membership on economic growth, which becomes apparent as soon as the influence of transfer payments is controlled for, is not just a statistical artefact, nor is it the result of an insufficient consideration of economic logic.

Summary and implications

Our earlier cross-national work, which contrasted members of the EU with a comparable set of other countries as benchmark, suggested that membership was beneficial for economic growth and may cause the faster economic convergence of less wealthy EU member states. Employing a newly collected data set on inter-state transfers in the EU, it was tested whether this faster economic convergence is due to access to the internal market (the proposition of economic logic) or rather a consequence of special forms of inter-state redistribution within the EU (the proposition of political logic).

According to the results reported in this chapter, the direct positive effect of EU membership on economic growth found in my previous analyses and in the previous chapter is more precisely explained by transfer payments than by EU membership years. In short, if EU countries grew faster in the 1980s and 1990s, this was mainly due to transfers within the community, and these benefit the poorer EU countries.

The beneficiary countries of the EU transfers are relatively smaller, and thus the question arises as to whether the taxes paid by the bigger and richer countries in order to fund these transfers did not create a loss for the EU taken as a whole. However, the net effect for the entire EU has to be clarified in another study. Of course, this will need a different methodology, since the regression techniques applied so far automatically attribute the same weight to each EU country – independent of its size.

The policies of cohesion and convergence, which have received a lot of attention within the Union, did not just have the character of wishful thinking, nor did they serve only as ideological cement. Due to the large amount of transfer payments that were made in order to implement these policies, EU membership actually did lead to faster convergence among member states. In the period from 1980 until 1998, the poorer EU members did indeed grow faster than comparable countries outside the Union.

This has a far-reaching significance for the possible convergence of new EU members in Central and Eastern Europe which joined the union in 2004. Social, regional and cohesion assistance will be, it now appears, less generous than in the past enlargements. The EU is not planning to increase the spending ratio for regional policy beyond the current figure of 35 per cent of its total spending, and the contributions of the newcomers to the EU budget will be rather small. Thus, an only 'slightly bigger cake' (Delhey 2001) has to be distributed among a significantly larger number of less-developed regions. However, the main recipient countries of the EU with fifteen member states seem to be unwilling to accept a cutback in their assistance. Delhey (2001) is probably right in arguing that the outbreak of the conflict over distribution will put an enormous pressure on the enlargement process; moreover, its result will determine the prospects for the convergence of the new EU members.

Our hypothesis regarding community logic, on which the EU is based, implies that solidarity has a price. This price has to be paid by the richer and bigger countries. According to a narrow economic calculation of costs and benefits, the advantages and disadvantages of members due to the transfer system should match in the aggregate. From a political point of view, however, this need not necessarily be the case. Solidarity based on cohesion is a valuable good, since it improves the bargaining position of the EU as well as its impact on defining regulation in the world political economy, and, last but not least, in creating a peace zone in Europe. Thus, such advantages may well be weighted more than the short-term economic price of achieving solidarity.

Implication for late development in world society

To what extent might the EU policy of cohesion be a model for late development in world society? Supranational integration can add to faster convergence, the catching up of the poor countries of world society. In this project, however, one cannot trust the consequences of market mechanisms; the political sphere must be called upon to bring this about by effective transfers from rich to poor. Transnational corporations, in the case of Western Europe, pushed integration in the 1980s (see Chapter 8) but they themselves did not manage the faster equilibration of prosperity which was found in this chapter. This was the political project of the supranational actors.

PART IV

Persisting differences and the change in the societal model

Societies at a roughly similar level of economic development differ in political style as well as in terms of culture, both at the level of individuals and as manifested in their institutional practices. Will such differences in the developed world – sometimes quite considerable in extent – vanish in the course of time as standard convergence arguments would say, or will they persist? If so, why? This is a very interesting question for our evolution theory. As a test, I consider the change in political styles as represented by different degrees of negotiated capitalism over the 1960–95 period. Such an analysis is pertinent to the claim of a general restructuring of the state in the era of economic globalization. We will conclude that differences between varieties of capitalism not only persist but that there tends to have emerged an even stronger polarization in the developed world during the last decades. Thus the two theses on the state–economy relationship under the aegis of economic globalization, i.e. the 'thesis of erosion' and the 'thesis of compensation', need to be reflected upon again. Both seem to receive some empirical support, depending, however, on different trajectories of political development.

I conclude the book with a chapter on the difficulties of the transition from the Keynesian societal model to the new societal model of the extended market sphere in the telematics era. Why is this transition so difficult and why does it take so much time? How has social change been brought about for different groups of developed countries and what role has the EU played in that change in Western Europe? Do the different patterns of economic growth in the 1990s make sense in the light of the theory of discontinuous change that is applied? This chapter fits together several arguments and findings which have accumulated throughout the book.

11 The persistence of varieties of capitalism in rich democracies

Remarks on varieties and overview

My use of the term 'varieties of capitalism' does not put 'capitalism' in plural. I agree with the classic position[1] – from Karl Marx, Max Weber and Werner Sombart to Karl Polanyi and Joseph Schumpeter – that capitalism in both its sociological and economic meaning is one system with the whole earth as its stage, as Schumpeter (1939, II: 666) once put it. Yet, it is also clear that capitalism does not exist without a state. The very fact that many states exist means that the economic and the political spheres are necessarily linked and form what I call the world political economy. My world market for protection and social order argument (see pp. 6–7 and 159–62) suggests that in this competitive setting political and economic entrepreneurs have to bargain to come to terms. Governments, which can be viewed as political businesses, produce 'order' and sell this public utility to capitalist enterprises as well as to citizens under their rule. By means of supplying this utility, governments affect the quality of their territory in the framework of the world political economy. This makes for the possibility that the whole set of institutional arrangements, be it at the level of the nation-states or unions of states (like the EU), differs. This is what the study of comparative capitalism is about. It cannot be the task of this introduction to overview these comparative studies of capitalism, but let me inform the reader that there are three main directions so far which the analysis of this quality of institutional sets took.

There are first the 'Three Worlds of Welfare Capitalism' introduced by Gøsta Esping-Andersen's (1990) influential work, later detailed, for example, by Robert Goodin et al. (1999). The focus is here on the value of equality and the wellbeing of people. The distinction between a 'socialist welfare regime', a 'liberal welfare regime' and a 'conservative welfare regime' in rich democracies reveals in detailed single-case analysis over time by Goodin et al. (1999: 259ff.) that in all three regimes government is a 'force for good', albeit the 'social democratic welfare regime turns out to be the best choice'. The original classification of the eighteen developed democracies suggested by Esping-Anderson (1990, see also his later work:

1999) was: Liberal (USA, Canada, Australia, Japan, Switzerland), Social Democratic (Norway, Sweden, Denmark, Finland, the Netherlands), Conservative (Italy, France, Belgium, Austria, Germany), Not Classified (Ireland, New Zealand, UK). As the reader notices, there is an overlapping with our three basic types from Chapter 7: high degrees of negotiated capitalism (corresponding with Esping-Andersen's social democratic welfare regime), a low degree of negotiated capitalism without Anglo-Saxon cultural heritage (considerable overlapping with his conservative category), and a low degree of negotiated capialism with the presence of Anglo-Saxon cultural heritage (somewhat overlapping with his liberal category). I cannot go into details here, but let me add that in Hicks and Kenworthy's (2003) recent 'Varieties of Welfare Capitalism' the original dimensions of Esping-Andersen are put into question, and Esping-Andersen (2003) seems to agree in his reply to some of the objections. The dispute is whether 'liberal' and 'social democratic' are two dimensions or one, where the role of political parties is the distinguishing factor, running from liberal (low strength of the left) to progressive liberal (high strength). This brings us to the second, political, classification.

The classification of varieties of capitalism from a political point of view has been introduced in detail in Chapter 7 on political styles, and I can, therefore, be brief here. The focus is on conflict resolution – in political decision-making and taking into account the degree of inclusion in that – be it in the broader understanding of politics, as in the rich literature on democratic corporatism, or in the narrower field of politics, as indicated by Lijphart's distinction between consensus democracy and rule of majority democracy. We overviewed that and pointed to the considerable overlapping between both political scales. As the reader will remember, we used Hicks and Kenworthy's 1998 scale based on cooperative economic institutions to achieve our measure of degree of negotiated capitalism, and this measure corresponds to a very high degree with the democratic corporatism measures suggested so far in the literature (see Figure 7.1). To this distinction we added the Anglo-Saxon cultural heritage variable which, however, clearly separates the group of low negotiated capitalism into two: with and without Anglo-Saxon cultural heritage.

Finally, there is the study of the variety of clusters of competitive advantages of institutional settings in what I call the world market for protection and social order. Here the focus is on efficiency and the performance of the economy, although I stress the role of legitimacy which is in my view the ultimate source of competitive edge. Furthermore, beside the people, firms and states enter (see above and also Chapter 8).[2] The general model and exemplifications with detailed single case studies (Japan in comparison with the Atlantic West) was first introduced in Bornschier (1988, see also the later extended editions). This 'Regulatory Impact of the World Market' argument (for the historical roots of the idea, see 1996: Chapter 3) is also present in Michael Porter's (1990) seminal work on 'The

Competitive Advantage of Nations'. Recently Peter Hall and David Soskice (2001) have started to participate in this kind of analysis.[3] In their widely praised work (which they modestly call work in progress) they, too, call into question the simple assumption that world economic integration will force institutions and regulatory regimes to converge on a common model. This is, as I argued earlier (1988), because diverse sets of institutional arrangements with their historically grown complementarities may deliver the sources of competiveness to a similar extent – if they are functionally equivalent. Only if they are clearly superior will they become a standard on which societies converge in the longer run, and if such institutional settings are not competitive, they will hardly last for long.

In their classification of twenty-two cases (from the OECD world) Hall and Soskice (2001: 19f.) build on the not so new distinction between 'liberal market economies' (they list six Anglo-Saxon cases, i.e. exactly the same six we label as cases with Anglo-Saxon cultural heritage) and 'coordinated market economies' (ten cases on their list which also figure on all standard lists of democratic corporatism, and indeed on my list of medium to high degrees of negotiated capitalism, too). In addition they report six 'more ambiguous positions' (France, Italy, Spain, Portugal, Greece and Turkey, which are all on my list of low negotiated capitalism without Anglo-Saxon cultural heritage, except for Turkey which we do not consider in our study). Beside the conceptual gap in classifying the Mediterranean cases, there is another shortcoming, since Hall and Soskice do not consider the new rich democracies in East Asia, Korea and Taiwan, which we will include in this chapter alongside with Japan. Certainly, Japan, Korea and Taiwan represent cases of negotiated capitalism, but it is less the industry-level coordination as in the Atlantic West that counts there, and more the firm group-based coordination, i.e. the *Keiretsus* in Japan, the *Chaebols* in Korea and the extended family clans in Taiwan.

After these remarks on the notion of variety and influential classifications in the literature let me explain the plan of this chapter. First, we investigate in more detail the main differences between rich democracies regarding the political and cultural spheres. While these societies have all achieved a high level of material wealth (most of them long since, the rest over the last quarter of a century) and can be considered to have become at least recently democratic, there are significant political differences within democracy as a political form; the type of the states and their political styles differ significantly. As we will see in this chapter, these differences have become not less but rather more pronounced over the last two decades. One obvious reason for that increased diversity is European unification, which has added a new state form to the old ones and made the once dominant nation-state almost obsolete. The impact of European unification on political styles is less clear. While there exist arguments that unification should have an effect, cross-national evidence is, thus far, lacking. I here report such an investigation. Data that inform us about the change of political styles over the 1960–95 period have become available only recently. They show that, while there is hardly any general trend, there is an obviously increased difference between Anglo-Saxon capitalism and the rest.

Beside differences in political style, we will observe differences in the cultural sphere beyond political culture as manifested in state structures and political styles. Such differences pertain especially to the cultural resource of generalized trust, which I have addressed several times in this book. A combined classification of rich democracies according to political styles and to the proliferation of generalized trust among the citizens results in a rather clear grouping of five cultural patterns: the Anglo-Saxon, the Latino–Mediterranean European, the East-Asian, the Middle–West European, and the Northern–Scandinavian European. These five cultural clusters also differ in several other aspects, but not in all. This is then an indication that culture differs in many respects, but that very little of that diversity may be important for studies of economic sociology.

After we have elaborated somewhat on these cultural clusters we come to the issue of change over time. The available data on cultural change is not yet enough to draw sensible conclusions, but the data on change in political styles allows firmer conclusions. Therefore, we concentrate on that in our analysis. We need to theoretically explain our findings from that analysis by looking more closely at the accomplishments of different political styles regarding economic development. We very briefly summarize the findings accumulated in the literature and relate these to social evolution theory. Our conclusion from the findings will be that the main lines of differentiation with regard to political styles have remarkably resisted the political changes, consequent upon technological revolution and increased economic globalization, which have been heralded. This then suggests that we need to reflect afresh on the opposing propositions concerning changes in the political sphere as a consequence of greater transborder openness of economies.

The findings in this chapter have implications for the changes in the societal model which has been going on for two decades. We discuss this in the final chapter: how have different political styles managed that transition so far? I will suggest in the concluding chapter that the EU has had a decisive influence on the ability of the majority of rich democracies to continue.

New and persistent distinguishing characteristics between rich democracies

Configurations of the state

Since I have addressed the remarkable development of European integration in the last three chapters, we will start with the consequence of this for state configurations in rich democracies. The striking differences between rich democracies are represented by at least three groups: united states, union of nations and nation-states. All three forms are important insofar as considerable portions of the population of developed Western society are citizens of one of these three state types. The smallest proportion of the population of rich democracies is by now the one living in nation-states, which, however, was once the prevailing form. Since the EU was established, this union of nations has become, for the largest single group of the total population, the supreme form of statehood, as the following summary compilation indicates.

In 1992 when the internal market programme of the EU was accomplished, the distribution of populations was as follows:

	In millions	
United states	310	(of which the *USA* 255)
Union of nations	370	(*EU* of 15 members)
Nation-states	193	(of which *Japan* 125)

Note that the populations of countries have been assigned to one of the three groups according to the characteristics of the highest level of statehood. Thus the members of the EU are assigned to that goup. Almost all rich democracies can be assigned to one of the three types. Difficulties might only arise in assigning Switzerland and Canada to the group of united states, because both cases mix core elements of united states with one of union of nations. New Zealand has not been classified.

United states

These are characterized by strong federal elements. Historically they have all, more or less, been immigration countries, the majority of them built by settlers of mainly European extraction. They are characterized by a dual culture; the hegemonic culture, as expressed in language, coexists with explicitly tolerated cultural diversity. The following countries belong to this group: the United States of America, the Commonwealth of Australia, Canada (borderline case because of two official languages and privileges of 'nations'), Switzerland (again a borderline case because of four official languages and privileges of 'nations'). One half of the cases is characterized by the peculiarity of not having their own heads of state; the English monarch functions as such in Australia and Canada.

Union of nations

A union of nations with, in many respects, equal rights not only shows pronounced federal aspects but acknowledges cultural segmentation (as evidenced, for example, by the equal rights of languages within the Union). At present, there exists only one case: the EU, with a total of fifteen nation-states in 2003; ten candidates joined in 2004, and many further applicants await. Within the Union, the single nation-states may exhibit variable degrees of a plurality of cultures, but this is mainly due to immigration from outside the Union. Thus, for instance, Spaniards normally live in Spain and do not constitute a substantial minority in any of the member states of the Union. The EU does not regard itself as a classical immigration area although it has become one, not least for demographic reasons. And this unexpected and swift change is also true and experienced in formerly traditional emigration countries, such as Italy, Spain, and Ireland.

Nation-states.

This classical state form, which was most fully developed during the nineteenth century, currently coincides with centralistic state authority and a strong myth of a common ethnic origin, and the latter seems to be more or less true for those cases that have been left in this group, and all tend to be comparatively reluctant to admit immigrants. The following countries belong to this group: Japan, South Korea, Taiwan (although differences exist between mainland and island Chinese), Norway, Iceland.

The listing by population shows that the once dominant nation-state is somewhat in retreat. Nowadays, the main form is represented by the EU, which has emerged only recently and represents, as was the nation-state, a European innovation. Will the EU become a 'United States of Europe'? I have recently argued in my concluding chapter of *State-building in Europe* that this will not be the case for a long time to come. The European state project rests, and needs to rest, on the acknowledgement of its constituent nations, which have developed in the course of its history. There is simply not enough support among the citizens to proceed to a 'united states' model. Furthermore, the imitation of European innovation is not likely to diffuse soon, since NAFTA (the EU's North American counterpart) will long remain merely a free trade association. Finally, the diffusion of the European model through enlargement has natural limits, as indicated by the first letter in the acronym EU.

Therefore, for the foreseeable future, three different state forms will coexist in rich democracies. There also seems to be no economic force that favours any one model, since that would provide a competitive edge for economic development. Our comparative results on the growth contribution of EU membership showed that the positive effect of EU membership does not pertain to the union as a whole but has spurred the growth of less-developed members as a consequence of redistribution; you will recall that the effect for technological development was found to be neutral (see Chapters 9 and 10).

So far we have discussed the new, and probably persisting, political differences between rich democracies. What about the older differentiations of political styles in rich democracies? Will they persist? Before we come to the latter question I would like to elaborate on these differences and their links with other elements of culture.

Political styles in rich democracies

We find different political styles in two of the political forms mentioned in the first part of this chapter, i.e. in the group of federal states as well as in the federation of the (then) fifteen nations of the EU. Only in the group of nation-states is the variation of political styles small, ranging from medium to high negotiated capitalism. The European Union as a whole is a case of negotiated capitalism or of consensus democracy as Lijphart (1999) puts it.

The differences in political styles of single countries go together with notable differences in societal characteristics which I started to analyse in Chapter 7. Before I continue with these structural characteristics, after the section that investigates whether the styles have actually changed over time, I would like now to point to some very interesting relationships between political styles and cultural patterns.

Let us start with Figure 11.1, which plots the empirical observations for the degree of negotiated capitalism with the observed proliferation of generalized trust (see also Chapter 7 for background).

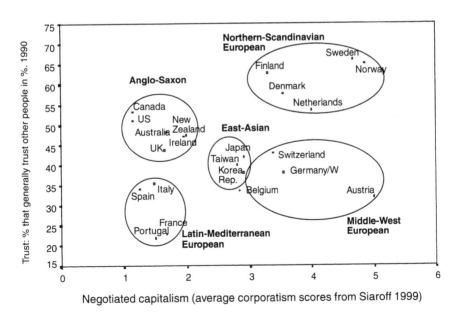

Figure 11.1 Varieties of capitalism and trust.

Figure 11.1 allows us to distinguish five cultural patterns into which rich democracies can be classified:

1   The Anglo-Saxon cultural pattern, which combines low values for negotiated capitalism with slightly above-average levels of trust. The six cases are: Canada, United States, Australia, New Zealand, Ireland and the United Kingdom.
2   The Northern–Scandinavian cultural pattern. The Netherlands tends in many other respects to cluster together with this group and not with the Middle–Western cluster. The five cases are: Sweden, Norway, Finland, Denmark and the Netherlands.
3   The Middle–West European cultural pattern, which is the one that shows the greatest dispersion of the values displayed in Figure 11.1 and represented by four cases: Switzerland, Germany (values for West G.), Belgium and Austria.
4   The Latino–Mediterranean cultural pattern, with four cases: Italy, Spain, France and Portugal.
5   The East Asian cultural pattern, represented in Figure 11.1 by three cases: Japan, South Korea and Taiwan

These five cultural patterns differ not only with regard to political culture but also by the cultural resource of generalized trust. Generalized trust is a core element in a much broader cluster of moral standards, which was analysed in Chapter 4. These cultural attitudes were called 'liberal individualism' and 'amoral egoism', and the various items used to establish these factors were presented in Chapter 4. At the individual data level as well as when one compares average values for societies, trust goes together with high values for liberal individualism and low values for amoral egoism. There exists, then, a large group of moral standards that are clearly linked to the culture of trust. The configuration of the five groups in Figure 11.1 would look very similar if one included the numerous items on moral standards which are part of the factors 'liberal individualism' and the civil virtues represented in 'absence of amoral egoism.'

In Figure 11.2 below I add further cultural attitudes so as to compare their distribution across the five clusters. This is not intended to be an exhaustive list of cultural matters, though they cover, together with the many items merged to liberal individualism and amoral egoism, a considerable portion of the cultural spectrum. Rather, I wish to demonstrate that in some respects cultures differ considerably, in others less. More specifically, I am interested in the differences and similarities between the cultural groupings that follow from those cultural differences which are the main interest of this book, political styles and trust. One can distinguish between three types of variables on the basis of how they cluster with political style and trust.

First, there are cultural variables that clearly distinguish the five groups

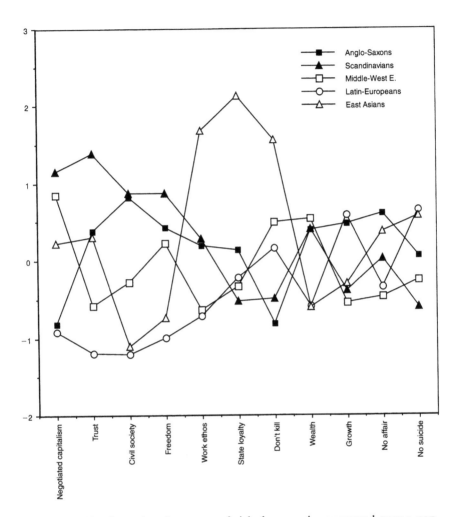

Figure 11.2 The five cultural patterns of rich democracies compared over a non-exhaustive field of cultural characteristics and material level of development.

of rich democracies. The differences between the groups are pronounced and are clearly greater than between societies within that group (the latter is not displayed). These are:

- negotiated capitalism (see also Chapter 7),
- trust (and liberal individualism and absence of amoral egoism, as discussed above and in Chapter 4),
- culture of a rich civil society (see also Chapter 7),
- freedom preferred to social equality (introduced in Chapter 7).

A second type of cultural variable distinguishes only between part of the five groups; more precisely, it is the East Asian cultural pattern that deviates from the rest, i.e. the societies of the Atlantic West. The questions from the *World Values Survey* 1990, on which these figures are based, are in an endnote.[4] These are:

- work ethos (importance of work in life),
- loyalty towards the state (as measured by honesty in paying taxes),
- killing taboo (which may also grasp some aspect of a conflict taboo).

A third type of variable shows that the differences between the five groups are comparatively small as compared to differences between societies of the same group (I give an example in endnote 2). The three cultural attitudes which are taken as examples are supplemented by a structural variable measuring average material wealth (indicated by per capita economic product corrected for purchasing power parities):

- average wealth
- importance of the goal of economic development
- moral standards, two examples:
  - Married person having an affair, never justified
  - Suicide, never justified

In order to be able to fully grasp the information condensed in Figure 11.2, one should add the following. A sample of twenty-three countries is used (in some comparisons a case may be lacking due to missing data). The values for the different indicators have been standardized (technically: z-standardization). This is easy to understand since it has the convenient consequence of making variables comparable: the mean value for all countries on a variable is assigned the value 0, a country with, for instance, one standard deviation above the mean is given the value 1, and another example country having an observed value one standard deviation below the mean is awarded the value −1. Then the standardized values for individual societies are averaged for each of the five groups (see classification in Figure 11.1). If there were no differences between the five groups of countries, they would all have the value zero (indicating that means for the five groups would not differ between the five groups). Clearly, this is far from the case in Figure 11.2.

Figure 11.2 shows that the degree of differences between groups differs. Take, for example, trust. The range of the means for the five groups differs by slightly more than two and a half points on the vertical scale (indicating standard deviations), whereas the emphasis on the goal of maintaining a high level of economic growth differs at the maximum in a range of only one point (or one standard deviation) on the scale. A last note: when differences between the five groups of countries are small, this by no means implies that there are no differences between the twenty-three rich democracies, but simply expresses the fact that such differences do not cluster according to the five cultural patterns. Let me point to an example for the latter before we discuss the findings in Figure 11.2. One of the cultural indicators where we observe little dispersion according to the five cultural groups is the moral standard of having an affair when being married. At the same time, there are amazing differences between societies, but this pertains to societies in all five cultural groups.[5] This example then shows that for several cultural attitudes the differences are low between the five groups but quite large within these groupings.

Let us now continue with some considerations of the first class of differences, which include negotiated capitalism, trust and the complex of attitudes of 'liberal individualism' and of absence of 'amoral egoism' which are closely related to trust (not in Figure 11.2 but mentioned above and in Chapter 4).

The richness of civil society and generalized trust correlate very highly, as mentioned in Chapter 7; this corresponds to arguments in the literature. The five cultural patterns could also be established by plotting negotiated capitalism against richness of civil society instead of trust (as was done in Figure 11.1). Figure 11.2 demonstrates this and shows that Anglo-Saxons and Latino-Europeans, although both living in societies with little negotiated capitalism, differ greatly with respect to civil society (networking beyond the family and the work sphere). The Anglo-Saxons are very high on that civil society index and only marginally surpassed by the Scandinavians (the Netherlands included). East Asians are also very low on this indicator, like the Latino-Europeans.

We observe a similar pattern for the relative importance of freedom. Remember the question from Chapter 7: 'Both freedom and equality are important, but if I were to choose one or the other, I would consider personal freedom more important, that is, everyone can live in freedom and develop without hindrance.' Anglo-Saxons, and even more the Scandinavians, opt for freedom, while Latino-Europeans and East Asians tend not to.

In the foregoing it has been established that East Asians do not differ from citizens in all societies of the Atlantic West; they share a relatively lower attachment of significance to freedom and to civil society (replaced instead by a greater importance of family relationships and, in the case of Asia, also workplace relationships) with Latino-Europeans. The people in these two groups of countries do not, of course, live like monads. This finding simply reflects the fact that the bonds of family and workplace relations (the latter especially important in East Asia) substitute for those of civil society.

What is it, then, that makes a cultural difference between the old or Atlantic West and the 'new West' of the East Asians? These are the cultural items that are indicated in Figure 11.2: work ethos, loyalty vis-à-vis the state, and the killing taboo, which is very strong among East Asians even in the case of an imagined situation of self-defence (for the indicator questions, see endnote 1). The proverbial industry of East Asians is not merely a common stereotype; it is also reflected in their answers to the question in the interview about whether one thinks that the decrease in the importance of work is a good thing. Furthermore, they are much more loyal to the state, as indicated by our indicator question: 'Cheating on tax if you have a chance'; 'Never justified', answer considerably more citizens in East Asia than in any of the cultural groups of the Atlantic West, which only mildly differ among each other. Finally, there is the remarkable difference in responses regarding the killing taboo. This may also be extended in interpretation by suggesting that it may express to some extent the aversion to express conflict, reflecting a greater need for harmony. This search for harmony is well established in the literature on Japanese culture.

Loyalty towards the state may have long standing cultural roots in some Asian societies, but it seems also to reflect the very important role that the state had in organizing the extremely successful late development of, first, Japan, and then Korea and Taiwan. Without a strong leading role on the part of the state, together with a loyal citizenry, this would have been simply impossible. There exists no single example of successful late development that contradicts this claim. Thus, East Asian rich democracies are not merely geographically separated from the Atlantic West. While there are a couple of distinctions that really do not completely distinguish them from all other cultural patterns also present in the old West (the role of civil society, relatively less importance attached to freedom, medium values of negotiated capitalism), these three issues make a telling difference.

Regarding loyalty towards the state, one may guess that the rich East Asian democracies might be well equipped for a new round in international competition, wherein a proactive 'Schumpeterian competitive state' is becoming more important, one that provides targets of where to go as well as the means of accomplishing the journey, such as focusing on education and technology development. In this respect, the societies of the Atlantic West may have somewhat converged to the East Asian pattern, and may well do so more. The supranational technology policy in Europe which was addressed in Chapter 8 is a case in point; I mentioned there that the Japanese experiences were a clear point of reference for the reformers.

So much for the differences. Figure 11.2 also considers examples of little diversity between the five cultural groups. By 1990 the differences in average wealth between the five cultural groupings had become rather small. Certainly, East Asian societies like Korea and Taiwan were still somewhat behind, like Portugal and Spain in the group of Latino-Europeans, but these differences are less spectacular than the huge ones we have addressed so far. Furthermore, economic growth is a goal held in common by citizens in all rich democracies. Answers to this issue ('Maintaining a high level of economic growth, is this an important goal?') may differ from society to society to some extent and are probably less affirmative when post-materialism is widespread, but the different answers do not significantly cluster with the five cultural groups. At least it is interesting that the somewhat still poorer Latino-Europeans, together with the largely quite rich Anglo-Saxons, have the strongest support for the goal of economic growth in common.

Finally, I added to Figure 11.2 two cultural standards which are examples of comparatively little difference. The one was taken as an example already earlier, the stance on having an affair while being married (see endnote 4 for the details), the other pertaining to the taboo against killing oneself. In both cases the cultural variation, which is there, does not cluster with the five groupings we considered in this section.

In short, culture in rich democracies remains diverse. Some aspects of it – but not all – are especially relevant to the questions of economic sociology regarding economic development. How do they change?

Cultural change: the case of political styles

It would be nice to have sufficient data to analyse how trust changes over time, but we do not have enough of that data at the moment. Among the twenty-three rich democracies studied so far in this chapter, there are only nine cases which were included in all three waves of the *World Values Surveys*, 1981, 1990, 1995, which is the data source for our measure of trust. These nine cases are far too few from which to draw conclusions over the 1981–95 period, given the sampling error implicit in surveys. The nine cases do not show any common pattern of change; some increase their level of trust (two cases) or increase it first to bring it back to the old level, or even lower (three cases), some are very stable, or at least over two points in time, then drop (three cases), and for only one case is a steady decline reported (one case). We simply have to wait for the next wave of the *World Values Survey*, expected to appear in 2004, to improve the data situation.

For political styles, and specifically the strong predictors of generalized trust that were established in Chapter 7, we have, however, data on the change between 1960–95 which has become available only recently. It was the admirable effort of Hicks and Kenworthy (1998) and Kenworthy and Hicks (2000) which provided this data. Their indicator of cooperative institutions at the macro-level which was used in Chapter 7 over the 1968–89 period to indicate negotiated capitalism (Hicks and Kenworthy 1998) has later been made available by the authors for five time periods between 1960–95, including eighteen rich democracies (Kenworthy and Hicks 2000: Table 1).[6] This is the data I consider here to evaluate the change in the degree of negotiated capitalism. This is a completely new step in research, since democratic corporatism, i.e. negotiated capitalism, which I use as the measure, has always been considered as a rather constant trait of developed political economies. Single cases and their shifts over time have certainly been discussed in the literature, and we will come to that later, but a systematic study of the change in the group of rich democracies has never been undertaken. Even Kenworthy and Hicks (2000), who provided this very valuable data, have not done such an analysis. Perhaps they will do so later, and so correct the shortcomings in my subsequent analysis.

Before we start, a remark seems appropriate. Political styles represent a set of institutions that are highly relevant for the political economy (see Chapter 7). To the extent that they deliver valuable inputs for economic development, they are sustainable; otherwise the selection mechanism of competition between social orders in the world political economy will force them, in the long run, to change. This follows from my social evolution approach outlined in Bornschier ([1988] 1996). Given the accomplishments of the different styles regarding the cultural resource of generalized trust, I rather expect these styles not to change very much. Yet, before we develop further our analysis of how that stability could actually be explained, let us deal with the facts of change.

Did political styles actually change from 1960–95?

Here we are not talking about the normative theories that are guidelines for the politico-economic regime. They have changed since the Keynesian era, and that has had consequences for the new configuration of what the state is thought to have to do in order to support the economy. This change is quite obvious and I demonstrated that in the case of the reconfiguration of European integration in Chapter 8. What we analyse here are the different political styles that are applied in pursuing this new configuration of targets and priorities. So we come to the next questions: did the styles change over the period 1960–95? If so, to what extent and into what direction? Afterwards, possible explanations and implications will be discussed.

Figure 11.3 presents a graphical plot of the scores for negotiated capitalism, also referred to as neocorporatism, over five time periods between 1960–95, provided by Kenworthy and Hicks (2000: Table 1). In Chapter 7 the scores for 1968–89 from Hicks and Kenworthy (1998) were taken as our indicator for negotiated capitalism, and we do the same here, except for the fact that now a look at change over time in this variable is the topic.

Over the 1960–95 period, we observe a comparatively stable pattern in Figure 11.3. We find the smallest correlation of scores for different periods between 1968–73 and 1990–5, with a still extremely high correlation coefficient of $r = 0.96$. Between 1960–7 and the heyday of the Keynesian societal model, 1968–73, there is almost no change in scores at all, except for the fact that two cases even increased their level of negotiated capitalism slightly (France and Finland).

Having said this about a quite stable overall pattern, one needs to add that there is one very noteworthy movement. All cases that ranked comparatively low on negotiated capitalism during the heyday of the Keynesian era (1960–73) have quite uniformly decreased their already low level even further; see Figure 11.3. Note that all these cases are Anglo-Saxons. On middle and high levels of negotiated capitalism, the changes are more

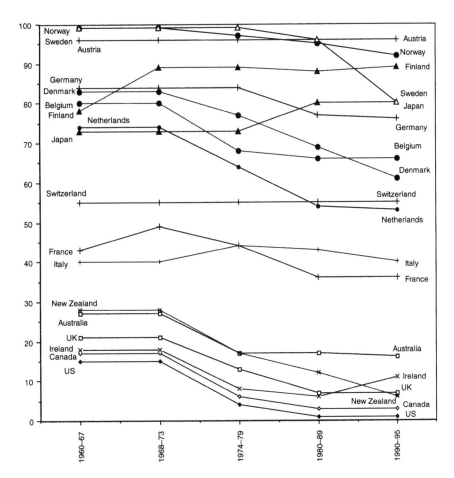

Figure 11.3 Negotiated capitalism 1960–95 for eighteen rich democracies.

Notes
The measure is the neocorporatism scores of Kenworthy and Hicks 2000: Table 1. See note 6 for the source on Internet. Further details on the descriptive statistics for the eighteen observations over five periods between 1960–95 are given in Table 11.1. Note that the scores for the eighteen societies in different time periods correlate very highly, the smallest being r = 0.96.

complex. One finds constancy (for example Switzerland, Austria, Italy) as well as decrease (for example the Netherlands, Belgium, Sweden) and increase (Japan, Finland).

Overall, despite considerable constancy between 1960–73, there is a slight decrease in average scores for negotiated capitalism, which are shown together with other statistics in Table 11.1. Note that together with the somewhat decreasing average values, the dispersion of the values around the mean increases (as evidenced by the coefficient of variation: standard deviation in relation to the mean).

We come to our initial conclusions. Yes, negotiated capitalism in rich democracies analysed over the 1960–95 period changed after the golden era of Keynesianism, i.e. since 1973, but the overall change was small. What is more important is the direction of change and whether it was the same for all rich democracies; this was not the case. For one thing, in all Anglo-Saxon societies the earlier low level of negotiated capitalism declined even further on that index. The development for the other cases, however, is mixed with a very mild overall decrease.

In Table 11.2 the values measured in 1990–95 are expressed as a percentage of the values of 1968–73, and the findings are astonishing. In

Table 11.1 Averages and other descriptive statistics for negotiated capitalism, 1960–95, eighteen rich democracies

Period	Mean	Standard deviation	Coefficient of variation	Range	Minimum	Maximum
1960–7	0.57	0.31	0.55	0.84	0.15	0.99
1968–73	0.58	0.31	0.54	0.84	0.15	0.99
1974–9	0.53	0.35	0.65	0.95	0.04	0.99
1980–9	0.50	0.35	0.71	0.95	0.01	0.96
1990–5	0.48	0.34	0.71	0.95	0.01	0.96

Source: The measure used for this computation is the neocorporatism scores of Kenworthy and Hicks 2000: Table 1 (see also Hicks and Kenworthy 1998 as well as the Internet source given in endnote 6).

Table 11.2 Change of negotiated capitalism in two groups of the eighteen cases. Average values for change expressed by the ratio, i.e. values for 1990–5 divided by those for 1968–73, times 100

	Ratio as a measure of change (%)
The 6 Anglo-Saxon cases	33
All other (12) rich democracies	90
All 18 cases	71

Notes
A country has the value 100 when its level of negotiated capitalism is the same in 1990–5 and 1968–93, the heyday of the Keynesian societal model. The figures listed are averages for the groups indicated.

Anglo-Saxon societies, on the average only 33 per cent of their earlier level of negotiated capitalism was left by the early 1990s; the other twelve rich democracies come out with 90 per cent of their earlier level.

Thus, what we can say is that over the last decades rich democracies have not become more alike with regard to political styles, but more dissimilar. The earlier split between negotiated capitalism and the Anglo-Saxon way of running a political economy has widened. There is, then, no common pattern in the change of political styles.

How can we explain the pattern of change in negotiated capitalism over time?

After looking at the actual pattern of change, this question seems less thrilling than might have been thought. There is, certainly, one explaining factor of pre-eminence, belonging to the group of Anglo-Saxon societies. In addition, I want to investigate whether that is due to hegemony, a structural position in the world system, or rather culturally rooted. Furthermore I wish to investigate whether one can generalize from the proposition regarding the impact of Western European integration on the political styles in member states.

The hegemonic position of a state in the world system implies that the dominant power can structure external matters by its sheer weight and leadership, while smaller powers have to adapt to external circumstances. In order to do so better, small powers tend to develop strategies for closing ranks internally so as to increase internal legitimacy, to be stronger against the rest of the world. This tends to be reflected – inter alia – in a well-organized mediation of interests through associations, initiated and coordinated by the state; this is called neocorporatism or democratic corporatism in the literature and I term it, as discussed in Chapter 7, negotiated capitalism. Small and rich democracies which belong neither to a powerful politico-military pact (e.g. NATO) nor to an economic treaty system (e.g. European integration) are under particular pressure, because they cannot take part as junior partners in the power of blocs in the world political economy. This is why membership in the EU might affect the political style. This will be elaborated further below.

In contrast, a hegemonic position tempts elites to neglect the domestic legitimacy on which initial success on their way to the top rested. Therefore, hegemons, or dominant powers, can be less expected to maintain negotiated forms of capitalism that restrict economic elites. The hegemons of the industrial era have been Anglo-Saxon countries, Britain in the nineteenth century, and the US in the twentieth century. We will explore whether this structural position of a hegemon (and the historical residuum in the case of Britain) is a factor that adds to an explanation of the decrease in negotiated capitalism in the case of Anglo-Saxon cultural heritage.

Single cases of a decrease in negotiated capitalism have been discussed, especially the Netherlands (see Ritter 1989: 168; Bornschier 1996: 292ff.; Wilensky 2002: 114f) and Sweden (Wilensky 2002: 110ff.). In both cases, the decrease discussed in the literature is also evidenced in our Figure 11.3. This change, however, did not make either cases new members of the Anglo-Saxon variant of capitalism. Wilensky (2002: 14) summarizes for Sweden: 'Despite undergoing the most change of all corporatist democracies, relative to the least-corporatist democracies Sweden's consensual style is still evident.' And, with respect to the Netherlands, he states (p. 115) that there are:

> signs of continuing consensual bargaining ... Despite some erosion of formal bargaining structures, as in Sweden, both informal and formal interaction among social partners persists. The celebrated Dutch civility is very much alive; a high level of trust prevails; pragmatic accommodations are the continuing custom.

What are the reasons for some change in former top scorers on the scale of negotiated capitalism? Earlier I suggested that it might be European integration, and we will test whether that proposition, deduced from the single case of the Netherlands, also holds in general. The argument was as follows (Bornschier 1996: 294). In observing in the shift of earlier excellent conflict management in the Netherlands I argued:

> The Netherlands was one of the founding members of the European Community (1957). Due to the European integration process and the shift of power from the capitals to the institutions in Brussels, Luxembourg and Strasbourg, the relevance of the national framework diminished for economic actors. Over time, the parent organizations of employers and workers which had been guided by national economic policy distanced themselves from them progressively to join the European parent organizations with their European goals. The result was a dismantling of neocorporatist and social partnership institutions, applying primarily to the Netherlands, because the other strongly neocorporatist countries are to date not members of the EC or became members long after the Netherlands.
>
> (Denmark in 1974)

The consequences for Dutch conflict management have been observed by Gerhard Ritter (1989: 169) who, however, does not mention EC integration as a possible explanation:

> In central institutions in which employers' and the employees' bodies were represented either alone or together with persons designated by the government, legislation regarding government economic and social

policy was substantially influenced and in 1964 a central wage policy was agreed upon. Then, and particularly since the wave of unofficial strikes in September 1970, the system of labour relations in The Netherlands has changed toward a withdrawal of the state from wage policy and a more pronounced polarization of the relationships between employers and labour unions. Thus, the Dutch system more closely came to resemble those of most Western and Central European countries.

(my translation)

We will then test whether EU membership has in general been a cause for weakening negotiated capitalism at the national level, and this will be evaluated together with the proposition of the impact of the structural position of a hegemon. I have elaborated these considerations a bit more than would otherwise have been necessary to demonstrate that not all plausible arguments find empirical support in cross-national designs. The test itself is presented in some detail for these pedagogical reasons. Many times in this book we have found empirical support for our arguments. This is not always the case, actually it is more frequent than the reader may imagine, simply because no-findings are seldom published.

Actually, we do not find any, or sufficient, empirical support for factors explaining the shift towards less negotiated capitalism other than for the single factor that really counts: Anglo-Saxon cultural heritage. Hegemonic position, whether past or present, does not matter. Membership of the EU has a small effect which is, however, less than convincing in statistical terms. The results are displayed in Table 11.3.[7] Note that 'ratio' indicating stability is high if there is no or little change in the degree of negotiated capitalism. In Table 11.3, a negative coefficient of a predictor then indicates that it reduces stability or, in other words, makes for less negotiated capitalism in the 1990s as compared to the late 1960s and early 1970s.

Comments on the results in Table 11.3

1   EU membership is hardly significant and becomes completely insignificant if level of wealth is not included in the model. Wealth also becomes insignificant if the EU variable is not included. Therefore, the only robust and highly substantial predictor of little stability in negotiated capitalism is, in fact, Anglo-Saxon cultural heritage; see also the telling figures in Table 11.2.

2   Anglo-Saxon cultural heritage and low initial level of negotiated capitalism go closely together (see also Figure 11.1). Therefore, one could argue that it was not Anglo-Saxon culture as such but the low institutionalization of negotiated capitalism that was adverse for its survival. Our finding that the initial level becomes insignificant once Anglo-Saxon cultural heritage is in the model rather speaks for the importance of the Anglo-Saxon variable.

Table 11.3 Explaining the stability of negotiated capitalism up to 1995 for eighteen rich democracies. The variable 'ratio' (see Table 11.2) is the dependent; the predictors are explained in endnote 7. Relative importance of predictors of the stability of negotiated capitalism (beta-weight in the multiple regression). Final cleared up estimations after the insignificant predictors were removed

Predictors	*Beta-coefficients and significance*
Anglo-Saxon cultural heritage	−0.94***
Hegemonic position actual and once	not signifcant
EU membership weighted for years	−0.23*
Openness, trade as a share in GDP	not significant
Wealth per capita, 1990	−0.28**
Initial level of negotiated capitalism	not significant
Total explanation	
R-squared (corrected)	0.78***

Notes
*   symbolizes a statistically barely trustworthy result (probability of error of only about 10 per cent in the above case);
**   means a statistically satisfying effect (probability of error below 5 per cent);
*** indicates that the result is very convincing statistically (error probability below 1 per cent).

3   It was also tested what happens when change is measured differently, as in the difference in scores of neocorporatism instead of 'ratio'. Even then, Anglo-Saxon culture is by far the most important predictor of decrease. EU membership is somewhat more substantial for decrease. The initial level of negotiated capitalism enters with a small negative contribution on stability. This would then mean that Anglo-Saxon culture was very adverse to stability. On high levels of negotiated capitalism, there was a tendency to reduce somewhat that high level, and EU members tended to reduce the previous level to some extent, too. As compared to the model listed in Table 11.3, however, the total explanation for this alternative measure of change is, however, very small (R-squared 0.21). One should therefore prefer the model specification as displayed in Table 11.3.

I mentioned why I dwelled a bit more on these tests. The reader should take one basic message after these considerations of possibilities: 73 per cent of all measured changes in negotiated capitalism can be associated with the single variable Anglo-Saxon cultural heritage. The other effects are not substantial; EU membership and wealth account together only for another 5 per cent.

Why do styles change comparatively little?

The results are obvious. Except for Anglo-Saxon societies, there has been little change in negotiated capitalism. How does social evolution theory account for this stability? First of all, there is an inherent tendency in culture to remain stable. This resistance to change will be a topic of the concluding chapter.

But a cultural practice will change in the end, if the forces bearing on it are strong enough. Where do such forces come from? In my theory of evolutionary change, which I mentioned only briefly at the beginning of this chapter, such forces also come from the competition of social orders in the world political economy.[8] This competition enforces convergence of the accomplishments of different social orders. The pressure for convergence, in other words, does not act on the arrangements of institutions as such but on their outcomes relevant for competition in the world political economy.

Therefore, institutional arrangements, for example, pronounced negotiated capitalism, will be stable not only through inertia but because they deliver crucial inputs to the political economy; these must be competitive in the long run. Whatever they do, if the outcomes meet the benchmark in international competition, the culture embodied in the political style will most probably survive for quite a while; if not, it will not.

The question of the survival of the cultural pattern of negotiated capitalism is then translated to one of competitiveness. There exists an impressive body of literature available on the economic merits of democratic corporatism, recently overviewed by Harold Wilensky (2002: 430–93), who himself contributed to the field. The conclusion is obvious. Neocorporatist or democratic corporatist systems, which I call negotiated capitalism, were an important source of good economic performance over the last decades (Wilensky 2002: 482). Such bargaining arrangements did more for the people, especially for those represented in, and admitted to, the power cartel. This is evidenced by lower inequality, not only due to redistribution but also due to the fact that strong federations of labour unions are part of the power cartel and put a brake on wage differentials. And, most importantly, this advantage (for the people) is not traded off against lower economic growth in the long run. Negotiated capitalism is neutral with regard to economic growth.[9] For evidence regarding such a view, see Hicks and Kenworthy (1998) and Wilensky (2002).

Such is the knowledge accumulated from studies that, in part, go back quite a while in time. In more recent times everything is different, one could argue. There are plenty of arguments in the media as well as on the side of concerned liberals or social democrats why that should now be different; mostly they cluster around the spectre of globalization.

Kenworthy and Hicks (2000) have the first empirically based answers. This is because they have made negotiated capitalism a variable over time and can therefore pool different periods in what have been termed panel designs. With such a design you can reveal whether the effect of a variable has changed over time. For a broad time spectrum between 1960–98, they test the effects of negotiated capitalism (which they term neocorporatism) They find two things that are relevant here: (a) that the positive effect of negotiated capitalism on social security spending did not change in the 1990s; and (b) that the absent effect of negotiated capitalism on economic growth also holds for the 1990s.

Let us conclude. Political styles are associated with different societal characteristics (see also Chapter 7), but they do not result in different economic growth rates over time. This consensus from the literature is supported by our findings in this book. We find both Anglo-Saxon cultural heritage as well as more negotiated forms of capitalism associated with the cultural resource of generalized trust (Chapter 7). Trust is, next to the classic factors of production, a source that makes for faster economic growth (Chapter 2). This makes it likely that the two contrasted political styles – negotiated capitalism versus Anglo-Saxon capitalism – do not differ in long term economic growth. The prediction for the least negotiated capitalist systems not of Anglo-Saxon cultural origin is different. They have less favourable long-term growth prospects. But for quite some time this will become less visible – and therefore be of little political relevance – since they take advantage of the still strong straggler effect and from the transfers they get from the EU. This will help to keep growth above their predicted lower long term steady growth level for quite a while.

The same applies to the second component of economic development, i.e. techno-economic change, on which future growth will be based. Remember that the accomplishments of the Anglo-Saxons and those high on negotiated capitalism are similar with regard to trust. Furthermore, we found that trust is a very forceful predictor of early adoption of Internet usage (Chapter 3) and also helps to foster innovation in general (Chapter 4). Thus, political styles act indirectly on economic change via their positive influence on the level of trust. When we add the political style variables to the predictors of technological change (as in Chapter 3), they have no effect once trust is included as a predictor. I have done this, but think it is better not to bore the reader with an additional table. For the third group, those being low on negotiated capitalism but not Anglo-Saxons, the conclusions are similar to the ones for economic growth.

So, the implication of our findings, in terms of social evolution theory that can account for what we find, is that differentiation according to political styles will persist.

Implications for the state–economy relationship

Some comments on the implications for the debate on the state–economy relationship are warranted. Much has been said about the inevitable change of this relationship since the collapse of the once hegemonic Keynesian doctrine and the increasing openness of societies to transborder exchange (often imprecisely termed globalization). Concerning the politico-cultural trait of political styles, much has been exaggerated and falsely generalized. We draw this insight from our analysis, which revealed – with one exception – a remarkable stability of negotiated capitalism. Outside the Anglo-Saxon world, this established pattern of consensus seeking politics bolstered by social security still plays an important role and is not in retreat as critics have thought and liberals and social democrats have feared.

The arguments of an inevitable erosion of the state's capacity to regulate, on the one hand and, on the other, the argument of increasing state action as a complement to openness may turn out to be overgeneralizations which need to be freshly thought over in the light of persisting differences in political styles.[10] I broadly agree with Neil Fligstein, who speaks of 'Globalization and Neo-liberalism as an American project' in his critical analysis (2000: 373) of the falsely assumed and generalized consequences of globalization. But I would add that this mushroomed in the whole Anglo-Saxon world, for historical reasons that I touched on in Chapter 7. Globalization has not produced a new capitalism; instead it has accentuated again the older split in the realms of capitalism. Anglo-Saxon societies have, in a way, moved back to their roots, since capitalism there has always been less mediated and more competitive – maybe for a while the Keynesian era pushed them nearer to the world of capitalism practised elsewhere.

Political styles in democracies and, therefore, the worlds of capitalism, differ. That sounds a bit paradoxical in times when everything is global and thought to become therefore alike. But these differences are real, not virtual like many things in the new economy, and likely to persist. Since different political styles respond in different ways, we wonder how they have managed one of the epochal changes in recent decades, the move towards the new societal model. This societal model has not yet received a palatable label. I still need to give it, therefore, a complicated name: the extended market sphere in the telematics era. This is simply the social world in which we have been living since the mid-1990s.

12 Transition towards the new societal model

Framing the Question[1]

Before concluding this book I would like to venture one last question. This relates to what can be called the big changes, not the ones we continuously experience over time, but the transition to a new societal model that significantly modifies social life. One hardly needs to have read my thesis of discontinuous social change, i.e. that developed Western societies renew their structures in a cyclical way,[2] to notice that, since the 1970s, signs of change have been unmistakable. They first became apparent in the realm of technology, increasingly accentuated in the course of the 1980s, then in the political spheres, both at the level of individual states and in their new relationships among each other in economic matters. This is manifested both in the surge of European integration since the mid-1980s and in the remarkable renewal of international institutions, most obvious in the case of the remodelled GATT regime in the new World Trade Organization, when the major powers struck a hitherto unexpected bargain in 1993 in Marrakesh.

Supranational political entrepreneurs, for example Europe's Commission, not only observed the early signs of this transition but were also the all-important protagonists who brought technology, economy and the state together in a new configuration. I discussed this in Chapter 8, on the renewal of Western European integration. The example shows that the transition to a new societal model involves the coming together of three spheres: new normative theories, a new technological style and a new politico-economic regulatory regime.

So far the model seems straightforward and quite simple, despite the amazingly long period this transition takes. In terms of economic growth, the transition is manifested in a downswing phase of the long economic waves, of a duration between forty-five and sixty years, called Kondratiev cycles. The long upswing and the golden era of the postwar Keynesian societal model before is evidenced by the data on economic growth presented in Chapter 1. The growth rate between 1950–72 was almost double the size of the one in the long downswing from 1973–92. Only after 1992 did growth again start to have a long-term rising trend. We will return to this issue at the end of this chapter.

The question can then be stated in the following way: why was there such a long period of decay of the old order? Or, to put it another way, why do modern societies not learn continuously? They are thought of as highly differentiated, and this should enable them to adapt continuously to new situations. In seeking answers, we will build on the two complexes which have been the central themes of this book: culture and politics. The rather simple way of looking at the mechanics of discontinuous social change that are suggested by the current development of our models needs to be enriched by a consideration of the cultural resources of citizens and societies. We will show that political styles interacted with new political forms in a very interesting way, i.e. that the latter ultimately made the change for most of the rich countries possible. Therefore, quite a bit of what we have discussed in this book collocates in this chapter.

We proceed as follows. First, we address general reasons why societies are rather reluctant to embrace fundamental change. But we will also see that this applies in widely differing degrees to different societies, depending on their culture. Then, we briefly discuss the reasons for this, inherent in the dynamics of technological style and its embeddedness in the whole society. Distinct spheres of society can thus be thought of as being open to change to different extents. The political sphere is often most reluctant towards fundamental change, due to the circumstances inherent in collective action in democracies. Following this exposition we explicitly introduce our three variables: generalized trust, political styles and the new political form at the supranational level. This suggests a ranking of societies regarding their differential progress in the transition process. Since this should be reflected in different levels of economic growth, as explained in the introductory chapter (pp. 23–8), we can look at the data when asking whether the economic growth patterns of different groups of countries since the 1990s actually support this thesis.

In the conclusion, on our efforts to extend the model of difficult and therefore long-term social transition, we briefly mention a peculiarity of the present transition that makes it more difficult as compared to an earlier great transition, i.e. that from agrarian to industrial society.

The inertia of societies

Considerations in general

Why do surges in innovation occur in the techno-economic and the politico-institutional spheres? One possible answer is that societal power, intended to cope with uncertainty, hinders innovation.

Let us try to understand social relationships as attempts to come to terms with uncertainty. Society can then be thought of as a kind of problem-solving community[3] whose task it is to provide security in a physical sense (safety and ensuring basic needs) as well as security for action, i.e. the meeting of expectations. Such functions are reflected and institutionalized in a sanctioning apparatus that punishes wrong and rewards correct behaviour, in a production apparatus that regulates how things are to be done, and in outlooks that define the perception of the social world. A common understanding of the world is made possible by encompassing and binding conceptions.

This is what a societal model does, and some sort of an umbrella for that is provided by the hegemonic normative theories. By way of a system of institutional routines, a societal model meets expectations and regulates action. Societal routines relating to how the world is seen – normative theories – and how it is engaged – technological style and politico-economic regime – constitute societal power to cope with uncertainty. Although such power favours certain groups, it is not the attribute of any particular group or person. Why, then, is social power so persistent?

The persistence of societal power can be explained by applying conflict theory as well as learning theory. Conflict theory would have it that as certain actors are privileged by societal power, they develop a vested interest in maintaining the existing order. They combat opposing interests and do not react innovatively or invent novel situations within the framework of a given politico-economic regime. This argument can be extended by distinguishing, for example, between two further types of interest: interest in the distribution of material wealth and interest in different conceptions of the world.

Learning theory at a macro level stresses the more abstract conflict between meeting expectations and autonomy of action. Thus, societal institutionalization of power is greatest if no alternative possibilities of action exist at all, because then the meeting of expectations is at its maximum. There is, thus, an exchange relationship between meeting expectations and alternative action possibilities. In this perspective the routinization of institutions and conceptions of the world create maximum certainty, yet at the cost of restricting alternative actions (see also Giesen 1980: 96).

Societal power, rooted in a societal model, resists change and alternatives because power stems precisely from restriction. For this reason, such power is simultaneously an advantage and a disadvantage. Societal power creates strong social cohesion – solidarity – and suppresses conflicts of interest. But, as Bernhard Giesen (1980: 99) has pointed out in another context, routines and a rigid conception of the world can lead to a crisis of interpretative knowledge. Only if the contradictions between conventionality and reality exceed a certain threshold does societal power enter a crisis and begin to dissolve.

The opposition of certainty and autonomy of action can also be put in terms of Schumpeter's notion of statics and dynamics in social life. In order to refute the critique of Schumpeter that statics are characterized solely by traditional behaviour and not by rationality, two kinds of rationality must be considered: (a) bounded, traditional rationality, which does include rational elements even though embedded within conventional wisdom and institutional routines representing social power; and (b) free rationality. As the latter's means and ends are not bound to conventional wisdom, it can radically open up new perspectives and future-oriented scenarios.

The implications for change

As mentioned, societal power may be both an advantage and a disadvantage, as it creates strong social cohesion and suppresses conflicts of interest. If it fulfils this function optimally, it is rather adverse for social change. But not all societies have an equal need to maximize the advantages of societal power in the medium run, which are traded-off against long-term problems of lower adaptability to the new.

In the competitive milieu of the world political economy, those societies with fewer power resources are forced more to maximize internal social power as a compensation for a relative lack of external power resources. Here one of our political style variables enters. The more pronounced forms of negotiated capitalism, characterized by consensus seeking and measures for the enhancement of internal cohesion, are a case in point. Therefore, one would expect that more pronounced systems of negotiated capitalism will tend to be laggards with regard to fundamental transition. However, this is only one social force at work. This political style is at the same time favourable to innovation due to the high level of generalized trust it supports, as evidenced in this book. But the very collective culture of consensus and cohesion puts a brake on this individual potential, so that it cannot be fully and effectively expressed in terms of collective action. We will come to this again later.

From the argument outlined above, one can develop the proposition that there are forces at work, stemming from the political style, that may retard the transition. Yet, this does not explain why it takes so long in general.

The dialectics of technological style development

Inherent in technological style development are brakes that hinder a smooth transition from the old to the new. I have mentioned the epochal contribution of Carlota Perez in developing our present understanding of discontinuous technological change (see Chapter 3). Let me briefly recapitulate. Carlota Perez designates two interrelated subsystems as follows. The techno-economic subsystem is characterized by faster adaptation due to the logic of more individualized choices, while the socio-institutional subsystem, based on the collective logic of political choices, is more conjunctive. Both the techno-economic and the socio-institutional subsystems need to adjust to each other during a long-term economic upswing, i.e. become matched. Thus, the adjustment of the socio-institutional subsystem is a necessary part of the evolution and diffusion of the new technological style. In Perez's understanding it is, however, not only the lagging support of the socio-institutional sphere that makes for the delay but a conflict between institutional orders, because even if advantages of the new style become obvious, it cannot come into effect immediately.

Let me add here a few remarks on the lack of coherence that is the main reason for the delay. This will also take into account the role of fascination necessary for the proliferation of the new. Before, let me briefly recapitulate the four phases in the evolution of a technological style (Bornschier [1988] 1996) by giving a periodization for the last cycle:

1   During the prosperity–recession phase (late 1960s and early 1970s) new elements of heterogeneity in the technological style appear as a consequences of basic innovations, their dissemination remaining restricted.
2   During the interim recovery phase (1980s), an accelerated unfolding and linkage of the new elements of the style takes place, but their diffusion remains restricted.
3   Full crystallization of the new style with an innovative range of products occurs only at the outset of the upswing phase (after 1992); old products are produced in a new way and new products emerge in large numbers. Still, the upswing only succeeds in connection with matching investments in economic infrastructure and social regulations within the framework of a novel politico-economic regime.
4   The new technological style spreads quickly during the upswing and prosperity phases. During prosperity (in the years to come) this permeation process tends towards saturation. No later than during the prosperity–recession phase, new elements of an emerging style appear, thus completing the cycle.

It should be noted that it is only the crystallization phase which brings about a novel range of products and services which fascinate consumers and, thus, a new match between productive opportunities and consumption that leads to the unfolding of a new technological style. By the fascination of novel goods and services I mean inventions which put people under their spell because they complement human capacities. They render possible things that people would not naturally be able to do. Thus, their fascination stems from an amplification of human action and experience. It is therefore not surprising that changes in transport and communications have been key projects lending substantial impulse to the development of technological style. Railways were the key project of the development of technological style during the first wave following the liberal revolts of 1830/48, whereas it was electrification during the second and cars during the third wave. Finally, the digital informatization of society is the key project of the new technological style.

The model of technological style development suggests several reasons why the change takes time. After all, the style cannot flourish without political procurement of the social and material infrastructure. Why is the political sphere reluctant to adopt quickly?

Politico-economic rigidities

Societal power, as developed at the beginning of the treatment in this chapter, falls into crisis and is undermined when the discrepancy between conventionality and reality surmounts thresholds. However, modern societies are differentiated and the metaphor of societal power needs therefore to be specified according to different areas of social life. In these areas, innovation does not arise simultaneously, because social power and risks that inhibit innovation have different strengths.

Scientists in the natural sciences bear few risks, since originality and invention is part of their social remit. The frequency of scientific discoveries might be governed by intra-professional forces but is affected comparatively little by what society takes to be a matter of course and the decay of such certainties. Scientific inventions which will one day become highly relevant for the economy and society therefore cluster little over time, quite in contrast to the later innovations which follow from them (for evidence, see Gerhard Mensch [1975] 1978).

Innovators with regard to views of life – social scientists, men and women of letters, intellectuals and leaders of social movements – confront quite a great risk. As long as stable and unquestioned normative theories govern social life they have no auditorium, no readers, and no following. As soon as the officially held worldviews begin to crumble, such innovators have their finest hours, since the demand for interpretation surges; and the new competition of different interpretations undermines what was once common sense even more (for evidence with regard to utopian literature, see Kizer and Drass 1987).[4]

Economic entrepreneurs bear a great risk due to sanctions following from unsatisfactory gains or from losses. They react defensively and, therefore, innovate in the long downturn primarily to bring their costs down. Such innovations increase and do not overcome the crisis, as mentioned before.[5]

Under the rule of democracy, political entrepreneurs confront the risk of losing public support; the crumbling of societal power thus also affects the stability of support. Various new political potentials emerge in the citizenry and become framed in new ideologies and articulated by political movements. These new political potentials are then for a long time unable to find significant support among the electorate, and remain partly outside the parliamentary system. In general, the opportunities for fundamental political change in democracies remain rather feeble. This, then, is why the political system remains a stronghold of conventional societal power for so long, albeit accompanied by increasing estrangement between political elites and the ordinary people (something that populist new political entrepreneurs regularly try to exploit).

In general, the proposition that the greatest obstacle to change is the political system may have some merits. Yet, it would be necessary to qualify it according to many variables that affect the political process and which are studied by our colleagues in political science. To include such complexity is beyond what can be done at the end of this book. But I would like to draw attention at least to some significant variables which are here relevant.

Constitutional particularities not only affect the specific shaping of politico-economic regimes but also the ease with which it can be changed. The power distribution between parliament, government, and head of state varies greatly amongst Western societies (for this and the following see Schmidt 1983; 1992; Hartmann 1983; Lijphart 1999), which influences the formation of a coherent and stable politico-economic regime. There are two basic forms of parliamentary democracy: the parliamentary system, which originated in Britain, and the presidential system founded in the United States. France's Fifth Republic is a mix of both types, a parliamentary–presidential hermaphrodite, since the president can appoint and dismiss the prime minister and the party affiliation of the president does not have to coincide with the majority in the parliament. In addition, there is consociational democracy (Lehmbruch 1992: 206ff.), which is found in Switzerland, Austria, the Netherlands and Belgium. In the political system of Switzerland, which basically belongs to the presidential type, the Bundesrat (Council of Ministers) is a comprehensive body, i.e. the head of state, government, and head of government all in one. The central decision-making mechanism is not the majority principle, but rather techniques of compromise and mutual accommodation. The participation of important minorities in government as well as proportionality in appointments to public offices is typical of Switzerland.

Consociational democracy and negotiated capitalism (democratic corporatism) are not identical, as I mentioned in passing in Chapter 7. It is true that consociational democratic systems are more or less characterized by high degrees of negotiated capitalism, i.e. by the recruitment of organizations into politics, but the negotiated systems of Scandinavia are not consociational democracies. Rather, their political culture is characterized by a deep distrust of broad coalitions, which leads to a predominance of minority cabinets. Systems of negotiated capitalism and consociational democratic systems prevent the fragmentation of political culture and thus favour continuity in the shaping of the societal model. However, these systems limit the access of groups with weak electoral support to the power circle. Issues which have not been put on the agenda by the governing groups (the political power bloc) thus lead to political opposition outside established party channels.

In the United States there is a separation of powers because executive power and Congress are independently elected. In the legislation process, however, executive power and Congress must work together. Congress can and does introduce legislation on many issues quite independently of the president, and in such cases the President must endorse or veto. The president may also propose legislation, but has to introduce it via members of Congress. Yet, the Congress does not endorse all of the President's propositions. In parliamentary systems, the government would be overthrown in a comparable situation. In the United States, the search for compromise and negotiation between president and Congress – itself bicameral, composed of the House of Representatives and the Senate – is necessary. Both chambers have similar rights in legislation (except that the House has sole power to introduce legislation to raise revenue for government, Section 7 of the Constitution). Furthermore, the difference between US and European parties has to be mentioned, i.e. the absence of party programmes in a European sense, and the complete absence of party discipline in terms of voting or positions on issues. The aforementioned elements of the political system can easily lead not only to blockages but also to abrupt changes if charismatic presidents take office. The outset of the past societal model, Roosevelt's New Deal (1932), is a case in point. Eisenhower in 1953, Kennedy in 1961 and Reagan in 1980 are examples of later abrupt changes. Reagan, after all, was important for initiating the basic political change in America in the 1980s.

A further important institutional influence originates from the administration. In the United States, for example, the federal administration includes '... a conglomerate of various agencies which, in part, are structured by departments (equivalent to the ministries in parliamentary systems) and, in part, enjoy independence' (Hartmann 1983: 186). In addition, the American administration is not staffed by a higher civil service. About 800 political officials are appointed by the President, among them the secretaries (ministers). These appointments have to be agreed by the Senate, which it normally does. A further two thousand political officials are appointed by the secretaries, i.e. indirectly by the President. Contrary to Western Europe and particularly Japan, the body of senior officials does not lead to continuity because it changes with each new President. In Europe, on the other hand, tenured civil servants staff the ministries, and in Japan one may even say that the legislative and governmental process is dominated by an elite senior civil service which cooperates closely with economic bodies.

Finally, election procedures must be discussed (Nohlen 1992: 519f.; Lijphart 1999: Chapters 2, 3, 5). In most of the Western industrial countries (according to Nohlen: fifteen out of twenty-three) elections are held on a proportional basis. Thus, parliamentary representation mirrors, more or less, voting patterns. The less frequent majority rule, on the other hand, is aimed at producing strong governments and thus tolerates a disproportion between votes and deputies. Such a disproportion may be even more substantial in the case of relative majority rule in single-candidate constituencies (United Kingdom, Canada, New Zealand and the United States). In Britain the 'Iron Lady', Thatcher, gained political power with a very comfortable majority in parliament with only 38 per cent of the British electorate's vote.[6]

Having mentioned all these additional variables for a minimal account of the differences that may result in the political process, let me suggest two generalizations. In the Anglo-Saxon political style it is easier, due to constitutional peculiarities, that fundamental political change can be pushed through early. In systems of greater negotiated capitalism the opposite holds. The inhibition of pronounced societal power is also reflected in the political institutions. This is no wonder, since institutions, in my understanding, reflect culture.

The matching of the techno-economic and the politico-institutional spheres in comparative perspective

Looking back at the beginning of the 1990s, one can state that the preference for fundamental change in the economy is present to quite different extents in rich democracies. In about half of the rich democracies this inclination is small or only moderate. Furthermore, independent of the level, only in seven out of twenty rich democracies is this about equally distributed among the citizenry and not more pronounced on the political left or right. This would make it quite difficult to predict the fundamental socio-economic change that actually took place. The data for the observations are from the 1990 wave of the *World Values Survey* (see Inglehart *et al.* 1998), and were used in Chapter 4. In that chapter it could be established that citizens in rich democracies with more generalized trust were more in favour of such changes, but that also the general level of trust in society counted very much. This is then the first link we can establish in modelling the likelihood of early transition to the new societal model; see the centre of Figure 12.1.

Sometimes the complex interrelationship of arguments may become clearer if we show it graphically. We do that with Figure 12.1, which is intended to bring together some of the arguments put forth in this chapter and add information from other chapters of this book. The first link between generalized trust and the preference for change, also with respect to the economy, was established in Chapter 4. Furthermore, it could be demonstrated that both little negotiated capitalism of the Anglo-Saxon type as well as pronounced negotiated capitalism foster generalized trust

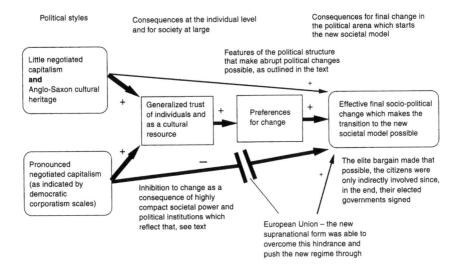

Figure 12.1 A synopsis of the arguments linking politics, culture, and fundamental social change.

Notes
The different hypotheses for the implications for economic growth in the 1990s are in the text. For consequences of pronounced negotiated capitalism without EU membership, see the examples of Switzerland and Japan in the text (pp. 238–40).

in the citizenry (see Chapter 7). Taking only these relationships, one would predict that effective politico-economic change will have a similar likelihood in both types of political styles.

Yet, the arguments developed earlier in this chapter add the proposition that Anglo-Saxon societies have a greater ease in bringing about fundamental political change due to constitutional reasons. On the other side, negotiated systems of capitalism contain inhibitions to change that are also reflected in the structure of their political decision-making.[7] Taking these additional aspects, one would predict that Anglo-Saxon societies were earlier prepared to make such changes, and this is what actually happened. However, many, if not most, of the others were not so much later. How could they manage this?

The thesis that the inhibitions to fundamental socio-political change inherent in negotiated capitalism were overcome is straightforward. The political dimension of European integration developed precisely during an era of dramatic change in information technologies and intensified economic globalization. In this respect the Union was a timely undertaking. More specifically, the EU as a supranational state-level was unique in meeting that challenge, since it did something that most of the member states were not willing or able to do on that scale. Actually, undemocratic as it was, the elite bargain that reshuffled Western Europe overcame the inhibitions of established societal power, since many of the member states have at least moderate levels of negotiated capitalism. It was not, then, the citizens of Western Europe that made possible the largest deregulation project ever in economic history. The governments had a correct premonition of that, since they hardly needed to be pressed. Let me cite only two references from our work on European integration, which was also outlined in Chapter 8:

> As the Commission has never ceased to affirm European undertakings must be assured that their activities will be able to develop in an economic unit similar in size to the American market and distinctly bigger than the Japanese market ... To date, this has not been achieved. Although the problem issues have been clearly identified and fully discussed, the decisions have not yet been taken.
> (Communication of the Commission on the *Re-Activation of the European internal market,* November 12, 1982/COM (82) 735 final, page 1.)

> The Council's [the representatives of the governments of member states] inaction cannot relieve the Commission of its obligation to take whatever measures are necessary to ensure the free movement of goods within the Community under conditions which are consistent with the aims of the treaty.
> (*Consolidating the Internal Market,* Communication of the Commission to the Council of 13 June, 1984/COM (84) 305 final, page 14. (Sources in detail, see: Bornschier 1996: 360.))[8]

The conclusions so far are that Anglo-Saxon societies were first in reshuffling the political sphere as a prerequisite of the change to the new technological style. Yet the EU was not very much later in pushing through deregulation of the market – the Internal Market Programme, finished by the end of 1992 – and pursuing a new technology policy. Thus, in terms of matching the techno-economic with the politico-institutional sphere, the Anglo-Saxon societies had a little edge over the EU. This should translate into increasing economic growth rates during the 1990s for both, although starting somewhat earlier and at a somewhat higher level for the Anglo-Saxon group. Note that I refer to all the members of that group and not only to the United States. Before we come to the figures, let us discuss two cases which are neither of Anglo-Saxon cultural origin nor members of the EU.

Negotiated capitalism without EU membership

How were the inhibitions regarding fundamental societal transition overcome in rich democracies that did not participate in the EU integration process? Let us consider here Switzerland and Japan, both ranked fairly high on consensus-seeking in politico-economic matters.

Switzerland, similar to many of the EU member states, is characterized by marked societal power built up over the past and adapted intensively to bolster the Keynesian societal model. At the turn of the 1980s to the 1990s an approach towards the EU was an option. The Swiss government suggested that and had a specific timetable, first joining the European Economic Area (EEA) and later the EU itself. Both issues where highly controversial in the Swiss political arena, especially the Swiss government's proposal to become a member of the European Union. On 6 December 1992 the Swiss electorate turned down the proposal to join the EEA. During the long political campaign on that issue the Swiss government, at the federal and cantonal level, had already started to adapt to EU standards of deregulation since acceptance of the first step (EEA) seemed certain. The autonomous adoption of the new EU standards to complete the internal market by the end of 1992 resulted, de facto, in a similar deregulation as in EU member states, albeit with a time lag and maybe less thoroughly. Thus, the effectively chosen reform path was moderate and cautious, typical for Swiss political culture. In the course of the 1990s, joining the EU became a less immediate political target, and instead bilateral treaties with the EU were chosen, the first wave becoming effective in 2002. From the actual approach to the new EU norms, one can deduce that the new formation of the politico-economic regime was only slightly delayed as compared to the EU. Economic growth in Switzerland should therefore surge later in the 1990s and approach a somewhat lower level in the second half of the 1990s.

Japan is, not in all respects but in the following sense, a special case. Economic growth was for a long period very much higher than in Western Europe, not only in the immediate post-war decades but also during the long downturn 1973–92. This had reasons beyond Japan's spectacular economic convergence. With regard to the new technological style, several of Japan's leading firms belong, together with US–American ones, to the co-innovators, especially with regard to the new methods of organizing firms and of managing inter-firm relations. The terms 'lean management' and 'kaizen' are cases in point. Looking back at the turn of the 1970s and 1980s, concerned European leaders feared an imminent technological superiority on the part of Japan (see Chapter 8).

How could it be that a society with such marked societal power was technologically so innovative? Well, first of all societal power is in general less a problem in the decentralized world of firms. For a long time, Japanese firms had practised an interesting mixture between fierce competition and collaboration in developing basic technologies, the so-called 'coopetition'. Furthermore, a special economic institution deserves attention, since it makes continuous technological change much easier.[9] The special kind of labour relations in Japan most probably contributed considerably to the country's development into one of the leading economic powers. Permanent employment is characteristic for the large enterprises, which recruit their staff primarily from schools and universities and keep them until retirement age. Other characteristics are payment according to seniority, mobility of workers and managers within the enterprises, generous corporate social benefits and the central role played by the firms' unions, next to which associations across particular sectors are only of limited importance. This special system of labour relations has the advantage of facilitating technological change. When new technologies are introduced, employees are not disqualified or fired but retrained. Due to permanent employment, firms are able to invest more in continuing education, which in turn positively influences labour morale and the quality of personnel.

Japan's spectacular economic growth results after the Second World War – enduring even when Europe and the USA were in decline in the 1970s and 1980s – produced quite a bit of turmoil among concerned contemporaries in the Atlantic West, several augurs even going so far as to predict a shift in hegemony, a 'Pax Nipponica' following the 'Pax Americana'. The 1990s showed a quite different picture. Japan, whose spectacular economic growth made it the great challenger of the seventies and eighties, featured in very different newspaper headlines in the 1990s. The crisis in Japan has affected societal self-confidence and exposed the rotten pillars of its post-war order. The years of extreme self-confidence are over, and Japan has entered a phase of deep self-doubt.[10] The sticky societal power becomes all too evident during the 1990s and commentators do not tire of producing headlines such as: 'Report from the country of missed reforms', 'Not only the stock exchange is going downhill, the whole country suffers from reform blockage', 'Japanese malaise – self-doubts of an uncertain nation', and so on.

Throughout the post-war era it has been not so easy for Western commentators to remain sober when reporting on Japan. While the accomplishments were first underestimated, in the later 1980s the opposite was the case. A lot has been written on that issue recently and I will be brief. I think Japan suffers from delayed reforms, which are understandable taking into account its once leading position in aspects of the new technological style and the very comfortable growth record until the early 1990s.

In contrast to Japan, Western Europe has already carried out much of the task of deregulation that started in the Anglo-Saxon world during the early 1980s, and produced a timely vision at the beginning of the 1990s. This vision is evidenced by the White Paper of December 1993 entitled *Growth, Competitiveness, Employment – The Challenges and Ways Forward into the 21st Century*. This report calls for a 'new model of European society' (White Paper 1993: 15, 150f.).

Empirical expectations

When we apply the dynamic model outlined at the end of Chapter 1 and include the information that has been gathered in this chapter, the predictions are straightforward. There will be a growth take-off in the Anglo-Saxon world starting soon after the beginning of the 1990s. If our reasoning is correct, this should not only apply to the United States but to all Anglo-Saxon cases. The EU will follow next with a somewhat less steep increase in growth rates and rather lower average growth rates. This is because the imitator of the new politico-economic regime still suffers somewhat from the rigidities of several of its member states, the reasons for which were outlined in this chapter. There should also be a growth take-off in Switzerland, but with a time delay. For Japan I do not expect a take-off during the 1990s, because the final reform of the politico-economic regime is still lacking.

Empirical evidence

We start by looking briefly at the historical accomplishment of societies which have become rich democracies (based on information given by Maddison 1995). Some figures were given already in Chapter 1 to provide evidence that growth oscillates over long time periods. Between 1870 and before the Second World War, the US (and the other Western Offshoots) had a clear edge over Western Europe in terms of level of economic growth. But this was due to the much higher population growth in the Western Offshoots. Western Europe and Japan had about the same economic growth. The 1950–73 period was exceptional in terms of level of growth. The high economic growth in the US (and the other Western Offshoots) and in Western Europe with figures between 4 per cent and 4.5 per cent was considerably surmounted by Japan's figures, which amounted to 8 per cent to 9 per cent. During the downturn phase of 1973–92 economic growth came down but much less so in Japan which continued with a 3.5 per cent figure. We will analyse the new upswing phase since the 1990s in more detail by taking data from the International Monetary Fund (IMF) with the most recent ones from its *World Economic Outlook* from 29 March 2002. It shows the rank order which we expect from the theoretical considerations outlined in this chapter.

Details of the 1990s

For all groups and individual countries except Japan, we find an increase in economic growth since 1991, a high level in the second part of the decade and a downturn in 2001 and 2002. This intermediate downturn is most probably not the end of the long-term upswing but a normal business cycle trough (called Juglars, of 8 to 10 years' length). The data is presented in the following order: US, the EU, Switzerland and Japan. The rate of increase in the early 1990s differs according to our expectations, and the same is true for the average level of growth within this thirteen-year period. The only completely different pattern is, as predicted, the one for Japan. At the beginning of the 1990s, Japan's growth still reflected somewhat the edge it had over the other countries until 1992, but since then it has been in decline.

The four displays – Figures 12.2–12.5 – are self-explanatory with regard to what I theoretically proposed and what we actually find by looking at the economic growth figures from 1991 to 2003 (the figures for 2002 and 2003 are projections). The only thing I wish to add is the demonstration that the swift surge of growth in the 1990s, as well as the high level of growth reached over the whole period, is a pattern common to all Anglo-Saxon societies see Figure 12.6. Ireland is not included in this comparison, since the straggler effect is still at work there and makes for remarkably high growth rates in Ireland. The recently widened split of the worlds of capitalism, which has been indicated in Chapter 11, is then not a distinction between the US and 'good old Europe', but between the Anglo-Saxon way of running an economy and the different degrees of negotiated capitalism that are present not only in Western Europe but also in developed East Asia.[11]

Comment to the following figures:[12] The horizontal line indicates the average growth rates for the 13 years 1991 to end of 2003. Note that the figures for 2002 and 2003 are projections, as of March 2002, which does not affect, however, my argument, see endnote on the impact of September 11, 2001.[13] The other line indicates the trend in growth. The source for the basic data is: IMF. These figures relate to total economic growth, and we will come to per capita growth as an indicator of wealth after the figures (see Table 12. 1).

In the Figures 12.2–12.6 we use total economic growth, as does my growth model that was applied in this book. However, in doing so we controlled for growth in labour input – outlined in Chapter 1 and first applied in Chapter 2. From Figures 12.2–12.6 it becomes obvious that total economic growth in Anglo-Saxon countries was higher over the last dozen years. To infer from this that also growth of wealth per capita was superior is not warranted; see Table 12.1 for examples.[14]

As Table 12.1 shows, the EU could well keep pace in terms of per capita economic growth, which is a welfare rather than an efficiency measure. Why, then, should an imagined average citizen of the EU want to switch to the Anglo-Saxon way of capitalism?

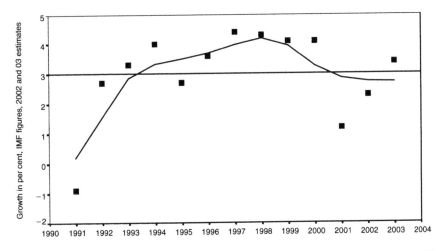

Figure 12.2 USA: economic growth 1991–2001 and projections (sources: IMF figures; 2002/3 are estimates).

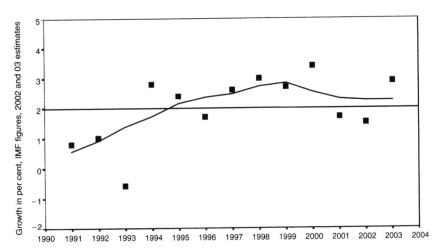

Figure 12.3 EU: economic growth 1991–2001 and projections (sources: IMF figures; 2002/3 are estimates).

Table 12.1 Total economic growth and per capita economic growth, examples for the eight years average, 1995–2002 (%)

	Total economic growth	*Economic growth per capita*
Canada	3.44	2.44
USA	3.20	2.04
EU	2.34	2.15

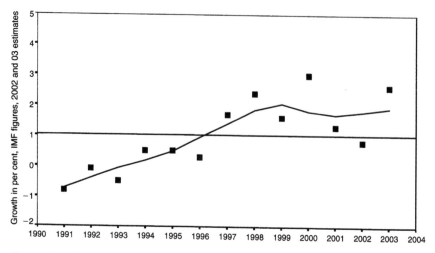

Figure 12.4 Switzerland: economic growth 1991–2001 and projections (sources: IMF figures; 2002/3 are estimates).

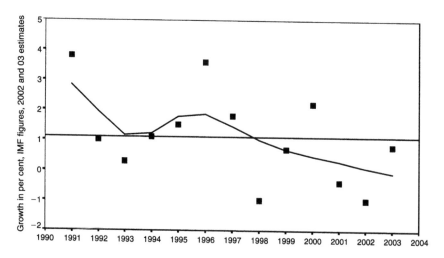

Figure 12.5 Japan: economic growth 1991–2001 and projections (sources: IMF figures; 2002/3 are estimates).

Concluding remarks

Originally I planned to discuss the peculiarities which make the transition to the new way of social life in the modern world especially difficult, as compared with the former great transition from agriculture to industry. Indeed, some very brief reflections on specificities which make the transition to the new societal model particularly difficult can be made here.

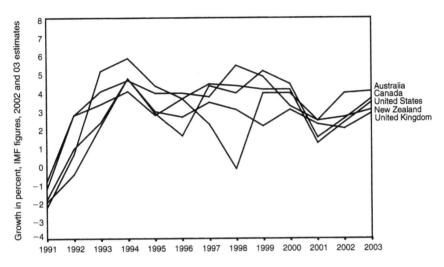

Figure 12.6 Economic growth in the Anglo-Saxon world, 1991–2001 and projections (sources: IMF figures; 2002/3 are estimates).

Epoch-making social transitions are nothing new in capitalism. Let me point only to the radical changes from agrarian to industrial society in the nineteenth century which affected our ancestors. No less dramatic was the transition from industrial to information society, starting during the last third of the twentieth centrury. There seems to be at least one fundamental difference between the two transitions. While the people that moved from agriculture to the booming industries had a lot of valuable manual skills immediately applicable in the new industries, the situation is quite different for the second epoch-making shift. Excess labour from the old industries is by no means easily absorbed by the new economic activities of the information age, even given all the retraining programmes. For quite a while then, excess labour from older industries coexists with a labour shortage of the highly qualified. And this is one of the reasons why income inequality will remain high on the way to the new societal model for quite a while; see also Bornschier 2002b.

The concluding chapter investigated some of the obstacles to a swift transition from one societal model to the next. Some of the basic themes of this book could be related to a dynamic modelling that predicts different economic growth patterns. While generalized trust is an excellent and broadly applicable cultural resource for economic development, it might not be enough to spur the transition to a new societal model. As demonstrated, political styles favour, in the case of the Anglo-Saxon cultural pattern, or inhibit, in the case of pronounced negotiated capitalism, that transition. My interpretation is that, whatever the accomplishments of negotiated capitalism, these systems would not have made the transition so fast if the new political form of the EU had not been brought into existence. Recasting the European bargain was, however, an arrangement made between elites. Of course, democratically elected governments had to sign, but the majority of the European citizenry was not directly involved.

Those who have read as far as this have been presented with a variety of arguments which relate a broad spectrum of topics to economic development: the nature and importance of trust as a cultural resource; the significance of political forms and political styles; the emergence of supranational political forms, chiefly the EU; and the persistence of cultural and political heterogeneity in a globalized world. What is central to the purpose of this book is that, across this diverse spectrum, each of the links between culture, politics and the development of economies has been investigated by reference to sources of empirical data. The reader will have remarked that this is not, and was never intended to be, an exhaustive study. A great deal of research remains to be done in the immensely complex field of the interaction between cultures and economies, and in this sense I hope that, for the readership, this book more closely resembles a starting point than the last word on the topic.

Finally, let me point out that, while it has been demonstrated that culture, broadly understood to include political culture too, matters for economic development, this should not be understood in the sense that the supreme task of culture is to serve the economy. Culture is something that reflects degrees of freedom independent of the level of material development. It has to do with the richness of life and, in my view, that is what really counts in the end. However, some forms of culture also have significant side-effects, and to demonstrate this for economic development was the task of this book.

Notes

1 Topics of economic sociology in this book

1 See Richard Swedberg (1987), see also Swedberg (2003). Mention should also be made of compilations of influential work like those by Alberto Martinelli and Neil Smelser (1990), Mark Granovetter and Richard Swedberg (1992), and last but not least to handbook treatments, see Neil Smelser and Richard Swedberg (1994). Recent contributions to the field which are relevant to the questions to be addressed in this book will be quoted at the appropriate places.

2 Dahrendorf (1983) points to a similar distinction in the writings of Karl Marx, who combines Aristotelian and Kantian elements to set the empire of necessity against the empire of freedom.

3 I would like to draw the reader's attention again to the fine work of Richard Swedberg (1987) on this issue. See also his most recent work: Swedberg (2003).

4 The question is not new. Let me point to two recent examples. While Ronald Inglehart (1997) in a chapter carefully looks at the influence of culture on economic growth, Lawrence E. Harrison and Samuel P. Huntington (2000) already have the answer, as evidenced in the title of their collection: *Culture Matters.*

5 See Bornschier, first 1988, with extended versions in English (1996), German and Chinese (1998).

6 The period 1870–1992 are from Maddison 1995: 60. They represent annual compound growth rates of real GDP growth in the periods. For the most recent period we take estimates of the IMF – Economic Outlook (from 29.3.2002: 158, Table 2). These figures represent a ten-year average, available for 1994 to 2001, with projections for 2002 and 2003. The weighted average for Western Offshots include the United States, Canada, Australia, New Zealand. The figures for Europe refer to the weigted average for Western Europe until 1992, and for the European Union of fifteen members since 1994.

7 These figures for Switzerland are compiled from various sources: 1910–43 from either Maddison 1982 or Maddison 1995; 1943–8 from Kleinewefers; 1949–93 from BAK (a Swiss Federal Office); 1994–2003 estimates from IMF – Economic Outlook, 29.3.2002. The moving average represent a nine-year moving average, at the beginning or the end of the series: five-year moving average or the effective yearly figures.

8 Note that for this comparison in Figure 1.4 each country attains the same weight. If one would weigh cases according to their share in total world population and total world product, the tendency of dispersion over time would be different, depending on the influential single case of China. Without China the weighted dispersion would still increase over 1980–97, albeit to a considerable smaller extent, with China it would decrease due to the very high economic

growth there since 1980 and the fact that China represents about one quarter of the world population.

9   Such statements are not the exception in the recent literature, as is revealed in the title of Charles Kenny and David Williamson's (2000) contribution: 'What Do We Know About Economic Growth? Or, Why Don't We Know Very Much?'

10   Or take Haiti and the Dominican Republic as an example, both on the same island once in Spanish colonialism called Española [Hispaniola], actually the first colonial settlement of the Spanish in the New World. Someone who is fascinated by the idea that geography counts is Ricardo Hausmann, who teaches development economics at Harvard University.

11   Cross-national analyses neglect the fact that national as well as regional economies are part of the embracing world economy. But since I have extensively worked on global political and economic processes I will not repeat all that here; see, for example, Bornschier and Chase-Dunn (1985), Bornschier (2002).

12   The study, as should have become clear, is on modern economic development and growth. Due to this focus and also due to lack of data I consider in most yet not all chapters only developed and newly industrializing countries. The problem of late development was a topic in my recent book on world society. So-called transformation societies are in almost all analyses not included since our analyses focus on long-term changes from 1980–2000. The revolutionary shifts in the political economy of the transformation societies make them incomparable for the type of analyses we are performing here.

13   Distributional questions are not the focus because these are unimportant: quite the contrary. The reason is that I have recently started a large-scale research project on the perception and evaluation of inequality in comparative perspective. The results of this research are not yet available but would be necessary for a fuller treatment of distributional questions.

14   This is an exaggeration, since Mankiw, Romer and Weil (1992) did an excellent job in bringing economic growth theory to the data. For a comprehensive overview of economic growth theory, see also Mankiw (1992), with an emphasis on findings, see Temple (1999), and for a specific issue that will also be of interest in our Chapter 2, see Whiteley (2000).

15   My reference comes from a book I read as a student, i.e. Max Weber (1905).

16   My first contribution to that field was the study of the growth, concentration and multinationalization of industrial enterprises (see Bornschier 1976) which was followed by a series of articles on transnational corporations in economic development, a debate that from the outset entered the top journal of our profession in the late 1970s and which is still going on in the 1990s. My final statement before I left the field open for debate was the book by Bornschier and Chase-Dunn (1985). During the 1990s this debate again grew very hot, see especially Firebaugh (1992) and Dixon and Boswell (1996) with comments by Firebaugh and a reply by Dixon and Boswell. A comprehensive overview of that debate now lasting more than one quarter of a century, together with fresh evidence, is presented by Mark Herkenrath (2003) as well as Herkenrath and Bornschier (2003). In my book of 2002 on world society there is also a whole chapter on that issue.

17   Examples are the studies within business firms by Tyler 2002, Kramer and Tyler 1996, or Fecker (2001).

18   See detailed references to the work of Joseph Schumpeter in Chapter 4.

19   The references to Carlota Perez's seminal work will follow in Chapter 3. Indeed, she is in my view – after Joseph Schumpeter – the second most original theoretician of innovation of the twentieth century. Her work is acknowledged

and continued in Bornschier ([1988] 1996), see also the later cited contributions by Christopher Freeman (who was Carlota Perez's academic teacher at Sussex and later helped to make her ideas more known) and, much later, Richard Lipsey (1999).

20 This is a prominent part in my longer treatment of discontinuous change in Western society; see Bornschier [1988] 1996.

2 Trust and growth

1 An earlier version of this chapter was published as: Volker Bornschier, 'Befähigung zu Sozialkapitalbildung und wirtschaftlicher Erfolg im entwickelten Kapitalismus – Neue Evidenzen aus Ländervergleichen 1980–1997', *Swiss Journal of Sociology/Schweizerische Zeitschrift für Soziologie* 26 (2): 373–400. This work received one of the prizes of the Fritz Thyssen Foundation for the best (German-language) social science articles of the volumes of 2000.

2 See, for example, Whiteley (2000: 448), Zak and Knack (2001: 295).

3 The works of James Coleman ([1990] 2000), Robert Putnam (1993) and Francis Fukuyama (1995) helped to popularize the discussion of the concept of social capital as a non-traditional source of economic growth, provoking a lively discussion among economists; for an overview, see Woolcock 1998; Portes 1998. For earlier contributions by economists and sociologists to the concept of trust see also the references given by Swedberg (1987: 131, 143f.). The continuing interest in recent times is also evidenced by, for example, Misztal (1996), Sztompka (1999), Hartmann and Offe (2001), Lin (2001) and Nuissl (2002).

4 For a detailed statement, see Bornschier ([1988] 1996; 1989).

5 The equation for estimation is deduced through logarithmization:

$$d \log Y_t = b_0 + b_1 \, d \log K_t + b_2 \, d \log L_t + b_3 \log ¥ + b_4 \log T + b_5 \log H + b_6 \log S + e_t$$

Here e_t is the residual of the regression; d is the operator of forward differences (dX equals $X_{t+1} - X_t$). The variables are mentioned in the text, details on the variables are in notes at the appropriate places. The above listed equation for estimation can be applied to use the ordinary least-squares regression technique, what would not be possible with the Cobb–Douglas function. The extended Cobb–Douglas function would read:

$$Y_t = K_t^{b1} \, L_t^{b2} \, ¥^{b3^t} \, T^{b4^t} \, H^{b5^t} \, S^{b6^t \exp(b_0 t} + v_t) \qquad \text{[with } e_t \text{ equals } dv_t \text{]}$$

6 See also Fecker 2001: Chapter 10; Bornschier 1996: 76.

7 This is argued in detail in Bornschier [1988] 1996.

8 A point first noted by Leicht (2000) in his conceptualization of social capital.

9 Erich Weede (1996) did not succeed with a strict replication of Bornschier's study, because he failed to transform logarithmically the dependent variable. Bornschier's earlier study consistently used a multiplicative model.

10 In order to maximize comparability we take exactly the same data as Knack and Keefer (1997) use, i.e. the values for 1980 and, in three cases where data from the 1980 wave are lacking, the ones from the 1990 wave.

11 The responding categories range from 0 = low to 100 = high. The index was constructed by Michael Leicht (2000) and represents the factor scores of the first factor representing 66.2 per cent of the total variance represented by the four items. The data become available only after 1988. The means for the items for the years 1989, 1990 and 1991 were considered.

12 For Australia only trust values are reported in the first (1981) and third wave (1995) of the *World Values Survey* (*WVS*). We take the average of the two figures as a reasonable estimate for 1990.

13 The relationship between logarithmic and non-logarithmic variables is as follows. We use rate of economic growth as the example. $Yt + 1/Yt = 1 + r$, where $r =$ the growth rate between t and $t + 1$. Through logarithmic transformation, we obtain: $\log Yt + 1 - \log Yt = \log (1 + r)$. Then r can be determined as anti-log minus 1 and is represented – after multiplying by 100 – as the percentage growth rate.

An expert, (acting as reviewer) once noted that the logarithmic transformation of all variables is unorthodox in multiple regression in sociology and econometrics. But it was used in my previous work on theoretical grounds (cf. among others Bornschier 1989, 1996: 328–38, 2000). In order to clarify the question of whether the effects that we will interpret would persist in the absence of this logarithmic procedure, we have also tested all variables in their non-logarithmic form. These results in no way alter our conclusions.

14 Human capital through education (scope and quality) is a subjective indicator, a factor analytically determined on the basis of evaluation of the scope and quality of the primary schools, economic literacy, and computer literacy. The underlying items come from the *World Competitiveness Report*, which assessed these specific items for the first time in 1992. When drawing conclusions about the effect of human (educational) capital (measured as a subjective evaluation of informants), one has to take into account that five of the values in the sample of thirty-three cases were estimated by us. Thus this variable presents a somewhat preliminary measure.

15 *Economic growth*: d log $Y = \log$ Y 1998 – log Y 1980. Source for Y: GDP according to World Development Indicators 1999, World Bank, on CD-ROM (values for 1998 are taken from IMF estimates). *Growth in capital stock (physical capital)*: d log $K = \log$ K 1993 – log K 1985; source: Herkenrath (1999). Values are estimated according to the method of Bornschier and Heintz (1979). Depreciation of capital goods is included in the calculations. *Growth of manpower (labour force)*: d log $L = \log$ L 1997 – log L 1980; source: World Development Indicators 1999. Note: Since we construct growth rates, the main problem of this indicator, namely that differential inputs of labour (working time and part-time work) are not covered, is almost completely neutralized. *Convergence*: log GDP per capita 1990 = real GDP per capita in international prices of 1985 (purchasing-power parity corrected) according to Summers and Heston (The Penn World Table, Mark 5.5). The measure is recoded: difference to maximum value in the sample. *Technology capital*: log technology capital, average for 1985–95. Operational definition: scientists and engineers in R&D per million inhabitants during the period 1985–95; source: *World Development Report* 1999/2000: 266f. *Human (educational) capital quality*: log education quality 1992. For this subjective indicator, see previous note. The index measure was constructed by Leicht (2000) and also used in Bornschier (2000). *Trust & Tolerance* 1981/90 = (log trust 1981 + log tolerance 1990)/2. The question for trust from the *World Values Survey* as mentioned in the text. Percentage of answers: 'Can be trusted' (without including the answer 'Don't know'). Here, the source is Knack and Keefer (1997), which uses the data of 1981 and, for three cases, data for 1991. Tolerance: scores of the main component of a factor analysis of different non-discrimination test items:

- Foreigners are treated equally in all respects;
- Women have similar career opportunities as men;
- Extent to which the country facilitates integration of professional women in the workforce;
- The degree of equal opportunity – the extent to which an individual can get ahead irrespective of background or sex.

The responding categories range from 0 = low to 100 = high. The index was constructed by Michael Leicht (2000) and respresents the factor scores of the first factor representing 66.2 per cent of the total variance represented by the four items. The data become available only after 1988. The means for the items for the years 1989, 1990, and 1991 were considered; source of basic data: *World Competitiveness Reports*. The data were collected by Leicht (2000) and can also be found in Bornschier (2000). This index bases on subjective evaluations of informants. Trust 1990: data from the 1990 wave of the *WVS*, see Inglehart *et al.* 1998. The value for Australia is the average from the figures from the *WVS* in 1981 and 1995. The trust values for Taiwan and New Zealand are from Pippa Norris (2000, 2003).

Estimating the missing values: Economic growth: missing information in the data sources was estimated, i.e, for Greece, Iceland and the Federal Republic of Germany. In these cases, the missing information is estimated by a procedure that proceeds from the average growth rate (from sources such as the World Bank and Fischer Weltalmanach. Through this method, we can determine the logarithm from an algorithm of the quotients Y1997/Y1980. Economic growth in case of Germany relates to the old FR before unification and to the new FR afterwards. *Convergence*: the value for Taiwan was estimated according to information in Fischer, Weltalmanach and Maddison (1995). *Technology Capital*: data are missing in five cases of the sample. Missing values for Chile, Hong Kong and Switzerland were estimated by using data on Internet host density as an indicator taken from the same *World Development Report* (correlation with technology capital is .86). The value for Taiwan was estimated according to expenditure for R&D, data based on Word Competitiveness Report, 1992: 555, 1995: 651. Iceland was given the average value of Western European countries. *Trust & Tolerance*: lacking data on the trust 1981 variable were substituted by the values for Tolerance. *Trust 1990*: Lacking data were estimated by using Trust & Tolerance as an instrument.

16 All tests proceed as follows. We first estimate the full model and then clean the estimation by excluding all insignificant predictors. The level of statistical significance we fix at a 5 per cent level (two-tailed test). Here is an example of one of the test runs: dependent variable: economic growth between 1980 and the end of 1998. Procedure: stepwise exclusion of non-significant predictors. Estimations for the sample of twenty-four developed countries

Predictors	First step, all predictors in the equation, $N = 24$				Final step, only significant predictors, $N = 24$			
	b	beta	t	p	b	beta	t	p
Capital stock growth	1.10	0.65	5.00	0.00	1.17	0.69	6.59	0.00
Labour force growth	0.05	0.02	0.17	0.87	–	n.s.	–	–
Convergence effect	0.62	0.69	4.17	0.00	0.53	0.59	5.26	0.00
Technology capital	0.04	0.08	0.44	0.67	–	n.s.	–	–
Educational capital	0.14	0.16	1.18	0.26	–	n.s.–	–	–
Trust & Tolerance social capital index	0.05	0.39	3.05	0.00	0.05	0.44	3.98	0.00
Constant	−0.17	–	–	–	0.04	–	–	–
R-squared, adjusted	–	0.75	–	–	–	0.75	–	–
Significance	–	F = 12.49	–	0.00	–	F = 24.60	–	0.00

17 This effect is, however, open to question due to collinearity. While the other predictors of growth are rather independent (i.e. do not correlate), technology capital correlates high with the level of material development ($r = 0.76$ for $N = 24$ and $r = 0.87$ for $N = 33$). Remember that our measure of the convergence effect is the reverse of the level of material development.

18 In earlier work (Bornschier 2000) I also tested what happens if the two components Trust & Tolerance are entered separately into the regression equation. The individual components are useful predictors of economic growth. In the case of trust, results are significant for nineteen cases; tolerance is significant for twenty-three cases, which corroborates Leicht's finding (2000).

19 The few sociological studies which estimate the stock of physical capital, which then allows the consideration of measures of the growth of physical capital over time are: Bornschier and Heintz 1979; Bornschier 1980 (as well as subsequent studies based on it, for example, Bornschier and Chase-Dunn 1985); Firebaugh 1992; Dixon and Boswell 1996; Herkenrath 1999, 2003; Graff 1996, 1999. Firebaugh as well as Dixon and Boswell use the data from the early Bornschier and Heintz study, Herkenrath updates these data; only Graff has independently constructed data for the stock of physical capital.

20 The listing is as follows:

Knack and Keefer (1997)

Growth period:	1980–92: annual growth in per capita income
Sample:	Twenty-nine countries, market economies
Social capital measure:	Generalized trust
Effects found:	Positive and significant effect on growth
Further finding:	Effect stronger in less developed countries
Characteristic:	Linear regression

Leicht (2000: 111ff.)

Growth period:	1990–8, annual growth in total income
Sample:	Twenty-nine to thirty-nine countries, market economies
Social capital measure 1:	Trust, factor score of factor analysis: nine items for trust in specific institutions
Effect:	Positive and significant effect on growth ($N = 39$)
Social capital measure 2:	Trust, the same measures as Knack and Keefer used
Effect:	Positive, but just fails to reach significance ($t = 1.93$, $N = 29$)
Social capital measure 3:	Tolerance (the same measure we use here to estimate missing trust values)
Effect:	Positive and significant ($N = 32$ cases)
Characteristic:	Linear regression

Bornschier (2000)

Growth period:	1980–97: growth of total real economic output (controlling for labour force growth)
Sample:	Twenty-four developed market economies
Social capital measure:	Trust & Tolerance as in this chapter beside Trust
Effect:	Positive and significant
Characteristic:	Regression of logarithms (non-linear model)

Kunz (2000)

Growth period:	1985–95
Sample:	Seventeen industrialized democracies
Social capital measure:	Trust in fellow nationals 1990 [compatriots] (not generalized trust as generally used, and in this chapter)

Effect:	Positive but not significant
Characteristic:	Linear regression

Whiteley (2000)

Growth period:	1970–92: mean growth rate of per capita income
Sample:	Thirty-four developed and developing countries, including also three non-market economies (Poland, Romania, Soviet Union)
Social capital measure:	Trust in other people, factor score from a factor analysis including three items: trust in other people in general, trust in family members, trust in fellow nationals
Effect:	Positive and significant effect on growth
Characteristic:	Regression of logarithms (non-linear model)

Zak and Knack (2001)

Growth period:	1970–92: average annual growth in per capita income
Sample:	Forty-one countries, market economies
Social capital measure:	Generalized trust (as in Knack and Keefer and in the study reported in this chapter), measurements between 1981 and 1996, earliest available measure of trust taken
Effect:	Positive and significant
Further finding:	Effect stronger in less-developed countries
Characteristic:	Linear regression

Study in this chapter [replication and extension of Bornschier (2000)]

Growth period:	1980–1998, growth of total real economic output (controlling for labour force growth)
Sample:	Twenty-four developed countries, and thirty-three cases including developing countries, market economies
Social capital measure:	Trust & Tolerance 1981/90, as well as Trust 1990
Effect:	Positive and significant for both measures and both samples
Further finding:	Impact on economic growth larger in more developed countries
Characteristic:	Regression of logarithms, i.e. a non-linear model as explained and justified in this chapter

21 The disagreement whether trust is more important for growth in developed or developing countries can hardly be settled at the moment since the earlier waves of the *WVS* underrepresented the less-developed countries (LDCs) in numbers (less so in terms of world population). Even though more recent waves include more LDC cases we have to wait until more time elapses to specify growth over a decent period after the measurement of trust.

3 Trust and technogical change: the case of Internet diffusion

1 An earlier version of the materials in this chapter was published as: Volker Bornschier, 'Generalisiertes Vertrauen und frühe Verbreitung der Internetnutzung im Gesellschaftsvergleich', *Kölner Zeitschrift für Soziologie und Sozialpsychologie* 53 (2), 2001: 233–57.
2 The more explicit discussion of social capital begins with James Coleman (1990: 300f.), who appreciated Glenn Loury (1977) who is assumed to have used the

term for the first time. Only a bit later Pierre Bourdieu (1983) used the term, too, albeit in a specific way. Coleman (1988: 88) defines social capital by its function. According to him its various elements have two things in common: they all consist of some aspect of social structures and they facilitate certain actions within the structure.

3 First argued in Bornschier (2000: 376).

4 While the findings of the pioneering work of Knack and Keefer (1997) have been corroborated in later work (see this chapter), it seems to be difficult to replicate the results of seminal work of Putnam (1993) beyond the context of Italian provinces. The study of Schneider, Plümper and Baumann (2000) finds it difficult to confirm the findings generated in the Italian context when the economic growth in the European regions is related to trust, controlling for the standard predictors of economic growth. Actually, their cross-sectional findings cast doubts on whether Putnam's bold claim holds in general.

5 There is evidence for this based on individual level data (variable v50 of the *WVS* covers the positive evaluation of the future: respondents from all countries and all waves result in 22,000 valid cases). Postmaterialists and materialists as well as those who cannot be associated with one of these categories perceive the future more optimistically if they are trusting (variable v94).

6 Georg Simmel (1908: 346) argues as follows: 'Vertrauen, als die Hypothese künftigen Verhaltens, die sicher genug ist, um praktisches Handeln darauf zu gründen, ist als Hypothese ein mittlerer Zustand zwischen Wissen und Nichtwissen um Menschen' 'Trust as the hypothesis of future behaviour, which is reliable enough to base practical action on, is, as a hypothesis, a middle condition between knowledge and ignorance about the human being' (my translation). For a new edition of Georg Simmel 1908, see Bibliography.

7 These are two examples which were presented by Thomas Volken in one of my seminars on technological change in the early 1990s. The exact reference I do not have at hand but I trust that he, who is a scientist himself, has correctly researched.

8 The source of this is from the Internet itself: www.cyberatlas.internet.com, 7 April, 1999.

9 Source: www.cisco.com, January 2000.

10 For the development of this model in the line of Perez's original idea, see Bornschier [1988] 1996: Chapter 5.

11 Crystallization is discussed in more detail in Bornschier [1988] 1996.

12 The source is: www.nua.ie/surveys/how_many_online.

13 Inglehart *et al.* 1998 report correlations between generalized trust and level of education for all the societies included in the 1990 wave of the *WVS*. Alesina and La Ferrara 2000 also find a strong association between trust and education comparing a panel of representative data in the USA; see also our own findings for fifteen rich democracies in Chapter 4. In the samples we use in this chapter we do not generally find, however, substantial correlations between the level of education and trust in the population.

   For the total sample of thirty-four cases the correlation between mass education and trust is 0.61 (significant) and 0.39 (significant only at a 8 per cent level) for twenty-one rich societies. The correlations of trust with early proliferation of tertiary education is almost absent, 0.27 (not significant) in the thirty-four cases sample and 0.05 (not significant) for the twenty-one rich countries.

14 In reanalyses and extensions of the research reported in this chapter, Thomas Volken (2002a, b) used Internet access costs as an additional predictor of diffusion. The effects were non-existent in rich countries and in transformation countries; only in samples covering a large range of material wealth does this variable turn out to have a small negative effect.

15 The thirty-four cases are the following; the twenty-one cases of the rich-country subsample are in italics.

	Internet hosts per 10,000	
	July 1997	*January 1999*
USA	*442.11*	*1,131.52*
Finland	*653.61*	*1,058.13*
Norway	*474.63*	*717.53*
Denmark	*259.73*	*526.77*
Sweden	*321.48*	*487.13*
Australia	*382.44*	*420.57*
Canada	*228.05*	*364.25*
New Zealand	*424.34*	*360.44*
Netherlands	*219.01*	*358.51*
Switzerland	*207.98*	*315.52*
United Kingdom	*149.06*	*240.99*
Singapore	*196.30*	*210.02*
Austria	*108.25*	*176.79*
Belgium	*84.64*	*162.39*
Germany	*106.68*	*160.23*
Republic Ireland	*90.89*	*148.70*
Japan	*75.80*	*133.53*
Hong Kong	*74.84*	*122.71*
France	*49.86*	*82.91*
Spain	*31.00*	*67.21*
Italy	*36.91*	*58.80*
Portugal	19.26	50.01
Greece	18.76	48.81
Republic Korea	28.77	40.00
South Africa	30.67	34.67
Malaysia	19.30	21.36
Chile	12.12	20.18
Argentina	5.32	18.28
Brazil	4.20	12.88
Mexico	3.72	11.64
Turkey	3.60	4.30
Thailand	2.11	3.35
Indonesia	0.54	0.75
India	0.05	0.13

16 Very few cases in the randomly chosen sample of thirty-four poor(er) countries, such as Uruguay or Costa Rica, have at least achieved low levels of Internet diffusion and would therefore qualify to be included in the test sample, but we have no data for these cases on our predictor variables from the *WVS* and from the *World Competitiveness Reports*.

17 The multiplicative equation from which the linear logarithmic form was obtained would read:

$$I_t = V_t^{b1} \, U_t^{b2} \, T_t^{b3} \, ¥_t^{b4} \, H_t^{b5}$$

18 Let me give some more details on the statistics: Internet diffusion, as for example measured in January 1999, predicted by multiple regression (OLS). The first set of columns presents the results for all variables in the equation, the

second considers only significant predictors in the final estimate. The level of statistical significance is 5 per cent in a two-tailed test.

The first set of results refers to the sample of thirty-four countries and the second to the subsample of twenty-one rich countries.

Dependent variable: Internet hosts per 10,000 population

Predictors	Internet diffusion, January 1999, N = 34			Internet diffusion, January 1999, N = 34, insignificant, predictors excluded		
	beta	t	p	beta	t	p
Trust	0.24	3.43	0.00	0.26	4.29	0.00
University education	0.26	2.58	0.02	0.31	4.44	0.00
Average wealth	0.53	4.68	0.00	0.58	7.77	0.00
Technological capital	0.12	0.82	0.42	not included		
Mass education	−0.01	0.11	0.92	not included		
R-square, corrected	0.90	–	0.00	0.91	–	0.00

Predictors	Internet diffusion, N = 21 rich countries			N = 21 final estimate only sign. predictors		
	beta	t	p	beta	t	p
Trust	0.59	3.63	0,00	0.67	5.28	0.00
University education	0.43	2.64	0.02	0.49	3.87	0.00
Average wealth	0.01	0.04	0.97	not included		
Technological capital	0.18	0.86	0.40	not included		
Mass education	−0.03	0.20	0.85	not included		
R-square, corrected	0.65	–	0.00	0.68	–	0.00

19 Note that the part of Internet diffusion not explained by trust is significantly related to early proliferation of university education, which is independent of the level of trust.
20 More details on the predictors of Internet usage in the course of diffusion. Reduced form of results: beta coefficients (t-values in brackets), only significant predictors are listed, see below.

Internet diffusion	July 1997	Jan. 1999	Jan. 2001
Full sample of thirty-four rich and newly industrializing developing countries			
Predictors			
Trust	0.33 (4.75)	0.26 (4.29)	0.19 (3.12)
University education	0.26 (3.13)	0.31 (4.44)	0.31 (4.41)
Material development	0.56 (6.31)	0.58 (7.77)	0.63 (8.37)
Total explanation (R-square)	0.87	0.91	0.91
Subsample of twenty-one rich countries			
Predictors			
Trust	0.69 (4.89)	0.67 (5.29)	0.61 (4.49)
University education	0.38 (2.68)	0.49 (3.87)	0.50 (3.70)
Total explanation (R-square, corrected)	0.61	0.68	0.62

21 In an earlier version of the study reported in this chapter we also evaluated whether the results are due to logging the variables. For model estimations without logged variables, very high and significant effects were also found; see Bornschier 2001a: 253.
22 In the sample of rich countries, no effect of growth on Internet diffusion was detected, and in the sample of thirty-four countries growth was somewhat negatively (but not significantly) related to Internet diffusion.

4 Trust, innovation, and entrepreneurship

1 This chapter relies on two papers by Volker Bornschier and Thomas Volken: 'Social Change and Entrepreneurship – The Role of Trust', presented at the 15th World Congress of Sociology, Brisbane (Australia), July 2002, Research Committee on Economy and Society, session 8. Further research: Volker Bornschier and Thomas Volken reported in: 'Trust and the Proneness to Change. A Research Note' (volken@soziologie.unizh.ch).
2 On the aggregate level, individual countries have been classified as countries with high or low levels of trust according to their position above or below the mean value (0.45).
3 The detailed results for these estimations are available from the authors (volken@soziologie.unizh.ch). In order to get unbiased estimates for the individual and the societal effect of trust we also employed hierarchical models with bootstrap bias-corrected estimates in the further research. We checked these results also with hierarchical models with maximum likelihood estimates and came to the same conclusion.
4 Indeed our ongoing research on the topic (with Thomas Volken: volken@-soziologie.unizh.ch) shows that in terms of predictive power the aggregate level of trust (what we also term: culture of trust) is *far more* important than individual trust. But this context effect does not reinforce the effects of individual trust, rather the culture of trust makes *all* individuals more prone to change.
5 The detailed results which were presented at the World Congress of Sociology in Brisbane, 2002 (for details, see first note to this chapter) are available from the authors (volken@soziologie.unizh.ch).
6 Consequently at least two alternative theoretical interpretations of the finding are possible. On the one side, one can think of accumulating life experience with increasing age, which allows more adequate evaluation of social environments. Insecurity may thus be lower and trust more generalized. Trust in this case would be considered as an individual disposition which may be built up through social learning (Rotter 1980). On the other hand, it is also plausible to assume that specific period and cohort effects produce the finding, as exemplarily expounded by Robert Putnam (1995, 1996). He claims that the proliferation of TV was the cause of the shrinking of the cultural resource of trust and the participation in voluntary associations, and thus responsible for the relative decay of civil society.
7 Opportunity structure: what are the opportunities for the growth of the entrepreneurial firm? Capabilities: what are the capacities of the founding entrepreneur? Resources: does the founding entrepreneur have sufficient resources at hand?

5 Democracy's indirect role for growth and technological change

1 This chapter draws on materials in Volker Bornschier, *Weltgesellschaft (World Society)* published in 2002 (Chapter 13) and on results presented in the paper by Volker Bornschier and Hanno Scholtz, 'Democracy, Economic Growth and

Techno-economic Change – Empirical Evidence for Neglected Indirect Effects', presented to the World Congress of Sociology, Brisbane (Australia), 7–13 July, 2002. IZA Research Committee 02: Economy and Society. Session XII: 'Politics and Markets: The Future of Institution-Building'. A reworked version of the paper with Hanno Scholtz is in preparation, more information is available from the authors (hs@idemo.org).

2 For example, in an often-quoted reference, Mr Lee Kuan Yew in May 1962 disclosed his opinion about the relative efficiency of democratic institutions compared to his own decision-making at the Royal Society of International Affairs: 'If I were in authority in Singapore indefinitely without having to ask those who are being governed whether they like what is being done, then, I have not the slightest doubt that I could govern much more effectively in their own interests.' And, with Mr Lee Kuan Yew as its highest official for almost forty years, Singapore enjoyed something near the highest growth ever in the entire world. So, if one is heading for growth, are democratic institutions to be avoided?

3 Bornschier and Iwan Gmünder have specified and estimated a model linking democracy to socio-political stability, which itself affects physical investment as an important predictor of economic growth. This is clear evidence from a world sample of seventy-eight countries that democracy indirectly affects growth via conflict and investment (see Bornschier 2002: 407–13).

4 But in a simpler view which merely examines the relationship between the citizen and the state, these institutional subtleties resolve themselves into two broad characteristics of democracy: that the citizen can control what the state does (involving pluralism, participation and responsibility), and that the state cannot control what the citizen does (involving civil rights). These two dimensions go together, though not very closely; when citizens only have civil rights, they will use them to demand democratic control, and when only democratic control is granted, they will try to use it to secure civil rights, too. However, popular interest does not necessarily lead to success; in the processes leading to so-called 'formal' re-democratization starting in Southern Europe and Latin America, for example, a number of regimes have endured a formally institutionalized democratic procedure without giving way to demands for civil rights (Suter 1999; Collier and Levitsky 1997). Completely excluding civil rights when defining democracy, as Lipset (1959: 71) did, has not gained much support in the literature. But, with Robert Dahl, most scientists place more emphasis on the first part of the definition.

5 Earlier overviews of the studies are: Sirowy and Inkeles 1990; Przeworski and Limongi 1993; Brunetti 1997; Obinger 2000; Plümper and Martin 2000; Martin and Plümper 2001). A recent overview including about twenty studies in more recent years is Bornschier and Scholtz (2002).

6 This piece has also become available in various English versions, see Volker Bornschier, 'The Civilizational Project and Its Discontents: Toward a Viable Global Market Society?' *Journal of World-Systems Research* 1999. An electronic journal on the Internet, http://csf.colorado.edu/wsystems/jwsr.html 5: 160–75. ISSN 1076–156X. See also: http://www.unizh.ch/suz/bornschier/; see also: 'The Globalization of Market Society – Will it be Viable?,' pp. 59–80 in Peter Herrmann (ed.), *Challanges for a Global Welfare System.* Commack (NY): Nova Science Publishers, 1999.

7 My translation of Luhmann's phrase: 'Die Hochbauten des Vertrauens müssen auf der Erde stehen.'

8 The argument is based on my fresh reading of Luhmann ([1968] 1974) who made the interesting distinction between trust and mistrust. He did not, however, establish a link between democracy and trust but pointed to: 'Das Vertrauen in die Funktionsfähigkeit von Systemen schliesst Vertrauen in die

Funktionsfähigkeit ihrer immanenten Kontrollen ein' (p. 65) and: 'Das Vertrauen in Systeme als Ganzes kann, wie wir sahen, entscheidend davon abhängen, dass an kritischen Stellen das Vertrauen unterbrochen und Mistrauen eingeschaltet wird' (p. 104).

9 There is no perfect index of democracy. Due to the small number of observed characteristics Vanhanen's (2000) index is sensitive to biasing errors and has only a small correlation with those of Jaggers and Gurr, Freedom House, and the World Bank (Vanhanen correlates 0.57 with World Bank, 0.44 with Jaggers and Gurr, and 0.53 with Freedom House). Though the Freedom House data are widely used to study democracy effects (for example: Kormendi and Meguire 1985; Marsh 1988; Scully 1988; Grier and Tullock 1989; Pourgerami 1992; Helliwell 1994; Knack and Keefer 1995; Barro and Sala-i-Martin 1995; Barro 1996), their quality has been debated: The rating of codified institutions induces a large number of arbitrary decisions, and the empirical fit with other measures of political rights and civil liberties does not seem to be beyond doubt; for Latin American evidence, see Suter and Nollert 1996; Suter 1999.

10 The Polity project suffers a bit from its focus on the institutional side and a 'certain coding bias favoring an American type of democracy with a strict separation of powers' (Berg-Schlosser 2002: 7). But since we are here discussing political institutions and trying to avoid both subjectivity and data availability problems, in the following sections we present results based on the Polity index, except for the last, where this would drop about one-third of the number of observations.

11 The sample is available on the World Bank's website at http://www.worldbank.org/research/growth/ddlevren.htm.

12 The details of the following operation are found in Bornschier and Scholtz (2002).

13 Hanno Scholtz, with whom I work on this issue, and I are aware of the limitations of the present state of analysis. These pertain to causality. Both trust as a cultural resource as well as the proliferation of education may be not only the outcome of democracy but they are also likely to be favourable to further democratization. The question of two-way causation could be addressed by panel data (measuring all variables at different points in time) which is still hard to realize due to the lack of enough observations for trust over time. Furthermore, we like to consider specific policy outcomes of democracy in future steps.

14 This earlier study in my research seminar (1999) with my then graduate student Iwan Gmünder addressed the question of causality by measuring all predictor variables earlier than the dependent ones (including the intermediate variables).

6 The double dividend of expanding education for development

1 For a full treatment of the theoretical reasoning, see Bornschier [1988] 1996: Chapter 9; German edition in 1998 (based on the extended American edition of 1996).

2 Sometimes 'findings' even of top researchers in the field are not immune to grotesque errors. Does female education hamper development? The 'strange finding' mentioned in the text suggests it does. But this is nonsense. Since this book serves also as a coursebook, let me explain a bit in detail why. We start with the finding reported by Barro and Sala-i-Martin (1995: 431) and Barro (1996: 6). Robert Barro (Harvard University) is a skilled member of the cross-national econometric community and once suggested an influential paradigm to account for growth in cross-sections of countries (Barro 1991). With regard to

the effect of female education he arrived a bit later at that mentioned 'puzzling finding'. Roberto Perotti (1996) repeated and extended some of the analyses by Barro and Sala-i-Martin and came to the same 'finding'. To shorten up, in reviewing the new growth literature, Norman Gemmel (1998) reported that 'strange and puzzling finding' and communicated it to a broader professional audience.

The 'strange and puzzling finding' that male education is a positive predictor of economic growth while female education is significantly negatively related to growth rests on *two* errors of the involved researchers: false application of the regression technique, and lack of common sense. In other words, the way the researchers specified their estimation models must automatically lead to the nonsense result.

First error: multicollinearity, i.e. a very high correlation between predictors makes regression technique inappropriate to estimate 'different' effects of the highly collinear varriables. Look at a section of the correlation matrix Perotti (1996: 156) reported for a cross-section of sixty-seven countries. Female education and male education are extremely correlated (0.94, with a variance in common of 88.4 per cent).

	GR	FSE	MSE
1 Economic growth (GR)	—	—	—
2 Female secondary education (FSE)	0.14	—	—
3 Male secondary education (MSE)	0.30	0.94	—

MSE: average years of secondary schooling in the male population, 1960
FSE: average years of secondary schooling in the female population, 1960
GR: average yearly growth rate of per capita GDP, 1960–85

Now, we look at the standard formula to compute a partial correlation coefficient, in our case between female education and growth, controlling for male education:

$$r_{12.3} = \frac{r_{12} - (r_{13} \times r_{23})}{\sqrt{(1 - r_{13}^2)(1 - r_{23}^2)}}$$

From the correlation matrix we take the values and insert them into the formula:

$$r_{12.3} = \frac{0.14 - (0.30 \times 0.94)}{\sqrt{(1 - 0.30^2)(1 - 0.94^2)}}$$

$$r_{12.3} = \frac{0.14 - 0.282}{0.3254}$$

$$r_{12.3} = -0.436$$

The resulting significant negative partial correlation between female education and growth for sixty-seven cases is not sensible information. When you look at the above formula, the partial coefficient is a function of the extremely high correlation (multicollinearity) between male and female education in the cross-section *and* of the difference in the correlation of both education variables with growth. This leads us to the second error.

Second error: lack of common sense. The correlation between female education in the population and growth in the economy must necessarily be smaller than the corresponding for males since female participation in the economy (beyond the household) is everywhere lower than male participation in the work force. Necessarily, female education cannot directly affect growth to the same extent as male education does. Therefore, the differences in the correlations which affect the partial effect do not represent relevant empirical information, but follow on logical grounds. Assume that female and male education have the same effect on productivity of the economically active population, even then both cannot affect growth in the aggregate to the same extent. Thus, the 'strange and puzzling finding' is not a finding at all but a combination of two errors. Starting from our discussions in a research seminar, two of my graduate students have elaborated and extended these points in their MA theses; see Karin Baumann (2000) and Vera Haag (2000).

3 This analysis is called preliminary – as compared to the second test in the chapter – because it did not yet apply the non-linear model to estimate economic growth, developed in Chapter 2 and usually applied in this book. Furthermore, albeit this analysis has the advantage that it considers the extent to which the population is integrated via the educational system – by specifying the effect of illiteracy – it does not yet include the average education attained in the whole population. This is however necessary to test directly the human capital argument.

4 The measures employed in Figure 6.3 are the following. Economic growth per capita 1970–85: logged quotient for the figures at the beginning and the end of the growth period (data based on Summers and Heston, taken here from Barro and Lee 1994). Socio-political instability over the 1964–82 period, index covering various dimensions of political instability, taken from Gupta (1990), the original scale was inverted to represent here stability. Government spendings on education as a share of all government expenditures, averaged for the years 1965, 1970 and 1975, as well as the share of population without schooling, again averaged for 1965, 1970 and 1975, from the data compilation of Barro and Lee (1994).

5 The source is Bornschier, Herkenrath and König, 'The Double Dividend of Expanding Education for Development – Further Tests'. Paper presented at the 6th European Sociological Conference in Murcia (Spain), 23–6 September 2003. In this paper we employed the extensions which are summarized in the text. Note that we employ now the non-linear specification of total economic growth (based on an extended Cobb–Douglas production function) introduced and employed in this book. In order to apply linear regression technique all variables have been logged. The measurement of the variables as well as the controls included the number of cases, and last but not least the specification of the economic growth model differ in the different studies reported and in Figure 6.3 and 6.4. The fact that both results basically tell the same story can be regarded as a robustness check.

6 *Economic growth* 1975–95 is measured as introduced in Chapter 2 (see also endnote 15); the source is again *World Development Indicators* (World Bank 1999, CD-Rom). *Public spending on education*, average for the years 1975, 1980, 1985, 1990 and 1995, is weighted by the geometric mean of GDP and population size for each of the five years. Weighting is necessary to capture the great differences in the capacities of government to finance schooling and to control for the number of citizens who have to be educated. *Secondary schooling* is for 1980; see text. *Conflict events* over the years 1975–95 are explained in the text, too. The control variables: *labour force growth* 1975–95 (from *World Development Indicators*, World Bank 1999, CD-Rom), *growth of physical capital* 1975–95 (from Herkenrath 1999, 2003), *level of economic development* 1975, is, as always in this book, purchasing power corrected (from *World Development Indicators*, World Bank 1999, CD-Rom). Note that all variables have been logged, as explained and justified in Chapters 1 and 2. Further details on the study are available from the authors (herky@access.unizh.ch; claudia@konig.ch).

7 Political styles and the production of trust in rich democracies

1 This chapter draws in part on Volker Bornschier, 'Gesellschaftlicher Zusammenhalt und Befähigung zu Sozialkapitalbildung – Determinanten des generalisierten Vertrauens im explorativen Vergleich demokratischer Marktgesellschaften.' *Swiss Journal of Sociology/Schweizerische Zeitschrift für Soziologie* 27 (3), 2001: 441–73.

2 The following remark is necessary. Even if we design the time of measurements in this chapter in such a way as to make causal inferences less problematic, actually we are observing only correlates of generalized trust. The problem of cause and effect is, of course, a general one. I like to remind the reader that we can never empirically prove causality. It is just a category of our thinking and not observable. What we can do, however, is to apply devices that disprove false (or one-sided) causal inferences. For that we need, however, panel data (different observations on cases over time). Yet, trust figures have become available only recently for larger samples, and panel observations are still not possible for a sensible number of cases. It is true that meanwhile time series from three waves of the *WVS* (the fourth is expected to become available by April 2004). The number of democratic societies included both in the 1981 and 1990 wave is not very large. For the twenty societies (democatic and non-democratic as well as rich and developing) which were included in both of the first two waves the correlation of average trust is very high (r = 0.91). According to Thomas Volken (personal communication) the same is true for the 1995 wave.

3 As is not often acknowledged, Emil Durkheim early suggested ideas on what democratic corporatism is about (French original 1893). Quotes from the foreword to the second edition of *The Division of Labor in Society*, the Macmillan Company, New York, 1933:

> Human passions stop only before a moral power they respect. If all authority of this kind is wanting, the law of the strongest prevails, and latent or active, the state of war is necessarily chronic. That such anarchy is an unhealthy phenomenon is quite evident, since it runs counter to the aim of society, which is to suppress, or at least to moderate, war among men, subordinating the law of the strongest to a higher law. ... Only social rules can prevent abuses of power .... [more specifically, on corporatism and the relations between employers and employees].... Finally, the syndicates of employers and the syndicates of employees are distinct from each other, which is *legitimate and necessary*, but with no regular contact between them. There exists no common organization for their union where they can develop a common authority, fixing their mutual relations and commanding obedience, without a consequent loss of individuality. Consequently, it is always the law of the strongest which settles conflicts, and the state of war is continuous. Save for those of their acts which arise from common ethics, employers and workmen are, in relation to each other, in the situation as two autonomous states, but of unqual power. They can form contracts, but these contracts express only the respective state of their military forces. They sanction a condition of fact; they cannot make it a condition of right.

4 Some further comments on the notion of democratic corporatism. Early and pioneering work on democratic corporatism goes back to Schmitter (1974, 1981), Wilensky (1976a, 1981a, 1981b), Schmitter and Lehmbruch (1979), Schmidt (1982), Kriesi (1982) and Katzenstein (1985). The literature over time has grown considerably; new summary statements or overviews are found in Czada (1992), Lehmbruch (1992), Nollert (1992), Siaroff (1999) and Wilensky

(2002: Chapter 2). The reader not acquainted at all with this rich literature may wish to start by consulting the new overviews.

5 Very good introductory texts are: Lehmbruch (1992: 206–11), and the chapter entitled 'The Consensus Model of Democracy' in Lijphart (1999).

6 Nollert (1992) combines the mentioned notion of democratic corporatism of Philippe Schmitter with the notion of Gerhard Lehmbruch and arrives at a seven-step rank scale which corresponds very much with the scores Hicks und Kenworthy (1998) have obtained for democratic corporatism at the macro level (with a correlation of r = 0.86 for eighteen rich democracies).

7 Also the operationalization of the new concept 'Integrated Economies' Siaroff (1999) suggests to overcome certain ambiguities of democratic corporatism scales correlates extremely high with the average scores on neo-corporatism which Siaroff has compiled from twenty-three studies.

8 Also Lijphart's consensus democracy scale corresponds highly with the average figures which Siaroff has compiled from the literature. Lijphart (1999: 181f.) correlates the democratic corporatism scores (from Siaroff, and adds own estimates for another twelve cases) with his measure of consensus democracy and finds for thirty-six democratic countries: democracies with stronger majoritarianism have less bargained capitalism and the consensus democracies have more (r = 0.68 for thirty-six cases). See also the earlier work of Lijphart and Crepaz (1991).

9 For a detailed treatment of this issue in the context of state development and capitalist development, see Bornschier 1988: 297ff., extended American edition 1996: 259ff.

10 This historical pattern corresponds with the liberal notion of the state in political philosophy. The state is seen as a subsystem ideally expressing the needs of the citizens and delivering public goods according to people's preferences. Such a conception of the state as pragmatic problem-solver contrasts with the notion of the state as a mystic actor striving after glory and autonomy in a system of states.

11 For the role of liberalism and individualism in historical perspective, see also my chapter entitled 'The State of the European Union' in Bornschier (2000b: Chapter 10).

12 We consider nineteen rich democracies by 1981, i.e. Austria, Australia, Belgium, Canada, Denmark, Germany, Finland, France, Ireland (Rep.), Italy, Japan, the Netherlands, Norway, Portugal, Spain, Sweden, Switzerland, the United Kingdom and the United States. Not included because lack of data: New Zealand and Greece (both no figures for trust 1981). Since we relate political styles measures from 1960–89 to social characteristics we had to exclude Spain and Portugal from this first step of the analysis because they were not democracies over this whole period. We have then a maximum of seventeen cases for the first step, and nineteen for the second.

13 We rely on the 1981 wave of the *WVS*, supplemented in three cases not included in the surveys by their values from the 1990 wave (Austria, Portugal, Switzerland). This procedure (the same as Knack and Keefer 1997) is not problematic since the correlation between the trust figures for 1981 and 1990 are very high; for the twenty cases (developed as well as underdeveloped) with information in both years: r = 0.91 (Knack and Keefer 1997: 1262).

14 The details of the tests for indirect links between political styles and trust, mediated by five societal characteritics are in Bornschier (2001b).

15 This variable is based on the frequency of political mass protest and political violence events (per million population) which come from Taylor's (1985) data collection. The period from 1968–82 is chosen in order to measure conflict before the measurement of trust but within the period for the measure of negotiated capitalism. Due to the 'spiral of conflict' (conflict is not only determined by exogenous factors but also by the level already manifested) the

variable has been normalized through logarithmization (the only variable that was transformed in the analyses which are reported in this chapter). Nevertheless, the Irish Republic and even more so the United Kingdom are outliers on the political conflict variable. This is due to the civil war in Northern Ireland. We controlled for these outliers either by recoding or by excluding them. The basic findings which we report here are the same for both procedures.

16 The richness of civil society was measured on the basis of self-report in the 1981 wave of the *WVS*, supplemented as Knack and Keefer (1997: 1285) did by some figures from the 1990 wave. The index measures the average number of associations in which the interviewees participate; the whole range of civic activities in the professional, cultural and social field is covered. Unfortunately, however, the intensity of participation is not included. The distinction between 'Putnam-Type' 'Olson-Type' of associations which were also considered by Knack and Keefer is not considered here since their results were inconsistent and insignificant.

17 The involvement of citizens in different associations with different goals in the first place implies heterogeneity, but at the same time such links transcend specific groups which may add to generalized trust as we suggested in Chapter 2. This is not to say that face-to-face interactions in voluntary associations as such is the main reason for building up trust, but in my opinion it is the experience of diversified interactions transcending goal-specific groups which enforces *generalized* trust.

18 Already Alexis de Tocqueville undertook in the first half of the nineteenth century a transatlantic societal comparison and was astonished about the richness of civil society in the United States. On civil society, see also Seligman (1993).

19 Source is the data collection of Barro and Lee (1994). We evaluated this indicator in detail and tested also for alternative measures (details in Bornschier 2001b). There I explain also why the average years of education in the population is not a possible indicator since no distinction is made between levels of schooling and average figures are not only influenced by the proliferation of higher education but also by the duration of obligatory education.

20 But the link between Anglo-Saxon cultural heritage and access to higher education needs further inquiry. The proliferation of tertiary education in Anglo-Saxon societies may be higher due to the BA system, which makes the tertiary level more open than the more exclusive MA system. It is unclear whether the data of the Barro and Lee compilation are controlled for that. In any case, the BA system potentially gives access to higher education for more citizens. And Continental European societies are eager to imitate that, as witnessed by the so-called Bologna Declaration.

21 The data relate to the so-called circulation mobility and were compiled by Nollert (1991: 170) on the basis of comparative research findings of Slomczynski und Krauze (1987). Unfortunately, this informative variable is only available for fourteen cases of our sample. Alternatives are hardly possible because they would not fit into our causal design which measures the predictor of trust at an earlier time point. Michael Leicht and I have worked also with a non-discrimination index (factor scores based on the chances to achieve status in society independent of social background, gender, and citizenship). This index would be a very sensitive measure to capture the openess of the opportunity structure, and, indeed, it correlates very highly with trust ($r = 0.74$, see Chapter 2). But these data became available only since 1989. Therefore, we do not suggest the measure of non-discrimination 1989–91 as a 'predictor' of trust in 1981.

22 These data are taken from Swank and Hicks (1985: 134). The measure is the difference between the Gini coefficient of income distribution *before* taxation and social policy transfer and the resulting Gini coefficient *after* taxation and

transfers. Unfortunately, these very informative data for the 1970s are only available for thirteen rich democracies.

23 A note on the procedure (we outlined in detail in Bornschier 2001b) seems appropriate here. The two measures for political styles are the degree of negotiated capitalism 1960–89 (measured with democratic corporatism scores of Hicks and Kenworthy 1998) and the dummy variable for liberal Anglo-Saxon cultural heritage (taking the values 1 for the Anglo-Saxon cases and 0 for the others) are statistically not independent, but are highly negatively correlated (with r = –0.87). This can already be seen in Figures 7.2a and 7.2b. Therefore, we do not put them into the regression simultaneously. We filter out the common variance by taking the residuals from negotiated capitalism regressed on the Anglo-Saxon dummy. The residualized variable for negotiated capitalism does not correlate any more with the other political style variable. In regressing the five societal characteristics on the two political style measures we control for the level of development (economic product per capita corrected for purchasing-power parities, 1980).

24 With individual data from seven countries Delhey and Newton (2002: 1) also found evidence for the subjective side of such a link: 'First and foremost, social trust tends to be high among citizens who believe that there are few severe social conflicts and where the sense of public safety is high.'

25 Remember that there is a high correlation between his measure of consensus democracy and our measure of negotiated capitalsm, mentioned earlier in a note to this chapter.

26 As mentioned in the second note to this chapter, the problem of cause and effect is a general one which, however, might be very salient in theoretically linking civil society and trust.

27 Their cases for the individual-level analysis are: South Korea, Switzerland, East Germany, West Germany, Spain, Hungary and Slovenia. Note that Delhey and Newton (2002: 19) find a medium-strong link between voluntary organizations and trust for respondents in Switzerland whereas Freitag (2003) is unable to find a significant one at all. Finally, I would like to mention that Delhey and Newton find membership in informal social networks to be a significant predictor of trust in all the seven countries.

28 Delhey and Newton (2002: 21) are, in studying individuals in seven countries, so far the exception. They report: 'The absence of an association with education is surprising and not consistent with many other studies. The explanation may be that education is closely related to, and a major cause of, success and well-being in life, and it is the latter that is more closely associated with trust.'

29 Note that trust is, of course, not the only predictor of economic growth (see details in Chapter 2). Controlling for other growth predictors, trust shows its clear effect in a multiple regression analysis. Lack of trust may then for quite a while be substituted by other growth factors. More specifically, growth may also be spurred by the straggler effect for quite a while, which means that disadvantages due to low levels of trust may become less obvious. Furthermore, growth supported by transfers, as we will discuss in Chapter 10, may also mask the lack of endogenously provided trust.

8 Transnationals and supranationals: the elite bargain towards European union

1 This chapter is based on a larger research that resulted in various publications also beyond the topics which are the focus of this chapter. Bornschier (2000a, b) offers an overall picture; see also Box 8.1, pp. 167–8.

2 The source is *Neue Zürcher Zeitung*: 28–9 June 1997, p. 23: 'Kleine Vertragsänderungen mit grosser Wirkung.' 'Vor zehn Jahren, am 1. Juli 1987, ist die

Einheitliche Europäische Akte über die Reform der Römer Verträge in Kraft getreten. Entgegen den Erwartungen vieler Experten haben die eher bescheidenen Vertragsänderungen grosse Wirkung gehabt. . . .'

9 Regional integration and economic growth: the case of the EU

1 For an earlier version of this research, including more technical details, see Volker Bornschier, 'Ist die Europäische Union wirtschaftlich von Vorteil und eine Quelle beschleunigter Konvergenz? Explorative Vergleiche mit 33 Ländern im Zeitraum von 1980 bis 1998'. *Kölner Zeitschrift für Soziologie und Sozialpsychologie*, Special issue 40/2000 entitled *Die Europäisierung nationaler Gesellschaften*, edited by Maurizio Bach. Opladen and Wiesbaden: Westdeutscher Verlag, 2001: 178–204.

2 *Years of EU Membership*: this variable represents the years of EU or EEC membership. The earlier integration of Benelux countries was not included since it only meant a small market expansion. The European Coal and Steel Community (ECSC) was also excluded since it only meant the integration of two sectors. Our account of membership year starts with the EEC in 1958. The maximum number of membership years until 1997 is forty and the minimum is three. The measure was logged, but before this procedure 1 was added to the original values of all countries and, additionally, 6 to the values of the member nations. Thus, nonmembers receive the value 0 and recent members at least receive the value 1. *EU Dummy*: This dummy variable shows the value '1' for EU members and the value '0' for the twenty-one non-members. Finland, Sweden and Austria are treated as non-members here, since they did not join the EU until 1995.

3 EU membership and level of development do not significantly correlate ($r = 0.30$).

4 Let me briefly introduce the new variables (see also Bornschier 2001): *Size of the Economy*: log GDP, average of 1980 and 1997. Total output in GDP has been calculated in ppp-corrected values; source: *World Development Report* 1998/99: 234 f. *Openness*: log trade ratio, average of 1980 and 1997. Trade ratio measures imports plus exports as a percentage of GDP; source: *World Development Report* 1998/99: 272f. Handling of missing data: *Openness of the national economy*: the missing figures in the source for Germany (1980), Iceland and Taiwan (1980 and 1996) were estimated by data drawn from different editions of Fischer Weltalmanach. *National Market Size:* two cases had to be estimated: Taiwan according to data from the *World Competitiveness Report* 1992, Iceland according to information in Fischer Weltalmanach.

5 Details for the ex-ante multiple regression (OLS) in Table 9.1, growth of capital stock 1985 until end of 1993 is the dependent variable.

Predictors	$N = 33$			
	b	*beta*	*t*	*p*
Openness of the national economy	0.28	0.81	4.54	0.00
Absolute size of the national market	0.08	0.46	2.67	0.01
Convergence (low level of development)	0.22	0.50	3.43	0.00
Population growth	not significant and therefore excluded			
Constant	−0.64	3.77	0.00	
R-square, corrected for d.f.	0.40	0.00		

Note
National market size and openness of the national economy correlate in the sample of thirty-three cases with $r = -0.56$.

6 Details for the results in Table 9.2: multiple regression (OLS):

Dependent variable: economic growth 1980 and end of 1998

Predictors	N = 33			
	b	beta	t	p
Growth of physical capital	0.99	0.70	8.48	0.00
Growth of workforce	0.77	0.34	2.30	0.03
Covergence (low level of develpment)	0.51	0.81	5.42	0.00
Technology capital	0.15	0.51	3.37	0.00
Quality of education	0.09	0.08	0.88	0.39
Social capital (trust and tolerance)	0.05	0.38	4.30	0.00
EU years	0.06	0.30	2.68	0.01
Constant	−0.60	3.57	0.00	–
R-square, corrected for d.f.	0.86	–	0.00	–

Note
Market size and economic openness have no additional effects. They mediate their impact as determinants of the growth of the stock of physical capital.

7 Stability of finding: this effect of EU membership remains very stable when the sample is varied in several steps by excluding each time other poor countries (non-EU members). This was tested since membership in the EU is somewhat correlated with level of material development in the sample of thirty-three cases; see text.

8 Further results from Bornschier (2001): when we take the growth of physical capital, how is that affected by EU membership? We present the OLS estimates. The dependent variable is the growth of physical capital from the end of 1985 to the end of 1993.

Predictors	N = 33			
	b	beta	t	p
Growth of labour force	positive effect but not significant and therefore excluded			
Market size, national	0.09	0.53	3.88	0.00
Openess of the national economy	0.30	0.86	6.15	0.00
Convergence	0.16	0.38	3.15	0.00
EU years*)	−0.07	−0.49	4.34	0.00
Constant	−0.65	–	4.84	0.00
R-square, corrected	0.63	–	–	0.00

Note
* The EU membership variable was adjusted and contains only cases which were members already over the 1986–93 period.

9 As a measure we took the z-standardized residuals of the regression of each of the three technology indicators on per capita income.

10 Also, our dummy variable version of membership, which we used *en passant*, had a less significant effect.

10 The political and economic logic of integration: the convergence policies of the EU

1 Earlier work on which this chapter is based: Volker Bornschier, 'Ist die Europäische Union wirtschaftlich von Vorteil und eine Quelle beschleunigter Konvergenz? Explorative Vergleiche mit 33 Ländern im Zeitraum von 1980 bis 1998.' *Kölner Zeitschrift für Soziologie und Sozialpsychologie*, Special issue 40/2000 entitled *Die Europäisierung nationaler Gesellschaften*, edited by Maurizio Bach. Opladen/Wiesbaden: Westdeutscher Verlag, 2001: 178–204. Later extensions of the research were presented by Volker Bornschier, Mark Herkenrath and Patrick Ziltener under the title 'Political and Economic Logic of Western European Integration. A Study of Convergence Comparing Member and Non-Member States, 1980–1998' at the 5th conference of the European Sociological Association in Helsinki, 2001, forthcoming in *European Societies*. For a published German version, see Bornschier, Herkenrath and Ziltener 2003.

2 The economic integration theory based on neo-classical assumptions predicts short- and medium-term growth effects; approaches based on the endogenous growth theory postulate a sustained 'growth bonus'.

3 The source we used was: *Statistical Yearbooks of the German Federal Bureau of Statistics*, various volumes. Exchange rate: 1 Euro equals 1.956 DM.

4 The construction of the variables is explained earlier in the chapter; see also the publication: Bornschier, Herkenrath and Ziltener 2003. Further information is available from the authors (pziltener@hotmail.com).

5 The new members that joined the EU in 1995 (Austria, Finland, Sweden) are here assigned the value '1' for our membership variable. The rationale is that the prospective membership had an impact well before 1995, since the applications for membership were made many years before. These three new members were affected for only part of the examined time period by measures of the EU, but this is reflected by the fact that they receive the lowest value on our variable EU years. If they were assigned the value '0' as non-members, the interaction effect (column 2 in Table 1) would be significant only on a 10 per cent level.

6 The effect on the size of the labour force, which is seen as another intermediate variable in the integration–growth nexus by conventional economic theory, is neglected here, as labour migration takes on surprisingly modest dimensions in the EU.

11 The persistence of varieties of capitalism in rich democracies

1 Let me add some references: Karl Marx ([1859] 1974) in *Das Kapital*, Max Weber (1923) in *Wirtschaftsgeschichte*, Werner Sombart (1928) in *Der moderne Kapitalismus*, Polanyi ([1944] 1978) in *The Great Transformation* and Joseph Schumpeter (1939) in *Business Cycles*, as well as later in *Capitalism, Socialism and Democracy*.

2 Not only the relationship between firms, the state and other interest groups can be clustered but also the types of (big) business networks. This is what Michael Nollert (forthcoming) is doing. There he discusses also typologies of capitalism, especially those which take into account the organization of property rights and the diverse patterns of the separation of ownership from control in capitalism.

3 Hall and Soskice's (2001) claim that they offer 'a new approach to the comparison of national economies' is in my view not warranted and they could have related their work more to the existing literature. Nevertheless, this is an important recent contribution to the theory of comparative institutional advantage.

4 Questions from the *WVS* 1990 (the source is Inglehart *et al.* 1998), on which the

indicators are based, are the following (only for those variables which have not been introduced and described earlier):

Work ethos, according to answers to the question (*WVS*, 1990, v265): 'Here is a list of various changes in our way of life that might take place in the near future. Please tell me for each one, if it were to happen whether you think it would be a good thing, a bad thing, or don't know?' 'Decrease in the importance of work in our lives' (percentage who do not answer 'good' is the measure).

Loyalty toward the state (*WVS*, 1990, v298): 'Please tell me for each of the following statements whether you think it can be justified, never be justified, or something in between?' 'Cheating on tax if you have a chance.' (indicator is: percentage responding 'never justified' – code 1 from a ten-point scale where 1 = never and 10 = always).

Killing taboo (don't kill) (*WVS*, 1990, v316): 'Please tell me for each of the following statements whether you think it can be justified, never be justified, or something in between.' 'Killing in self-defence' (indicator is: percentage responding 'never justified' – code 1 from a ten-point scale where 1 = never and 10 = always).

Importance of the goal of economic growth (*WVS*, 1990, v257): 'There is a lot of talk these days about what the aims of this country should be for the next ten years. On this card are listed some of the goals which different people would give top priority. Would you please say which one of these you, yourself, consider the most important?' (indicator is: percentage responding 'Maintaining a high level of economic growth').

Moral issue 1: having an affair (*WVS*, 1990, v304): 'Please tell me for each of the following statements whether you think it can be justified, never be justified, or something in between?' 'Married man/woman having an affair.' (indicator is: percentage responding 'never justified' – code 1 from a ten-point scale where 1 = never and 10 = always).

Moral issue 2: (don't commit suicide) (*WVS*, 1990, v313): 'Please tell me for each of the following statements whether you think it can be justified, never be justified, or something in between? 'Suicide' (indicator is: percentage responding 'never justified' – code 1 from a ten-point scale where 1 = never and 10 = always).

5 *Married persons having an affair* is the issue, and the per cent answering: '*never justified*' the indicator (code 1 from a ten-point scale where 1 = never and 10 = always justified, see also previous note):

'Never justified', range and average of answers expressed as percentage, 1990

Cultural group	Highest value in (%)	Lowest value in (%)	Average in the cultural group (%)
Anglo-Saxon	71 (US)	53 (UK)	62
Northern-Scandinavian	63 (Sweden)	42 (Finland)	56
Middle-West European	56 (Switzerland)	43 (Germany)	51
Latin-Mediterranean European	62 (Portugal)	35 (France)	52
East Asian	72 (Korea)	47 (Japan)	60

Notes
The average value for our twenty-three rich democracies is a bit less than 56 per cent, and for all forty-three societies included in the 1990 wave of the *WVS* is 58 per cent.

This example of a moral issue shows that for several cultural attitudes the differences are low *between* the five groups but quite large *within* these groupings.

6 The data are available from: http://www.emory.edu/SOC/Lkenworthy/ajs98.htm (last download May 2003).

7 The variables used for the test in Table 11.3 are the following:

> *Ratio*: Level of liberal corporatism (neocorporatism) 1990–5 devided by the level 1968–73, times 100, computed after the figures given in Kenworthy and Hicks (2000: Table 1, see for the Internet source the previous note).
>
> *Anglo-Saxon cultural pattern*: 1 for USA, UK, Canada, Australia, New Zealand, Ireland; 0 for the other cases.
>
> *Hegemonic position actual and once, weighted*: USA: 2, UK: 1; other cases: 0.
>
> *Openess*: Trade as a share in GDP averaged for 1980 and 1996 (from Bornschier 2001).
>
> *EU-membership, weighted for years until 1995*: Belgium, France, Germany, Italy, the Netherlands: 37; Denmark, Ireland, United Kingdom: 22; other cases: 0.
>
> *Wealth per capita*: GDP per capita in purchasing-power parities (from Bornschier 2001).
>
> *Initial level of negotiated capitalism*: neocorporatism scores for 1968–73 from Kenworthy and Hicks (2000: Table 1).

8 I had the opportunity to give a full treatment of this subject in my book *Western Society in Transition*, first published in 1988, with expanded editions in 1996 and 1998. Furthermore, treatments on evolution theory can be found in my recent book (2002) on *Weltgesellschaft* (World Society), and in my encyclopedia article on social change (2002a).

9 The same conclusion is drawn by Lijphart (1999: Chapter 15). He uses consensus democracy as the measure which is highly correlated with negotiated capitalism in his sample of thirty-six democracies (see also note 8 to my Chapter 7). After addressing the question: 'Does Consensus Democracy Make a Difference?' Lijphart concludes that consensual systems stimulate economic growth, control inflation and unemployment, and limit budget deficits just as well as majoritarian democracies do. And he adds that consensus democracies clearly outperform majoritarian systems on measures of political equality, women's representation, citizen participation in elections, and proximity between government policies and voter preferences. Last but not least they outperform in controlling violence.

10 The notion of 'footloose capital', which was a kind of buzzword for quite a while, seems too little informed by the diversity even in the world of transnational corporations (TNCs). One fact is that on the *average* even the world's leading TNCs have 60 per cent of their equity still invested in their headquarter country (Bornschier 2002: Chapter 14.1). They need and (maybe only tacitly) appreciate the advantages of the institutions of their home countries. It is thus unrealistic to assume that business in general is in favour of deregulation along the lines of Anglo-Saxon capitalism. This is also what Hall and Soskice (2001: 63), whose work we appreciated at the beginning of this chapter, are suggesting: 'business communities of coordinated market economies will not automatically support deregulation, since many firms may want to retain competitive advantages that depend on high levels of regulation'.

12   Transition towards the new societal model

1 This chapter draws on materials from my concluding lecture entitled 'Western Society in Transition' at the University of Zurich, summer semester 2002.

2 Outlined with full details in my book *Western Society in Transition*, first published 1988, with expanded editions and translations 1996 and 1998.

3 When I started to work on this (Bornschier 1988) I was stimulated by ideas exposed in Bernhard Giesen (1980) on social evolution theory which are still reflected in my arguments, and I would like to acknowledge this stimulus.

4 For a cyclical interpretation of social movements, see Brand (1990) and, with regard to their role in cyclical social development, see Bornschier (1996: 173f. and especially pp. 189ff.).

5 See also 'Monopolization and the Neglect of Basic Innovations' in my book *Western Society in Transition* (1996: 105ff.).

6 Another example for disproportional results of the election process – one party may win without the majority of the popular vote – is New Zealand (see Lijphart 1999: 21ff.).

7 My hypothesis that negotiated systems put a brake on early adaptation to the new is recently also suggested in the work of Hall and Soskice (2001: 65): 'In "negotiated economies" adjustment is often slower than it is in economies coordinated primarily by markets; but markets do not necessarily generate superior outcomes.'

8 Further details, not only from the analysis of documents but also underpinned by interviews with protagonists, are in Nicola Fielder (2000), Chapter 3 of my book on *State-building in Europe*.

9 The source is Bornschier (1996: Chapter 12), where I also rely on the research of Gerhard Ritter (1989). See also David Chiavacci (2002) for the challenges this system is experiencing in present times.

10 On Japan's indecisiveness of the 1990s, see also David Chiavacci (2002) and Bai Gao (2000), and on the reforms in labour marker institutions in comparison with major OECD countries, see Mari Miura (2001). The crisis of Japanese and German capitalism is discussed in Steven K. Vogel (2001). Vogel argues that even if both Germany and Japan are lagging behind the Anglo-Saxon reform steps, Germany, in contrast to Japan, has realized more reforms (especially in the finance sector and in corporate governance), and Vogel sees that related also to the impact of the EU.

11 With David Chiavacci I have started to investigate in more detail the similarities and differences of Japanese, Korean and Taiwanese capitalism, as well as the differences with regard to European ways of negotiated capitalism which they have in common. This will result in comparative case studies similar to those I did earlier on Japan and Malaysia (Bornschier [1988] 1996, 2002). But detailed results will not be ready soon. Readers who wish to start reading on the issue we are referred to: Jeffrey Henderson (1992), Jong-Il You (1998), T.J. Pempel (1999), Patrick Köllner and Rüdiger Frank (1999), Erich Weede (2000), Markus Pohlmann (2002).

12 The data are from: International Monetary Fund (IMF) – *World Economic Outlook*. Internet version of 29 March, 2002, for the years 1994–2003 (2002 and 2003 are estimates). The source for the years 1991–3 are also from IMF, *International Financial Statistics*.

13 Certainly, the tragic events of September 11, 2001 had a drastic impact on economic growth, particularly in the United States. In my view it has considerably accentuated the cyclical downturn in the Juglar cycle (of about 8–10 years). In the long run, however, economic growth will remain high for quite a while – this is what my theory predicts. Below I present the more recent projections and the revisions concerning economic growth from the IMF (*World Economic Outlook*, as of 19 March, 2003, available on Internet) together with the ones from the same source as of 29 March, 2002, which were used for the figures in the text. The latter are the first entry in the list, while the

second entry relates to the revised estimates and new projections, as of 19 March, 2003, again from the Internet. Figures are in percentage; figures in italics are projections:

	2001	*2002*	*2003*	*2004*
USA	1.2	*2.3*	*3.4*	–
	0.3	2.4	2.2	*3.6*
EU (of 15)	1.7	*1.5*	2.9	–
	1.6	1.0	1.3	*2.4*
Switzerland	1.3	*0.8*	2.6	–
	1.1	0.1	0.6	1.7
Japan	−0.4	−1.0	0.8	–
	0.4	0.3	*0.8*	*1.0*

14 Computed from the figures given in the *World Economic Outlook* of the IMF, as of 19 March, 2003, pp. 172 and 176; available on the Internet.

Bibliography

Alesina, Alberto and Eliana La Ferrara (2000). 'The Determinants of Trust'. *Working Paper 7621*. Cambridge, MA: National Bureau of Economic Research, http://www.nber.org/papers/w7621.

Almond, Gabriel and Sidney Verba (1963). *The Civic Culture: Political Attitudes and Democracy in Five Nations*. Princeton: Princeton University Press.

Anderson, Jeffrey J. (1995). 'Structural Funds and the Social Dimension of EU Policy: Springboard or Stumbling Block?' in Stefan Leibfried and Paul Pierson (eds), *European Social Policy: Between Fragmentation and Integration*. Washington, DC: Brookings, pp. 123–58.

Arrow, Kenneth (1970). *Essays in the Theory of Risk Bearing*. Amsterdam: North-Holland.

Arrow, Kenneth (1974). *The Limits of Organization*. New York: Norton.

Baldwin, Richard E. and Elena Seghezza (1996). 'Growth and European Integration: Towards an Empirical Assessment'. Centre for Economic Policy Research, London. *Discussion Paper No. 1393*.

Banks, Arthur (2002). Cross-national Time–Series Data Archive. CD-ROM, distributed by Databanks International, 1634 Hering Avenue, Bronx, NY 10461, USA. Website: http://www.scc.rutgers.edu/cnts/about.cfm.

Barro, Robert (1991). 'Economic Growth in a Cross Section of Countries'. *The Quarterly Journal of Economics* 106, May 1991: 407–43

Barro, Robert (1996). 'Democracy and Growth'. *Journal of Economic Growth* 1, 1: 1–27.

Barro, Robert J. and Jong-Wha Lee (1994). *Data Set for a Panel of 138 Countries*. Revised edition of January 1994. Download: http://www.nber/pub/barro.lee, file Server of the National Bureau of Economic Research.

Barro, Robert J. and Xavier Sala i Martin (1995). *Economic Growth*. New York: McGraw-Hill.

Barro, Robert J. and Jong Wha Lee (2000). 'International Data on Educational Attainment: Updates and Implications'. Manuscript, Harvard University.

Baumann, Karin (2000). *Die direkten und indirekten Beiträge der Frauen zum wirtschaftlichen Erfolg. Eine empirisch-quantitative Querschnittsanalyse zum Wirtschaftswachstum der Periode von 1975–1995*. MA thesis, University of Zurich, Sociological Institute: Library.

Benhabib, Jess and Mark M. Spiegel (1994). 'The Role of Human Capital in Economic Development. Evidence from Aggregate Crosscountry Data'. *Journal of Monetary Economics* 34: 143–73.

Berg-Schlosser, Dirk (2002). 'Indicators of Democratization and Good Governance as Measures of the Quality of Democracy – A Critical Appraisal'. Paper presented at the IZA World Congress of Sociology, Brisbane, 2002

Bornschier, Volker (1976). *Wachstum. Konzentration und Multinationalisierung von Industrieunternehmen.* Frauenfeld and Stuttgart: Huber.

Bornschier, Volker (1980). *Multinationale Konzerne, Wirtschaftspolitik und nationale Entwicklung im Weltsystem.* Frankfurt/M. and New York: Campus.

Bornschier, Volker (1989). 'Legitimacy and Comparative Economic Success at the Core of the World System'. *European Sociological Review* 5, 3: 215–30.

Bornschier, Volker (1994). *Institutionelle Ordnungen – Markt, Unternehmung, Staat und Schule – und soziale Ungleichheit.* Scripts of lectures at the University of Zurich, Sociological Institute: Library.

Bornschier, Volker ([1988] 1996). *Westliche Gesellschaft im Wandel.* Frankfurt/M. and New York: Campus.

Bornschier, Volker (1996). *Western Society in Transition.* New Brunswick and London: Transaction Publishers. German and Chinese translations based on this new American edition, both 1998.

Bornschier, Volker (1997). 'Zivilisierung der Weltgesellschaft trotz Hegemonie der Marktgesellschaft?' in Dieter Senghaas (ed.), *Frieden machen.* Frankfurt/M.: Suhrkamp, pp. 421–43 (also on the Internet: www.unizh.ch/suz/bornschier).

Bornschier, Volker (2000). 'Befähigung zu Sozialkapitalbildung und wirtschaftlicher Erfolg im entwickelten Kapitalismus – neue Evidenzen aus Ländervergleichen 1980–1997'. *Schweizerische Zeitschrift für Soziologie* 26, 2: 373–400.

Bornschier, Volker (2000a). 'Western Europe's Move Toward Political Union'. And: 'The State of the European Union'. Chapters 1 and 10 in Volker Bornschier (ed.), *State-building in Europe – the Revitalization of Western European Integration.* Cambridge: Cambridge University Press.

Bornschier, Volker (ed.) (2000b). *State-building in Europe – the Revitalization of Western European Integration.* Cambridge: Cambridge University Press.

Bornschier, Volker (2001). 'Ist die Europäische Union wirtschaftlich von Vorteil und eine Quelle beschleunigter Konvergenz? Explorative Vergleiche mit 33 Ländern im Zeitraum von 1980 bis 1998'. *Kölner Zeitschrift für Soziologie und Sozialpsychologie.* Special issue 40/2000 entitled 'Die Europäisierung nationaler Gesellschaften' edited by Maurizio Bach. Opladen and Wiesbaden: Westdeutscher Verlag, pp. 178–204.

Bornschier, Volker (2001a). 'Generalisiertes Vertrauen und die frühe Verbreitung der Internetnutzung im Gesellschaftsvergleich'. *Kölner Zeitschrift für Soziologie und Sozialpsychologie*, 53, 2: 233–57.

Bornschier, Volker (2001b). 'Gesellschaftlicher Zusammenhalt und Befähigung zu Sozialkapitalbildung – Determinanten des generalisierten Vertrauens im explorativen Vergleich demokratischer Marktgesellschaften'. *Schweizerische Zeitschrift für Soziologie*, 27, 3: 441–73.

Bornschier, Volker (2002). *Weltgesellschaft.* Zurich: LVB.

Bornschier, Volker (2002a). 'Sozialer Wandel', in Günter Endruweit and Gizela Trommsdorff (eds), *Wörterbuch der Soziologie.* Stuttgart: Lucius & Lucius. 2nd edn., pp. 681–6.

Bornschier, Volker (2002b). 'Changing Income Inequality in the Second Half of the 20th Century – Preliminary Findings and Propositions for Explanations'.

Journal of World-Systems Research (electronic journal: http://csf.colorado.edu/ jwsr, Special Issue on Global Inequality. VIII, 1: winter 2002: 100–27.

Bornschier, Volker and Peter Heintz (1979). *Compendium of Data for World System Analysis*. Zurich: Special Issue of the *Bulletin of the Sociological Institute at the University of Zurich*: Library.

Bornschier, Volker and Christopher Chase-Dunn (1985). *Transnational Corporations and Underdevelopment*. New York: Praeger.

Bornschier, Volker and Doris Aebi (1992). 'Rolle und Expansion der Bildung in der modernen Gesellschaft – Von der Pflichtschule zur Weiterbildung'. *Schweizerische Zeitschrift für Soziologie* 18, 3: 539–67.

Bornschier, Volker, Mark Herkenrath and Patrick Ziltener (2001). 'Political and Economic Logic of Western European Integration. A Study of Convergence Comparing Member and Non-Member States, 1980–1988'. Paper presented at the 5th conference of the European Sociological Association in Helsinki. Forthcoming in *European Societies*.

Bornschier, Volker and Thomas Volken (2002). 'Trust – Consequences for Social Change and Its Roots. A Study of Individual Characteristics and Contextual Effects in 15 Rich Democracies'. Paper presented at the IZA RC on Economy and Society, Session 8: *The Entrepreneurial Society*, World Congress of Sociology, Brisbane, Australia.

Bornschier, Volker and Hanno Scholtz (2002). 'Democracy's Indirect Growth Fuelling'. Paper presented at the IZA World Congress of Sociology, Brisbane, Australia.

Bornschier, Volker, Mark Herkenrath and Patrick Ziltener (2003). 'Politische Klubs als Tauschgemeinschaft: Eine Untersuchung der Konvergenz der Mitglieder der Europäischen Union im Vergleich zu Nichtmitgliedern', in Thomas Plümper (ed.), *Politische Integration. Beiträge zu einer Theorie politischer Klubs*. Wiesbaden: Westdeutscher Verlag, pp. 134–70.

Bornschier, Volker, Mark Herkenrath and Claudia König (2003). 'The Double Dividend of Expanding Education for Development – Further Tests'. Paper presented at the 6th European Sociological Conference in Murcia (Spain), 23–6 September 2003.

Borrás, Susana and Helle Johansen (2001). 'Cohesion Policy in the Political Economy of the European Union'. *Cooperation and Conflict* 36, 1: 39–60.

Bourdieu, Pierre (1983). 'Ökonomisches Kapital, kulturelles Kapital, soziales Kapital', in Reinhard Kreckel (ed.), *Soziale Ungleichheiten*. Göttingen: Schwartz & Co, pp. 183–98.

Bourdieu, Pierre ([1980] 1993). *Sozialer Sinn. Kritik der theoretischen Vernunft*. Frankfurt/M.: Suhrkamp.

Bourdieu, Pierre and Jean-Claude Passeron (1970). *La reproduction*. Paris: Editions de Minuit.

Boyer, Robert (1988). 'Technical Change and the Theory of "Régulation"', in G. Dosi, Ch. Freeman, R. Nelson, G. Siverberg and L. Soete (eds), *Technical Change and Economic Theory*. London and New York: Pinter Publishers.

Brand, Karl Werner (1990). 'Zyklische Aspekte neuer sozialer Bewegungen', in Volker Bornschier *et al.* (eds), *Diskontinuität des sozialen Wandels*. Frankfurt/M.: Campus, pp. 139–64.

Brunetti, Aymo (1997). *Politics and Economic Growth: A Cross-country Data Perspective*. Paris: OECD.

Cameron, David R (1992). 'The 1992 Initiative: Causes and Consequences', in Alberta M. Sbragia (ed.) *Euro-Politics. Institutions and Policymaking in the EC.* Washington, DC: Brookings Institution, pp. 23–74.

Cecchini, Paolo (1988). *EUROPA '92. Der Vorteil des Binnenmarktes.* Baden-Baden: Nomos.

Chiavacchi, David (2002). *Der Boom der ausländischen Unternehmen als Arbeitgeber – Paradigmenwechsel in Japan?* Munich: Iudicium.

Cockfield, Lord (1994). *The European Union. Creating the Single Market.* Chichester: Wiley Chancery Law.

Coleman, James S. (1988). 'Social Capital in the Creation of Human Capital'. *American Journal of Sociology* 94: 95–210.

Coleman, James S. ([1990] 2000). *Foundations of Social Theory.* Cambridge, MA: Belknap Press of Harvard University Press.

Collier, David and Steven Levitsky (1997). 'Democracy with Adjectives. Conceptual Innovation in Comparative Research'. *World Politics* 49: April, 430–51

Commission of the European Communities (1991). *Informations- und Kommunikationstechnologien. Die Rolle Europas.* Brussels: General Directorate XIII.

Commission of the European Communities (1993). *White Paper: Growth Competitiveness, Employment: The Challenges and Ways Forward into the 21st Century.* Brussels and Luxembourg: Office for Official Publications of the European Communities.

Communication of the Commission on the *Re-activation of the European Internal Market*, 12 November, 1982/COM, 82: 735 final.

Communication of the Commission, *Consolidating the Internal Market*, to the Council of 13 June, 1984/COM, 84: 305 final.

Crédit Suisse (2000). 'Geschenkt wird es oft, käuflich ist es nicht: Vertrauen'. Bulletin. *Das Magazin der Crédit Suisse*, August/September 2000, no. 4.

Czada, Roland (1992). 'Korporatismus', in Manfred G. Schmidt (ed.), *Die westlichen Länder.* Vol. 3 of *Lexikon der Politik.* München: Beck, pp. 218–24 .

Dahl, Robert A. (1971). *Polyarchy. Participation and Opposition.* New Haven, CT: Yale University Press.

Dahl, Robert A. (1998): *On Democracy.* New Haven: Yale University Press.

Dahrendorf, Ralf (1979). *Lebenschancen.* Frankfurt/M.: Suhrkamp.

Dahrendorf, Ralf (ed.) (1981). *Trendwende: Europas Wirtschaft in der Krize.* Vienna: Molden.

Dahrendorf, Ralf (1983a). *Die Chancen der Krize: Über die Zukunft des Liberalismus.* Stuttgart: Deutsche Verlagsanstalt.

Davignon, Etienne (1981). 'Europa am Ende oder vor einem neuen Aufschwung', in Ralf Dahrendorf (ed.) *Trendwende. Europas Wirtschaft in der Krize.* Vienna: Molden, pp. 167–91.

De Melo, J., C. Montenegro and A. Panagariya (1992). *Regional Integration Old and New: Issues and Evidence.* Mimeo. Washington, DC: World Bank.

Delhey, Jan (2001). *The Prospect of Catching Up for New Members. Lessons for the Accession Countries to the European Union from Previous Enlargements.* Social Science Research Centre Berlin (WZB) Paper FS III 01–403, Berlin: WZB.

Delhey, Jan and Kenneth Newton (2002). *Who Trusts? The Origins of Social Trust in Seven Nations.* Social Science Research Centre Berlin (WZB) Paper FS III 02–402, Berlin: WZB.

Dixon, William J. and Terry Boswell (1996). 'Dependency, Disarticulation, and

Denominator Effects: Another Look at Foreign Capital Penetration'. *American Journal of Sociology* 102, 2: 543–62.

Dosi, Giovanni and Luigi Orsenigo (1988). 'Coordination and Transformation: An Overview of Structures, Behaviours and Chance in Evolutionary Environments', in G. Dosi, Ch. Freeman, R. Nelson, G. Siverberg and L. Soete (eds), *Technical Change and Economic Theory*. London and New York: Pinter Publishers.

Durkheim, Emile ([1893] 1977). *Über soziale Arbeitsteilung. Studie über die Organization höherer Gesellschaften*. Frankfurt/M.: Suhrkamp.

Easterly, William and Ross Levine (2000). 'It's Not Factor Accumulation: Stylized Facts and Growth Models'. World Bank Research Paper. Appeared also in 2002 as Working Paper No. 164 of the Banco Central de Chile. Available at: http://www.bcentral.cl/Estudios/DTBC/164/dtbc164.pdf. Revised version published in 2001: 'What Have We Learned from a Decade of Empirical Research on Growth? It's Not Factor Accumulation: Stylized Facts and Growth Models'. *World Bank Economic Review* 15: 2.

Elias, Norbert (1969). *Über den Prozess der Zivilization*. Vol. II: *Wandlungen der Gesellschaft und Entwurf eine Theorie der Zivilization*. Bern: Francke.

Emerson, Michael *et al.* (1988). *The Economics of 1992. The EC Commission's Assessment of the Economic Effects of Completing the Internal Market*. Oxford: Oxford University Press.

Esping-Andersen, Gøsta (1990). *The Three Worlds of Welfare Capitalism*. Princeton: Princeton University Press.

Esping-Andersen, Gøsta (1999). *Social Foundations of Postindustrial Economies*. New York: Oxford University Press.

Esping-Andersen, Gøsta (2003). 'Why No Socialism Anywhere? A Reply to Alex Hicks and Lane Kenworthy'. *Socio-Economic Review* 1: 63–70.

European Commission (1996). *First Report on Economic and Social Cohesion*. Luxembourg: Office for Official Publications of the European Communities.

Fecker, Lukas (2001). *The Innovative Firm. A Cybernetic Approach*. Bern: Peter Lang.

Fielder, Nicola (1997). *Western European Integration in the 1980s. The Origin of the Single Market*. Bern: Peter Lang.

Fielder, Nicola (2000). 'The Origins of the Single Market', in Volker Bornschier (ed.), *State-building in Europe. The Revitalization of Western European Integration*. Cambridge: Cambridge University Press, pp. 75–92.

Firebaugh, Glenn (1992). 'Growth Effects of Foreign and Domestic Investment'. *American Journal of Sociology* 98, 1: 105–30.

Firebaugh, Glenn and Frank D. Beck (1994). 'Does Economic Growth Benefit the Masses? Growth, Dependence, and Welfare in the Third World'. *American Sociological Review* 59: 631–53.

Fligstein, Neil (2000). 'Verursacht Globalisierung die Krise des Wohlfahrtsstaates?' *Berliner Journal für Soziologie* 10, 3: 349–78.

Freeman, Christoper (1988). 'Japan: A New National System of Innovation?', in G. Dosi, Ch. Freeman, R. Nelson, G. Siverberg and L. Soete (eds), *Technical Change and Economic Theory*. London and New York: Pinter Publishers.

Freeman, Christopher (1989). 'Die Verbreitung neuer Technologien in Unternehmen, Wirtschaftsbereichen und Ländern', in Arnold Heertje (ed.), *Technische und Finanzinnovationen. Ihre Auswirkungen auf die Wirtschaft*. Frankfurt/M.: Campus, pp. 34–63 .

Freeman, Christopher (1992). 'Changes of techno-economic paradigm', in Ch. Freeman, *The Economics of Hope. Essays on Technical Change, Economic Growth and the Environment*. London: Pinter, pp. 132–42 .

Freitag, Markus (2003). 'Beyond Tocqueville: The Origins of Social Capital in Switzerland'. *European Sociological Review* 19, 2: 217–32.

Fukuyama, Francis (1995). *Trust: The Social Virtues and the Creation of Prosperity*. New York: Free Press.

Gambetta, Diego (ed.) (1988). *Trust: Making and Breaking Cooperative Relations*. Oxford: Basil Blackwell.

Gao, Bai (2000). 'Globalization and Ideology: The Competing Images of the Contemporary Japanese Economic System in the 1990s'. *International Sociology* 15, 3: 435–53.

Gastil, Raymond D. (1982). *Freedom in the World*. Westport, CON: Greenwood

Gates, Bill, in collaboration with Nathan Myhrvold and Peter Rinearson (1995). *The Road Ahead*. New York: Viking Penguin.

Gehrig, Thomas (1999). *Humankapital und Legitimation als Vorteil im Weltsystem*. Research paper in Volker Bornschier's research seminar.

Gehrig, Thomas and Iwan Gmünder (2000). 'Kapitalstockdaten 1950–2000. Erläuterungen, Vergleich vorhandener Datensätze'. Research paper, University of Zurich: Sociological Institute.

Gemmel, Norman (1998). 'Reviewing the New Growth Literature'. *New Political Economy* 3, 1: 129–33.

George, Stephen (1992). 'Intergovernmentalism, Supranationalism and the Future Development of the European Community'. Paper presented to the Pan-European Conference on International Relations, Heidelberg, September.

George, Stephen (1993). 'Supranational Actors and Domestic Politics: Integration Theory Reconsidered in the Light of the Single European Act and Maastricht'. Paper presented to the Political Studies Association Annual Conference, University of Leicester, April.

Gerschenkron, Alexander (1962). *Economic Backwardness in Historical Perspective*. Cambridge, MA: Harvard University.

Giddens, Anthony (1990). *The Consequences of Modernity*. Oxford: Polity Press.

Giesen, Bernhard (1980). *Makrosoziologie. Eine evolutionstheoretische Einführung*. Hamburg: Hoffmann und Campe.

Gilpin, Robert (1975). *US Power and the Multinational Corporation – The Political Economy of Foreign Direct Investment*. London: Fontana/Collins.

Glaeser, Edward L., David Laibson, José A. Scheinkman and Christine L. Soutter (2000). 'Measuring Trust'. *Quarterly Journal of Economics* 3: 811–46.

Goodin, Robert E., Bruce Headey, Ruud Muffels and Henk-Jan Dirven (1999). *The Real Worlds of Welfare Capitalism*. Cambridge: Cambridge University Press.

Graff, Michael (1996). 'Die Bedeutung der Bildung im Prozess der wirtschaftlichen Entwicklung'. *Kölner Zeitschrift für Soziologie und Sozialpsychologie* 48, 2: 274–95.

Graff, Michael (1999). *Financial Development and Real Economic Growth*. Postdoctoral thesis at the TU Dresden.

Grande, Edgar and Jürgen Häusler (1994). *Industrieforschung und Forschungspolitik. Staatliche Steuerungspotentiale in der Informationstechnik*. Frankfurt/M.: Campus.

Granovetter, Mark S. (1973). 'The Strength of Weak Ties'. *American Journal of Sociology*, 78, 6: 1360–80.

Granovetter, Mark S. (1985). 'Economic Actions and Social Structure: The Problem of Embeddedness'. *American Journal of Sociology* 91: 481–510.

Granovetter, Mark S. and Richard Swedberg (eds), (1992). *The Sociology of Economic Life*. Boulder, CO: Westview.

Granovetter, Mark (2000). 'Ökonomische Institutionen als soziale Konstruktionen – ein Analyserahmen' in Dieter Bögenhold (ed.), *Moderne amerikanische Soziologie*. UTB, Stuttgart: Lucius & Lucius, pp. 199–217.

Green Cowles and Maria L. (1995). 'Setting the Agenda for a New Europe: The ERT an EC 1992'. *Journal of Common Market Studies* 33, 4: 501–26.

Grier, Kevin B. and Gordon Tullock (1989). 'An Empirical Analysis of Cross-national Economic Growth, 1951–80'. *Journal of Monetary Economics* 24: 259–76.

Gurr, Ted Robert (1974). 'Persistence and Change in Political Systems, 1800–1971'. *American Political Science Review* 68: 1482–504

Gupta, Dipak K. (1990). *The Economics of Political Violence. The Effect of Political Instability on Economic Growth*. New York: Praeger.

Haag, Vera (2000). *Die Effekte der Frauenbildung auf das Wirtschaftswachstum. Eine Reanalyse des Barro–Lee-Modells*. MA thesis, University of Zurich, Sociological Institute: Library.

Hall, Peter A. and David Soskice (2001). 'An Introduction to Varieties of Capitalism', in Peter A. Hall and David Soskice (ed), *Varieties of Capitalism. The Institutional Foundations of Comparative Advantage*. New York: Oxford University Press, pp. 1–68 .

Halpern, David (2001). 'Moral Values, Social Trust and Inequality: Can Values Explain Crime?' *British Journal of Criminology* 41: 236–51.

Harrison, Lawrence E. and Samuel P. Huntington (2000). *Culture Matters. How Values Shape Human Progress*. New York: Basic Books.

Hartmann, Jürgen (1983). *Politik und Gesellschaft in Japan, USA, Westeuropa*. Frankfurt/M.: Campus.

Hartmann, Martin and Klaus Offe (eds) (2001). *Vertrauen. Die Grundlage des sozialen Zusammenhalts*. Frankfurt/M.: Campus.

Heintz, Peter (1972). 'A Formalized Theory of Social Systems', in Peter Heintz (ed.), *A Macrosociological Theory of Societal Systems: With Special Reference to the International System*. Bern: Huber, pp. 13–38.

Heintz, Peter with the collaboration of Suzanne Heintz (1973). *The Future of Development*. Bern: Huber.

Helliwell, John F. (1994). 'Empirical Linkages Between Democracy and Economic Growth'. *British Journal of Political Science* 24: 225–48.

Helliwell, John F. (1996). *Do Borders Matter for Social Capital? Economic Growth and Civic Culture in US States and Canadian Provinces*. National Bureau of Economic Research, Cambridge M., Working Paper 5863.

Henderson, Jeffrey (1992). 'Situating the State in the East Asian Development Process', in Richard P. Appelbaum (ed.), *States and Development in the Asian Pacific Rim*. London: Sage, pp. 1–26.

Henrekson, Magnus, Johan Torstenson and Rasha Torstenson (1997). 'Growth Effects of European Integration'. *European Economic Review* 41: 1537–57.

Herkenrath, Mark (1999). *Transnationale Konzerne und nachholende Entwicklung. Ein empirisch-quantitativer Ländervergleich.* MA thesis, University of Zurich, Sociological Institute: Library.

Herkenrath, Mark (2003). *Transnationale Konzerne im Weltsystem. Globale Unternehmen, nationale Wirtschaftspolitik und das Problem nachholender Entwicklung.* Wiesbaden: Westdeutscher Verlag.

Herkenrath, Mark and Volker Bornschier (2003). 'Transnational Corporations in World Development – Still the Same Harmful Effects in an Increasingly Globalized World Economy?' *Journal of World-Systems Research* IX, 1, winter 2003: 105–39.

Herrmann, Peter (ed.) (1999). *Challenges for a Global Welfare System.* Commack, NY: Nova Science Publishers.

Hicks, Alexander and Duane H. Swank (1992). 'Politics, Institutions, and Welfare Spending in Industrialized Democracies, 1960–1992'. *American Political Science Review* 86: 658–74.

Hicks, Alexander and Lane Kenworthy (1998). 'Cooperation and Political Economic Performance in Affluent Democratic Capitalism'. *American Journal of Sociology* 103, 6: 1631–72.

Hicks, Alexander and Lane Kenworthy (2003). 'Varieties of Welfare Capitalism'. *Socio-Economic Review* 1: 27–61.

Hintze, Otto ([1929] 1964). 'Wirtschaft und Politik im Zeitalter des modernen Kapitalismus', in Otto Hintze, *Staat und Verfassung.* Vol. II, *Gesammelte Abhandlungen zur Soziologie, Politik und Theorie der Geschichte*, edited and introduced by Gerhard Österreich. Göttingen: Vandenhoeck & Ruprecht, 2nd edn, pp. 427–52.

Hirschman, Albert O. (1993). 'Wieviel Gemeinsinn braucht die liberale Gesellschaft?' in Körber-Stiftung (ed.), *Protokoll Nr. 100 des Bergedorfer Gesprächskreizes.* Hamburg, pp. 18–29.

Huang, H., C. Keser, J. Leland and J. Shachat (2003). 'Trust, the Internet, and the Digital Divide'. *IBM Systems Journal* 42, 3: 507–18.

Inglehart, Ronald (1977). *The Silent Revolution. Changing Values and Political Styles among Western Publics.* Princeton: Princeton University Press.

Inglehart, Ronald (1990). *Culture Shift in Advanced Industrial Society.* Princeton: Princeton University Press.

Inglehart, Ronald (1997). *Modernization and Postmodernization.* Princeton: Princeton University Press.

Inglehart, Ronald, Miguel Basañez and Alejandro Moreno (1998). *Human Values and Beliefs: A Cross-cultural Sourcebook.* Ann Arbor: University of Michigan Press.

Inglehart, Ronald *et al.* (1998). *World Values Survey and European Values Survey,* 1981–4, 1990–3 and 1995–7. ICPSR 2790.

International Monetary Fund (IMF) (2002/2003). *World Economic Outlook.* Internet version of 29 March, 2002; and of 19 March, 2003.

Jaggers, Keith and Ted Robert Gurr (1995). 'Tracking Democracy's Third Wave with the Polity III Data', *Journal of Peace Research* 32: 469–82

Jaggers, Keith and Ted R. Gurr (1996). 'Polity III: Regime Type and Political Authority, 1800–1994'. Inter-University Consortium for Political and Social Research. Ann Arbor: Michigan.

Kahin, Brian (1996). 'The Internet and the National Information Infrastructure', in

Günter Müller, Ulrich Kohl and Ralf Strauss (eds), *Zukunftsperspektiven der digitalen Vernetzung*. Heidelberg: dpunkt. Verlag für digitale Technologie, pp. 39–54.

Katzenstein, Peter J. (1985). *Small States in World Markets: Industrial Policy in Europe*. New York: Cornell University Press.

Kaufmann, Daniel, Aart Kraay and Pablo Zoido-Lobatón (2001). 'Governance Matters II: Updated Indicators for 2000–2001'. World Bank Development Research Group, 2001. http://www.worldbank.org/wbi/governance/pubs/govmatters2001.htm

Kenny, Charles and David Williamson (2000). 'What Do We Know About Economic Growth? Or, Why Don't We Know Very Much?' *World Development* 29, 1: 1–22.

Kenworthy, Lane and Alexander Hicks (2000). 'Neocorporatism, Income Distribution, and Macroeconomic Performance'. Paper, March 2000. kenworthyl@mail.edu/kenworthyl and ahicks@emory.edu. Data available from: http://www.emory.edu/SOC/Lkenworthy/ajs98.htm (last download May 2003).

Kerr, Clark *et al.* (1960). *Industrialism and Industrial Man*. Cambridge, MA: Harvard University Press.

KIG (Koordinationsgruppe Informationsgesellschaft). Bericht an den Bundesrat vom 16.5.2000 (see: www.isps.ch).

Kizer, Edgar and Kriss A. Drass (1987). 'Changes in the Core of the World-System and the Production of Utopian Literature in Great Britain and the United States, 1883–1975'. *American Sociological Review* 52: 286–93.

Kleinewefers, Henner and Regula Pfister (1982). *Die schweizerische Volkswirtschaft*. Frauenfeld and Stuttgart: Huber. 3rd revised edition.

Knack, Stephen and Philip Keefer (1995). 'Institutions and Economic Performance: Cross-country Tests Using Alternative Institutional Measures'. *Economics and Politics* 7: 207–27.

Knack, Stephen and Philip Keefer (1997). 'Does Social Capital Have an Economic Payoff? A Cross-country Investigation'. *Quarterly Journal of Economics* 112, 4: 1251–88.

Köllner, Patrick and Rüdiger Frank (1999). *Politik und Wirtschaft in Südkorea*. Hamburg: Institut für Asienkunde (Mitteilungen des Instituts für Asienkunde Hamburg, 304).

Kollock, Peter (1994). 'The Emergence of Exchange Structures: An Experimental Study of Uncertainty, Commitment, and Trust'. *American Journal of Sociology* 100, 2: 313–45.

Kormendi, Roger C. and Philip G. Meguire (1985). 'Macroeconomic Determinants of Growth. Cross Country Evidence'. *Journal of Monetary Change* 35: 35–76.

Kramer, R. M. and Tom R. Tyler (1996). *Trust in Organizations*. Thousand Oaks, CA: Sage.

Kriesi, Hanspeter (1982). 'The Structure of the Swiss Political System', in Gerhard Lehmbruch and Philippe C. Schmitter (eds) *Patterns of Corporatist Policy-Making*. Beverly Hills, pp. 133–61.

Kunz, Volker (2000). 'Determinanten der wirtschaftlichen Entwicklung im internationalen Vergleich'. *Kölner Zeitschrift für Soziologie und Sozialpsychologie* 52, 2: 195–225.

Kuznets, Simon (1958/59). 'Quantitative Aspects of the Economic Growth of Nations'. *Economic Development and Cultural Change* 7 (3, Part II) April: 1–100.

282 *Bibliography*

Lane, Peter J. and Michael Lubatkin (1998). 'Relative Absorptive Capacity and Interorganizational Learning'. *Strategic Management Journal* 19: 461–77.

Landau, Daniel (1995). 'The Contribution of the European Common Market to the Growth of its Member Countries: An Empirical Test'. *Weltwirtschaftliches Archiv* 131: 4.

Larson, Andrea (1992). 'Network Dyads in Entrepreneurial Settings: A Study of the Governance of Exchange Relationships'. *Administrative Science Quarterly* 37: 76–104.

Lehmbruch, Gerhard (1977). 'Liberal Corporatism and Party Government'. *Comparative Political Studies* 10: 91–126.

Lehmbruch, Gerhard (1992). 'Konkordanzdemokratie', in Manfred G. Schmidt (ed.), *Die westlichen Länder*. Vol. 3 of *Lexikon der Politik*. Munich: Beck, pp. 206–11.

Leicht, Michael (2000). *A Reformed European Model – Social Capital as Competitive Advantage*. Zurich: PhD thesis at the University of Zurich, Faculty of Philosophy.

Levine, Ross and David Renelt (1992). 'A Sensitivity Analysis of Cross-Country Growth Regressions'. *American Economic Review, Papers and Proceedings* 82: 942–63.

Lijphart, Arend (1968). 'Typology of Democratic Sytems'. *Comparative Political Studies* 1, 1: 3–44.

Lijphart, Arend (1984). *Democracies: Patterns of Majoritarian and Consensus Government in Twenty-One Countries*. New Haven: Yale University Press.

Lijphart, Arend (1999). *Patterns of Democracy. Government Forms and Performance in Thirty-Six Countries*. New Haven: Yale University Press.

Lijphart, Arend, M. Markus and L. Crepaz (1991). 'Corporatism and Consensus Democracy in Eighteen Countries: Conceptual and Empirical Linkages'. *British Journal of Political Science* 21, 2: 235–46.

Lin, Nan (2001). *Social Capital. A Theory of Social Structure and Action*. Cambridge: Cambridge University Press.

Lipset, Seymour Martin (1959). 'Some Social Prerequisites of Democracy: Economic Development and Political Legitimacy'. *American Political Science Review* 53, 1: 69–105

Lipsey, Richard G. (1999). 'Sources of Continued Long-run Economic Dynamism in the 21st Century'. *Organization for Economic Co-operation and Development. The Future of the Global Economy. Towards a Long Boom?* Paris: OEDC, pp. 33–76.

Lorenz, Edward (1999). 'Trust, Contract and Economic Cooperation'. *Cambridge Journal of Economics* 23: 301–15.

Lounsbury, Michael and Mary Ann Glynn (2001). 'Cultural Entrepreneurship: Stories, Legitimacy, and the Acquisition of Resources'. *Strategic Management Journal* 22: 545–64.

Loury, Glenn (1977). 'A Dynamic Theory of Racial Income Differences', in P. A. Wallace and A. Le Mund (eds), *Women, Minorities, and Employment Discrimination*. Lexington, MA: Lexington Books, Chapter 8.

Lucas, R. E. (1988). 'On the mechanics of economic development'. *Journal of Monetary Economics* 22: 42.

Luhmann, Niklas ([1968] 1974). *Vertrauen: Ein Mechanismus zu Reduktion sozialer Komplexität*. Stuttgart: Enke.

Luhmann, Niklas (1979). *Trust and Power*. Chichester: Wiley.
Luhmann, Niklas (1984). *Soziale Systeme. Grundriss einer allgemeinen Theorie*. Frankfurt/M.: Suhrkamp.
Macy, Michael W. and John Skvoretz (1998). 'The Evolution of Trust and Cooperation Between Strangers: A Computational Model'. *American Sociological Review* 63: 638–60.
Maddison, Angus (1982). *Phases of Capitalist Development*. Oxford: Oxford University Press.
Maddison, Angus (1995). *Monitoring the World Economy 1820–1992*. Paris: OECD.
Maddison, Angus (2001). *The World Economy. A Millennial Perspective*. Paris: OECD (Development Centre Studies).
Mahler, Alwin and Matthias W. Stoetzer (1995). 'Innovation und Diffusion in der Telekommunikation', in A. Mahler and M. W. Stoetzer (eds), *Die Diffusion von Innovationen in der Telekommunikation*. Heidelberg and New York: Springer.
Mankiw, N. Gregory (1992). *Macroeconomics*. New York: Worth.
Mankiw, N. Gregory, David Romer and David N. Weil (1992). 'A Contribution to the Empirics of Economic Growth'. *Quarterly Journal of Economics* 107, 2: 407–37.
Mankiw, N. Gregory (1995). 'The Growth of Nations'. *Brookings Papers on Economic Activity*, No. 1: 275–310.
Markoff, John (1996). *Waves of Democracy*. Pine Forge Press, CA.
Marsh, Robert M. (1988). 'Sociological Explanations of Economic Growth'. *Studies in Comparative International Development* 23: 41–77.
Marshall, Thomas H. ([1950] 1965). *Class, Citizenship, and Social Development*. Garden City: Anchor Books.
Martin, Christian and Thomas Plümper (2001). 'Regimetyp und Wirtschaftswachstum. Ein Kommentar (nicht nur) zu Herbert Obinger'. *Swiss Political Science Review* 7, 3: 45–66.
Marshall, Monty G. and Keith Jaggers (2000). 'Political Regime Characteristics and Transitions, 1800–1999. Dataset Users Manual'. Polity IV Project Integrated Network for Societal Conflict Research (INSCR) Program, www.bsos.umd.edu/cidcm/inscr/polity, 2000
Martinelli, Alberto and Neil J. Smelser (eds). 1990. *Economy and Society: Overviews in Economic Sociology*. London: Sage Publications. Also published in *Current Sociology*, Vol. 28, Nos 2–3.
Marx, Karl ([1859] 1974). *Das Kapital. Zur Kritik der politischen Ökonomie*. Berlin: Dietz Verlag.
Maskell, Peter (2000). 'Social Capital, Innovation, and Competitiveness', in Stephen Baron, John Field and Tom Schuller (eds), *Social Capital. Critical Perspectives*. New York: Oxford University Press.
Mathieu, Philipp (2003). *Generalisiertes Vertrauen und die frühe Verbreitung der Internetnutzung im Gesellschaftsvergleich*. MA thesis, Faculty of Philosophy of the University of Zurich, Sociological Institute: Library.
Mensch, Gerhard ([1975] 1978). *Stalemate in Technology*. Cambridge, MA: Ballinger. German edition: *Das technologische Patt*. Frankfurt/M.: Umschau.
Meyer, John W. (1977). 'The Effects of Education as an Institution'. *American Journal of Sociology* 83, 1: 55–72.
Meyer, John W., Francisco Ramirez, Richard Rubinson and John Boli-Bennett

(1977). 'World Educational Revolution, 1950–1970'. *Sociology of Education* 50: 242–58.

Meyer, John W. and Michael T. Hannan (eds) (1979). *National Development and the World System. Educational, Economic, and Political Change, 1950–1970.* Chicago: University of Chicago Press.

Miller, Damina and Elizabeth Garnsey (2000). 'Entrepreneurs and Technology Diffusion. How Diffusion Research Can Benefit From a Greater Understanding of Entrepreneurship'. *Technology in Society* 22, 4: 445–65.

Misztal, Barbara A. (1996). *Trust in Modern Societies.* Cambridge: Polity Press.

Miura, Mari (2001). 'Globalization and Reforms in Labor Market Institutions: Japan and Major OECD Countries'. Tokyo: University of Tokyo, Institute of Social Science (Discussion Paper, F-94).

Molle, Willem T. M. (1990). 'Will the Completion of the Internal Market Lead to Regional Divergence?', in Horst Siebert (ed.), *The Completion of the Internal Market.* Tübingen: Mohr, pp. 174–96

Molle, Willem T. M. (1991). *The Economics of European Integration. Theory, Practice, Policy.* Dartmouth: Aldershot.

Molm, Linda D., Nobuyuki Takahashi and Gretchen Peterson (2000). 'Risk and Trust in Social Exchange: An Experimental Test of a Classical Proposition'. *American Journal of Sociology* 105, 5: 1396–427.

Moravcsik, Andrew (1991). 'Negotiating the Single European Act: National Interests and Conventional Statecraft in the European Community'. *International Organization* 45, 1: 19–56.

Moravcsik, Andrew (1998). *The Choice for Europe. Social Purpose and State Power from Messina to Maastricht.* Ithaca, NY: Cornell University Press.

Moravcsik, Andrew (1999). 'A New Statecraft? Supranational Entrepreneurs and International Cooperation'. *International Organization* 53, 2: 267–306.

Müller, Günter (1996). 'Aufbau und Entstehen der Infobahn – Technische Realität durch politische Initiativen', in Günter Müller, Ulrich Kohl and Ralf Strauss (eds), *Zukunftsperspektiven der digitalen Vernetzung.* Heidelberg: dpunkt, Verlag für digitale Technologie, pp. 17–38.

Narjes, Karl-Heinz (1988). 'Europe's Technological Challenge: A View from the European Commission'. *Science and Public Policy* 15, 86: 395–402.

Nohlen, Dieter (1992). 'Wahlsysteme', in Manfred G. Schmidt (ed.), *Die westlichen Länder.* Vol. 3 of *Lexikon der Politik* (ed. by Dieter Nohlen). Munich: Beck, pp. 519ff.

Nollert, Michael (1991). 'Zwischen Konvergenz und Variation. Zur Berufsmobilität im internationalen Vergleich', in Volker Bornschier (ed.), *Das Ende der sozialen Schichtung?* Zürich: Seismo, pp. 154–86.

Nollert, Michael (1992). *Interessenvermittlung und sozialer Konflikt.* Pfaffenweiler: Centaurus.

Nollert, Michael (2000). 'Biotechnology in the European Union: A Case Study in Political Entrepreneurship', in V. Bornschier (ed.), *State-building in Europe. The Revitalization of Western European Integration.* Cambridge: Cambridge University Press, pp. 210–43.

Nollert, Michael (Forthcoming). *Unternehmensverflechtungen in Westeuropa. Nationale und transnationale Netzwerke von Unternehmen, Aufsichtsräten und Manager.* Postdoctoral thesis at the University of Zurich, Faculty of Philosophy. Manuscript to be published.

Nollert, Michael in collaboration with Nicola Fielder (2000). 'Lobbying for a Europe of Big Business: The European Roundtable of Industrialists', in V. Bornschier (ed.), *State-building in Europe. The Revitalization of Western European Integration.* Cambridge: Cambridge University Press, pp. 187–209.

Norris, Pippa (2000). 'Making Democracies Work: Social Capital and Civic Engagement in 47 Societies'. Paper for the EURESCO Conference on Social Capital, Exeter, 15–20 September 2000. Available on the Internet.

Norris, Pippa (2003). *Democratic Phoenix: Reinventing Political Activism.* Cambridge, MA: Cambridge University Press. An earlier version of Chapter 8 was delivered as 'Making Democracies Work: Social Capital and Civic Engagement in 47 Societies', at the EURESCO Conference on Social Capital, Exeter, 15–20 September 2000.

Nuissl, Henning (2002). 'Bausteine des Vertrauens – eine Begriffsanalyse'. *Berliner Journal für Soziologie* 12, 1: 87–108.

Obinger, Herbert (2000). 'Politische Regime, politische Stabilität und Wirtschaftswachstum'. *Swiss Political Science Review* 6, 2: 1–26.

Organization for Economic Co-operation and Developement (2001). *The Well-being of Nations. The Role of Human and Social Capital – Education and Skills.* Paris: OECD.

Organization for Economic Co-operation and Developement (1999). *Managing National Innovation Systems.* Paris: OECD.

Parker, Simon (2000). 'Esprit and Technology Corporatism in European Technology Policy', in V. Bornschier (ed.), *State-building in Europe. The Revitalization of Western European Integration.* Cambridge: Cambridge University Press, pp. 93–121.

Paulsen, Andreas (1968). *Allgemeine Volkswirtschaftslehre.* Bd. 1. Berlin: Walter de Gruyter & Co.

Pelkmans, Jacques (1997). *European Integration. Methods and Economic Analysis.* Harlow: Longman.

Pempel, T. J. (1999). 'The Enticement of Corporatism: Appeals of the "Japanese Model" in Developing Asia', in Dennis L. McNamara (ed.), *Corporatism and Korean Capitalism.* London: Routledge, pp. 26–53.

Perez, Carlota (1983). 'Structural Change and Assimilation of New Technologies in the Economic and Social Systems'. *Futures* 15, 5: 357–75.

Perez, Carlota (1985). 'Microelectronics, Long Waves and World Structural Change: New Perspectives for Developing Countries'. *World Development* 13, 3: 441–63.

Perez, Carlota (2000). *Technological Change and Opportunities for Development as Moving Target.* UNCTAD X, Bangkok, 12 February, 2000: TD(X)/RT.1/9.

Perotti, Robert (1996). 'Growth, Income Distribution, and Democracy: What the Data Say'. *Journal of Economic Growth* 1: 149–87.

Plümper, Thomas and Christian W. Martin (2000). 'Political Participation, Government Spending and Economic Growth'. Paper presented at the Congress of the German Sociological Association, Cologne.

Plümper, Thomas and Christian W. Martin (Forthcoming). 'Democracy, Government Spending, and Economic Growth: A Political–Economic Explanation of the Barro-Effect'. *Public Choice*, forthcoming 2003.

Pohlmann, Markus (2002). *Der Kapitalismus in Ostasien: Südkoreas und Taiwans Wege ins Zentrum der Weltwirtschaft.* Münster: Westfälisches Dampfboot.

Polanyi, Karl ([1944] 1978). *The Great Transformation: The Political and*

Economic Origins of Our Times (1944; reprint, Boston: Beacon, 1957). German edition: *Politische und ökonomische Ursprünge von Gesellschaften und Wirtschaftssystemen.* Frankfurt/M.: Suhrkamp.

Porter, Michael E. (1990). *The Competitive Advantage of Nations.* New York: Free Press.

Portes, Alejandro (1998). 'Social Capital: Its Origins and Applications in Modern Sociology'. *Annual Review of Sociology* 24: 1–24.

Pourgerami, Abbas (1992). 'Authoritarian Versus Nonauthoritarian Approaches to Economic Development: Update and Additional Evidence'. *Public Choice* 74: 365–77.

Przeworski, Adam and Fernando Limongi (1993). 'Political Regimes and Economic Growth'. *Journal of Economic Perspectives* 7.

Putnam, Robert D. (1993). *Making Democracy Work: Civic Traditions in Modern Italy.* Princeton: Princeton University Press.

Putnam, Robert D. (1995). 'Bowling Alone: America's Declining Social Capital'. *Journal of Democracy* 6, 1: 65–78.

Putnam, Robert D. (1996). 'Who Killed Civic America?' *Prospect*, March 1996. http://www.prospect-magazine.co.uk/highlights/civic_america.html.

Rennstich, Joachim K. 2002a). 'The New Economy, the Leadership Long Cycle and the Nineteenth K-Wave'. *Review of International Political Economy* 9, 1: 150–82.

Rennstich, Joachim K. (2002b). 'The Phoenix Cycle: Global Leadership Transition in a Long-Wave Perspective'. Paper presented at the 26th Political Economy of World-Systems 2002 Conference at the University of California at Riverside. Riverside, CA: 3–4 May 2002.

Rieger, Elmar (1996). 'The Common Agricultural Policy', in Helen Wallace and William Wallace (eds), *Policymaking in the European Union.* Oxford: Oxford University Press, pp. 97–123.

Ritter, Gerhard A. (1989). *Der Sozialstaat: Entstehung und Entwicklung im internationalen Vergleich.* Munich: Oldenbourg Verlag.

Robinson, Jeffrey J. (1995). 'The State of the (European) Union. From the Single Market to Maastricht, from Singular Events to General Theories'. *World Politics* 47: 441–65.

Rogers, Everett M. (1962). *Diffusion of Innovations.* New York: The Free Press.

Rogers, Everett M. (1995). 'Diffusion of Innovations: Modifications of a Model for Telecommunications', in Alwin Mahler and Matthias W. Stoetzer (eds), *Die Diffusion von Innovationen in der Telekommunikation.* Heidelberg and New York: Springer.

Romer, Paul M. (1986). 'Increasing Returns and Long-run Growth'. *Journal of Political Economy* 94, 5: 1002–37.

Romer, Paul M. (1990). 'Endogenous Technological Change'. *Journal of Political Economy* 86, 2: 71–102.

Romer, Paul M. (1994). 'The Origins of Endogenous Growth'. *Journal of Economic Perspectives* 8, 3: 22.

Rostow, Walt. ([1960] 1990). *Stages of Economic Growth – A Non-Communist Manifesto.* Cambridge: Cambridge University Press, 3rd edn.

Rotter, Julian B. (1980). 'Interpersonal Trust, Trustworthiness, and Gullibility'. *American Psychologist* 35: 1–7.

Sanderson, Stephen K. (1995). *Social Transformation. A General Theory of Historical Development.* Oxford. Blackwell.

Sandholtz, Wayne and John Zysman (1989). '1992 – Recasting the European Bargain'. *World Politics* 42: 819, October.

Sandholtz, Wayne (1992). *High-tech Europe. The Politics of International Cooperation.* Berkeley: University of California Press.

Scheidegger, Jürg (1981). *Bildung und nationale Entwicklung: Eine kritische Würdigung der Literatur, eine Erweiterung des analytischen Rahmens und neue Analysen.* MA thesis. University of Zurich Sociological Institute: Library.

Schmidt, Manfred G. (1982). 'Does Corporatism Matter? Economic Crisis, Politics and Rates of Unemployment in Capitalist Democracies in the 1970s', in Gerhard Lehmbruch and Philippe C. Schmitter (eds), *Patterns of Corporatist Policy-making.* Beverly Hills, pp. 237–58.

Schmidt, Manfred G. (ed.) (1983). *Westliche Industriegesellschaften. Wirtschaft – Gesellschaft – Politik.* Vol. 2: Dieter Nohlen (ed.), *Pipers Wörterbuch zur Politik,* Munich: Piper.

Schmidt, Michael G. (ed.) (1992). *Die westlichen Länder.* Vol. 3: Dieter Nohlen (ed.) *Lexikon der Politik.* Munich: Beck.

Schmitter, Philippe C. (1974). 'Still the Century of Corporatism?', in F. B. and T. Stritch Pike (eds), *The New Corporatism: Social–Political Structures in the Iberian World.* Notre Dame, IN: University of Notre Dame Press, pp. 85–131.

Schmitter, Philippe C. (1977). 'Modes of Interest, Intermediation, and Models of Societal Change in Western Europe'. *Comparative Political Studies* 10: 3–38.

Schmitter, Philippe C. (1981). 'Interest Information and Regime Governability in Contemporary Western Europe and North America', in Suzanne Berger (ed.), *Organising Interests in Western Europe: Pluralism, Corporatism and the Transformation of Politics.* Cambridge: Cambridge University Press, pp. 287–327.

Schmitter, Philippe C. and Gerhard Lehmbruch (eds) (1979). *Trends Towards Corporalist Intermedation.* London.

Schneider, Gerald, Thomas Plümper and Steffen Baumann (2000). 'Bringing Putnam to the European Regions. On the Relevance of Social Capital for Economic Growth'. *European Urban and Regional Studies* 7, 4: 307–17.

Scholtz, Hanno (2002). *Effiziente politische Aggregation.* Opladen: Leske & Budrich

Schumpeter, Joseph A. (1939). *Business Cycles.* 2 Vols. New York: McGraw-Hill.

Schumpeter, Joseph A. ([1947] 1989a). 'The Creative Response in Economic History', in Clemence, Richard V. (ed.), *Essays on Entrepreneurs, Innovations, Business Cycles, and the Evolution of Capitalism.* New Brunswick und Oxford: Transaction Publishers.

Schumpeter, Joseph A. ([1949] 1989b). 'Economic Theory and Entrepreneurial History', in Richard V. Clemence (ed.), *Essays on Entrepreneurs, Innovations, Business Cycles, and the Evolution of Capitalism.* New Brunswick and Oxford: Transaction Publishers.

Scully, Gerald W. (1988). 'The Institutional Framework and Economic Development'. *Journal of Political Economy* 96: 652–62.

Seligman, Adam (1993). *The Idea of Civil Society.* Princeton: Princeton University Press.

Siaroff, Alan (1999) 'Corporatism in 24 Industrial Democracies: Meaning and Measurement'. *European Journal of Political Research* 36: 175–205.

Simmel, Georg (1900). *Philosophie des Geldes.* Leipzig: Duncker & Humblot.

Simmel, Georg (1908). *Soziologie. Untersuchungen über die Formen der Vergesellschaftung.* Leipzig: Duncker & Humblot. New edition: 1992. *Soziologie:*

Untersuchung über die Formen der Vergesellschaftung. In Otthein Rammstedt (ed.), *Georg Simmel Gesamtausgabe,* Band 11. Frankfurt/M.: Suhrkamp.

Sirowy, Larry and Alex Inkeles (1990). 'The Effects of Democracy on Economic Growth and Inequality: A Review'. *Studies in International Development* 25: 126–57.

Slomczynski, Kazimierz M. and Tadeusz K. Krauze (1987). 'Cross-National Similarity in Social Mobility Patterns: A Direct Test of the Featherman-Jones-Hauser Hypothesis'. *American Sociological Review* 52: 598–611.

Smelser, Neil and Richard Swedberg (eds) (1994). *The Handbook of Economic Sociology.* Princeton, NY: Russell Sage Foundation New York.

Smith, Adam ([1776] 1975). *The Wealth of Nations.* London: Dent.

Sombart, Werner (1928). *Der moderne Kapitalismus,* 3 Vols in 6 parts, 2nd edn. Leibzig: Duncker & Humblot.

Solow, Robert M. (1956). 'A Contribution to the Theory of Economic Growth'. *Quarterly Journal of Economics* 70: 65–94.

Solow, Robert M. (1957). 'Technical Change and the Aggregate Production Function'. *Review of Economics and Statistics* 39: 312–20.

Solow, Robert M. (1995). 'But Verify'. *The New Republic.* 11 September: 36–38.

Stern, Scott, Michael E. Porter and Jeffrey L. Furman (2000). *The Determinants of National Innovative Capacity. National Bureau of Economic Research.* Cambridge: NBER Working Paper 7876. http://www.nber.org/papers/w7876.

Summers, Robert and Alan Heston (1988). 'A New Set of International Comparisons of Real Product and Price Levels: Estimates for 130 Countries, 1950–1985'. *Review of Income and Wealth* 34, 1: 1–25.

Summers, Robert and Alan Heston (1996). 'International Price and Quantity Comparisons: Potentials and Pitfalls'. *American Economic Review* 86, 2: 20–4.

Suter, Christian and Michael Nollert (1996). 'Demokratien ohne Menschenrechte: Eine empirische Analyse des Demokratisierungsprozesses in Lateinamerika', in Hans Peter Müller (ed.), *Weltsystem und kulturelles Erbe. Gliederung und Dynamik der Entwicklungsländer aus ethnologischer und soziologischer Sicht.* Berlin: Reimer, pp. 197–225.

Suter, Christian (1999). *Gute und schlechte Regimes. Staat und Politik Lateinamerikas zwischen globaler Ökonomie und nationaler Gesellschaft.* Frankfurt/M.: Vervuert.

Swan, T. W. (1956). 'Economic Growth and Capital Accumulation'. *Economic Record* 32: 334–61.

Swank, Duane H. and Alexander Hicks (1985). 'The Determinants and Redistributive Impact of State Welfare Spending in the Advanced Capitalist Democracies, 1960–1980', in Norman J. Vig and Steven E. Schier, *Political Economy in Western Democracies.* New York and London: Holmes & Meier.

Swedberg, Richard (1987). 'Economic Sociology: Past and Present'. *Current Sociology* 35, 1: 1–215.

Swedberg, Richard (2003). *Principles of Economic Sociology.* Princeton: Princeton University Press.

Sztompka, Piotr (1999). *Trust. A Sociological Theory.* Cambridge: Cambridge University Press.

Taylor, Charles L. (1985). *World Handbook of Political and Social Indicators.* Third Edition ZA no. 1130–2. Cologne: Zentralarchiv für Empirische Sozialforschung.

Temple, Jonathan (1999). 'The New Growth Evidence'. *Journal of Economic Literature* 37, 1: 112–56.

Tyler, Tom R. (2002). 'Höhere Produktivität dank prozeduraler Gerechtigkeit. Überschätzte Rolle monetärer Anreize', in Ernst Fehr and Gerhard Schwarz (eds), *Psychologische Grundlagen der Ökonomie*. Zurich: Verlag Neue Zürcher Zeitung, pp. 61–3.

Vanhanen, Tatu (1997). *Prospects of Democracy: A Study of 172 Countries*. London: Routledge.

Vanhanen, Tatu (2000). 'A New Dataset for Measuring Democracy, 1810–1998'. *Journal of Peace Research* 37, 2: 251–65.

Vanhout, Patrick (1999). 'Did the European Unification Induce Economic Growth? In Search of Scale Effects and Persistent Changes'. *Weltwirtschaftliches Archiv* 135, 2: 193–220.

Vogel, Steven K. (2001). 'The Crisis of German and Japanese Capitalism: Stalled on the Road to the Liberal Market Model?' *Comparative Political Studies* 34, 10: 1103–33.

Volken(-Reinert), Thomas (2002a). *Elemente des Vertrauens. Internetdiffusion in den Transformationsländern als Paradigmatest*. Bern: Peter Lang.

Volken(-Reinert), Thomas (2002b). 'Elements of Trust: The Cultural Dimension of Internet Diffusion Revisited'. *Electronic Journal of Sociology* 6, 4: http://www.sociology.org.

Weber, Axel A. (1998). 'Humankapital, Schulbildung und Wirtschaftswachstum: Eine kritische Betrachtung der Literatur', in Robert K. Weizsäcker (ed.), *Bildung und Wirtschaftswachstum*. Berlin: Duncker & Humblot, pp. 49–76.

Weber, Max (1905). *Die protestantische Ethik und der Geist des Kapitalismus*. Tübingen: Mohr/Siebeck. English: (1958): *The Protestant Ethic and the Spirit of Capitalism*. New York: Scribners.

Weber, Max ([1921] 1972). *Wirtschaft und Gesellschaft*. Tübingen: Mohr (Siebeck).

Weber, Max (1923). *Wirtschaftsgeschichte. Abriss der universalen Sozial- und Wirtschaftsgeschichte*. Edited by S. Hellmann and M. Palyi. München and Leibzig: Duncker & Humblot. American edition: *General Economic History*. New York: Transaction Books, 1981.

Weede, Erich (1996). 'Legitimacy, Democracy and Comparative Economic Growth Reconsidered'. *European Sociological Review* 12, 3: 217–25.

Weede, Erich (2000). *Asien und der Westen. Politische und kulturelle Determinanten der wirtschaftlichen Entwicklung*. Baden-Baden: Nomos.

White Paper (1993). See under Commission of the European Communities.

Whiteley, Paul F. (2000). 'Economic Growth and Social Capital'. *Political Studies* 48: 443–66.

Wilensky, Harold L. (1976a). *The 'New Corporatism', Centralization and the Welfare State*. London: Sage.

Wilensky, Harold L. (1981a). 'Democratic Corporatism, Consensus, and Social Policy: Reflections on Changing Values and the "Crisis" of the Welfare State', in *The Welfare State in Crisis: An Account of the Conference on Social Policies in the 1980s*. Paris: OECD, pp. 185–95.

Wilensky, Harold L. (1981b). 'Leftism, Catholicism, and Democratic Corporatism: The Role of Political Parties in Welfare State Development', in Peter Flora and Arnold J. Heidenheimer (eds), *The Development of Welfare States in Europe and America*. New Brunswick, NJ: Transaction Books, pp. 345–82.

Wilensky, Harold L. (2002). *Rich Democracies. Political Economy, Public Policy, and Performance*. Berkeley: University of California Press.

Woolcock, Michael (1998). 'Social Capital and Economic Development: Toward a Theoretical Synthesis and Policy Framework'. *Theory and Society* 27: 151–208.

World Development Report see World Bank.

World Bank (1997). *World Development Report/Weltenwicklungsbericht*. Washington, DC.

World Bank (1998). *World Development Report 1998/1999*. Washington, DC.

World Bank (1999). *World Development Report 1999/2000*. Washington, DC.

World Bank (1999a). *World Development Indicators* CD-ROM. Washington, DC.

World Values Survey (1981–4 and 1990–3). World Values Study Group. Interuniversity Consortium for Political and Social Research. Ann Arbor, MI.

Yamagishi, Toshio, Karen S. Cook and Motoki Watabe (1998). 'Uncertainty, Trust, and Commitment Formation in the United States and Japan'. *American Journal of Sociology* 104, 1: 165–94.

Yli-Renko, Helena, Erkko Autio and Harry J. Sapienza (2001). 'Social Capital, Knowledge Acquisition, and Knowledge Exploitation in Young Technology-Based Firms'. *Strategic Management Journal* 22: 587–613.

You, Jong-Il (1998). 'Income Distribution and Growth in East Asia'. *The Journal of Develoment Studies* 34, 6: 37–65.

Zak, Paul J. and Stephen Knack (2001). 'Trust and Growth'. *The Economic Journal* 111: 295–321.

Ziltener, Patrick (1999). *Strukturwandel der europäischen Integration. Die Europäische Union und die Veränderung von Staatlichkeit*. Münster: Westfälisches Dampfboot.

Ziltener, Patrick (2000a). 'Tying up the Luxembourg Package of 1985 – Prerequisites and Problems of its Constitution', in V. Bornschier (ed.), *State-building in Europe. The Revitalization of Western European Integration*. Cambridge: Cambridge University Press, pp. 38–72.

Ziltener, Patrick (2000b). 'EC Regional Policy: Monetary Lubricant for Economic Integration?', in V. Bornschier (ed.), *State-building in Europe. The Revitalization of Western European Integration*. Cambridge: Cambridge University Press, pp. 122–51.

Ziltener, Patrick (2001). 'Wirtschaftliche Effekte der europäischen Integration – Theoriebildung und empirische Forschung'. MPIfG Working Paper 01/7, November 2001. Cologne: Max-Planck-Institut für Gesellschaftsforschung.

Index